Edited by Letitia R. Naigles

Innovative Investigations of Language in Autism Spectrum Disorder

Language and the Human Lifespan Series

Bilingualism Across the Lifespan
Factors Moderating Language Proficiency
Edited by Elena Nicoladis and Simona Montanari

Innovative Investigations of Language in Autism Spectrum Disorder
Edited by Letitia R. Naigles

Innovative Investigations of Language in Autism Spectrum Disorder

Edited by
Letitia R. Naigles

DE GRUYTER
MOUTON

American Psychological Association • Washington, DC

Published by

American Psychological Association
750 First Street, NE
Washington, DC 20002-4242
www.apa.org

Walter de Gruyter GmbH
Genthiner Strasse 13
10785 Berlin / Germany
www.degruyter.com

To order in the United States and Canada:
APA Order Department
P.O. Box 92984
Washington, DC 20090-2984
Tel: (800) 374-2721; Direct: (202) 336-5510
Fax: (202) 336-5502; TDD/TTY: (202) 336-6123
Online: www.apa.org/pubs/books/
E-mail: order@apa.org

To order in Europe:
HGV Hanseatische Gesellschaft für Verlagsservice mbH
Holzwiesenstr. 2
72127 Kusterdingen / Germany
Tel.: +49 (0)7071 9353 – 55
Fax.: +49 (0)7071 9353 – 93
Online: www.degruyter.com
E-mail: orders@degruyter.com

Other customers, including those in the United Kingdom, may order from either publisher.

Typeset in DG Meta Serif Science by Circle Graphics, Inc., Columbia, MD

Printer (U.S. & Canada): Edwards Brothers, Inc., Lillington, NC
Printer (Europe): CPI books GmbH, Leck, Germany
Cover Designer: Mercury Publishing Services, Inc., Rockville, MD

Library of Congress Cataloging-in-Publication Data
Names: Naigles, Letitia R., editor.
Title: Innovative investigations of language in autism spectrum disorder / edited by Letitia R. Naigles.
Description: Washington, DC : American Psychological Association, [2017] | Series: Language and the human lifespan | Includes bibliographical references and index.
Identifiers: LCCN 2016018805 | ISBN 9783110409789 | ISBN 311040978X
Subjects: LCSH: Autistic people—Language.
Classification: LCC RC553.A88 I576 2017 | DDC 616.85/882—dc23
LC record available at https://lccn.loc.gov/2016018805

British Library Cataloguing-in-Publication Data
A CIP record is available from the British Library.

Bibliographic Information published by the Deutsche Nationalbibliothek
The Deutsche Nationalbibliothek lists this publication in the Deutsche Nationalbibliografie; detailed bibliographic data are available in the internet at http://dnb.dnb.de

Printed in the United States of America and Germany
First Edition

http://dx.doi.org/10.1037/15964-000

For Sheila E. Blumstein, who first taught me about language disorders.
For Lila R. Gleitman, who first taught me about language acquisition.
For Deborah A. Fein, who first taught me about autism spectrum disorder.

Contents

Contributors

Leonard Abbeduto, PhD
MIND Institute and Department of Psychiatry and Behavioral Sciences
University of California, Davis

Emma K. Baker, BPsySc (Hons)
School of Psychology and Public Health
La Trobe University
Melbourne, Australia

Janet Bang, BS
School of Communication Sciences and Disorders
McGill University
Montreal, Quebec, Canada; and
Centre for Research on Brain, Language and Music
Montreal, Quebec, Canada

Graham Barrington, MBBS, MAppSc (CogSci)
School of Languages and Linguistics
The University of Melbourne
Melbourne, Australia

Marie-Anne Barthez, MD
Language Reference Center
Clocheville Hospital
Tours Regional University Hospital Center
Tours, France

Edith L. Bavin, PhD
School of Psychology and Public Health
La Trobe University
Melbourne, Australia

Frédérique Bonnet-Brilhault, MD, PhD
Tours Regional University Hospital Center
Tours, France

Morgane Burnel, MSc
French National Centre for Scientific Research
Laboratoire de Psychologie et NeuroCognition
University of Grenoble Alpes
Grenoble, France

Allison Canfield, MA
Department of Psychological Sciences,
University of Connecticut, Storrs

Marie Moore Channell, PhD
MIND Institute and Department of Psychiatry and Behavioral Sciences
University of California, Davis

Kerrie Delves, BA (Hons), PhD candidate
School of Languages and Linguistics
The University of Melbourne
Melbourne, Australia

Susan Douglas, PhD
School of Languages and Linguistics
The University of Melbourne
Melbourne, Australia

Stephanie Durrleman-Tame, PhD
Department of Psycholinguistics
Faculty of Psychology and Educational Sciences
University of Geneva
Geneva, Switzerland

Inge-Marie Eigsti, PhD
Department of Psychological Sciences
University of Connecticut, Storrs

Deborah Fein, PhD
Department of Psychological Sciences
University of Connecticut, Storrs

Sandrine Ferré, PhD
Université François Rabelais de Tours
Department of Language Science
Tours, France

Christina Irvine, MA
Department of Psychological Sciences
University of Connecticut, Storrs

Vikki Janke, PhD
English Language and Linguistics
School of European Culture and Languages
University of Kent
Canterbury, England

Elizabeth Kelley, PhD
Psychology Department
Queen's University
Kingston, Canada

Joëlle Malvy, MD, PhD
Tours Regional University Hospital Center
Tours, France

Andrea McDuffie, PhD
MIND Institute and Department of Psychiatry and Behavioral Sciences
University of California, Davis

Aparna Nadig, PhD
School of Communication Sciences and Disorders
McGill University
Montreal, Quebec, Canada; and
Centre for Research on Brain, Language and Music
Montreal, Quebec, Canada

Letitia R. Naigles, PhD
Department of Psychological Sciences
University of Connecticut, Storrs

Courtenay Frazier Norbury, DPhil
Psychology and Language Sciences
University College London
London, England

Alexandra Perovic, PhD
Department of Linguistics, Division of Psychology and Language Sciences
University College London
London, England

Philippe Prévost, PhD
Université François Rabelais de Tours
Department of Language Science
Tours, France

Anne Reboul, PhD
French National Centre for Scientific Research
Institute for Cognitive Sciences
University of Lyon
Lyon, France

Jillian M. Schuh, PhD
Division of Neuropsychology
Department of Neurology
Medical College of Wisconsin, Milwaukee

Lesley Stirling, PhD
School of Languages and Linguistics
The University of Melbourne
Melbourne, Australia

Joyce Suh, PhD
Department of Psychological Sciences
University of Connecticut, Storrs

Helen Tager-Flusberg, PhD
Center for Autism Research Excellence
Department of Psychological and Brain Sciences
Boston University
Boston, MA

Angela John Thurman, PhD
MIND Institute and Department of Psychiatry and Behavioral Sciences
University of California, Davis

Laurice Tuller, PhD
Université François Rabelais de Tours
Department of Language Science
Tours, France

Foreword

When Leo Kanner introduced the clinical syndrome we now call *autism* or *autism spectrum disorder* (ASD), he was of two minds about whether language should be considered a core symptom. Initially, he did not seem to think language was central to how autism should be defined (Kanner, 1943), but within a few years, he devoted his second publication on this new syndrome to describing the "peculiarities of language" (Kanner, 1946, p. 242) that he observed in his patients. In addition to "mutism," echolalia, and pronoun reversals, Kanner described the "metaphorical" phrases or sentences that appeared meaningless in the contexts in which they were spoken. Hans Asperger (1944/1991) also described some of the "unnatural" language of his patients, such as odd vocal quality, unusual choice of words and expressions, and failure to engage in reciprocal conversations. Both Kanner and Asperger highlighted the idiosyncratic nature of linguistic expression in the children they observed; from their clinical vantage point, atypical language was a core feature that defined autism in their patients.

It took another 3 decades for researchers to begin investigating language in autism building on the theories and methods introduced in the newly created field of "developmental psycholinguistics." This was about the time that I began my own research career as a doctoral student, convinced that language and related cognitive deficits were the most important features of autism. Studies published in the early 1970s by Rutter, Bartolucci, and their colleagues were my primary inspiration. We adapted paradigms and tools that were developed and validated in studies of phonology, grammar, or semantics in typically developing toddlers and children.

The findings were somewhat disappointing and mixed: Yes, children with autism were impaired in these structural aspects of language compared with their typical peers, but their impairments were not so evident when compared with children with other disorders, suggesting that we were not finding unique differences in the language of children with autism. In hindsight, one of the major issues was the enormous heterogeneity within the population, which likely obscured anything that might have been revealed had we taken a more careful look at individual variation.

Christine Baltaxe (1977) was the first to describe in detail impairments in pragmatic functioning, connecting Kanner's and Asperger's original observations to models of pragmatic development that were emerging at that time. Although it would take several more years before systematic research was carried out on pragmatic aspects of language in autism, Baltaxe's observations were a turning point in confirming from a linguistic perspective which areas of language were more universally and specifically different in autism.

Forty years on and we now have a new wave of researchers, theories, and methodologies that together are providing fresh insights into language in autism, as is evident in this volume. Letitia R. Naigles has brought together a stellar group of scientists who are taking on the challenge of studying language in ASD by extending the boundaries of earlier work. Several key themes are threaded through the chapters, including how language is processed, the intricate interplay between pragmatics and syntax, interactions between language and other cognitive domains (particularly theory of mind and working memory), and the comparison of ASD to other language disorders. It is exciting to see some of these themes explored in languages other than English as well as in written, not just spoken, language. Moreover, several chapters illustrate how the addition of eye-tracking technology and the visual-world paradigm has transformed studies on language processing in children with ASD, underscoring the importance of novel methods for advancing research in ways we could not have imagined when I began working in this field.

Today we are still somewhat divided in our view of how language fits into our understanding of ASD. A few years ago, deficits in language and communication were eliminated from the definition of ASD in the fifth edition of the *Diagnostic and Statistical Manual of Mental Disorders* (*DSM*; American Psychiatric Association, 2013), leaving only a slimmed down category of deficits in social communication. Under this category, the only mention of language is poor pragmatics, or impairment in conversation skills. Although the definition of autistic disorder has not been changed in the *International Classification of Diseases*, language impairment is also no longer a required symptom used in diagnosis. As we read the chapters in this volume, we can see why language itself may no longer be considered a core deficit; for the most part, verbally fluent children with ASD are not that different from carefully matched control children in their use and processing of language.

Yet there are still open questions that the *DSM* does not address. For example, even individuals who have intact linguistic skills often rely on different neural circuitry for processing language, such as greater reliance on the right hemisphere or reduced functional connectivity (Tager-Flusberg, Lindgren, & Mody, 2008). Do such differences suggest distinct underlying mechanisms that should be included in core definitions of ASD? Looking more broadly at the population, this volume focuses on those children who do acquire spoken language, but what about those who do not? Even Kanner (1946) reported that about one third of his patients were mute, and although this proportion is declining, there are still many children who, despite access to early interventions, remain minimally verbal. The absence of language in about one quarter of all children with ASD suggests that we still have a great deal to learn about the place of language in our definition of ASD. I look forward to what we will be learning in the coming decades as our field builds further on future advances, some of which we have yet to imagine. In the meantime, this rich set of chapters offers important insights into how language reveals new ways of conceptualizing ASD and, in turn, how ASD itself can lead to new ways of thinking about language.

—Helen Tager-Flusberg, PhD

References

American Psychiatric Association. (2013). *Diagnostic and statistical manual of mental disorders* (5th ed.). Washington, DC: Author.

Asperger, H. (1991). "Autistic psychopathy" in childhood. In U. Frith (Ed. & Trans.), *Autism and Asperger syndrome* (pp. 37–91). Cambridge, England: Cambridge University Press. (Original work published 1944)

Baltaxe, C. (1977). Pragmatic deficits in the language of autistic adolescents. *Journal of Pediatric Psychology, 2*, 176–180.

Kanner, L. (1943). Autistic disturbances of affective contact. *Nervous Child, 2*, 217–250.

Kanner, L. (1946). Irrelevant and metaphorical language in early infantile autism. *American Journal of Psychiatry, 103*, 242–245.

Tager-Flusberg, H., Lindgren, K., & Mody, M. (2008). Structural and functional imaging research on language disorders: Specific language impairment and autism spectrum disorders. In L. Wolf, H. Schreiber, & J. Wasserstein (Eds.), *Adult learning disorders: Contemporary issues* (pp. 127–157). New York, NY: Psychology Press.

Acknowledgments

This volume was launched via conversations with Maureen Adams and Julia Frank-McNeil, senior acquisitions editor and senior director (retired) at APA Books, respectively, and I am very grateful for their inspiration and encouragement. Christopher Kelaher took over midway through the project and provided invaluable information and support, as did the two manuscript reviewers. Moreover, the chapter authors have done a fantastic job to help make this an "innovative" work; they have also been responsive to both the letter and spirit of comments and suggestions coming from a number of ports. I am happy to acknowledge the input of my students, with whom each chapter was read and discussed: Ahmed Abdel-Aziz, Nora Alpers-Leon, Iris Chin, Tabitha d'Souxa, Manya Jyotishi, and Kacie Wittke. Thanks also to the indexer (WordCo Indexing Services, Inc.), copyeditor (Elizabeth Sirimarco Budd), and development editor (Ida Audeh).

Edited by Letitia R. Naigles

Innovative Investigations of Language in Autism Spectrum Disorder

Letitia R. Naigles

Introduction: Perspectives on Language in ASD

Diagnoses of neurodevelopmental disorders, and particularly autism spectrum disorder (ASD), have been increasing over the past 20 to 30 years (Fombonne, Quirke, & Hagen, 2011); hence, more and more children and adolescents are carrying an ASD diagnosis. Deficits in social interaction, together with excessive restricted and repetitive behaviors, are key components of ASD. Language impairment, broadly defined, has also been considered a core component of ASD (American Psychiatric Association, 2000), yet the precise nature of this impairment, and its current status within the ASD diagnosis, is unresolved (American Psychiatric Association, 2013; World Health Organization [WHO], 1992; see also Eigsti & Schuh, Chapter 9, this volume). One reason for this lack of resolution is the enormous variability that is observed when language use is assessed in individuals with ASD. In somewhat oversimplified terms, some studies report language impairments ranging from minimal to severe, and other studies report language that looks completely intact. From a person-centered standpoint, some individuals with ASD rarely speak and appear not to understand the language of their community, whereas others speak and understand at levels that appear indistinguishable from typically developing (TD) individuals—and many, many others present with language in between these two extremes. This variability has intrigued and inspired the contributors to this volume, who have brought their expertise in fields ranging from communication disorders to developmental and clinical psychology to theoretical linguistics to bear on innovative investigations concerning the nature and origins of linguistic knowledge and use in individuals, especially children, with ASD.

Why Does Variability in Language Use Matter?

Variability in the development and use of language in children with ASD matters to clinicians, linguists, and developmental psychologists for somewhat different reasons. Clinicians, who diagnose, assess, design, and carry out interventions, are directly affected by recent changes in the core diagnostic characteristics of ASD (for an excellent historical review, see Goldstein & Ozonoff, 2009). That is, deficits and delays in language per se are no longer designated as core components of ASD in the current U.S.-based *Diagnostic and Statistical Manual of Mental Disorders* (fifth edition [*DSM–5*]; American Psychiatric Association, 2013); the *International Statistical Classification of Diseases* (10th revision [*ICD–10*] for "Childhood Autism"; WHO, 1992), which is now considered the standard for diagnosis, focuses more on deficits in the social uses of language. Both

http://dx.doi.org/10.1037/15964-001
Innovative Investigations of Language in Autism Spectrum Disorder, L. R. Naigles (Editor)

of these sources cite *communication* as a core component of ASD or Childhood Autism, particularly with reference to nonverbal behaviors in social interaction, such as eye contact and facial expressions, body language, and gesture. Developmental disorders of speech and language (SLDs) are designated as separate from ASD, with the possibility available that a child presents with both disorders comorbidly. It is important, therefore, to clarify some distinctions between *communication* and *language*.

Communication may be considered the broader term because many uses of language (e.g., telling and understanding stories, metaphors, puns, and jokes; disputing, conversing about external events and internal thoughts and feelings) are communicative in that they convey intentional messages between producers and comprehenders. Additionally, there are nonlinguistic forms or media of communication, such as body language and gesture.[1] Language use also exists outside of interpersonal communication, as speakers may exploit their linguistic knowledge during, for example, self-reflection and examination, social and cognitive problem solving, creative engagement, and (for students of language) linguistic analysis (Altmann, 1996; Chomsky, 2006). A key point, however, is that both communicative and noncommunicative language use includes all four levels of language, including sounds and signs, words, sentences, and discourse (also termed *phonology*, *lexical semantics*, *morphology and syntax*, and *semantics/pragmatics*). Salient questions for clinicians, then, may involve the extent to which children with ASD's delays in language-related milestones (first words, first phrases) and/or difficulties with stories and metaphors reflect linguistic as well as communicative deficits. Moreover, to the extent that language is a dominant medium for interventions for children with ASD, intervention design must take account of their linguistic as well as communicative skills. Finally, it is important to point out that many of the studies described in these chapters were carried out by researchers who were studying children diagnosed as ASD under the criteria of the previous edition of the *DSM* (*DSM–IV*; American Psychiatric Association, 2000), in which language delay is a specific criterion (note that, changes in *DSM–5* notwithstanding, these individuals are still considered to carry the ASD diagnosis). An interesting question for future research concerns the extent to which findings such as those discussed in this volume are replicated with children with ASD whose diagnosis is restricted to *DSM–5*/*ICD–10* criteria.

Variability in the development and use of language in children with ASD raises questions for linguists that involve theory and structure. For example, when language impairment occurs, does the coherent system of highly regular relationships between linguistic forms (sounds, morphemes, words, sentences, discourse) and meanings (concepts, events, relationships, propositions, interactions) break down in ASD in similarly systematic patterns, such that only one level is impaired or all levels are impaired? Language deficits in ASD can look quite systematic, especially at the lowest and highest

1 Sign languages, by virtue of their reliance on the visual-tactile modalities, include both linguistic and nonlinguistic manifestations of these forms (Goldin-Meadow, 2015). See Shield (2014) for a recent discussion of how ASD may be manifested in American Sign Language.

verbal extremes. For example, a sizeable minority (15%–30%) of children diagnosed with ASD remain nonverbal (i.e., apparently without language) into adulthood (Pickett, Pullara, O'Grady, & Gordon, 2009); moreover, many children who acquire language nonetheless show substantial delays in their onset of speech compared with TD age mates (Tager-Flusberg, Paul, & Lord, 2005; Tek, Mesite, Fein, & Naigles, 2014). Among high-verbal children with ASD, neither speech-sound nor articulation errors are commonly reported, supporting an intact system of phonology (Tager-Flusberg et al., 2005), although recent research has begun to question this conclusion (Suh et al., Chapter 11, this volume; Tuller et al., Chapter 6, this volume). Scrutiny of the pragmatic level, in contrast, yields the most consistent evidence of difficulties, including weaknesses in story connectedness, humor and metaphor use, and adjustments of speech in line with the perspectives of the listener (for comprehensive summaries, see Naigles & Chin, 2015; Stirling, Douglas, Leekam, & Carey, 2014), supporting a pervasive deficit in the pragmatic component of language. Four chapters in the current volume further explore the origins of this deficit. For example, researchers investigate whether ASD perspective-taking difficulties might actually be rooted in challenges with complex syntax (Durrleman-Tame, Burnel, & Reboul, Chapter 8, this volume) or low-level nonsocial functions such as working memory (see in this volume Eigsti & Schuh, Chapter 9; Suh et al., Chapter 11). Researchers also deploy novel methods, such as written retelling of familiar narratives and eye tracking during tasks accessing speaker–listener common ground to illuminate unexpectedly good—and poor—pragmatic usage (see in this volume Eigsti & Schuh, Chapter 9; Stirling, Barrington, Douglas, & Delves, Chapter 10).

Studies focusing on the components of lexicon and grammar, including both morphology and syntax, have generated the most mixed findings with respect to their degree of intactness/strength versus deficit/weakness in ASD and are discussed at length in the current volume. One prominent example in the literature concerns the degree to which a subgroup of children with ASD might manifest the same language impairments as children without ASD who have specific language impairment (SLI). In brief, classic SLI can be diagnosed in preschool-aged children whose language scores are below the normal range for their age but whose nonverbal IQs are within the normal range—that is, they present without frank cognitive deficits. These children typically demonstrate significant impairments in articulation and grammatical expression, frequently omitting sounds from consonant clusters; morphemes, such as those for tense and aspect; and required elements, such as direct objects, from sentences (Leonard, 2015; Tomblin, 2015). Tager-Flusberg and colleagues (Kjelgaard & Tager-Flusberg, 2001; Roberts, Rice, & Tager-Flusberg, 2004; Tager-Flusberg, 2006; Tager-Flusberg & Joseph, 2003; see also Gernsbacher, Geye, & Ellis Weismer, 2005) have proposed that a subgroup of children with ASD also fit this profile, such that they carry both ASD and SLI (or in *DSM–5/ICD–10* terms, SLD) diagnoses. This proposal has been controversial, with other researchers arguing that the "structural language" impairments associated with ASD are different in kind from those in SLI (Riches, Loucas, Baird, Charman, & Simonoff, 2010; Taylor, Mayberry, & Whitehouse, 2014;

Williams, Botting, & Boucher, 2008); however, Tuller et al. (Chapter 6, this volume) garner some support for the proposal while recasting the grammatical deficit as one involving computational complexity rather than specific constructions. Still other researchers point out that similarities in overt grammatical use may have different underlying roots or developmental pathways (Eigsti & Bennetto, 2009; Taylor et al., 2014; Whitehouse, Barry, & Bishop, 2008; see also Norbury, Chapter 1, this volume). The existence of an ASD–SLI subgroup would provide evidence of linguistic systematicity in language breakdown (i.e., a specifically grammatical impairment; see van der Lely, 2005); however, because human language also manifests interfaces between language levels, evidence of the interdependency of, say, the lexical semantic and syntactic levels in the language of children with ASD is also highly relevant for investigations of systematicity (e.g., Naigles, Kelty, Jaffery, & Fein, 2011; see also in this volume, Janke & Perovic, Chapter 7; Nadig & Bang, Chapter 5; Naigles & Fein, Chapter 3; Norbury, Chapter 1).

Variability in the development and use of language in children with ASD raises questions for developmental psychologists that may involve the processes of change and growth. For example, when some children with ASD have difficulty developing more advanced language, is this because they are using some different processes of language acquisition or because they are using the same processes as TD children but at lower levels of efficiency? Processes exploited during the language acquisition of TD children include, but are by no means limited to, statistical learning (Höhle, 2015; Thiessen & Erickson, 2015), which enables children to discover the configural patterns of their input language; social interaction (Clark, 2015; Tomasello, 2015), which facilitates children's attention to the linguistic signal and its concomitant meanings; and working memory (Archibald & Noonan, 2015; Snedeker & Huang, 2015), which enables children to track and organize the plethora of external and internal data that goes into acquiring, producing, and understanding language. Thus, because both engagement in and inferencing from social interactions are, by definition, impaired in children with ASD, such children might illuminate how much language development and use is dependent on these interactions. Indeed, the social impairments of children with ASD have been cited as the primary cause of their language impairments (Tager-Flusberg et al., 2005): If children are not sufficiently socially engaged even to pay attention to the speech of others in their milieu, they are not going to process that speech sufficiently to determine its sound structure, syntactic patterning, and semantic–pragmatic relationships. Yet social engagement cannot be the definitive "gatekeeper" to language development because many socially impaired children with ASD nonetheless acquire functional, if not advanced, language skills (Akhtar & Gernsbacher, 2007; Naigles & Chin, 2015). Possible interpretations of these findings include postulating that (some) children with ASD acquire language by relying more on statistical learning or working memory processes than social interactional processes or that the social processes may exert their primary influence at developmentally restricted time points (Gernsbacher, Stevenson, Khandakar, & Goldsmith, 2008; Naigles, 2013).

Overarching Research Questions

From all three perspectives (linguistic, clinical, and that of developmental psychologists), two overarching questions recur: Is the variability of language development and use in children with ASD a function of the *language*, such that some linguistic domains are more vulnerable to ASD than others? Is the variability a function of the *individual*, such that some characteristics predispose those with ASD to have more versus less difficulty with language development and use? The investigations presented in this volume address both of these questions. In particular, contributors consider and assess language as a system of interdependent levels (phonology, lexical semantics, grammar—morphology, single-clause syntax, complex syntax—and semantics/pragmatics), and scrutinize the structures in these levels in sufficient detail to (a) observe pockets of strengths or weaknesses possibly unique to a specific level or (b) observe connections across levels that are linguistic-theoretic or processing based. Naigles and Fein's (Chapter 3) discovery that highly verbal children with ASD nonetheless have difficulty using a shape bias to extend word meanings is an example of (a); Janke and Perovic's (Chapter 7) demonstration of children with ASD's success in identifying referents that require tapping both syntactic and pragmatic information is an example of (b).

Contributors also target the psychological underpinnings or precursors to successful language acquisition and use, scrutinizing characteristics within the child such as processing speed, attention, and working memory. For example, Bavin and Baker (Chapter 2) demonstrate that while both TD children and children with ASD display anticipatory looking to referent objects based on prior speech, the ASD group's looking occurred significantly more slowly. Characteristics of the child in his or her milieu, such as social-interpersonal interaction and the linguistic richness of the input, are also discussed, with McDuffie, Thurman, Channell, and Abbeduto (Chapter 4) intensively exploring the role of social cues in word learning by children with ASD as well as children with fragile X syndrome. Intriguingly, the superficially similar social impairments of the two groups nonetheless seem coupled with different patterns of word learning. Nadig and Bang (Chapter 5) highlight the increasingly compelling evidence that, despite their generally poor social skills, children with ASD nonetheless are able to use their parents' linguistic or social input (or both) in the service of learning language.

Finally, conventional standardized testing lacks the methodological techniques and range of stimuli that could help reveal the origins and extent of the language variability in children with ASD. The contributors of this volume deploy new and exciting methods that allow us to observe language development and language processing in real time, as well as both within and independently of the social milieu. For example, studies involving eye tracking during language use are covered in five chapters in this book (Norbury, Chapter 1; Bavin & Baker, Chapter 2; Naigles & Fein, Chapter 3; McDuffie et al., Chapter 4; Eigsti & Schuh, Chapter 9), with the general goal of using a task that is both less socially taxing (thereby tapping linguistic knowledge less fettered by communicative demands) and more finely tuned to the time course of speech production and comprehension (thereby illuminating when language processing might go awry). Intriguingly, researchers have revealed both typical and atypical looking patterns during language use in children and adolescents with ASD.

Plan of the Volume

This volume will be of interest to students and researchers from all language-relevant disciplines, including linguists, psychologists, sociologists, and behavioral and cognitive neuroscientists, from the graduate student to the professional level. Although each of the three perspectives included here has its own terminology and assumptions, chapter authors have made considerable effort to present their research in ways that will be comprehensible to those outside their specific disciplines. Examples are plentiful throughout, and jargon has been kept to a minimum (see also the section on terminology at the end of this chapter). All contributors include both discussions of background literature and descriptions of their state-of-the-art empirical results, and many include suggestions of how to extend their findings for use in interventions.

The following 11 chapters are ordered somewhat in line with the levels of language they focus on, with investigations of lexical semantics and single-clause syntax presented first (Chapters 1–5), followed by investigations of computationally complex phonology and syntax (Chapter 6) and the syntax-pragmatics interface (Chapters 7 and 8), and then investigations of pragmatics (Chapters 9 and 10). The final chapter (Chapter 11) considers a wide range of language structures and processes with respect to one extremely intriguing subgroup: children originally diagnosed with ASD who no longer carry the diagnosis (i.e., “optimal outcome”; Fein et al., 2013). Additional prominent subthemes of the chapters include discussions of what eye-tracking methods, cross-disorder comparisons (Norbury, Chapter 1; McDuffie et al., Chapter 4; Nadig & Bang, Chapter 5; Tuller et al., Chapter 6; Suh et al., Chapter 11), and examinations of what the contexts of language development (Naigles & Fein, Chapter 3; McDuffie et al., Chapter 4; Nadig & Bang, Chapter 5; Suh et al., Chapter 11) have revealed about the variability and uniqueness of ASD language use.

Most of the chapters consider the language of children with ASD who are school age (6–11 years) or adolescents, although two (Chapters 3 and 5) discuss children as young as 2 years of age. The dominant language under investigation is English; however, another innovation of this volume is to reflect the increasing inclusion of additional languages to the study of language development and representation in ASD: three of the 11 chapters (Nadig & Bang, Chapter 5; Tuller et al., Chapter 6; Durrleman-Tame et al., Chapter 8) present findings from French learners. Investigations of the language use of children and adults with ASD who are exposed to the many other languages of the world are, of course, of great need and importance (e.g., Su, Jin, Wan, Zhang, & Su, 2014).

In sum, these chapters provide a wealth of detailed information about the language development, processing, and production of children with ASD. Some authors aimed for breadth, taking readers through beautifully integrated surveys of recent research, whereas other authors chose depth, showing readers how they generated and analyzed specific linguistic findings. Variability of language use, as suspected, is accounted for in multiple ways, including language centered (e.g., some concepts and constructions are indeed more resilient than others), child centered (e.g., more efficient speech processing and social referencing enable better word learning and conversational interaction), and situation centered (e.g., parental behaviors and intensive interventions can facilitate the language development of children with ASD). Building on these findings, many of the chapters call for a fourth category of innovative investigation, involving longitudinal studies (e.g., Anderson, Liang, & Lord, 2014). For example, children should be followed over time to discover the *effects*—weeks, months, and years later—of more versus less efficient speech processing, parental responsivity, and richness of linguistic input. Moreover, concepts, constructions, and conversation topics that are challenging for children with ASD to produce or understand at one age can be reassessed at later ages to see whether and when they are mastered. The language of children with ASD is still a puzzle in need of solutions, but the chapters in this volume illuminate many of the tools needed to identify the puzzle pieces and fit them together.

Explanation of Some Linguistic Terminology

For additional information on terminology, see Hoff (2008).

Grammatical morphology is the structure of words that results from combining word roots with prefixes or endings that mark grammatical relations, such as the *–s* at the end of verbs to mark agreement with a third-person subject (he runs) or the *–ed* at the end of verbs to mark the past tense.

A *mental lexicon* is the "dictionary" of words and associated knowledge that speaker–hearers have.

Phonology is the sound system of a language. Phonological segments include sonorants (*s, z*), glides (*w, y*), liquids (*l*), and obstruents (*p, b, d, t*). Phonological syllables can appear at onset (beginning), medial (middle), and coda (final) positions in words.

Pronouns (*she, they, his*), clitics (*le, la, les* in French), and empty categories (phonologically null) refer to full noun phrases (antecedents) in surrounding discourse; their reference is governed by syntactic and pragmatic principles.

Syntax is a system of rules for building phrases out of words (which belong to particular grammatical categories such as *noun* and *verb*) and for building sentences out of those constituent phrases.

Complex sentences are composed of a main clause plus at least one subordinate/ dependent clause. Sentence complements are subordinate clauses that modify or further specify the verb phrase in the main clause. Relative clauses are subordinate clauses that modify or further specify one of the noun phrases in the main clause.

Syntactic bootstrapping is the process of acquiring aspects of the meanings of words based on the ways those words appear in sentences.

Wh-questions are questions that begin with *who, what, where, why, when,* or *how.* In "movement" languages, these wh-words usually appear at the beginning of the question. In "in situ" languages, the wh-words usually appear at the location in the sentence of the phrase, which the wh-word is asking about. For example, "What is she wearing?" in English is produced as "She [is] wearing what?" in Chinese.

References

Akhtar, N., & Gernsbacher, M. A. (2007). Joint attention and vocabulary development: A critical look. *Language and Linguistics Compass, 1,* 195–207. http://dx.doi.org/10.1111/j.1749-818X.2007.00014.x

Altmann, G. (1996). *The ascent of Babel.* Oxford, England: Oxford University Press.

American Psychiatric Association. (2000). *Diagnostic and statistical manual of mental disorders* (4th ed., text rev.). Washington, DC: Author.

American Psychiatric Association. (2013). *Diagnostic and statistical manual of mental disorders* (5th ed.). Washington, DC: Author.

Anderson, D. K., Liang, J. W., & Lord, C. (2014). Predicting young adult outcome among more and less cognitively able individuals with autism spectrum disorders. *Journal of Child Psychology and Psychiatry, 55,* 485–494. http://dx.doi.org/10.1111/jcpp.12178

Archibald, L., & Noonan, N. (2015). Processing deficits in children with language impairments. In E. L. Bavin & L. R. Naigles (Eds.), *The Cambridge handbook of child language* (2nd ed., pp. 564–584). http://dx.doi.org/10.1017/CBO9781316095829.026

Chomsky, N. (2006). *Language and mind* (3rd ed.). http://dx.doi.org/10.1017/CBO9780511791222

Clark, E. V. (2015). Lexical meaning. In E. L. Bavin & L. R. Naigles (Eds.), *The Cambridge handbook of child language* (2nd ed., pp. 351–368). http://dx.doi.org/10.1017/CBO9781316095829.016

Eigsti, I. M., & Bennetto, L. (2009). Grammaticality judgments in autism spectrum disorders: Deviance or delay. *Journal of Child Language, 19,* 1–23.

Fein, D., Barton, M., Eigsti, I.-M., Kelley, E., Naigles, L. R., Schultz, R. T., . . . Tyson, K. (2013). Optimal outcome in individuals with a history of autism. *Journal of Child Psychology and Psychiatry, 54,* 195–205. http://dx.doi.org/10.1111/jcpp.12037

Fombonne, E., Quirke, S., & Hagen, A. (2011). Epidemiology of pervasive developmental disorders. In D. G. Amaral, D. H. Geschwind, & G. Dawson (Eds.), *Autism spectrum disorders* (pp. 90–111). http://dx.doi.org/10.1093/med/9780195371826.003.0007

Gernsbacher, M. A., Geye, H. M., & Ellis Weismer, S. (2005). The role of language and communication impairments within autism. In P. Fletcher & J. Miller (Eds.), *Developmental theory and language disorders* (pp. 73–93). http://dx.doi.org/10.1075/tilar.4.06ger

Gernsbacher, M. A., Stevenson, J. L., Khandakar, S., & Goldsmith, H. H. (2008). Why does joint attention look atypical in autism? *Child Development Perspectives*, *2*, 38–45. http://dx.doi.org/10.1111/j.1750-8606.2008.00039.x

Goldin-Meadow, S. (2015). From gesture to word. In E. L. Bavin & L. R. Naigles (Eds.), *The Cambridge handbook of child language* (2nd ed., pp. 183–204). http://dx.doi.org/10.1017/CBO9781316095829.009

Goldstein, S., & Ozonoff, S. (2009). Historical perspective and overview. In S. Goldstein, J. Naglieri, & S. Ozonoff (Eds.), *Assessment of autism spectrum disorders* (pp. 1–17). New York, NY: Guilford Press.

Hoff, E. (2008). *Language development* (4th ed.). Belmont, CA: Wadsworth/Cengage Learning.

Höhle, B. (2015). Crosslinguistic perspectives on segmentation and categorization in early language acquisition. In E. L. Bavin & L. R. Naigles (Eds.), *The Cambridge handbook of child language* (2nd ed., pp. 159–182). http://dx.doi.org/10.1017/CBO9781316095829.008

Kjelgaard, M. M., & Tager-Flusberg, H. (2001). An investigation of language impairment in autism: Implications for genetic subgroups. *Language and Cognitive Processes*, *16*, 287–308. http://dx.doi.org/10.1080/01690960042000058

Leonard, L. (2015). Language symptoms and their possible sources in specific language impairment. In E. L. Bavin & L. R. Naigles (Eds.), *The Cambridge handbook of child language* (2nd ed., pp. 545–563). http://dx.doi.org/10.1017/CBO9781316095829.025

Naigles, L. R. (2013). Input and language development in children with autism. *Seminars in Speech and Language*, *34*, 237–248. http://dx.doi.org/10.1055/s-0033-1353446

Naigles, L. R., & Chin, I. (2015). Language development in children with autism. In E. L. Bavin & L. R. Naigles (Eds.), *The Cambridge handbook of child language* (2nd ed., pp. 637–658). http://dx.doi.org/10.1017/CBO9781316095829.029

Naigles, L. R., Kelty, E., Jaffery, R., & Fein, D. (2011). Abstractness and continuity in the syntactic development of young children with autism. *Autism Research*, *4*, 422–437. http://dx.doi.org/10.1002/aur.223

Pickett, E., Pullara, O., O'Grady, J., & Gordon, B. (2009). Speech acquisition in older nonverbal individuals with autism: A review of features, methods, and prognosis. *Cognitive and Behavioral Neurology*, *22*, 1–21. http://dx.doi.org/10.1097/WNN.0b013e318190d185

Riches, N. G., Loucas, T., Baird, G., Charman, T., & Simonoff, E. (2010). Sentence repetition in adolescents with specific language impairments and autism: An investigation of complex syntax. *International Journal of Language & Communication Disorders*, *45*, 47–60. http://dx.doi.org/10.3109/13682820802647676

Roberts, J., Rice, M., & Tager-Flusberg, H. (2004). Tense marking in children with autism. *Applied Psycholinguistics*, *25*, 429–448. http://dx.doi.org/10.1017/S0142716404001201

Shield, A. (2014). Preliminary findings of similarities and differences in the signed and spoken language of children with autism. *Seminars in Speech and Language*, *35*, 309–320. http://dx.doi.org/10.1055/s-0034-1389103

Snedeker, J., & Huang, Y. T. (2015). Sentence processing. In E. L. Bavin & L. R. Naigles (Eds.), *The Cambridge handbook of child language* (2nd ed., pp. 409–437). http://dx.doi.org/10.1017/CBO9781316095829.019

Stirling, L., Douglas, S., Leekam, S., & Carey, L. (2014). The use of narrative in studying communication in autism spectrum disorders: A review of methodologies and findings. In J. Arciuli & J. Brock (Eds.), *Communication in autism* (pp. 171–215). http://dx.doi.org/10.1075/tilar.11.09sti

Su, Y., Jin, Y., Wan, G., Zhang, J., & Su, L. (2014). Interpretation of *wh*-words in Mandarin-speaking high-functioning children with autism spectrum disorders. *Research in Autism Spectrum Disorders*, *8*, 1364–1372. http://dx.doi.org/10.1016/j.rasd.2014.07.008

Tager-Flusberg, H. (2006). Defining language phenotypes in autism. *Clinical Neuroscience Research*, *6*, 219–224. http://dx.doi.org/10.1016/j.cnr.2006.06.007

Tager-Flusberg, H., & Joseph, R. M. (2003). Identifying neurocognitive phenotypes in autism. *Philosophical Transactions of the Royal Society B: Biological Sciences*, *358*, 303–314. http://dx.doi.org/10.1098/rstb.2002.1198

Tager-Flusberg, H., Paul, R., & Lord, C. (2005). Language and communication in autism. In F. R. Volkmar, R. Paul, A. Klin, & D. Cohen (Eds.), *Handbook of autism and pervasive developmental disorders* (3rd ed., pp. 335–364). New York, NY: Wiley.

Taylor, L., Mayberry, M., & Whitehouse, A. (2014). Do autism spectrum disorders and specific language impairment have a shared aetiology? In J. Arciuli & J. Brock (Eds.), *Communication in autism* (pp. 75–102). Amsterdam, the Netherlands: John Benjamins.

Tek, S., Mesite, L., Fein, D., & Naigles, L. (2014). Longitudinal analyses of expressive language development reveal two distinct language profiles among young children with autism spectrum disorders. *Journal of Autism and Developmental Disorders*, *44*, 75–89. http://dx.doi.org/10.1007/s10803-013-1853-4

Thiessen, E., & Erickson, L. (2015). Statistical learning. In E. L Bavin & L. R. Naigles (Eds.), *The Cambridge handbook of child language* (2nd ed., pp. 37–60). http://dx.doi.org/10.1017/CBO9781316095829.003

Tomasello, M. (2015). The usage-based theory of language acquisition. In E. L. Bavin & L. R. Naigles (Eds.), *The Cambridge handbook of child language* (2nd ed., pp. 89–106). http://dx.doi.org/10.1017/CBO9781316095829.005

Tomblin, B. (2015). Children with SLI. In E. L. Bavin & L. R. Naigles (Eds.), *The Cambridge handbook of child language* (2nd ed., pp. 527–544). http://dx.doi.org/10.1017/CBO9781316095829.024

van der Lely, H. K. (2005). Domain-specific cognitive systems: Insight from Grammatical-SLI. *Trends in Cognitive Science*, *9*, 53–59. http://dx.doi.org/10.1016/j.tics.2004.12.002

Whitehouse, A. J., Barry, J. G., & Bishop, D. V. (2008). Further defining the language impairment of autism: Is there a specific language impairment subtype? *Journal of Communication Disorders*, *41*, 319–336. http://dx.doi.org/10.1016/j.jcomdis.2008.01.002

Williams, D., Botting, N., & Boucher, J. (2008). Language in autism and specific language impairment: Where are the links? *Psychological Bulletin*, *134*, 944–963. http://dx.doi.org/10.1037/a0013743

World Health Organization. (1992). *The ICD-10 classification of mental and behavioural disorders: Clinical descriptions and diagnostic guidelines*. Geneva, Switzerland: Author.

Courtenay Frazier Norbury

1 Eye-Tracking as a Window on Language Processing in ASD

Introduction

In our everyday lives, the language that we hear and produce is situated within a rich environmental experience. The conversational context is shaped by the physical and visual landscape, our previous experiences and knowledge about the world, and our understanding of our social partners. In contrast, clinical assessment of language abilities most often occurs in the absence of rich contextual information. It is therefore unsurprising that scores on structured and standardized tests of language may not always reflect an individual's ability to use language in socially meaningful contexts (Norbury, Nash, Baird, & Bishop, 2004). This may be especially true in the case of autism spectrum disorder (ASD), in which there is variation in core language abilities and qualitative differences in how core language skills are used for the purposes of social communication.

In this chapter, I consider how innovations in eye-tracking technology can elucidate differences in language processing within ASD. I begin by outlining the rich variation that exists in language ability within ASD and then explain how eye-tracking methods work. Many eye-tracking studies of ASD have focused on precursor skills, such as visual and social attention, and I evaluate the evidence that early perturbations of attention may negatively affect language learning. I then provide a selective review of studies that have used eye-tracking methods with typically developing (TD) language users. Application of these techniques in studies of language processing within ASD is just beginning but includes studies of lexical processing, sentence comprehension, language production, and discourse processing. Taken together, these studies have highlighted multiple factors that contribute to individual differences in language development within ASD.

Language Variation Within ASD

Impairments in using language for social purposes is a cardinal feature of ASD (American Psychiatric Association, 2013). Impairments in language content and structure, for example, vocabulary, phonology, and grammar, are considerably more variable (Norbury, 2013a). For example, a significant minority of children with ASD have limited expressive verbal skills (Wodka, Mathy, & Kalb, 2013). In contrast, Loucas et al. (2008) found that almost half of children with ASD with normal nonverbal reasoning skills scored within

http://dx.doi.org/10.1037/15964-002
Innovative Investigations of Language in Autism Spectrum Disorder, L. R. Naigles (Editor)

the normal range on standard tests of language structure and content. The remaining children in this sample had a profile in which language skills were significantly below expectations for age and nonverbal ability; grammar was strikingly impaired and vocabulary and nonsense word repetition were in the low-average range, while articulation skills were generally preserved. Such a profile is reminiscent of children without autism but with specific language impairment (SLI; Kjelgaard & Tager-Flusberg, 2001).

Historically, language impairments have been considered sequelae of core deficits in social interaction and social cognition. However, the identification of distinct language phenotypes within ASD (Tager-Flusberg & Joseph, 2003) has challenged this view and given rise to an influential theory positing that ASD with additional language impairment (ALI) represents a comorbid condition that shares neurobiological risk with SLI (Tager-Flusberg & Joseph, 2003). Similarities between the SLI and ALI groups are often mirrored by similar performance between children with ASD and language scores within the normal range (ALN) and their TD peers (for review, see Norbury, 2013a).

Our understanding of the sources of language variation within ASD is hampered by the limitations of traditional assessments of language competence; they can only ever reflect the outcome of a complex information processing chain and cannot elucidate where in that chain language processing breaks down. It is therefore possible that different clinical populations experience different vulnerabilities with the various skills that underpin language processing. The net result might be similar performance on a given task, but for very different reasons. For instance, Norbury (2005) asked children with ALI, ALN, and SLI and TD peers to complete a picture verification task. In this task, participants heard a simple declarative sentence and 1,000 ms later, a picture appeared on the screen. Participants were required to indicate whether the picture was an appropriate match for the sentence they just heard. In some instances, the sentences included an ambiguous word such as *bank*, which could be followed by a picture of a riverbank or a picture of a financial institution. Some sentences included a neutral verb (e.g., "John ran by the bank") in which either picture would be acceptable, and other sentences contained a verb that biased a particular interpretation of the ambiguous word (e.g., "John fished by the bank"). Overall, accuracy rates for the TD and ALN groups were much higher in the biasing condition relative to SLI and ALI groups, as children with SLI and ALI continued to accept either picture, even if the verb in the sentence context was inconsistent with the picture. The similarity in performance between SLI and ALI is theoretically and clinically interesting, but there are numerous reasons why children may not succeed at this task. Children may not understand the verb or understand the multiple meanings of the ambiguous words. Alternatively, they may understand the individual words in the sentence but fail to integrate those words or fail to remember the whole sentence when it is time to make a decision. It could be that understanding of sentences is intact, but problems with sustaining attention result in a focus on the final word rather than the entire sentence. It is therefore possible that the similar performances of the ALI and SLI groups do not reflect comorbidity but arise from different deficits in underlying mechanisms. Similarly, the "typical" performance of children with ALN may be characterized by subtle differences in the time course of language processing, which may contribute to differences in using language in everyday contexts.

Online methods of measuring social or language processing may take us closer to the source of linguistic errors, highlighting when and why language breaks down and whether the time course of language processing differs as a function of diagnostic status. Eye-tracking paradigms allow fine-grained analysis of language processing in real time and have enormous potential to elucidate the factors that influence language variation within the autism spectrum (Norbury, 2013b).

Eye-Tracking as a Window on Language Processing: Studies of Typical and Atypical Language Learners

How Eye-Tracking Studies Work

The world around us is packed with visually complex information from which we must filter out distractions and focus on the relevant aspects of any scene to understand what is happening and how best to pursue our goals. The sequence and duration of gaze is fundamental to gathering information because high-quality visual detail is only available from a limited spatial region surrounding the fovea (Henderson, 2003). Our visual attention requires a combination of top-down and bottom-up processes. For example, our eyes are drawn to movement, social beings, and otherwise visually salient objects (Henderson, 2003). However, classic experiments by Yarbus (1967) demonstrated that our internal goals also significantly influence the order and duration of gaze to different aspects of a visual scene. Yarbus presented adults with a painting to inspect and then asked viewers to report specific details about the picture. If the task was to establish the age of characters depicted in the scene, viewers increased looking time to faces relative to baseline. In contrast, if the goal was to establish how wealthy the characters were, looks to faces decreased while looking time to clothes and possessions increased.

The application of eye-tracking techniques to the study of language processing was pioneered by Cooper (1974) and Tanenhaus, Spivey-Knowlton, Eberhard, and Sedivy (1995) using the *visual world paradigm*. In this paradigm, viewers are presented with a visual scene, and their eye movements are recorded while they listen to spoken language because looking times to particular objects are influenced by what the viewers hear. For example, in Cooper's (1974) work, viewers began to gaze at a picture of a snake as the word *snake* unfolded. Interestingly, if the picture "snake" was not on screen, viewers would gaze at semantically related items, providing a window on the implicit semantic associations made as language is processed. Thus, by recording the eye movements of viewers as they perform language-related tasks, we can increase understanding of what information is available to the viewer, when that information becomes available, and how that information is related to spoken language production and comprehension.

The application of eye-tracking methods to explore language processing in young TD children or children with atypical language acquisition is a new and rapidly emerging field. To date, only a handful of studies that have applied these methods to children with ASD, yet these studies illustrate the potential of such methods to yield new insights into qualitative differences in foundational skills (visual and social attention) and in the timing of language processes that serve comprehension and production. Most eye-tracking studies of language processing in ASD to date have involved older, cognitively able children and have measured aspects of language comprehension. This largely reflects the attention demands of experimental tasks and the technical demands of linking spoken language with visual fixations. As methods for presentation (including unrestricted head movements and mobile eye-tracking) and analysis continue to develop, there is great potential for extending eye-tracking research to a wider variety of participants in ever more naturalistic environments.

What Are the Dependent Variables in an Eye-Tracking Study?

Eye movements are typically divided into *fixations*, the points at which gaze pauses at a certain position, usually for at least 100 ms, and *saccades*, rapid movements to a new position. The temporal order of fixations and saccades yields a *scanpath*, which provides important information about when and for how long the viewer gazed at different aspects of the visual display. *Fixation duration* to a particular area of interest is typically the first variable researchers include in their analyses. In the context of language and communication, there is much interest in the extent to which children with ASD fixate the eye and mouth regions of the human face, as these are purveyors of social cues important for language. *Latency of fixation* is also a key variable; for example, how long it takes a participant to look at a picture of CAKE on hearing the phrase "Jane will eat the . . ." (Nation, Marshall, & Altmann, 2003). We may also be interested in *first fixations* because these can tell us what is of immediate interest to the viewer. We can then investigate how long it takes to move the eyes from the first fixation to another area of interest. Using the pattern and timing of fixations, we can begin to infer a number of cognitive processes, such as cognitive intent, interest and attention, salience, and cognitive load (Aslin, 2007).

Eye-Tracking Studies of Visual and Social Attention in ASD: Links to Language Development

Visual Attention

To make inferences about underlying cognitive processes, we must first establish that individuals with ASD do not differ from peers with respect to basic oculomotor control processes. In general, studies of children and adults with ASD report intact basic oculomotor control (Kelly, Walker, & Norbury, 2013; Luna, Doll, Hegedus, Minshew, & Sweeney, 2007). However, studies of infant siblings at genetic risk for ASD have reported atypicalities in both visual orienting (disengagement from central fixation to peripheral cue) and oculomotor efficiency (fixation to peripheral cue in the absence of competing stimuli; Elsabbagh et al., 2009). Such studies have suggested that reduced attentional control may be an early marker of ASD that has consequences for how young children with ASD gather information about the world around them. It may also adversely affect social-communicative development because the child may not recognize or follow social-communicative cues such as eye gaze (cf. Brenner, Turner, & Müller, 2007). However, longitudinal studies directly linking early oculomotor anomalies to later socio-communicative function are currently lacking. In addition, early perturbations of visual attention are evident in other neurodevelopmental disorders, such as Down syndrome, Fragile X, and attention-deficit/hyperactivity disorder (Cornish, Scerif, & Karmiloff-Smith, 2007).

Measures of volitional oculomotor control are equally vital to understanding the interaction of vision and language. Most studies that use eye-tracking methods to explore language processing strip the visual scene to a bare minimum to avoid visual distraction. This allows a fairly "pure" estimate of how language influences eye movements (and vice versa) but is far removed from the challenges of language processing in everyday contexts. In the real world, we must actively select visual targets from a visually cluttered world and filter out extraneous visual information to focus on the task at hand. An important question, therefore, is to what extent are individuals with ASD able to do the same?

Volitional oculomotor control is typically assessed using an antisaccade task, a well-known measure of top-down attention control. A cue appears peripheral to a central fixation, but in this task participants are required to ignore the cue and fixate the opposite side of the screen. Kelly, Walker, and Norbury (2013) used this task in school-age children with ALI and ALN and comparison groups of TD age-matched peers and peers with SLI. ASD diagnosis was not predictive of task performance; only those children with language impairments showed significant impairments on the antisaccade tasks, as both the ALI and SLI groups had greater difficulty suppressing reflexive shifts of gaze to the cue. A similar pattern of performance was found on a visual search task in which children had to fixate a prespecified target and maintain fixation on that target while ignoring visual distractors. Although the ALI and SLI groups were just as quick as ALN and TD peers to find the target, they made significantly more fixations to distractor items than the groups without language difficulty. These findings echo Takarae, Luna, Minshew, and Sweeney (2008), who reported increased deficits on visual motor tasks in individuals with ASD with early language delay, relative to peers with ASD who met early language milestones.

These findings highlight the importance of parsing heterogeneity within ASD but do not speak to the direction of causation. It has been argued that early deficits in top-down visual attention can be deleterious to language development because such deficits alter the child's ability to learn from visual social cues and disrupt the establishment of joint attention, with cascading effects on language learning (Brenner et al., 2007). However, for older children and adults, performance on tasks of visual attention control may benefit from the ability to verbalize task rules (e.g., "look to the opposite side"). Longitudinal studies of infant siblings at risk for ASD may clarify the causal relations between early perturbations of visual attention and later language development.

Social Attention

Far more research interest has been directed at investigating differences in social attention within ASD. Although there are many contradictory findings in the literature, the emerging consensus is that the majority of individuals with ASD display less spontaneous attention to social cues, relative to peers (for a review, see Papagiannopoulou, Chitty, Hermens, Hickie, & Lagopoulos, 2014). Seminal work by Klin and colleagues (Klin, Jones, Schultz, Volkmar, & Cohen, 2002) investigated fixation patterns to human faces during dynamic scenes of social interaction. Highly verbal adults with ASD displayed reduced fixations to the eye region of faces but increased fixation to mouth regions relative to TD peers. Klin and colleagues (2002) argued that this reflects compensation; increased fixation on the mouth could increase linguistic competence, which could in turn provide overt strategies for dealing with confusing social cues conveyed by the eyes. Norbury et al. (2009) extended these findings by investigating fixation patterns in adolescents with ASD who did (ALI) or did not (ALN) meet clinical criteria for language impairment. Neither group showed increased fixation time to mouth regions relative to TD peers, although fixation duration to the mouth was significantly correlated with parent ratings of communicative competence. Fixations to eye regions also differed according to language status; those adolescents with ASD who had language scores within the normal range (ALN) displayed reduced fixations to eye regions and more fixations to objects in the background. In contrast, those with language impairments (ALI) did not differ from TD peers. Rice, Moriuchi, Jones, and Klin (2012) extended these findings in a younger and much larger sample of children with ASD. Fixation patterns varied considerably within the ASD group and aligned with cognitive profiles, rather than ASD symptom profile. Those with better verbal, relative to nonverbal, abilities preferentially fixated the mouth, again suggesting a possible focus on language detail at the expense of nonverbal social information.

These studies have clearly highlighted the importance of considering language variation within ASD as the group mean often masks significant, and clinically relevant, within group variation. These studies have also raised lingering questions about what the relationships between spontaneous social gaze and language competence mean. It is noteworthy that Norbury et al. (2009) also found that the ALN group had higher reported rates of restricted interests and repetitive behaviors. This raises an intriguing possibility that higher levels of restricted interests and repetitive behaviors may alter the viewing goals of some individuals with ASD. For example, increased looking time to the background may reflect efforts to find objects of particular interest (e.g., light switches) before attending to social information.

These findings also suggest that within-group variation in visual attention to social cues may be associated with different language outcomes for children with ASD, yet few studies have measured this relationship directly. Young, Merin, Rogers, and Ozonoff (2009) did report significant relationships between face scanning at 6 months of age and expressive language outcomes at 24 months. Specifically, eye–mouth index scores (i.e., amount of gaze to the eye region of a face divided by the combined amount of gaze to both eyes and mouth) were negatively related to language outcome, such that increased gaze to eyes yielded slower rates of expressive language development. The numbers of children later diagnosed with ASD was small ($n = 3$), with a further eight diagnosed with other clinical concerns. In addition, given the fluidity of language development within the early years, the long-term predictive power of early differences in social viewing is questionable. Nevertheless, many children with ASD appear to be attending to the world in a qualitatively different way. In particular, infants at high risk for ASD do not preferentially attend to social and linguistic cues evident on a speaker's face. Such cues are vital to establishing joint attention and mapping novel linguistic forms to referents in the environment; thus, it is reasonable to expect differences in viewing patterns may contribute to language learning difficulties. Follow-up of at-risk siblings will elucidate relationships between early gaze patterns and later language.

Eye-Tracking Studies of Language Processing

Word Learning

Given reported deficits in social orienting and joint attention, eye-tracking studies that elucidate the child's ability to utilize social cues to learn new words have yielded surprising findings. Norbury, Griffiths, and Nation (2010) investigated the use of social cues to word learning in 6-year-old children with ASD and their age-matched TD peers. Participants viewed static images of a woman standing behind three novel objects. In a neutral condition, the woman gazed straight to camera, whereas in a social cue condition, the woman gazed directly at one of the three objects. Participants heard sentences such as "Show me the kellow" and were asked to click on the appropriate object. Participants learned four words over six trials, the first of which was always presented in the neutral condition. There were no differences between the groups in the rate of learning over the course of six trials; importantly, accuracy increased dramatically for both groups when a social cue was present. There were no differences in the total number of fixations to the objects or to the eyes during the initial inspection period. Both groups increased fixation to the eyes in the social cue condition relative to the neutral condition, suggesting that these children at least recognized that the eyes were more informative in this context. However, subtle differences emerged as the sentence unfolded; TD children increased gaze to the eyes just before making their selection, in effect using the gaze information to check their own responses. In contrast, within the ASD group, looks to the eyes decreased during this period, suggesting that the children with ASD did not engage in social referencing to the same extent as their peers. Notably, the two groups were matched on raw and standard scores of a receptive vocabulary task, but the ASD group scored one standard deviation below their peers on an expressive vocabulary measure that required verbal definitions of target words. Thus, the ability to follow overt social cues may facilitate associative learning of words and referents, but more nuanced social skills may be required for developing detailed semantic knowledge and meeting the pragmatic demands of the assessment situation.

Tenenbaum, Amso, Abar, and Sheinkopf (2014) measured attention to eyes and mouths while viewing a dynamic video of an adult teaching new words to viewers. Participants included 2- to 5-year-old children with ASD, children with language delay matched for age and raw scores on expressive and receptive language assessment, and a much younger group of TD toddlers matched for language age (mean age 16 months). There were no group differences in attention to eyes, mouths, or referent objects. There were also no differences in latency to fixate the target novel object, suggesting that, again, children with ASD were learning from the social cues at the same rate as their peers. Caution is warranted, however, because the sample sizes were small and there was considerable within-group variation in latency to looks at target. Increased fixation time to the speaker's mouth positively correlated with standardized measures of language competence in children with ASD and their younger TD peers, but not in the group of children with language delay. An unexpected result was that increased looking time to the mouth was associated with lower standard scores, only in the group with language delay. This finding urges caution in how we interpret the looking behavior; looking at the mouth may be driven by differences in language competence, rather than driving those differences initially. On this view, fixations to the mouth might signal increased effort in processing the linguistic code. Attention to facial components shifts as a function of both age and language ability, so matching on language scores may have obscured important developmental changes in this study. It is thus necessary to study developmental trajectories, looking at the extent to which early differences in fixating social cues predicts individual differences in word learning and later language development.

Gliga et al. (2012) investigated word learning in 3-year-old children at high risk for ASD (by virtue of having an older sibling with ASD) and a low-risk comparison group. Ten of the high-risk children had significant social-communication deficits indicative of ASD at age 3; 25 remaining high-risk children scored within the normal range on social communication measures. As in the Tenenbaum et al. (2014) study, participants viewed video clips of an adult presenting novel objects with novel labels. Across all groups, the first fixation after attending to the speaker's face followed the speaker's direction of gaze, replicating the Norbury et al. (2010) findings that children with ASD are able to follow gaze cues. However, unlike these earlier findings, the at-risk group with poor social-communication skills looked less at target referents and were less able than comparison groups to learn the new words. These differences were not accounted for by differences in age or general cognitive ability. Gaze following and word learning were only moderately correlated across groups, although the numbers of high-risk children affected by ASD symptoms remains small.

Eye-tracking methods have provided convincing evidence that when learning new words, many children with ASD look at the speaker's face in a similar way to typical peers and are able to follow the direction of gaze to object referents. There is also some consistency in findings that the timing of looks to social cues on the face is similar across groups. However, these findings suggest that gaze following is not sufficient for word learning and raise questions about additional challenges that may be present in ASD that adversely affect word learning. Here, eye-tracking studies have yielded some novel insights into looking behaviors later in the joint attention episode; for example, looking times to object referents may differ. As a result, some children with ASD may not be gazing at the target when they hear the phonological form. Behavioral data in combination with eye-movement data can be particularly instructive. For example, Norbury et al. (2010) demonstrated superior recall of phonological information in newly learned words for verbally able children with ASD and postulated that children with ASD who experience language impairment may have additional phonological deficits (see also Tuller et al., Chapter 6, this volume). It is also worth remembering that as children get older, new words are more frequently encountered incidentally in text and television, rather than in ostensible social contexts. Thus, differences in the ability to use surrounding linguistic context to infer new meaning may further limit word-learning opportunities for children with ASD.

Sentence Comprehension

Several early studies have explored the extent to which TD adults were able to integrate the linguistic and contextual constraints on grammatical processing. Tanenhaus et al. (1995) recorded eye movements while listeners performed instructions that were either temporarily ambiguous (e.g., "put the apple on the towel in the box") or unambiguous (e.g., "put the apple *that's* on the towel in the box"), when both an apple on a towel and an empty towel were in the display. Looking times to the empty towel were much greater in the ambiguous condition relative to the unambiguous condition, demonstrating that listeners initially assume that *on the towel* is a destination, not a modifier. However, looking times to the empty towel dramatically decreased when an apple on a napkin was introduced to the visual scene; in this context, listeners immediately assumed that *on the towel* was a modifier of *apple*. Trueswell, Sekerina, Hill, and Logrip (1999) applied this methodology to young TD language learners. In contrast to adults, they found that 5-year-old children were less likely to attend to the referential context, instead displaying a strong tendency to interpret *on the towel* as the goal of *put* reflected in both their actions and in looks to the incorrect destination. When the syntactic ambiguity was removed, the children showed adult-like patterns of eye movements. Trueswell et al. (1999) argued that this finding might reflect the limited processing capacities of young children. In other words, young children may be unable to contemplate multiple interpretations of complex sentences simultaneously or to integrate contextual constraints with the linguistic stream rapidly enough to alter their interpretation of the incoming sentence.

Diehl, Friedberg, Paul, and Snedeker (2014) employed a similar experimental design to investigate the extent to which prosodic cues may support syntactic processing in adolescents with ASD. Diehl et al. found that, overall, children with ASD were able to use prosodic cues to resolve syntactic ambiguities of the type described by Tanenhaus et al. (1995). Difficulties in syntactic ambiguity resolution were more evident in young children (with or without ASD), especially if the interpretation was different from sentences they were exposed to earlier. In contrast, teenagers (with or without ASD) were able to use prosodic cues to rapidly shift their eyes (and therefore their interpretation) to the intended target. Fixation patterns to competitor objects in younger children with ASD, however, suggested that children with ASD were more likely than TD peers to experience continued interference from earlier exposures, perhaps reflecting difficulties inhibiting prior interpretations or shifting attention to new cues. The wide age range included in this study provided some important information about potential developmental trajectories of the prosody–syntactic interface. However, participants were required to have verbal ability scores greater than 80, although within group variation was considerable (81–140). Thus, we know little about how children with ASD and additional language impairments process prosodic cues or use linguistic and environmental context to resolve syntactic ambiguities.

Another body of work has highlighted that TD listeners are exquisitely sensitive to information contained in verbs and that this information is used to guide subsequent language processing by helping listeners to anticipate what is coming next in the sentence (cf. Altmann & Kamide, 1999). For instance, while listening to a sentence such as "Jane saw her mother eat the cake," viewers increased fixations to the cake (the only edible item on the screen) as soon as they heard the word *eat*, and long before the onset of the word *cake*. Further experiments indicated that listeners integrate their world knowledge with the linguistic information they hear to guide understanding. For example, Kamide, Altmann, and Haywood (2003) presented adults with a display including a chocolate milkshake and a glass of beer. When participants heard "The man drank the . . . ," fixations to the glass of beer increased. In contrast, when they heard "The girl drank the . . . ," fixations to the milkshake increased.

Anticipatory gaze in response to verbs has been replicated in TD children and in children with language-based disorders, such as poor reading comprehension (Nation et al., 2003) and SLI (Brock, Norbury, Einav, & Nation, 2008). However, subtle differences between TD language learners and those with language impairments were evident. For instance, Nation et al. (2003) reported that children with poor reading comprehension made more fixations overall, even after they had fixated the target. The authors attributed this either to difficulties in memory (i.e., the need to refresh memory traces of the spoken language or the other objects in the scene), or difficulties with attention (i.e., increased visual distraction).

Brock et al. (2008) extended this work in a study involving groups of adolescents with ALI and ALN and age- and ability-matched peers with SLI and TD. The investigators explored the use of linguistic context to drive anticipatory gaze to a target object or to inhibit looks to competitor items that were inconsistent with sentence context, and in particular verb meaning. Adolescents observed two pairs of phonological cohort competitors in a visual display (e.g., hammer and hamster, candle and cannon) while listening to sentences that were either neutral (e.g., "John chose the . . .") or biased one of the objects (e.g., "John stroked the . . ."). Brock et al. found that all groups demonstrated anticipatory gaze toward the target in the biased condition. However, when the target (e.g., *hamster*) was not visually displayed, participants with language impairment (both the ALI and the SLI groups) were unable to use the biasing context to inhibit looks to the phonological competitor (e.g., *hammer*). In other words, adolescents with SLI and ALI increased fixations to the *hammer* when they heard "John stroked the *hamster*" even though the verb "stroked" negated *hammer* as a potential referent. Adolescents with ALN and TD peers did not fixate the inappropriate competitor, nor did they differ on any eye-movement variable.

Hahn, Snedeker, and Rabagliati (2015) used a similar paradigm to explore lexical ambiguity resolution in highly verbal children with ASD (i.e., with standard scores on omnibus tests of language greater than 85). Children with ASD and their TD peers heard ambiguous words in sentence contexts that were either neutral or strongly supported one interpretation (e.g., John fed/saw the *bat*). Activation of the unintended meaning was measured by looks to a semantic associate (e.g., *baseball glove*). The application of eye-tracking methods in this study overcomes the limitations of Norbury (2005) by removing the possibility of strategic effects in responding and has the potential to reveal subtle qualitative group differences in the timing of ambiguity resolution. Across both groups, there was a reduction in fixations to the semantic associate when the linguistic context was inconsistent with the depicted meaning. There were no interactions with group, indicating that the speeds of association and inhibition were similar for these linguistically able children with ASD, replicating Brock et al. (2008). Hahn et al. (2015) did not include participants with language impairment, and it is interesting to consider what the pattern of performance would be for those with ALI or SLI. Brock et al.'s findings might lead us to anticipate that children with language impairment (ALI or SLI) would show increased fixations to the semantic associate relative to ALN and TD peers, even in the biasing condition. However, this hypothesis assumes that children with language impairment would be equally familiar with both meanings of the ambiguous words and would demonstrate typical patterns of semantic association. Further work is necessary to test these assumptions and whether children with ASD and language impairment can rapidly apply semantic knowledge in experimental tasks.

These studies suggest that the integration of vision and language is robust in younger language learners and those with ASD, provided the visual context is consistent with the verbal message. Importantly, these studies have demonstrated that individuals with ALN process language in sentential contexts in a qualitatively similar way to their TD peers. Similarly, the evidence to date is that the language impairments that characterize ALI are also qualitatively similar to those seen in SLI, at least with regard to timing and persistence of gaze on contextually inappropriate information. In addition, Brock et al. (2008) highlighted other potential sources of breakdown in language processing, which are neither universal nor specific to ASD. In addition to linguistic deficits, individual differences in memory (specifically memory decay), general social and world knowledge (or the ability to spontaneously integrate that knowledge with linguistic forms), inhibitory processes, and visual attention also impede language comprehension. Future studies using eye tracking may further narrow the possible contributions to individual differences in language processing within ASD.

Eye-Tracking Studies of Social Communication and Pragmatics

Two studies have explored aspects of social communication in ASD using eye-tracking methods. Nadig, Lee, Singh, Bosshart, and Ozonoff (2010) investigated conversational behaviors in school-age (mean age 11 years) children with ASD and their age- and ability-matched peers. They specifically asked whether the topic of conversation influenced social gaze to their conversational partner's face and how interpersonal gaze affected the quality of conversation. There were no group differences overall in looking times to the face of a conversation partner. Both groups increased social gaze when they were speaking about focused interests, relative to a generic conversational topic. In TD children, increased social gaze was accompanied by verbal reciprocity and seemed to signal increasing social engagement. In contrast, although children with ASD increased gaze to partner when talking about circumscribed interests, the proportion of reciprocal utterances they produced actually decreased, and their speech became more of a monologue than a conversation. On the other hand, those children with ASD who looked more at their partner's face produced fewer atypical utterances. Rather than increasing social engagement, the authors suggest this pattern of gaze reflects increased confidence when speaking about a familiar and well-rehearsed topic. Children in this study were selected to have average or above average structural language skills, and it would be clinically interesting to know whether social gaze is attenuated in those children who experience additional language impairments. In addition, the conversational partner in this study was a research assistant, usually older and presumably skilled in conversing with children who may present with communication difficulties. How children with ASD modulate gaze behavior with peers or familiar adults would further our understanding of how gaze and language development interact in this population.

Gesture is another aspect of social communication that is often reported to be compromised in children with ASD, particularly in the extent to which gestures are integrated with speech (de Marchena & Eigsti, 2010). Silverman, Bennetto, Campana, and Tanenhaus (2010) asked whether gesture deficits in ASD could reflect difficulties integrating information across auditory and visual modalities. To answer this question, Silverman et al. used the visual world paradigm to record the eye movements of highly verbal adolescents with ASD and age- and ability-matched peers as they watched an adult describing shapes, either with speech alone or with speech and co-occurring gesture. Viewers were asked to click on the object being described; this object was displayed with a speech competitor, a gesture competitor and an unrelated foil, with the video of the adult gesturing presented in the middle of the screen. When speech and gesture co-occurred, the gesture was visible before the point at which the verbal message disambiguated the target from the speech competitor. Thus, the investigators reasoned that if viewers benefited from the additional cues provided by gesture, they would be quicker to fixate the referent when gesture accompanied speech, relative to fixation times in the speech alone condition. Group differences were only evident in the gesture accompanying speech condition, where TD adolescents fixated the target object some 1,500 ms before the group with ASD. The authors suggest that processing information in multiple modalities slowed comprehension for individuals with ASD. However, fixations to the gesture video itself were similar across the two groups and increased in the gesture accompanying speech condition. The nature of the stimuli prevented a more nuanced investigation of what information within the video individuals with ASD preferentially attended because it was not possible to isolate fixations to face and to hands. The gestures were also redundant, in the sense that the information they conveyed was also expressed in speech. Future research could usefully investigate the extent to which individuals with ASD fixate gestures (as opposed to mouths) in situations in which gesture is crucial to comprehension, either because the speech signal is diminished or because the gesture provides additional semantic information that is not linguistically realized.

Eye-Tracking Studies of Language Production

In contrast to studies of language comprehension, far fewer studies have used eye-tracking paradigms to investigate processes of language production. This is not because eye movements are uninformative for language production but more likely because such studies require labor-intensive transcription of verbal utterances and challenges involved in linking verbal output to the eye-movement record for individual utterances (whereas in comprehension studies, the timing of verbal outputs is fixed and the same for all participants). Griffin and Bock (2000) pioneered this technique by asking TD adult speakers to describe simple cartoons depicting transitive events (e.g., "the woman is shooting the man"). Speakers demonstrated a highly consistent pattern of visual scanning, temporally linked to verbal description. They initially surveyed key aspects of the scene for approximately 300 ms, after which gazes to the agent (*woman*) and patient (*man*) characters began to diverge. Initially, looks to the sentential subject (typically the agent) increased; as articulation of the sentential object unfolded, gaze shifted to the patient. In contrast, when speakers were asked simply to identify the recipient of the action, looks focused almost exclusively on the patient. Griffin and Bock (2000) argued that this pattern of eye movements supported at least two distinct phases of sentence production: a rapid period of event apprehension, during which speakers comprehend the event, and a longer period of utterance formulation in which the specific lexical items and syntactic forms needed to describe the event are accessed and articulated. Importantly, in the formulation phase, objects are fixated in the order in which they are mentioned, looks at the object occur slightly in advance of articulation, and duration of looking time to objects appears to reflect the ease with which objects may be identified and names retrieved (Meyer, Sleiderink, & Levelt, 1998).

More recent work using similar paradigms has questioned whether apprehension of the event in its entirety is necessary for sentence planning. These studies have highlighted the more flexible nature of sentence production, which is subject to external influences such as manipulation of visual attention (Gleitman, January, Nappa, & Trueswell, 2007) and discourse effects, which may prioritize focus on particular sentential elements (Konopka, 2012; Konopka & Meyer, 2014). Such findings suggest that language production is continuously incremental, with linguistic messages updated as new information (visual or verbal) becomes available (Brown-Schmidt & Konopka, 2015).

The majority of production studies have involved TD adult speakers, raising questions about the extent to which children are able to integrate visual and verbal information into their speech production. Bunger, Trueswell, and Papafragou (2012) asked TD children (4-year-olds) and adults to describe short film clips depicting motion events (e.g., "the boy skated into the net") that included an agent (*the boy*), an instrument (*skates*), and an end path (*the net*). In the initial stages of event apprehension, eye-movement data revealed that both children and adults fixated the instrument and path regions of the screen to a similar extent. However, the children were less likely to mention both elements of the scene in their utterances, describing the target clip as "the boy went into the net" or "the boy skated." Thus, young TD children did not necessarily verbalize all aspects of a visual scene that they had attended. Bunger et al. (2012) argued that this reflects a limited capacity linguistic system, rather than developmental differences in attentional processes, in that younger children may not be able to hold in mind all possible sentential elements while formulating a sentence. It also raises the possibility, however, that processes of inhibition are also important for developing language production. We almost certainly do not want to articulate everything we may fixate in a scene but only those things that are relevant to the intended message. With regard to ASD, the findings of Kelly et al. (2013) and Brock et al. (2008) lead to the prediction that children with ALI may be more likely to fixate irrelevant objects in the visual scene, which may in turn lead to production of atypical or off-topic utterances. More generally, how children decide which aspects of a visual scene are relevant to report and which should be suppressed is currently an open question.

Norbury (2013b) investigated language production in children with ASD (ALI and ALN), children with SLI, and TD peers using a similar paradigm to that of Griffin and Bock (2000). However, unlike earlier studies, transitive events were embedded in a contextually appropriate background scene. Building on the work of Kelly et al. (2013), Norbury hypothesized that an inability to maintain fixations in the presence of competing stimuli could increase looks to irrelevant objects in the background. Fixating visual objects automatically activates the relevant semantic structures and phonological forms for such objects, increasing competition for items to be named in output (Huettig, Rommers, & Meyer, 2011). Thus, aberrant visual attention could contribute to increased production of irrelevant utterances in ASD in narrative tasks (Diehl, Bennetto, & Young, 2006).

Verbal descriptions were coded as *canonical* or *noncanonical* and the timing of each sentential element was recorded relative to the start of the trial. Canonical utterances were those that described the transitive event and mentioned both the agent and the patient. Utterances that included hesitations, false starts, and repetitions were also included in this group. Utterances that contained conjoined noun phrases (e.g., “the boy and the girl are playing on the beach”), passive constructions (e.g., “the girl was soaked by the boy”), or only one character noun phrase (e.g., “someone has a water gun on the beach”) were coded as noncanonical. Timing of sentential elements was then compared with the eye-movement data. Fixations were categorized as occurring before speech onset, after speech onset but before mention of the sentential subject, and after articulation of the subject noun phrase. Fixations were also allocated to one of four scene regions: the agent, the patient, the event core (the area of the image that signaled the event), and the background (everything else).

Children in the TD group demonstrated a pattern of eye movements that is consistent with TD adult speakers (cf. Griffin & Bock, 2000); before subject onset, there is a greater proportion of fixations to the agent, who is then realized in speech as the sentential subject. As the subject noun phrase is articulated, fixations shift to the patient, who is mentioned later in verbal output. Thus, to some extent, fixations mirror verbal output. However, approximately 25% of fixations were to objects in the background, despite the fact that these were never mentioned in output. Thus, TD individuals may inhibit mention of fixated items if they are not deemed relevant to the task at hand.

In general, children in the clinical groups produced similar utterances with relatively few irrelevant or unusual utterances in this fairly simple and structured task. However, there were subtle differences in all three clinical groups. Similar eye-movement patterns were obtained for children with ALN, although they tended to mention more items in the background relative to TD peers. Children with SLI showed a similar time course of fixations to agent and patient, although as a group they made considerably more fixations to the background. Children with ALI showed a qualitatively different pattern of fixations before speech onset; they did not prioritize looks to the agent initially, spending a similar amount of time gazing at both the agent and the patient. However, looks to scene protagonists were reduced relative to looking time at the background. Notably, the ALI group produced the most noncanonical utterances and were slower than any other group to articulate utterances. The performance of children with ALI appears to reflect additive effects of social and linguistic challenges in language production.

Summary and Future Directions

The use of eye-tracking methods to explore language processing is a new and rapidly emerging field. The handful of studies that have applied these methods to children with ASD illustrate the potential of such methods to yield new insights into qualitative differences in foundational skills (visual and social attention) and in the underlying mechanisms involved in processing language as it unfolds. We clearly have a long way to go, however. Studies of infants and toddlers at risk of developing ASD have yielded tantalizing (and sometimes contradictory) findings suggesting that there are early differences in visual attention and attention control processes that may fundamentally alter the types of visual information available to the child in communicative contexts. In addition, the ability to modulate visual attention in social situations, and particularly those social situations in which the child is exposed to language, also appears to be aberrant in a significant proportion of children who go on to receive an ASD diagnosis. The tempting conclusion is that these early differences in visual attention to social cues such as eyes and mouths, and the objects speakers refer to, disrupts the ability to engage in joint attention and learn language. However, we desperately need good longitudinal data to ascertain the extent to which these early perturbations of visual and social attention have lasting adverse consequences for language learning.

The majority of eye-tracking studies of school-age children and adolescents with ASD have focused on highly verbal and cognitively able participants with structural language scores on standard measures within the normal range. Several studies have now demonstrated that viewing patterns may vary according to linguistic or cognitive profiles within ASD, and thus there is an urgent need to distinguish language phenotypes early and relate our eye-movement variables to ecologically valid measures of language and discourse skills in everyday contexts. There is an urgent need to conduct more eye-tracking studies with nonverbal individuals with ASD and those with intellectual disabilities. One challenge in working with these populations is the need for task compliance, to remain relatively still, and to attend to information on the screen. In addition, like all reaction-time data, there tends to be wide intra- and interindividual variation in eye-movement metrics that may be greater in children with cognitive challenges and may obscure meaningful group differences. Advances in technology, both for presentation and analysis, may increasingly address these limitations. Of particular interest is continuing development of gaze contingent eye tracking, in which fixations to particular scene elements cause a contingent event. This may be particularly rewarding for children, including those with ASD, and may enhance task compliance.

Other studies have used eye-tracking paradigms in an effort to reveal qualitative differences in language processing when groups do not differ on more standard tests of language competence. In terms of language comprehension, the results are consistent and yet surprising; for children with ALN, the timing and pattern of language-mediated eye movements is identical to that of TD peers. Fewer studies have included children with ALI, but those that do have failed to identify qualitative differences between children with ALI and nonautistic peers with SLI. Studies of language production are urgently needed, but preliminary work suggests that qualitative differences may become more evident because language production taxes the integration of visual attention, social skill, and linguistic knowledge. Eye-tracking studies will be vital to determine what information becomes available to speakers, and when and how this information influences language production.

Cross-disorder comparisons are critically important, and eye tracking has potential to reveal qualitative differences and similarities among clinical conditions. Such studies are theoretically informative because they can pinpoint sources of language breakdown that are shared across disorders and those that might be specific to ASD. The studies reviewed in this chapter suggest that social differences associated with ASD may not necessarily be sufficient to derail language learning. Other factors are clearly necessary to explain the wide variation in language outcome that exists within ASD. These include differences in attention control, inhibition, phonological perception and memory, and the ability to integrate linguistic information with the environmental context and existing world knowledge (see also Eigsti & Schuh, Chapter 9, this volume).

Eye tracking can take us closer to the source of language breakdown, with obvious implications for clinical practice. For example, the studies reviewed here demonstrate that even those children with language impairment can use semantic information contained in the verb to anticipate potential referents but that they do not use this information to inhibit irrelevant responses. Eye tracking may also reveal subtle differences in the time course of language processing for those with apparently "typical" structural language abilities that may need attention or identify alternative routes to language competence that may be exploited in intervention. Any model of intervention will need to incorporate social supports for language learning and nonlinguistic behaviors (attention, inhibition) to develop linguistic skill. For example, Gleitman et al. (2007) provided evidence that manipulating attention can alter language production, and Wass, Porayska-Pomsta, and Johnson (2011) provided preliminary evidence that visual attention may be trained in infancy using gaze-contingent eye-tracking methods. In this study, increasing gaze duration (sustained attention) on relevant aspects of the scene yielded improvements in attentional control in novel contexts, although the follow-up period was relatively short (2 weeks). If such effects are sustained over a longer period, intervention using gaze-contingent methods may be beneficial in emphasizing social cues that support language and identify relevant aspects of the environment that may enhance communication. A strong prediction from current eye-tracking work is that altering visual attention early in development should change the developmental course of language learning for children with ASD.

References

Altmann, G. T., & Kamide, Y. (1999). Incremental interpretation at verbs: Restricting the domain of subsequent reference. *Cognition*, *73*, 247–264. http://dx.doi.org/10.1016/S0010-0277(99)00059-1

American Psychiatric Association. (2013). *Diagnostic and statistical manual of mental disorders* (5th ed.). Washington, DC: Author.

Aslin, R. N. (2007). What's in a look? *Developmental Science*, *10*, 48–53. http://dx.doi.org/10.1111/j.1467-7687.2007.00563.x

Brenner, L. A., Turner, K. C., & Müller, R.-A. (2007). Eye movement and visual search: Are there elementary abnormalities in autism? *Journal of Autism and Developmental Disorders*, *37*, 1289–1309. http://dx.doi.org/10.1007/s10803-006-0277-9

Brock, J., Norbury, C., Einav, S., & Nation, K. (2008). Do individuals with autism process words in context? Evidence from language-mediated eye-movements. *Cognition*, *108*, 896–904. http://dx.doi.org/10.1016/j.cognition.2008.06.007

Brown-Schmidt, S., & Konopka, A. E. (2015). Processes of incremental message planning during conversation. *Psychonomic Bulletin & Review*, *22*, 833–843.

Bunger, A., Trueswell, J. C., & Papafragou, A. (2012). The relation between event apprehension and utterance formulation in children: Evidence from linguistic omissions. *Cognition*, *122*, 135–149. http://dx.doi.org/10.1016/j.cognition.2011.10.002

Cooper, R. M. (1974). The control of eye fixation by the meaning of spoken language: A new methodology for the real-time investigation of speech perception, memory and language processing. *Cognitive Psychology*, *6*, 84–107. http://dx.doi.org/10.1016/0010-0285(74)90005-X

Cornish, K., Scerif, G., & Karmiloff-Smith, A. (2007). Tracing syndrome-specific trajectories of attention across the lifespan. *Cortex*, *43*, 672–685.

de Marchena, A., & Eigsti, I.-M. (2010). Conversational gestures in autism spectrum disorders: Asynchrony but not decreased frequency. *Autism Research*, *3*, 311–322. http://dx.doi.org/10.1002/aur.159

Diehl, J. J., Bennetto, L., & Young, E. C. (2006). Story recall and narrative coherence of high-functioning children with autism spectrum disorders. *Journal of Abnormal Child Psychology*, *34*, 87–102. http://dx.doi.org/10.1007/s10802-005-9003-x

Diehl, J. J., Friedberg, C., Paul, R., & Snedeker, J. (2014). The use of prosody during syntactic processing in children and adolescents with autism spectrum disorders. *Development and Psychopathology*, *27*, 867–884.

Elsabbagh, M., Volein, A., Holmboe, K., Tucker, L., Csibra, G., Baron-Cohen, S., . . . Johnson, M. H. (2009). Visual orienting in the early broader autism phenotype: Disengagement and facilitation. *Journal of Child Psychology and Psychiatry*, *50*, 637–642. http://dx.doi.org/10.1111/j.1469-7610.2008.02051.x

Gleitman, L. R., January, D., Nappa, R., & Trueswell, J. C. (2007). On the give and take between event apprehension and utterance formulation. *Journal of Memory and Language*, *57*, 544–569. http://dx.doi.org/10.1016/j.jml.2007.01.007

Gliga, T., Elsabbagh, M., Hudry, K., Charman, T., Johnson, M. H., & the BASIS Team. (2012). Gaze following, gaze reading, and word learning in children at risk for autism. *Child Development*, *83*, 926–938. http://dx.doi.org/10.1111/j.1467-8624.2012.01750.x

Griffin, Z. M., & Bock, K. (2000). What the eyes say about speaking. *Psychological Science*, *11*, 274–279. http://dx.doi.org/10.1111/1467-9280.00255

Hahn, N., Snedeker, J., & Rabagliati, H. (2015). Rapid linguistic ambiguity resolution in young children with autism spectrum disorder: Eye tracking evidence for the limits of weak central coherence. *Autism Research*, *8*, 717–726. http://dx.doi.org/10.1002/aur.1487

Henderson, J. M. (2003). Human gaze control during real-world scene perception. *Trends in Cognitive Sciences*, *7*, 498–504. http://dx.doi.org/10.1016/j.tics.2003.09.006

Huettig, F., Rommers, J., & Meyer, A. S. (2011). Using the visual world paradigm to study language processing: A review and critical evaluation. *Acta Psychologica*, *137*, 151–171. http://dx.doi.org/10.1016/j.actpsy.2010.11.003

Kamide, Y., Altmann, G. T., & Haywood, S. L. (2003). The time-course of prediction in incremental sentence processing: Evidence from anticipatory eye movements. *Journal of Memory and Language*, *49*, 133–156. http://dx.doi.org/10.1016/S0749-596X(03)00023-8

Kelly, D. J., Walker, R., & Norbury, C. F. (2013). Deficits in volitional oculomotor control align with language status in autism spectrum disorders. *Developmental Science*, *16*, 56–66. http://dx.doi.org/10.1111/j.1467-7687.2012.01188.x

Kjelgaard, M. M., & Tager-Flusberg, H. (2001). An investigation of language impairment in autism: Implications for genetic subgroups. *Language and Cognitive Processes*, *16*(2–3), 287–308. http://dx.doi.org/10.1080/01690960042000058

Klin, A., Jones, W., Schultz, R., Volkmar, F., & Cohen, D. (2002). Visual fixation patterns during viewing of naturalistic social situations as predictors of social competence in individuals with autism. *Archives of General Psychiatry*, *59*, 809–816. http://dx.doi.org/10.1001/archpsyc.59.9.809

Konopka, A. E. (2012). Planning ahead: How recent experience with structures and words changes the scope of linguistic planning. *Journal of Memory and Language*, *66*, 143–162. http://dx.doi.org/10.1016/j.jml.2011.08.003

Konopka, A. E., & Meyer, A. S. (2014). Priming sentence planning. *Cognitive Psychology*, *73*, 1–40. http://dx.doi.org/10.1016/j.cogpsych.2014.04.001

Loucas, T., Charman, T., Pickles, A., Simonoff, E., Chandler, S., Meldrum, D., & Baird, G. (2008). Autistic symptomatology and language ability in autism spectrum disorder and specific language impairment. *Journal of Child Psychology and Psychiatry*, *49*, 1184–1192. http://dx.doi.org/10.1111/j.1469-7610.2008.01951.x

Luna, B., Doll, S. K., Hegedus, S. J., Minshew, N. J., & Sweeney, J. A. (2007). Maturation of executive function in autism. *Biological Psychiatry*, *61*, 474–481. http://dx.doi.org/10.1016/j.biopsych.2006.02.030

Meyer, A. S., Sleiderink, A. M., & Levelt, W. J. (1998). Viewing and naming objects: Eye movements during noun phrase production. *Cognition*, *66*, B25–B33. http://dx.doi.org/10.1016/S0010-0277(98)00009-2

Nadig, A., Lee, I., Singh, L., Bosshart, K., & Ozonoff, S. (2010). How does the topic of conversation affect verbal exchange and eye gaze? A comparison between typical development and high-functioning autism. *Neuropsychologia*, *48*, 2730–2739. http://dx.doi.org/10.1016/j.neuropsychologia.2010.05.020

Nation, K., Marshall, C. M., & Altmann, G. T. M. (2003). Investigating individual differences in children's real-time sentence comprehension using language-mediated eye movements. *Journal of Experimental Child Psychology*, *86*, 314–329. http://dx.doi.org/10.1016/j.jecp.2003.09.001

Norbury, C. F. (2005). Barking up the wrong tree? Lexical ambiguity resolution in children with language impairments and autistic spectrum disorders. *Journal of Experimental Child Psychology*, *90*, 142–171. http://dx.doi.org/10.1016/j.jecp.2004.11.003

Norbury, C. F. (2013a). Autism spectrum disorder. In L. Cummings (Ed.), *The Cambridge handbook of communication disorders* (pp. 141–158). http://dx.doi.org/10.1017/CBO9781139108683.011

Norbury, C. F. (2013b). Sources of variation in developmental language disorders: Evidence from eye-tracking studies of sentence production. *Philosophical Transactions of the Royal Society B: Biological Sciences*, *369*, 20120393–20120393. http://dx.doi.org/10.1098/rstb.2012.0393

Norbury, C. F., Brock, J., Cragg, L., Einav, S., Griffiths, H., & Nation, K. (2009). Eye-movement patterns are associated with communicative competence in autistic spectrum disorders. *Journal of Child Psychology and Psychiatry*, *50*, 834–842. http://dx.doi.org/10.1111/j.1469-7610.2009.02073.x

Norbury, C. F., Griffiths, H., & Nation, K. (2010). Sound before meaning: Word learning in autistic disorders. *Neuropsychologia*, *48*, 4012–4019. http://dx.doi.org/10.1016/j.neuropsychologia.2010.10.015

Norbury, C. F., Nash, M., Baird, G., & Bishop, D. (2004). Using a parental checklist to identify diagnostic groups in children with communication impairment: A validation of the Children's Communication Checklist—2. *International Journal of Language & Communication Disorders*, *39*, 345–364. http://dx.doi.org/10.1080/13682820410001654883

Papagiannopoulou, E. A., Chitty, K. M., Hermens, D. F., Hickie, I. B., & Lagopoulos, J. (2014). A systematic review and meta-analysis of eye-tracking studies in children with autism spectrum disorders. *Social Neuroscience*, *9*, 610–632.

Rice, K., Moriuchi, J. M., Jones, W., & Klin, A. (2012). Parsing heterogeneity in autism spectrum disorders: Visual scanning of dynamic social scenes in school-aged children. *Journal of the American Academy of Child & Adolescent Psychiatry*, *51*, 238–248. http://dx.doi.org/10.1016/j.jaac.2011.12.017

Silverman, L. B., Bennetto, L., Campana, E., & Tanenhaus, M. K. (2010). Speech-and-gesture integration in high functioning autism. *Cognition*, *115*, 380–393. http://dx.doi.org/10.1016/j.cognition.2010.01.002

Tager-Flusberg, H., & Joseph, R. M. (2003). Identifying neurocognitive phenotypes in autism. *Philosophical Transactions of the Royal Society B: Biological Sciences*, *358*, 303–314. http://dx.doi.org/10.1098/rstb.2002.1198

Takarae, Y., Luna, B., Minshew, N. J., & Sweeney, J. A. (2008). Patterns of visual sensory and sensorimotor abnormalities in autism vary in relation to history of early language delay. *Journal of the International Neuropsychological Society*, *14*, 980–989. http://dx.doi.org/10.1017/S1355617708081277

Tanenhaus, M. K., Spivey-Knowlton, M. J., Eberhard, K. M., & Sedivy, J. C. (1995). Integration of visual and linguistic information in spoken language comprehension. *Science*, *268*, 1632–1634. http://dx.doi.org/10.1126/science.7777863

Tenenbaum, E. J., Amso, D., Abar, B., & Sheinkopf, S. J. (2014). Attention and word learning in autistic, language delayed and typically developing children. *Frontiers in Psychology*, *5*, 490. http://dx.doi.org/10.3389/fpsyg.2014.00490

Trueswell, J. C., Sekerina, I., Hill, N. M., & Logrip, M. L. (1999). The kindergarten-path effect: Studying on-line sentence processing in young children. *Cognition*, *73*, 89–134. http://dx.doi.org/10.1016/S0010-0277(99)00032-3

Wass, S., Porayska-Pomsta, K., & Johnson, M. H. (2011). Training attentional control in infancy. *Current Biology*, *21*, 1543–1547. http://dx.doi.org/10.1016/j.cub.2011.08.004

Wodka, E. L., Mathy, P., & Kalb, L. (2013). Predictors of phrase and fluent speech in children with autism and severe language delay. *Pediatrics*, *131*, e1128–e1134. http://dx.doi.org/10.1542/peds.2012-2221

Yarbus, A. L. (1967). *Eye movements and vision*. http://dx.doi.org/10.1007/978-1-4899-5379-7

Young, G. S., Merin, N., Rogers, S. J., & Ozonoff, S. (2009). Gaze behavior and affect at 6 months: Predicting clinical outcomes and language development in typically developing infants and infants at risk for autism. *Developmental Science*, *12*, 798–814. http://dx.doi.org/10.1111/j.1467-7687.2009.00833.x

Edith L. Bavin and Emma K. Baker

2 Sentence Processing in Young Children With ASD

Most frequently observed to be problematic in individuals with autism spectrum disorder (ASD) is the use of language in social situations, that is, the pragmatic aspects of language. However, there is extensive heterogeneity in the language abilities reported for individuals with ASD. A significant number are nonverbal, but others score in the normal range on structural language assessments (Tager-Flusberg, Paul, & Lord, 2005). There is also variability in the scores achieved on IQ tests; those individuals with ASD who achieve a score in the average range have typically been referred to as high functioning. Research on lexical development in young children with ASD who are verbal indicates similarities but delayed rather than deviant developmental paths. For example, Rescorla and Safyer (2013) showed that, although delayed, they acquire the same words as children with typical development (TD). In addition, young children with autism (at mean age 41 months) have also been found to comprehend the subject–verb–object basic word order and show evidence of syntactic bootstrapping, associating the word order with causative meaning, which is evident in younger children with TD (Naigles, Kelty, Jaffery, & Fein, 2011).

The extent to which communication problems in ASD arise from atypical language processing skills is not yet clear and has not been a major focus of research. Because we know comparatively little about the specific underlying factors that influence poor communication in this population, we can gain much insight from detailed investigation of their processing of language input, and systematically testing whether the language processing strategies and constraints that have been reported for individuals with TD also apply to individuals with ASD. Where differences are identified, a priority for future research will be to understand more about the nature and causes of those differences. Such knowledge will be valuable for developing intervention programs for children with ASD. Of particular importance would be research on developmental aspects of language processing in ASD so that children's progress can be monitored.

In this chapter, we present a brief overview of what is involved in processing sentences that people hear (see also Norbury, Chapter 1, this volume; Sedivy, Tanenhaus, Chambers, & Carlson, 1999) and discuss some of the research conducted with samples of individuals with TD and the limited research on sentence processing that has been

The research by Bavin and colleagues reported in the chapter was funded by the Australian Research Council (Grant DP1092668, awarded to Bavin, Kidd, Dissanayake, & Prior) and a small La Trobe University Academic Ranking of World Universities grant to the first author.

http://dx.doi.org/10.1037/15964-003
Innovative Investigations of Language in Autism Spectrum Disorder, L. R. Naigles (Editor)

conducted with ASD samples. We focus on research using eye-tracking methodology (the visual world paradigm; Tanenhaus, Spivey-Knowlton, Eberhard, & Sedivy, 1995) including research conducted with young children with ASD in our own laboratory (Bavin et al., 2014; Bavin, Kidd, Prendergast, & Baker, 2016; Bavin, Prendergast, Kidd, Baker, & Dissanayake, 2016; Gergis, 2013). For this research, we recruited comparatively large samples of children, using a narrower and younger age range than has been typical in ASD research on language processing. We investigated the time course of sentence processing focusing on lexical access, priming, identifying unique referents, and the verb bias.

Eye-tracking research with young school-age children with ASD is still in its infancy. This online method, in which integration of verbal and visual information is required, is extremely valuable because it is possible to identify when in the course of processing a sentence a breakdown occurs in understanding, or if different paths in processing the information are found across groups. Previous (non–eye-tracking) research has shown enhanced perceptual processing for individuals with ASD (e.g., see Mottron, Dawson, Soulières, Hubert, & Burack, 2006), and some researchers have discussed a preference for the visual-spatial domain over verbal (e.g., Kamio & Toichi, 2000). Because visual information is included, eye-tracking methodology provides an opportunity to identify whether individuals with ASD spend more time examining the items on display. If they do pay more attention to the visual stimuli, it would influence the time taken to integrate the auditory with the visual stimuli, using the available cues and constraints from the linguistic and nonlinguistic context.

The Incremental Nature of Language Processing

In interpreting what others say, people draw on and integrate information from multiple sources. As discussed by Sedivy et al. (1999), language processing is incremental and involves auditory, cognitive, and language mechanisms (Medwetsky, 2011). Over the course of the sentence, meanings are assigned. Interpretations of what is being said will be influenced by previous linguistic information, prior knowledge, and context. Thus, in addition to structural linguistic knowledge, attention and working memory are involved for successful processing of language input (e.g., Baddeley, 2003). When information can be anticipated, based on the individual's knowledge of words and structures as well as past experience with how people use language, it facilitates faster processing and reduces the load on working memory. Speed of information processing is considered fundamental to general intellectual functioning (Kail & Salthouse, 1994). Speech is extremely fast, and language processing needs to be rapid so that meaning and interpretation are updated during the course of a conversational exchange. Slow processing will affect what listeners can grasp as the discourse continues. A negative impact on children's academic achievements is likely if they do not keep up with information that is presented orally, for example, in classroom contexts.

The processing of language input is incremental. A word onset is a cue to likely candidates within the individual's lexicon (Marslen-Wilson & Welsh, 1978; Marslen-Wilson & Zwitserlood, 1989). Words sharing the same phonological onset are possible candidates, but as more of the word is heard, nonmatching items will be discarded. Even 24-month-olds have been found to identify a target faster when pictures of two objects are presented and the names of these objects do not share the same onset (e.g., access is slower for *doggie* if paired with *doll* than if it is paired with *tree*; Swingley, Pinto, & Fernald, 1999). In our own research, we tested whether 5- to 7-year-olds ($M_{age} = 6.4$) with ASD who were high functioning also showed evidence of accessing words with the same phonological onset before hearing the whole word. We tested 37 children with a diagnosis of ASD and 48 children with TD of the same age as the ASD group; all were attending mainstream schools. On the basis of symptom severity scores from the Autism Diagnostic Observation Schedule—Generic (ADOS–G; Lord et al., 2000), we used a median split to identify a "severe" group (ASD-S; $n = 16$) and a "moderate" group (ASD-M; $n = 21$). We included in the study the lifetime version of the Social Communication Questionnaire (SCQ; Rutter, Bailey, & Lord, 2003) to obtain a score of autistic-like behaviors, as reported by parents, for all 85 participants. None of the children in the TD group had a score on the SCQ that was indicative of ASD.

We used an eye-tracking task that included sentences of the form "Where's the X?" For each sentence, the visual display included four pictures: the named item (target), a picture that shared the same phonological onset as the target (competitor; e.g., target = *car*, competitor = *cat*), and two (unrelated) distractor items. For our analyses, we averaged percentage of looking time to each of the four pictures for each child over 200-ms intervals starting 200 ms before the word onset. Our analyses were conducted using R version 2.13.1 (R Core Team, 2013), and the data were modeled using generalized estimating equations (GEEs), specifically the package "geepack" (Højsgaard, Halekoh, & Yan, 2006). This allowed for both an ordinal response and repeated measures and for multiple comparisons and also we were able to assess the impact of possible confounds, that is, language, IQ, sustained attention, and memory (for details of the measures and analyses, see Bavin et al., 2014).

To determine whether the children did access both items with the same phonological onset, we compared mean percentage of looking at these two items versus looking at the two distractors. The results showed that all three groups initially accessed both the target and competitor before they identified the target, and there was significantly more looking at these two items than at the distractors. For the TD and ASD-M groups, this was evident in the 400- to 600-ms and 600- to 800-ms time intervals posttarget onset, whereas the ASD-S group were slower; a similar result was not found until the 600- to 800-ms interval. In addition, children in the ASD-S group were less likely to have fixated on the target by 1,000- to 1,200-ms posttarget onset, with fixation defined as looking for 80% of the time in any 200-ms time interval. We can conclude that for children with more severe behaviors associated with ASD, it is likely that they will be slower at processing language input. With 200 ms slower processing over the course of a word, processing over the course of a sentence is likely to have a major impact on their communication skills.

The results were supported by analysis for all participants using the SCQ scores. Those children with more behaviors associated with ASD looked less at the target in the later intervals; instead, they looked at the other pictures in the display, which is consistent with the view of a preference for visual information for individuals with ASD (e.g., Kamio & Toichi, 2000). However, from the current results, this is more likely to be identified with individuals with a more severe presentation of ASD characteristics, at least at the younger school ages. The findings suggest that the children with more severe ASD behaviors were examining the pictures in more detail because proportionally less looking time was spent on the target, which adds support to an enhanced perceptual processing style. Of interest is that language, memory, attention, and IQ scores did not have a significant effect on the results, most likely because this was a simple lexical access task.

Influences From Semantically Related Words on Interpretation: Priming

Priming influences processing time; that is, one word may influence how linguistic material later in the sentence is processed, and this reduces time to process (Tulving & Schacter, 1990). Some priming research has used verbs as primes; other studies have used nouns. A study with adolescents with ASD showed that the verb in a sentence influenced (primed) participants to anticipate the target word (the direct object) that followed (Brock, Norbury, Einav, & Nation, 2008). For example, the verb *stroke* primed the listener to something that can be stroked; that is, listeners were faster in identifying the object than when a neutral verb (e.g., *choose*) was used (see more details in the section Constraints on Sentence Processing later in the chapter).

In a semantic priming study with 5- to 7-year-old children with ASD, Gergis (2013) showed that they, like children with TD, could be primed by category labels (e.g., *fruit*), although processing was slower for the ASD group. The sentences contained either a semantic category label or in its place a more neutral word (e.g., *shopping*). Primes and nonprimes were presented in the format "She/he likes lots of ___," with either the prime or nonprime word filling the gap. Following the prime/nonprime was a test sentence. For example, the test sentence "She's going to eat the apple" followed both the *fruit* and *shopping* sentences. The visual display for both included the target (i.e., *apple*), a semantically related picture (i.e., *banana*), and two distractors. A priming effect was found, with both groups fixating significantly faster to the target in the priming than nonpriming condition. However, for the TD group, the effect of the prime emerged 300 ms earlier than for the ASD group. That the ASD group was slower indicates intact semantic organization but slower processing of the language input. This finding supports the slower processing found for children with ASD in Bavin et al. (2014), although it was not restricted to those children with more severe ASD characteristics.

Identifying the Intended Meaning or Referent

There has been some research on how the linguistic and nonlinguistic contexts can influence the processing of language. For example, research on lexical ambiguity has shown that the meaning most likely to be identified depends on the linguistic context. For example, in a study with 6- to 9-year-old children with ASD who were high functioning, Hahn, Snedeker, and Rabagliati (2015) used an implicit priming method with ambiguous words (e.g., *bat* [animal] vs. *bat* [in sport]) in sentences. Some of the sentences provided a biasing context. The children with ASD, like the children with TD, readily used the biasing context to interpret potentially ambiguous sentences.

We used eye tracking during auditory language processing to understand whether young, highly verbal children with ASD are indeed impaired at using context. We found that young children with ASD process ambiguous words in a similar manner to matched controls. Using an implicit priming method, we found that both ASD and TD children can use strong context to inhibit the inappropriate meanings of ambiguous words. Our data suggest that they do this quickly, with evidence for inhibition emerging within 500 ms of hearing the word. We used eye tracking during auditory language processing to understand whether young, highly verbal children with ASD are indeed impaired at using context. We found that young children with ASD process ambiguous words in a similar manner to matched controls. Using an implicit priming method, we found that both children with ASD and TD can use strong context to inhibit the inappropriate meanings of ambiguous words. Our data suggest that they do this quickly, with evidence for inhibition emerging within 500 ms of hearing the word.

A body of research with TD samples shows that if there is more than one item that could be identified as the intended target, listeners typically expect further information from the speaker to identify the intended target. "The car," for example, implies a unique interpretation (Crain & Steedman, 1985), but if there is more than one car that could be being referred to, some restricting information is needed to facilitate interpretation. For example, a prenominal adjective (e.g., as in "the *big* car") will be interpreted as contrastive (= not the small car), and a postnominal modifying prepositional phrase (e.g., "the car *that is red*") will specify a particular item.

Using eye-tracking methodology, Sedivy et al. (1999) found that responses were faster to auditory stimuli comprising a noun phrase containing a prenominal adjective when a contrastive item was also shown in the visual display (e.g., for the target *small dog*, both a small dog and a large dog were visible). The assumption on hearing "small dog" is that it is being compared and contrasted with another dog (Nadig, Sedivy,

Joshi, & Bortfeld, 2003); thus, having visible two items of the same kind facilitates identification of the intended target.

Bavin, Prendergast, et al. (2016) investigated whether young children with ASD process noun modifications similarly to children with TD. The children with ASD were all high functioning, with IQ scores ranging from 79 to 124. The children in both groups were aged 5 to 9 years. The study included sentences with pre- and postnominal modification; both modifications were required to identify a target from a set of four of the same kind, for example, four squares. The prenominal adjective in the early part of the sentence restricted the four items to two possibilities, whereas the preposition phrase later in the sentence distinguished one of these two (i.e., the target) from the other (i.e., the competitor). For example, for the test sentence "Look, there's a blue square with dots," the visual display included two blue squares and two red squares. Only one of the blue squares had dots (i.e., the target), whereas the other was a plain blue square (i.e., the competitor). One of the red squares also had dots.

The results provided insight into how the children integrated the modifying information as they were listening to each sentence. From 200 to 400 ms after the onset of the noun, the TD group looked significantly more at the two identified items than at the distractors; this pattern continued until the children had heard the prepositional phrase. However, the ASD group took 200 ms longer than the TD group to show significantly more looking at these two items. On the other hand, by 800 to 1,000 ms the proportion of looking at the two items was similar for the two groups. Independent of ASD status, from 400 to 800 ms after the noun onset, the covariates attention (measured by the Sustained Attention task from the Developmental Neuropsychological Assessment—Second Edition [Korkman, Kirk, & Kemp, 2007]) and age had some impact on the result. There was a higher proportion of looking time at the target and competitor for those children with higher attention scores and also for the children who were older.

The disambiguating information in the prepositional phrase started at approximately 700 ms following the noun onset. A clear trend for group differences began at the 200- to 400-ms interval after the onset of the disambiguating property, and this continued to the end of the trial, with a higher proportion of looking at target for the TD group. So both groups initially looked significantly more at the two items matching the description provided by the prenominal adjective and noun (e.g., *blue square*) and on hearing the modifying prepositional phrase they were able to integrate that information, looking more at the target than the competitor.

By taking longer to process, a deficit in integrating information from different sources for children with ASD is suggested, as proposed for example by Minshew, Goldstein, and Siegel (1997). However, this could be reflective instead or as well of a developmental delay. Of interest is that, independent of diagnosis, higher attention scores were associated with more looking. Good attention skills were required when integrating the information; to reach an accurate decision about the target, the initial noun phrase needed to be kept active while the participant attended to the description in the prepositional phrase. In addition, the older children looked more at the target with a trend evident from the 400- to 600-ms interval and significant differences continuing through to the end of the trial. There are implications of these effects for future research. When samples cover a wide age range, chronological age may need to be included as a covariate in the analyses. In addition, variability in attention within a sample may impact on the research findings.

Constraints on Sentence Processing

On the basis of studies with TD samples, a number of constraints (or biases) that influence language processing have been discussed. The major focus on constraints has been the verb bias (Altmann & Kamide, 1999, 2007; Mani & Huettig, 2012; Nation, Marshall, & Altmann, 2003). That is, listeners are influenced by the semantics of the verb in a sentence, and this constrains or biases what they expect will follow. For example, on hearing the verb *eat* listeners anticipate an edible object (even 2-year-olds will fixate on "a cake" in a visual scene soon after hearing the verb *eat* (Golinkoff, Hirsh-Pasek, Cauley, & Gordon, 1987). In contrast, with the verb *choose*, it is less predictable what the object will be. For *cut*, not only is a particular type of object predicted, the cutting instrument might also be anticipated (e.g., "She cut the wood with the saw"; "He chopped the tree with an axe"). The expectations are based on the listeners' knowledge of the verb and the syntactic construction in which it is likely to appear. However, such lexical biases can be overridden as additional information is processed. So in line with incremental processing, updates to interpretations are made as more of the sentence is processed; initial interpretations may be modified.

A study conducted with adolescents with ASD (previously mentioned) showed the influence of verb semantics in sentence processing; participants anticipated which item would be named as the object of the verb (Brock et al., 2008). In this study, adolescents with ASD who were high functioning were compared with a mixed group of adolescents with TD and adolescents with language impairment. The sentences either included a biasing verb (e.g., *stroke* in "Joe stroked the hamster quietly") or a neutral verb (e.g., *chose* in "Sam chose the hamster reluctantly"). The results of the study showed that both groups were influenced by the verb semantics; looking was quicker to the named object following a biasing verb.

As discussed by Sedivy et al. (1999), continuous updating can lead to temporary ambiguity in sentence processing, for example, if a linguistic element has different functions. Sentences with temporary syntactic ambiguity, in which initial interpretations need to be revised, have been discussed in the psycholinguistic literature as "garden path" structures. An eye-tracking study by Trueswell, Sekerina, Hill, and Logrip (1999) investigated how 4- to 5-year-old children with TD and adults resolved temporary ambiguity when verbs with strong biases were included (e.g., *put* biases a destination—where something is to be put). The participants were asked to perform the action indicated in the sentence; however, while an action reflects a final interpretation, listeners' eye movements indicate initial and updated interpretations as the sentence progresses. In Trueswell et al.'s study, participants heard as one of the sentences: "Put the frog on the napkin in the box" where *on the napkin* could be interpreted as the destination, but when *in* is processed, some reanalysis is needed. In one condition, a referential context with a contrast set of two frogs (with one sitting on a napkin) was provided; that is, the prepositional phrase "on the napkin" restricted reference to one of the frogs. Reanalysis would lead to the interpretation that *in the box* is the destination and *on the napkin* is modification of the noun *frog*. The 5-year-old children tested were not prepared to change their initial destination interpretation of *on the napkin*, but adults were. In summary, the children did not integrate the information from the nonverbal context with the linguistic input. Trueswell et al. (1999) proposed that it was by about age 8 years that the referential context is used to help interpretation.

Other prepositional phrases may lead to reanalysis of initial interpretations. For example "with a feather" is the instrument in "The boy tickled the cat with a feather." Snedeker and Trueswell (2004) showed that the verb *tickle* evokes an instrument, whereas for the verb *choose*, as in "Choose the pig with the stick," a noun-modifier interpretation is more likely. Although verb biases are strong, when an accompanying prepositional phrase labels an implausible instrument, as in "The woman cut the cake with the icing," a noun modification interpretation is more likely for adults (Snedeker & Trueswell, 2004). However, even with implausible instruments, as in "Cut the tree with the leaves," 5-year-old children follow the bias of the verb, as shown in a study by Kidd, Stewart, and Serratrice (2011)—that is, they interpret the leaves as the instrument.

Bavin, Kidd, et al. (2016) tested the verb bias in young children with ASD using instrument biasing verbs. The aim was to identify whether children would follow a verb bias with instrument verbs and whether they would override the bias in favor of a noun modification interpretation. In the first of two eye-tracking tasks, sentences either contained a biasing verb for the object, as in "The boy will *eat* the cake" or a more neutral verb, as in "The boy will *move* the cake." For each sentence, four objects were displayed on the monitor: the target (e.g., *cake* for the example sentence given) and three distractors: *toy*, *ball*, and *cup*. The participants (aged 5–9 years; 47 with ASD and 56 with TD) heard an equal number of biasing and nonbiasing sentences but only the biasing version or the nonbiasing version of each.

Group differences were found. For biasing verbs, the ASD group, compared with the TD group, looked away more rapidly after identifying the target. Across the sample, attention scores had an impact on the results with lower attention scores associated with more looking in the 800- to 1,200-ms interval following target onset. More attention may be required in making the linguistic connection between the verb and the direct object plus matching the auditory and visual stimuli for the children with lower attention scores in this task. In contrast, for the nonbiasing verbs, the ASD group took significantly longer than the TD group to look at the target for a similarly high proportion of time. Proportion of looking at the target dropped from the 800- to 1,000-ms interval after target onset for both groups. Looking away was then more rapid for the children with ASD, but not as rapid as with biasing verbs. Attention did not have an impact on the results with the nonbiasing verbs, indicating that it did not have as much influence when there was no bias from the verb to a particular item.

A second task included in this study (Bavin, Kidd, et al., 2016) involved a *with* prepositional phrase. In one set of sentences, a biasing verb and a prepositional phrase that named an expected instrument were included, as in "The girl will cut the cake with the knife." In the other set of sentences, the instrument phrase was switched to include an unlikely instrument, as in "The girl will cut the cake with the candle." As well as functioning as an instrument, in both sets of sentences, the prepositional phrase structurally could serve as noun modification, but this was more likely if the prepositional phrase contained an unlikely (implausible) instrument. For both versions of the "cut the cake" example, the display included a knife, a cake without a candle, a cake with a candle, and a candle on its own. The children heard either the likely instrument or the implausible instrument version of each sentence.

The results showed no significant group differences. Both groups of participants looked more at the target they heard named. That is, there was a significantly greater proportion of looking to the expected instrument when a likely instrument was named from the 400- to 600-ms interval postinstrument onset to the end of the trial. Similarly, in the same time period, there was a greater proportion of looking to the implausible instrument if an implausible target was named. However, looking patterns to the item that indicated a nominal modification interpretation (e.g., the cake with a candle on it) was greater when the named instrument was implausible—from the 800- to 1,200-ms interval through to the end of the trial. Across the sample, age and sustained attention had no impact on the results.

The absence of group differences indicates that 5- to 9-year-old children with ASD (mean age 6.71 years), as well as children with TD, are able to overcome the strong instrument bias imposed by the verb semantics. Although their looking patterns showed that they responded to the named instrument, the participants also considered the alternate function of the prepositional phrase. This was more likely if an implausible instrument was named, but it was also apparent toward the end of the analysis window when the named instrument was plausible. However, for the ASD group, switching to the alternative, nominal modification interpretation was not as quick as for the TD. Thus, overall the research results show that the verb bias is a strong constraint on processing for young children with ASD who are high functioning.

Conclusion

Language processing has been well researched in TD samples with adults and more recently children. With eye-tracking methodology, there have been developments in understanding the incremental nature of processing linguistic input and the linguistic and nonlinguistic factors that may influence it. There are many advantages of using eye tracking to capture how listeners process language input—that is, the real-time processing of language (e.g., Borovsky, Elman, & Fernald, 2012; Sedivy et al., 1999). In the course of processing what others say, listeners cannot backtrack as readers can if the text is still visible, but by using eye tracking, it is possible to observe which linguistic elements in the sentence influence the ongoing processing of sentences and whether the visual array affects interpretation; the method provides closely time-locked measure of ongoing cognitive processing through the course of the sentence. No verbal response is required, nor are the behavioral demands of pointing or using toys to act out a sentence (although some researchers do analyze a behavioral response in addition to the eye movements). By designing eye-tracking studies to include specific structures of interest to test young children, it is possible to identify where problems may arise in typical and atypical populations. For children with ASD, this may involve difficulties in integrating information within a sentence and with visual information. Such difficulties are likely to contribute to communication problems in real-life situations.

Overall findings from eye tracking in research with young children with ASD who are verbal and high functioning show that, like children with TD, they process incrementally upgrading interpretations through the course of the sentence. Moreover, they are influenced by linguistic and nonlinguistic context and follow biases, as do children with TD, but they can override the bias to consider alternative interpretations. However, at least in an experimental context, young children with ASD who are high functioning are likely to be slower in integrating information within a sentence and across domains. Slower processing affects how much information is taken in; there will be cumulative effects, resulting not only in possible miscommunication but also less opportunity to master the conventions of communicating with others. In the real world, sentences are connected and listeners respond appropriately to others if they have interpreted what they say. Some of the pragmatic difficulties reported for individuals with ASD may arise from slower processing when integrating information from different sources, linguistic and nonlinguistic.

Because of the heterogeneity in ASD, it is important to identify influencing factors that might affect their language processing. In some research, scores from standard language assessments have been reported to be associated with performance in processing sentences (e.g., Brock et al., 2008), but this link has not been found in all studies, as indicated in this chapter, possibly because of differences in the range of abilities within a sample. As shown in Bavin et al. (2014; Bavin, Kidd, et al., 2016; Bavin, Prendergast, et al., 2016), the contribution of attention and age on research results for children with ASD and children with TD depend on the particular processing task undertaken, indicating that it would be useful generally to include both age and attention as covariates in future studies. As they get older, children have more experience of how speakers are likely to provide unique identification and are able to draw more on the referential context, as discussed by Trueswell et al. (1999).

Further research with large samples of children with ASD who are not high functioning or that represent the heterogeneity of ASD would be valuable for providing more information on developmental trajectories for language processing skills in ASD. The incorporation of social scenarios to establish a context for the target items could be valuable because misunderstanding occurs primarily in social contexts. In addition, more processing research on complex structures will help identify strengths and weaknesses in the processing abilities of children with ASD (see in this volume Norbury, Chapter 1; Tuller et al., Chapter 6).

References

Altmann, G. T. M., & Kamide, Y. (1999). Incremental interpretation at verbs: Restricting the domain of subsequent reference. *Cognition*, *73*, 247–264. http://dx.doi.org/10.1016/S0010-0277(99)00059-1

Altmann, G. T. M., & Kamide, Y. (2007). The real-time mediation of visual attention by language and world knowledge: Linking anticipatory (and other) eye movements to linguistic processing. *Journal of Memory and Language*, *57*, 502–518. http://dx.doi.org/10.1016/j.jml.2006.12.004

Baddeley, A. (2003). Working memory and language: An overview. *Journal of Communication Disorders*, *36*, 189–208. http://dx.doi.org/10.1016/S0021-9924(03)00019-4

Bavin, E. L., Kidd, E., Prendergast, L., & Baker, E. (2016). Testing the verb and instrument biases in young children with ASD. *Frontiers in Psychology*, *7*, 171. Retrieved from http://journal.frontiersin.org/article/10.3389/fpsyg.2016.00171/full

Bavin, E. L., Kidd, E., Prendergast, L., Baker, E., Dissanayake, C., & Prior, M. (2014). Severity of autism is related to children's language processing. *Autism Research*, *7*, 687–694. http://dx.doi.org/10.1002/aur.1410

Bavin, E. L., Prendergast, L., Kidd, E., Baker, E., & Dissanayake, C. (2016). Online processing of sentences containing noun modification in young children with high functioning autism. *International Journal of Language & Communication Disorders*, *51*, 137–147.

Borovsky, A., Elman, J. L., & Fernald, A. (2012). Knowing a lot for one's age: Vocabulary skill and not age is associated with anticipatory incremental sentence interpretation in children and adults. *Journal of Experimental Child Psychology*, *112*, 417–436. http://dx.doi.org/10.1016/j.jecp.2012.01.005

Brock, J., Norbury, C., Einav, S., & Nation, K. (2008). Do individuals with autism process words in context? Evidence from language-mediated eye-movements. *Cognition*, *108*, 896–904. http://dx.doi.org/10.1016/j.cognition.2008.06.007

Crain, S., & Steedman, M. (1985). On not being led up the garden path: The use of context by the psychological parser. In D. R. Dowty & A. M. Zwicky (Eds.), *Natural language parsing: Psychological, computational, and theoretical perspectives* (pp. 320–358). Cambridge, England: Cambridge University Press.

Gergis, G. (2013). *Language processing in children with typical development and high-functioning-autism using eye-tracking* (Unpublished doctoral dissertation). La Trobe University, Bundoora, Australia.

Golinkoff, R. M., Hirsh-Pasek, K., Cauley, K. M., & Gordon, L. (1987). The eyes have it: Lexical and syntactic comprehension in a new paradigm. *Journal of Child Language*, *14*, 23–45. http://dx.doi.org/10.1017/S030500090001271X

Hahn, N., Snedeker, J., & Rabagliati, H. (2015). Rapid linguistic ambiguity resolution in young children with autism spectrum disorder: Eye tracking evidence for the limits of weak central coherence. *Autism Research*, *8*, 717–726.

Højsgaard, S., Halekoh, U., & Yan, J. (2006). The R Package geepack for generalized estimating equations. *Journal of Statistical Software*, *15*, 1–11.

Kail, R., & Salthouse, T. A. (1994). Processing speed as a mental capacity. *Acta Psychologica*, *86*, 199–225. http://dx.doi.org/10.1016/0001-6918(94)90003-5

Kamio, Y., & Toichi, M. (2000). Dual access to semantics in autism: Is pictorial access superior to verbal access? *Journal of Child Psychology and Psychiatry*, *41*, 859–867. http://dx.doi.org/10.1111/1469-7610.00673

Kidd, E., Stewart, A. J., & Serratrice, L. (2011). Children do not overcome lexical biases where adults do: The role of the referential scene in garden-path recovery. *Journal of Child Language*, *38*, 222–234. http://dx.doi.org/10.1017/S0305000909990316

Korkman, M., Kirk, U., & Kemp, S. (2007). *NEPSY–II: A developmental neuropsychological assessment.* San Antonio, TX: The Psychological Corporation.

Lord, C., Risi, S., Lambrecht, L., Cook, E. H., Jr., Leventhal, B. L., DiLavore, P. C., . . . Rutter, M. (2000). The autism diagnostic observation schedule—generic: A standard measure of social and communication deficits associated with the spectrum of autism. *Journal of Autism and Developmental Disorders*, *30*, 205–223. http://dx.doi.org/10.1023/A:1005592401947

Mani, N., & Huettig, F. (2012). Prediction during language processing is a piece of cake—But only for skilled producers. *Journal of Experimental Psychology: Human Perception and Performance*, *38*, 843–847. http://dx.doi.org/10.1037/a0029284

Marslen-Wilson, W., & Welsh, A. (1978). Processing interactions and lexical access during word recognition in continuous speech. *Cognitive Psychology*, *10*, 29–63. http://dx.doi.org/10.1016/0010-0285(78)90018-X

Marslen-Wilson, W., & Zwitserlood, P. (1989). Accessing spoken words: The importance of word onsets. *Journal of Experimental Psychology*, *15*, 576–585.

Medwetsky, L. (2011). Spoken language processing model: Bridging auditory and language processing to guide assessment and intervention. *Language, Speech, and Hearing Services in Schools*, *42*, 286–296. http://dx.doi.org/10.1044/0161-1461(2011/10-0036)

Minshew, N. J., Goldstein, G., & Siegel, D. J. (1997). Neuropsychologic functioning in autism: Profile of a complex information processing disorder. *Journal of the International Neuropsychological Society*, *3*, 303–316.

Mottron, L., Dawson, M., Soulières, I., Hubert, B., & Burack, J. (2006). Enhanced perceptual functioning in autism: An update, and eight principles of autistic perception. *Journal of Autism and Developmental Disorders*, *36*, 27–43. http://dx.doi.org/10.1007/s10803-005-0040-7

Nadig, A., Sedivy, J., Joshi, A., & Bortfeld, H. (2003). The development of discourse constraints on the interpretation of adjectives. In B. Beachley, A. Brown, & F. Conlin (Eds.), *Proceedings of the 27th Annual Boston University Conference on Language Development* (pp. 568–579). Somerville, MA: Cascadilla Press.

Naigles, L. R., Kelty, E., Jaffery, R., & Fein, D. (2011). Abstractness and continuity in the syntactic development of young children with autism. *Autism Research*, *4*, 422–437. http://dx.doi.org/10.1002/aur.223

Nation, K., Marshall, C. M., & Altmann, G. T. M. (2003). Investigating individual differences in children's real-time sentence comprehension using language-mediated eye movements. *Journal of Experimental Child Psychology*, *86*, 314–329. http://dx.doi.org/10.1016/j.jecp.2003.09.001

R Core Team. (2013). *R: A language and environment for statistical computing*. Vienna, Austria: R Foundation for Statistical Computing.

Rescorla, L., & Safyer, P. (2013). Lexical composition in children with autism spectrum disorder (ASD). *Journal of Child Language*, *40*, 47–68. http://dx.doi.org/10.1017/S0305000912000232

Rutter, M., Bailey, A., & Lord, C. (2003). *Social Communication Questionnaire*. Los Angeles, CA: Western Psychological Services.

Sedivy, J. C., Tanenhaus, M. K., Chambers, C. G., & Carlson, G. N. (1999). Achieving incremental semantic interpretation through contextual representation. *Cognition*, *71*, 109–147. http://dx.doi.org/10.1016/S0010-0277(99)00025-6

Snedeker, J., & Trueswell, J. C. (2004). The developing constraints on parsing decisions: The role of lexical-biases and referential scenes in child and adult sentence processing. *Cognitive Psychology*, *49*, 238–299. http://dx.doi.org/10.1016/j.cogpsych.2004.03.001

Swingley, D., Pinto, J. P., & Fernald, A. (1999). Continuous processing in word recognition at 24 months. *Cognition*, *71*, 73–108. http://dx.doi.org/10.1016/S0010-0277(99)00021-9

Tager-Flusberg, H., Paul, R., & Lord, C. (2005). Language and communication in autism. In F. R. Volkmar, R. Paul, A. Klin, & D. J. Cohen (Eds.), *Handbook of autism and pervasive developmental disorders* (Vol. 1, pp. 335–364). Hoboken, NJ: Wiley.

Tanenhaus, M. K., Spivey-Knowlton, M. J., Eberhard, K. M., & Sedivy, J. C. (1995). Integration of visual and linguistic information in spoken language comprehension. *Science*, *268*, 1632–1634. http://dx.doi.org/10.1126/science.7777863

Trueswell, J. C., Sekerina, I., Hill, N. M., & Logrip, M. L. (1999). The kindergarten-path effect: Studying on-line sentence processing in young children. *Cognition*, 73, 89–134. http://dx.doi.org/10.1016/S0010-0277(99)00032-3

Tulving, E., & Schacter, D. L. (1990). Priming and human memory systems. *Science*, *247*, 301–306. http://dx.doi.org/10.1126/science.2296719

Letitia R. Naigles and Deborah Fein

3 Looking Through Their Eyes: Tracking Early Language Comprehension in ASD

In this chapter, we focus on the nature and centrality of the language disorder in children with autism spectrum disorder (ASD). For example, is language impairment one result of the primary social impairment, or is the language delay or impairment itself primary? If the primary impairment in children with ASD is one of social motivation and attention, then once attention to language and other social input is forced (as in some behavioral interventions), linguistic development might be expected to follow, with the same course and the same principles as normal development (Allen & Rapin, 1992; Lord & Risi, 2004). In contrast, if some children with autism have primary disturbances of language, then deviant or atypical language development might be expected, such that the application of principles that seem to guide normal language development, and the generalization of semantic concepts and syntactic rules found in typically developing (TD) children, may be reduced or absent. In typical development, for example, the emergence of children's comprehension of specific concepts and rules usually precedes their production, and certain principles or strategies govern concept learning and syntactic rule application. In this chapter, we summarize findings from a longitudinal study of language development in children with ASD, designed to address this key question. We used a method called *intermodal preferential looking* (IPL), which enabled us to assess the children's language comprehension independently of their social skills.

Intermodal Preferential Looking

The social impairments of children with ASD frequently reveal themselves in a disinclination to talk or communicate with others and in difficulties with following the attentional focus of others (Lord, Rutter, DiLavore, & Risi, 1999; Mundy, Sigman, & Kasari, 1990). Thus, the "usual" language assessments, which involve spontaneous or

This research was funded by the National Alliance for Autism Research and the National Institute on Deafness and Other Communication Disorders (Grant No. R01 DC007428). We extend our gratitude to our collaborators on this project, including Rose Jaffery, Janina Piotroski, Andrea Tovar, Elizabeth Kelley, Lauren Swensen Meade, Saime Tek, Anthony Goodwin, Emma Kelty-Stephen, Jinhee Park, Laura Mesite, Emily Potrzeba, and Christian Navarro-Torres. Over the 15 years of this project, the undergraduates of the University of Connecticut Child Language Lab have provided consistently excellent assistance in data collection, eye-movement coding, and transcribing. Finally, we are profoundly grateful to the children and families who participated in the study.

http://dx.doi.org/10.1037/15964-004
Innovative Investigations of Language in Autism Spectrum Disorder, L. R. Naigles (Editor)

elicited speech, or experimenter-administered receptive language tasks, are unlikely to reveal everything that children with ASD, especially low-functioning or low-verbal children, know about language. For example, children who have difficulty following an experimenter's gaze or an experimenter's point to an array of pictures will also have difficulty choosing which of those pictures matches what the experimenter says (for more discussion, see Naigles & Chin, 2015). In contrast, IPL assesses children's language comprehension in a setting with very low social demands; it was first designed for use with TD infants and toddlers, who also have difficulty complying with adult directives and tasks (Hirsh-Pasek & Golinkoff, 1996; Piotroski & Naigles, 2012). In the IPL paradigm, children sit in front of side-by-side visual displays that are either static or dynamic; the use of dynamic video here enables more ecologically valid tests of the words and grammatical constructions describing events and relationships. A single linguistic stimulus is emitted from a box centered between the displays; this audio matches only one of the two displays. The children's eye movements are recorded and later coded offline. The core assumption is that if the child understands the linguistic stimulus, she or he will look more quickly or for longer periods of time at the matching display (Fernald, Perfors, & Marchman, 2006; Golinkoff, Ma, Song, & Hirsh-Pasek, 2013; Piotroski & Naigles 2012). The absence of any directives from live adults and any requirements that the child point to the displays makes this an easier task for children with social difficulties. In addition, viewing each video usually takes less than 6 minutes (across all trials) and so is well suited to the short attention spans of this population (Naigles & Tovar, 2012).

The video layout generally includes three sets of trials for each test item. The familiarization or teaching trials come first and appear alternately on each display (e.g., a girl tickling a boy, the boy tickling the girl). The baseline trials usually appear next, and present the contrasting test stimuli side by side with a nondirecting audio (e.g., "Look at them!"); these trials elicit looking based on the salience of the visual stimuli. The test trials usually appear third; during these trials, the side-by-side visuals are paired with the test audio (e.g., "The girl is tickling the boy!"). The side of the matching display varies by item in an XYYXXYYX pattern, which is counterbalanced across children. We code the children's eye movements during the baseline and test trials (sometimes during the teaching trials as well; see Ellawadi, Fein, & Naigles, 2015), with two assistants coding looking direction frame-by-frame, blind to which is the "matching" side for any given trial. Reliability between coders averages 0.95 ($p < .001$). Measuring children's eye movements allows for assessment of the speed of their language processing as well as accuracy; therefore, we usually report two measures of comprehension: proportion of looking to the matching (vs. nonmatching) scene during test (vs. salience/control) trials and latency to look at the matching (vs. nonmatching) scene. Children who understand the linguistic stimulus will look longer, and with shorter latencies, at the matching scene during test compared with baseline trials. We have used the IPL paradigm to investigate language comprehension in three cohorts of children with ASD (total $N = 42$), assessed every 4 months for four to six home visits spanning 1 to 2 years. The children were recruited from service providers in the northeastern United States to be within 6 months of their ASD diagnosis and the beginning of applied behavior analysis (ABA) therapy. We chose to restrict the sample to children receiving ABA to minimize any heterogeneity in performance due to receiving different forms of therapy. The children's ASD diagnosis (or lack thereof in the TD group) was confirmed with the Autism Diagnostic Observation Schedule (ADOS; Lord et al., 1999) at the first visit. Each ASD cohort was matched with a TD cohort, which included children with no reported developmental delays or concerns who were at the same level of language development as the ASD group at the first visit. As shown in Table 3.1 for all three cohorts combined, at Visit 1, both groups of children were functioning linguistically at an 18- to 23-month-old level, that is, with small vocabularies and just beginning to produce words in combinations. As expected given their usual delay in language development, the ASD group was approximately 1 year older than the TD group (Table 3.1).

Using IPL, we have investigated whether these young children with ASD displayed several well-established processes of typical language development. With respect

Tab. 3.1: Demographic Information Combining All Three Cohorts

	ASD V1	TD V1	ASD V6[a]	TD V6[a]
N	42	42	30	30
Age	32.88 (5.09)	19.4 (2.14)	53.32 (5.92)	40.94 (1.81)
MCDI–I	86.5 (101.24)	101.77 (105.44)		
Word types	34.6 (39.56)	29.86 (29.31)	97.32 (88.78)	166.29 (49.87)
MLU	1.39 (0.71)	1.29 (0.38)	1.99 (0.98)	2.95 (0.51)
Mullen *t* scores				
VisRec	34.19 (14.30)	56.27 (11.12)	37.75 (19.15)	64.97 (10.22)
RecLang	32.86 (17.12)	56.27 (12.41)	35.47 (19.08)	61.31 (10.40)
ExpLang	29.36 (11.47)	48.64 (12.66)	32.84 (18.86)	60.75 (10.75)
Mullen age equivalents				
VisRec	23.93 (6.99)	22.04 (4.53)	42.72 (15.18)	50.68 (7.66)
RecLang	21.19 (10.23)	23.04 (5.2)	37.63 (17.13)	49.12 (8.64)
ExpLang	18.19 (7.99)	19.58 (5.95)	32.88 (19.68)	48.56 (9.60)
MCDI–II			120.54 (131.27) (*n* = 13)	
MCDI–III			69.8 (22.68) (*n* = 15)	79.68 (15.53)
Vineland standard scores				
Comm	73.26 (15.38)	102.05 (9.73)	85.45 (18.74)	106.75 (10.93)
Daily Living	74.90 (13.47)	102.77 (8.82)	80.1 (19.02)	103.45 (9.91)
Social	72.4 (8.24)	101.7 (6.72)	77.13 (14.94)	101.31 (7.95)
Motor	83.19 (14.17)	101.02 (6.88)	89.06 (15.8)	103.36 (10.09)

Note: ASD = autism spectrum disorder; TD = typically developing; Comm = Communication; ExpLang = Expressive Language; MCDI = MacArthur Child Development Inventory; MLU = mean length of utterance; RecLang = Receptive Language; VisRec = Visual Recognition.
[a]Visit 6 columns include data from Cohorts 2 and 3 only.

Tab. 3.2: Intermodal Preferential Looking Videos Shown at Each Visit

Visit	ASD group	TD group
1	Shape bias	Shape bias
	Noun bias	Noun bias
	Word order	Word order
2	Shape bias	Shape bias
	Noun bias	Noun bias
	Word order	Word order
3	Shape bias	Shape bias
	Wh-questions	Wh-questions
	Syntactic bootstrapping	Syntactic bootstrapping
4	Shape bias	Shape bias
	Wh-questions	Wh-questions
	Syntactic bootstrapping	Syntactic bootstrapping
5	Shape bias	Syntactic bootstrapping
	Wh-questions	Wh-questions
	Aspect	Aspect
6	Shape bias	Syntactic bootstrapping
	Wh-questions	Wh-questions
	Aspect	Aspect

to grammar, we investigated whether they demonstrated evidence of understanding before producing specific constructions, namely, subject–verb–object (SVO) word order, subject and object wh-questions, and grammatical aspect. With respect to lexical development, we assessed three well-documented word-learning strategies, including the noun bias, the shape bias, and syntactic bootstrapping. Table 3.2 lists the visits at which each IPL video was presented.

Comprehension of Grammar

The phenomenon of comprehension of grammar preceding production is pervasive in the language development of TD children, who have been shown to understand simple sentences before they produce word combinations in speech (Hirsh-Pasek & Golinkoff, 1996) and to understand grammatical morphemes (e.g., *the* preceding nouns) that are months away from production (Gerken & MacIntosh, 1993; Shi, 2014). This reveals that TD children's analyses of their input are carried out "underground" (Maratsos, 1998, p. 438; see also Snyder, 2007), or out of direct view of the children's caregivers. The comprehension-preceding-production phenomenon reveals the typical toddler to be using language at one level to engage in the social-cognitive interactions that dominate their waking lives while also analyzing language at more sophisticated levels for no immediate social or interactional purpose, and it highlights that TD children's acquisition of linguistic forms does not depend on their ability to produce them. To the extent that comprehension requires only that the child access a stored representation (i.e., a pattern abstracted from specific lexical items) based on perceived sounds whereas production also requires a successful generation of that representation based on the desire to express a more-or-less well-formed meaning (Huttenlocher, 1974), comprehension of course seems easier.

Whether children with ASD also demonstrate this phenomenon has been unclear; see Naigles and Chin (2015) for a comprehensive discussion. In the current set of studies, we presented children with ASD with three grammatical constructions: SVO word order, wh-questions, and aspect, and compared their success at comprehension with their spontaneous production during naturalistic interactions. We collected the latter data via 30-minute mother–child play sessions at each visit. Half of each session was semistructured (based on the Screening Tool for Autism in 2-year-olds protocol; Stone, Coonrod, & Ousley, 2000) and included prompts that facilitated discussion of a variety of topics and constructions (e.g., looking through a bag for toys facilitated the production of wh-questions, building towers with cups facilitated aspectual markers usage). The other half of the session was free play.

The first construction we investigated was sentential word order. In English, the ordering of nouns in a sentence indicates the thematic roles of these nouns. For example, in active sentences the subject noun (S) is usually the agent and the object noun (O) the patient of the action. Hirsh-Pasek and Golinkoff (1996) showed that TD children at approximately 17 months of age demonstrate understanding of SVO word order, regardless of whether they had produced any words in combination yet (see also Gertner, Fisher, & Eisengart, 2006; Yuan, Fisher, & Snedeker, 2012). In our studies, we adapted Hirsh-Pasek and Golinkoff's design, showing the children side-by-side videos in which, for example, a girl pushing a boy was paired with the boy pushing the girl; the accompanying test audio was "Look, the girl is pushing the boy!" A total of six verbs in SVO frames were tested (*push*, *ride*, *hug*, *kiss*, *wash*, *tickle*). As Swensen, Kelley, Fein, and Naigles (2007) reported, at the first visit when they viewed this video, nine of the 10 children with ASD in Cohort 1 looked longer at the matching scene during the test trials relative to the baseline trials; across children, this pattern held for five of the six verbs. The children's level of SVO production at this same visit (V1) was much lower: Their overall mean length of utterance (MLU) was 1.45, and only one child produced any SVO constructions at all. Five children were nonverbal or producing only one-word utterances, and the multiword combinations of the other four children were highly stylized and formulaic (e.g., repetitions of "spin around" or "pop balloon"). These findings were replicated with the larger sample (n = 17) in Cohort 2 (Naigles, Kelty, Jaffery, & Fein, 2011); moreover, the Cohort 2 children also had shorter latencies to the match, indicating that once they heard the test audio, they consistently looked more quickly to the matching scene than the nonmatching scene. Only two of the children who demonstrated comprehension of SVO had MLUs longer than 2.0. In sum, across two cohorts of children with ASD the same pattern emerged, in which children who were not producing words in combinations, let alone utterances structured as SVO, nonetheless understood SVO sentences well enough to look longer and more quickly at, say, a girl pushing a boy when they heard "the girl is pushing the boy" and at the boy tickling the girl when they heard "the boy is tickling the girl."

Simple matrix wh-questions, such as "What did the apple hit?" (querying the *object* of the verb) and "What hit the flower?" (querying the *subject* of the verb), begin to emerge in the speech of TD children at the end of their third year (Stromswold, 1995). A study using IPL reported reliable comprehension of these sentences in much younger TD children (i.e., 20 months; Seidl, Hollich, & Jusczyk, 2003). In our study, we adapted Seidl et al.'s (2003) design; children first viewed an event in which, for example, an apple hits a flower, then were presented with side-by-side pictures of the apple and the flower and asked, in the test trials, "What did the apple hit?" and "What hit the flower?" Control trials were of two types: The apple and flower were presented side by side with (a) a nondirecting audio ("Look at them!") and (b) two "where" questions ("Where is the apple?" "Where is the flower?"). A second set of events, showing some keys hitting a book and including all of the same trial types, was also presented (Goodwin, Fein, & Naigles, 2012, 2015). With the proportion of looking to the match measure, the TD group demonstrated reliable comprehension with both subject and object wh-questions starting at Visit 3 (with an average age of 28 months). In contrast, the ASD group demonstrated reliable comprehension of each wh-question type only at Visit 6, when they averaged 54 months of age. Thus, the children with ASD were considerably delayed in their onset of wh-question understanding not only in terms of their chronological age but also in terms of their "language age." That is, their age-equivalent scores on the receptive and expressive language subscales of the Mullen Scales of Early Learning (Mullen, 1995) at Visit 6 averaged 33 to 36 months, whereas the TD group demonstrated reliable understanding at 28 months. However, the MLUs of the TD group at Visit 3 and the ASD group at Visit 6 were similar (2.28 vs. 2.01). Jyotishi, Fein, and Naigles (2015) recently replicated these findings with a new video and with the children in Cohort 3.

Some of the children with ASD (20%–33%) provided evidence of comprehension and production of wh-questions at the same visit; however, of the remainder, all children but one showed understanding at an earlier visit than producing. On average, comprehension of subject wh-questions was demonstrated one visit earlier than production of these same questions, and comprehension of object wh-questions was demonstrated about two visits earlier than production of these same questions. Thus, our findings confirm those who have found the production of wh-questions in children with autism to be unusually sparse (Eigsti, Bennetto, & Dadlani, 2007; Tager-Flusberg, 1994). Comprehension of wh-questions may also be relatively more challenging for children with ASD. However, a relative developmental advantage of *comprehension before production* has again been observed for children with ASD.

The third construction we investigated involved grammatical aspect. In English, the *-ing* suffix on verbs indicates an ongoing action, whereas the *-ed* suffix indicates a completed action, usually in the past. TD children produce these morphemes contrastively (i.e., with the same verb) after 3 years of age, while comprehension appears by about 2.5 years of age (Wagner, Swensen, & Naigles, 2009). In our study, we adapted Wagner et al.'s (2009) design, presenting children with side-by-side renditions of the same event, one of which was ongoing (e.g., a girl washing a doll) while the other was completed (e.g., the girl finished washing the doll and held it up). At Visit 5, two sets of events (*wash, drink*) were presented, and at Visit 6, four sets of events (*wash, drink, pick, draw*) were presented; at both visits, both *-ing* and *-ed/past* audios were tested. Across both visits, the 4-year-old children with ASD demonstrated reliable comprehension of both morphemes, looking consistently at different visuals when the test trials with the *ing* versus *past* audios were directly compared (Tovar, Fein, & Naigles, 2015).

The aspect videos were presented at the later visits of the study, and some of the children with ASD had already begun to produce some tense-aspect morphemes by these visits; therefore, we could not conduct as clear a test of the "comprehension before production" hypothesis as we did with the word order and wh-question videos. However, our examination of the children's spontaneous productions of these morphemes during the play sessions at Visits 5 and 6 revealed two findings: First, children who produced more tokens of *ing* and *past/ed* during the play sessions showed stronger comprehension of *ing* while viewing the aspect video. Tellingly, however, four children with ASD produced zero tokens of either morpheme during the play sessions yet nonetheless demonstrated comprehension of both morphemes by looking longer at the match during the test trials. At least for these four children, then, comprehension of grammatical aspect preceded production.

For these three English constructions, these children with ASD have demonstrated (a) successful comprehension and (b) comprehension earlier than production. All three components, which are part of core English grammar (Comrie, 1976; Radford, 1990), thus appear to be developing typically, albeit slowly, in these children with ASD. How can these findings of successful comprehension be reconciled with previous indications of grammatical impairments in ASD? We next consider three possible resolutions.

First, most previous reports of grammatical impairments have used measures from spontaneous or elicited speech through which children with ASD are found to produce specific morphemes at lower frequencies than TD children (Eigsti et al., 2007; Fein et al., 1996; C. J. Park, Yelland, Taffe, & Gray, 2012; Roberts, Rice, & Tager-Flusberg, 2004; Tager-Flusberg, 1994; Waterhouse & Fein, 1982). It is possible, however, that such lower frequency of usage is attributable to pragmatic difficulties rather than grammatical ones. For example, less past tense use could arise from a disinclination to talk about past events or misunderstanding that the context promoted talk about past events (Eigsti et al., 2007; Williams, Botting, & Boucher, 2008). Additionally, fewer wh-questions could arise from disinterest in the objects and activities of others (Tager-Flusberg, 1994). The IPL comprehension paradigm circumvented many of these pragmatic difficulties because the children could observe the contexts in the videos (e.g., completed events) without having to engage with them. Thus, we were able to demonstrate that the constructions themselves were part of the children's linguistic repertoires, even if they were not inclined to use them in conversations.

Second, it is possible that our ASD sample was different from those studied by other researchers. For example, the children with ASD in previous studies who demonstrated grammatical impairments may have had a comorbid specific language impairment (in this volume, see Janke & Perovic, Chapter 7; Norbury, Chapter 1; and Tuller et al., Chapter 6). Kjelgaard and Tager-Flusberg (2001) and Roberts et al. (2004) have reported that some children with ASD perform poorly on language tasks (autism language impaired or ALI), whereas others perform at age-appropriate levels (autism language normal or ALN; see also Norbury, 2005; Perovic, Modyanova, & Wexler, 2013). Given their overall good comprehension performance, the children with ASD in our three cohorts might all fit the ALN designation. However, this seems unlikely because the sample actually includes a wide range of language abilities, as revealed by the large variances in Mullen scores at Visits 1 and 6 (see Table 3.1). Moreover, Tek, Mesite, Fein, and Naigles (2014) scrutinized the spontaneous speech of the children in Cohort 2 in some detail and reported that although approximately half of the ASD sample demonstrates growth curves in MLU, noun and verb use, and grammatical morpheme frequency that parallel the curves of the TD children, the other half of the sample demonstrates much shallower curves, indicating much slower language development (see Fusaroli, Weed, Fein, & Naigles, 2014, for a replication with Cohorts 2 and 3 combined). Yet most of the children in this low-verbal subsample demonstrated successful comprehension of SVO, wh-questions, and aspect (i.e., they showed longer looking to the matching display during test compared with baseline). Thus, the children whose speech at 2 to 4 years of age suggests a language impairment nonetheless have shown understanding of three English constructions at levels not different from their TD peers.

Third, it is important to point out that thus far we have only assessed three English constructions. It is possible that grammatical impairments would be observed in our sample, or a subsample, if more complex constructions were assessed, such as reflexive pronouns or multiclause sentences (in this volume, see Durrleman-Tame, Burnel, & Reboul, Chapter 8; Janke & Perovic, Chapter 7; and Tuller et al., Chapter 6). Moreover, de Villiers, Roeper, Bland-Stewart, and Pearson (2008) argued that knowledge of wh-movement cannot be fully assessed unless multiclause wh-questions are presented (e.g., "What did the girl say that she saw?"). And although our children with ASD were able to use grammatical aspect to contrast "she's washing the doll" versus "she washed the doll," we have not yet investigated whether children with ASD command this aspectual contrast within, say, narrative contexts (Berman, 2009; Stirling et al., Chapter 10, this volume). Therefore, we cannot and do not claim our findings indicate that grammatical knowledge is completely intact in these children with ASD. What our findings do indicate, however, is that several core English constructions are acquired fairly early by a significant proportion of children with ASD and that these constructions seem to be acquired "offline," without needing to be used in conversation.

Demonstrating Word-Learning Principles

TD children appear to use principles or biases to facilitate their acquisition of the meanings of words (Golinkoff et al., 2000; Markman, 1989). These principles help children resolve the Quinian (Quine, 1960) problem of word learning, that is, that any given word used in conjunction with a scene could have a plethora of possible meanings (e.g., *rabbit* used while pointing to a rabbit could also mean *brown*, *ears*, *furry*, *puffy tail*, *point*, etc.). Some principles, such as extendability ([Golinkoff, Mervis, & Hirsh-Pasek, 1994]; also called *generalization* in the autism literature [Fein, Tinder, & Waterhouse, 1979; Minshew, Meyer, & Goldstein, 2002]), enable children to use a word to refer to a previously unlabeled referent (e.g., to use the word *dog* for a newly encountered dog). Others, such as the noun bias and shape bias, enable more specific predictions about the meaning of a new word. Furthermore, the strategy known as *syntactic bootstrapping* exploits children's syntactic knowledge to help determine the meaning of a new verb. In our longitudinal study, we investigated whether children with autism also use these principles in learning word meanings. These investigations were among the first to use novel (nonsense) words to investigate how children with autism acquire word meanings; the use of novel words allows researchers to simulate the word-learning process and thus determine whether general principles (abstracted from specific contexts) are being used by the child.

The noun bias has been proposed as a universal principle of language acquisition, that children find it easier to learn nouns than verbs because many nouns refer to static and concrete objects whereas many verbs refer to dynamic and less concrete relations (Gentner, 1982). Novel word-learning studies with TD English learners have revealed that when novel actions and objects are presented together in a single scene, 1- to 3-year-old children initially map a single novel word onto the novel object; novel actions take much longer to learn (for a comprehensive summary of these findings, see Waxman et al., 2013). In our study, we first presented "teaching trials" in which an unfamiliar animal puppet (e.g., an opossum) was engaged in an unfamiliar action (e.g., twirling on its nose), paired with a novel word (e.g., *toopen*; all novel words in this study ended with *en*, which afforded either a noun [*kitten*] or verb [*jumpin'*] interpretation). Baseline and test trials presented the original puppet performing a different action paired with a new puppet performing the original action; the baseline audio was "Look, they're different now," and the test audio was, for example, "Where's toopen?" Two-year-old children with ASD (i.e., at Visits 1 and 2) from Cohorts 1 and 2 looked significantly longer at the original puppet during the test trials than during the baseline trials, indicating that they had mapped the novel word onto the puppet rather than onto its original action (Swensen et al., 2007; Tek, Jaffery, Fein, & Naigles, 2008). They did this for five of the six novel words tested, indicating that this mapping was consistently performed over multiple items. Thus, children with ASD, at the beginning of language development, consistently display a noun bias.

The syntactic bootstrapping procedure has been proposed as an aid to verb learning. Verbs are typically produced in sentences, and the specific sentence structure has implications for the meaning of the verb. For example, causative verbs typically appear in transitive sentences (e.g., SVO: The girl drops the ball), whereas noncausative verbs appear in intransitive sentences (e.g., SV: The ball drops). TD children as young as 25 months of age have been shown to use syntactic bootstrapping in learning novel verbs (Arunachalam & Waxman, 2010; Naigles, 1990); moreover, Shulman and Guberman (2007) demonstrated the basic syntactic bootstrapping effect with high-functioning Hebrew-speaking 5-year-olds with autism. We adapted Naigles's (1990) video for our study, so that our child participants received only three teaching trials for each novel verb (instead of the 10 included by Shulman & Guberman); in addition, our Cohort 2 participants manifested a much wider range of language abilities than in the Hebrew study (see Table 3.1). In our study, children saw people dressed in duck and bunny costumes, performing novel causative and noncausative actions. For example, one set of teaching trials showed the duck kneeling behind the sitting bunny, pushing the bunny down (as if it was stretching its legs). Simultaneously, both characters were iteratively bending their arms in and out. The teaching audio was "Look, the duck is gorping the bunny!" The next trials split up the actions, so that the causative one appeared on one screen and the noncausative one on the other screen. After the baseline audio of "Look, they're different now!" the children heard the test audio "Where's gorping now? Find gorping," repeated for two trials. At both Visits 3 and 4, the children with ASD looked longer at the causative action (because the verb was in the transitive frame) during the test trials than during the baseline trials, demonstrating the basic syntactic bootstrapping behavior (Naigles et al., 2011).

Interestingly, this effect was seen most strongly during the second half of each test trial (Naigles et al., 2011). That is, when the actions were first separated, the children looked longer at the noncausative action, in which the two characters were doing the same action in synchrony; this initial "synchronous action" preference has also been observed in 2-year-old TD children (Naigles & Kako, 1993). Then, when the children with ASD heard the "find gorping" directive, they shifted their gaze to the causative action and did so more quickly for the second test trial than the first. Thus, mapping novel verbs onto novel actions seems to be tractable for children with ASD, at least as long as there are both syntactic and visual cues. The children's looking patterns also reveal what their nonlinguistic action preferences are and how quickly or slowly they are able to successfully process the linguistic stimulus.

The shape bias is the third word-learning strategy we investigated and the one that has produced the most puzzling results. The shape bias has been observed in TD children as young as 14 to 20 months of age; it seems to appear once children have acquired 50 to 100 object labels (Graham & Poulin-Dubois, 1999; Landau, Smith, & Jones, 1988; Smith, Jones, Landau, Gershkoff-Stowe, & Samuelson, 2002). TD children of this age construe a novel word to refer to a novel object—more specifically, its shape—in their environment, and to extend a novel word taught in reference to a novel object, to new objects *of the same shape*. In the usual paradigm, children are shown a novel object and told "This is a dax." They are then shown two new objects, one that matches the first in shape and the other that matches the first in color or pattern, and asked, "Which is the dax?" "No-name trials" ("Look at this one. Find another one") first establish the children's baseline preferences. Shape-guided word extension in TD children has been observed by both pointing to real objects (Landau et al., 1988; Smith, 2000) and eye gaze to pictures (Graham & Poulin-Dubois, 1999). In our first investigation of the shape bias with children with ASD, we conducted both "real object" and IPL tests (Tek et al., 2008). Following the paradigm just described, we showed the children three-dimensional objects, labeled them, held up three-dimensional color- and shape-matches, and asked the children to point to which object was also called that label. In the IPL task, we created videos of the same objects (moving slowly back and forth) and presented these first in no-name trials and then with the target objects labeled. The TD children in Tek et al. (2008) behaved as expected: They pointed to the shape-matched object more in the "name" than no-name trials first at 28 months of age and demonstrated the same pattern via eye gaze at 24 months of age (i.e., one visit earlier). In contrast, the children with ASD demonstrated no label-driven shape preferences with either task throughout the first four visits (Tek et al., 2008).

In a recent follow-up, we doubled the size of the samples (now with 30 or more children in each group) and generated similar findings. With the larger sample, TD children showed a shape preference when hearing the novel word at 20 months (i.e., at Visit 1), but the children with ASD, as a group, still did not look reliably longer at the shape match than color match (nor at the color match over the shape match) during the name trials relative to the no-name trials, even through Visit 6 (Potrzeba, Fein, & Naigles, 2015). Many of the children knew more than 100 object labels by parental report; moreover, because they frequently looked at the shape match during the no-name trials, they seemed to notice the shape similarity between the target and test objects. What they did not do, in contrast to the TD children, was highlight this shape similarity during the name trials; that is, they did not preferentially extend the novel word to objects of the same shape.

Summary of Basic IPL Findings

Taken together, these findings from the IPL tasks reveal both strengths and weaknesses in children with ASD: They show strengths in understanding SVO word order at 2 to 3 years of age and in using this sentence pattern to learn novel verbs. Their comprehension of wh-questions and of grammatical aspect develops later (i.e., at an average of 4 years of age), but nonetheless consistently emerges before their spontaneous production of these same constructions. They demonstrate a noun bias, mapping novel words onto objects rather than actions, but have thus far failed to demonstrate a shape bias, failing to extend object words to new objects of the same shape. The power of our multitask longitudinal design can be seen when we compare across videos: That is, children with ASD who successfully demonstrated a noun bias at Visits 1 and 2 did not demonstrate a shape bias at those same visits (although the TD children did). Moreover, children with ASD who demonstrated successful comprehension of wh-questions and grammatical aspect at Visit 6 did not demonstrate a shape bias at that same visit. Thus, the shape bias task revealed the most consistent group differences; this process is evidently challenging for children with ASD. We discuss the shape bias findings further once we have considered the effects of individual differences on all of our IPL tasks.

What Does IPL Reveal About Individual Differences Within the ASD Group?

The findings presented here were based on the entire group of children with ASD; however, as Table 3.1 shows, on standardized general language measures, our ASD sample displays the great heterogeneity frequently observed within this disorder. This heterogeneity was also observed in their speech production: Some of the children increased in their word use, MLU, and many grammatical morphemes at the same rates as the TD children, whereas other children with ASD demonstrated much flatter language growth patterns (Fusaroli et al., 2014; Tek et al., 2014). The question we addressed next was, can this variability be captured in the IPL measures?

Early descriptions of the IPL paradigm focused on group-level effects, and some researchers doubted whether this method could reveal individual variation because of the small number of test items in a given video (i.e., with only four to six items per child). The primary emphasis was on revealing that all or most children of a given age would demonstrate comprehension or perform consistently (Hirsh-Pasek & Golinkoff, 1996). However, more recent reports using IPL have found variability in both children's speed and strength of matching the linguistic and visual stimuli (Fernald & Marchman, 2012; Fernald, Perfors, & Marchman, 2006). In our studies, whereas 10 of the 15 children in Goodwin et al. (2012) demonstrated positive comprehension scores at Visit 6, they could be further divided into five "strong comprehenders" (i.e., children who showed a difference of 0.65 seconds or more between the baseline and test trials [in the correct direction]) and five "weak comprehenders" (i.e., children who showed a difference of between 0.64 and 0.01 seconds). In addition, as discussed earlier, children showed faster looking to the match in the syntactic bootstrapping task during the second test trial relative to the first. So the question we now turn to is, does variability in IPL performance manifest stable relationships with other language and language-related measures? Two IPL measures were examined: speed of comprehension (i.e., latency of the first look to the matching scene; Candan et al., 2012; Marchman & Fernald, 2008) and degree of comprehension (i.e., percentage looking to the match during test trials minus percent looking to the match during baseline trials; Gertner et al., 2006). The overall prediction was that children with higher general language scores should also demonstrate faster comprehension (i.e., shorter latency) or stronger comprehension (i.e., greater magnitude of shift in looking to the match from baseline to test) on the IPL tasks.

This prediction was supported multiple times across our longitudinal study. Children's vocabulary size, as measured by the MacArthur Child Development Inventory (MCDI; Fenson et al., 1993) or number of word types produced in spontaneous speech, correlated significantly and positively with their concurrent degree of comprehension with five of the six IPL tasks: wh-questions, syntactic bootstrapping, noun bias, shape bias, and aspect (Goodwin et al., 2012; Naigles et al., 2011; Potrzeba et al., 2015; Tovar et al., 2015). The children's scores on the Mullen Receptive Language subscale at Visit 6 correlated significantly and positively with their concurrent degree of comprehension of the shape bias and grammatical aspect (Potrzeba et al., 2015; Tovar et al., 2015). Thus, general language measures gleaned from maternal report (MCDI), naturalistic interactions (spontaneous speech), and experimenter-administered standardized tests (Mullen) all yielded significant relationships with IPL measures, essentially confirming that children with ASD with better general language showed stronger comprehension of almost all of the linguistic constructions we tested.

For two of the IPL tasks, the relationship with the MCDI held longitudinally as well. That is, children with higher MCDI scores at Visit 1 demonstrated stronger comprehension of syntactic bootstrapping 8 months later (Naigles et al., 2011). Moreover, children with higher MCDI scores at Visit 1 demonstrated a stronger shape bias at both Visits 2 and 6, even when controlling for their shape bias performances at Visit 1 (i.e., the relationship was not reducible to early shape bias performance predicting later shape bias performance). This latter relationship was found to be reciprocal: Children with ASD with stronger shape bias comprehension at Visit 4 had larger vocabularies at Visit 6, even when controlling for their vocabularies at Visit 4 (Potrzeba et al., 2015). Thus, a stronger shape bias at 3 years of age seems predictive of better lexical knowledge at 4 years of age.

If children's eye-gaze patterns on a given IPL task are reflective of individual differences in their degree or efficiency of language processing of that linguistic stimulus, then relationships between performances on IPL tasks might also be observed. For example, children who are more efficient at processing SVO sentences might also be better at using the transitive frame to learn novel verbs. We tested this hypothesis by comparing the Cohort 2 children with ASD's latency to first look at the match on the word order video at Visit 1 with their performance on the syntactic bootstrapping video at Visit 3. Indeed, a significant relationship was observed—namely, even after Visit 1 CDI scores were controlled, Visit 1 word order latency significantly predicted children's strength of syntactic bootstrapping at Visit 3 (Naigles et al., 2011). Including Visit 1 noun bias latency added nothing to the model; thus, the effect of word order processing efficiency was specific to this video and not indicative of general IPL performance (attention, ability to sit still, etc.). In future investigations, we plan to examine relationships between early word order and later wh-question performance; some hypotheses might predict that children who are more efficient at processing SVO word order might initially perform more poorly on object wh-questions because the ordering of the latter sentences is different (i.e., OSV: "What did the apple hit?"). The IPL thus does provide information concerning the levels of efficiency and accuracy with which children with ASD understand specific linguistic constructions.

In the TD literature, numerous components of parent–child interactions, including parental responsiveness, engagement in joint attention (JA), and frequency and complexity of parental speech, have been found to be predictive of TD children's lexical and syntactic growth, as measured by their speech or their performance on standardized tests (Clark, 2009; Hoff & Naigles, 2002; Huttenlocher, Vasilyeva, Cymerman, & Levine, 2002; Tamis-LeMonda, Bornstein, & Baumwell, 2001). ASD samples have manifested some of these predictive relationships as well. For example, parents who are more responsive to their child with ASD's gaze and communication bids have children who subsequently have larger vocabularies on parent report measures (McDuffie & Yoder, 2010; Siller & Sigman, 2008; see also McDuffie, Thurman, Channell, & Abbeduto, Chapter 4, this volume). Parents who use more complex utterances have children with ASD who later produce more words in naturalistic interactions (Bang & Nadig, 2015; see Nadig & Bang, Chapter 5, this volume). Moreover, children with more advanced JA skills subsequently display higher language scores on standardized tests (Charman et al., 2003; Mundy et al., 1990). These effects illustrate that many children with ASD are able to take advantage of rich social and linguistic input from their caregivers.

Are these relationships observed with IPL measures as the outcome variables? That is, do aspects of maternal input or child JA predict IPL performance? Fernald and colleagues have reported significant and positive relationships between maternal input levels and children's speed of object label comprehension in TD children (Weisleder & Fernald, 2013), and two of our IPL tasks yielded similar effects. Goodwin et al. (2015) coded the maternal wh-question usage at Visits 1 and 2 of the Cohort 2 children who viewed the wh-question IPL video at later visits and then performed regressions investigating whether any aspects of wh-question input predicted later degree of wh-question comprehension. For the TD group, mothers who produced more wh-questions with content-rich verbs (e.g., *eat*, *push*, *play*, *help*) had children with stronger wh-question comprehension, controlling for mother and child general language levels. The ASD group's significant relationships were essentially the same, albeit inverted: Mothers who produced more wh-questions with the copula (i.e., a verb bleached of semantic content) had children who subsequently showed weaker comprehension of wh-questions on the IPL task, again controlling for mother and child general language levels. The idea is that hearing wh-questions with a diverse set of verbs (as in the TD case) enables children to extract the wh-question structure independently of any specific verb and discover how the wh-word in the structure stands for a "missing" noun phrase. In the inverse relationship, hearing a large number of wh-questions that are all highly similar (e.g., "What's this? What's that? What is it?") may enable children with ASD simply to memorize the question as a frozen form in which the wh-word prompts the child for more specific reference; these questions can be understood without consideration of wh-movement or how wh-words stand for missing noun phrases (Goodwin et al., 2015).

Finally, we coded the children's number and duration of JA episodes during the play sessions at Visits 1 through 4 and performed correlations comparing these with their IPL measures at subsequent visits. As of this writing, only Cohort 2 has been included in these analyses; however, our general findings are that children who participated in more JA episodes at the early visits in which they responded to their parent's attention bid demonstrated faster looking to the matching display during both the wh-question and aspect IPL tasks (J. Park, Tek, Fein, & Naigles, 2011). It is possible that children who have more experience coordinating their own attention toward an object with that of their parent's become more efficient cognitive processors overall. These findings need replication with the combined Cohorts 2 and 3 sample, analyses that are currently underway.

Conclusion: How Can the IPL Be Useful to Researchers and Practitioners With ASD and Other Disorders?

Our findings with respect to the shape bias indicate that, unlike TD children, many children with ASD do not preferentially extend labels to objects of similar shapes. This difficulty with the shape bias may be symptomatic—and therefore an early diagnostic—of the well-known categorization deficits in this population (Klinger & Dawson, 2001). Some researchers have proposed that the shape bias emerges from offline processing that TD children perform on their early lexicons. As they "notice" that many of their words designate objects differentiated by shape, they induce that a shape bias would be a useful heuristic for acquiring new words (Smith, 2000). Children with ASD may fall short in noticing the commonalities of meaning in the words they have already acquired or in developing a heuristic based on those commonalities, especially if they have a domain-general problem with generalization, as suggested by many autism researchers (Fein et al., 1979; Minshew et al., 2002). Alternatively, the difficulty with the shape bias may be symptomatic of children with

ASD's social deficits; other researchers have proposed that the shape bias emerges in TD children from understanding when speakers are intentionally referring to classes of objects (Diesendruck, Markson, & Bloom, 2003). Children with ASD may fall short because they do not understand the differing intentions of other speakers. In addition, it may be speculated that their sensory differences may predispose them to focus more on sensory properties of objects (e.g., color) over functional properties that may be more related to shape. Research on the development and outcomes of children with ASD who manifest different levels of the shape bias may thus shed light on its origins. The generally low performance of preschoolers with ASD, however, indicates that lexical knowledge needs more and earlier interventions from ASD therapists. That is, children with ASD may need specific therapy to develop the functional semantic networks that go beyond learning to match words with objects.

In a different vein, the IPL findings provide more specific language constructs to examine with respect to neural correlates to language in young children with ASD. Much recent research has focused on the structural properties of the brains of individuals with ASD, investigating how variability in language performance correlates with variability in gray matter volume or white matter tract integrity. However, a number of studies have found no significant relationships between brain areas/activation and language level in their ASD group (Eyler, Pierce, & Courchesne, 2012; Knaus, Silver, Lindgren, Hadjikhani, & Tager-Flusberg, 2008; Verhoeven et al., 2012; Yoshimura et al., 2013), and the suggestion has been made that the usual measures of early language may be unstable in the ASD population, such that the standard or *t* scores usually used may not accurately reflect the children's varying levels of linguistic knowledge (Eyler et al., 2012; Kuhl et al., 2013). Given our demonstrations that IPL measures capture individual differences in lexical and grammatical knowledge in children with ASD, we propose that these measures have the potential to illuminate specific brain–language relationships in this population.

Finally, the IPL findings reveal that there is more language understanding than may be obvious even in low-functioning children with ASD. These findings highlight that some degree of language acquisition *is* occurring in these children, possibly promoting the refocusing of their language therapy on speech more directly. More broadly, demonstrations of linguistic knowledge in apparently nonverbal children suggest that researchers and practitioners can usefully employ nonsocial paradigms to assess the knowledge of children with ASD in linguistic and other cognitive domains.

References

Allen, D. A., & Rapin, I. (1992). Autistic children are also dysphasic. In H. Naruse & E. M. Ornitz (Eds.), *Neurobiology of infantile autism* (pp. 73–80). Amsterdam, The Netherlands: Elsevier Science.

Arunachalam, S., & Waxman, S. R. (2010). Meaning from syntax: Evidence from 2-year-olds. *Cognition*, *114*, 442–446. http://dx.doi.org/10.1016/j.cognition.2009.10.015

Bang, J., & Nadig, A. (2015). Learning language in autism: Maternal linguistic input contributes to later vocabulary. *Autism Research*, *8*, 214–223. http://dx.doi.org/10.1002/aur.1440

Berman, R. (2009). Beyond the sentence: Language development in narrative contexts. In E. L. Bavin (Ed.), *The Cambridge handbook of child language* (pp. 354–375). http://dx.doi.org/10.1017/CBO9780511576164.020

Candan, A., Küntay, A., Yeh, Y., Cheung, H., Wagner, L., & Naigles, L. (2012). Language and age effects in children's processing of word order. *Cognitive Development*, *27*, 205–221. http://dx.doi.org/10.1016/j.cogdev.2011.12.001

Charman, T., Baron-Cohen, S., Swettenham, J., Baird, G., Drew, A., & Cox, A. (2003). Predicting language outcome in infants with autism and pervasive developmental disorder. *International Journal of Language & Communication Disorders*, *38*, 265–285. http://dx.doi.org/10.1080/1368203100000104830

Clark, E. (2009). *First language acquisition*. http://dx.doi.org/10.1017/CBO9780511806698

Comrie, B. (1976). *Aspect*. Cambridge, England: Cambridge University Press.

de Villiers, J., Roeper, T., Bland-Stewart, L., & Pearson, B. (2008). Answering hard questions: Wh-movement across dialects and disorder. *Applied Psycholinguistics*, *29*, 67–103. http://dx.doi.org/10.1017/S0142716408080041

Diesendruck, G., Markson, L., & Bloom, P. (2003). Children's reliance on creator's intent in extending names for artifacts. *Psychological Science*, *14*, 164–168. http://dx.doi.org/10.1111/1467-9280.t01-1-01436

Eigsti, I.-M., Bennetto, L., & Dadlani, M. B. (2007). Beyond pragmatics: Morphosyntactic development in autism. *Journal of Autism and Developmental Disorders*, *37*, 1007–1023. http://dx.doi.org/10.1007/s10803-006-0239-2

Ellawadi, A., Fein, D., & Naigles, L. (2015, May). *Dynamic assessment of the looking patterns of toddlers with ASD during teaching*. Poster presented at the 2015 International Meeting for Autism Research, Salt Lake City, UT.

Eyler, L. T., Pierce, K., & Courchesne, E. (2012). A failure of left temporal cortex to specialize for language is an early emerging and fundamental property of autism. *Brain: A Journal of Neurology*, *135*, 949–960. http://dx.doi.org/10.1093/brain/awr364

Fein, D., Dunn, M., Allen, D. A., Aram, D. M., Hall, N., Morris, R., & Wilson, B. C. (1996). Language and neuropsychological findings. In I. Rapin (Ed.), *Preschool children with inadequate communication* (pp. 123–154). London, England: MacKeith Press.

Fein, D., Tinder, P., & Waterhouse, L. (1979). Stimulus generalization in autistic and normal children. *Journal of Child Psychology and Psychiatry*, *20*, 325–335. http://dx.doi.org/10.1111/j.1469-7610.1979.tb00518.x

Fenson, L., Dale, P., Reznick, J., Thal, D., Bates, E., Hartung, J. P., . . . Reilly, J. S. (1993). *MacArthur Communicative Development Inventories*. Baltimore, MD: Brookes.

Fernald, A., & Marchman, V. A. (2012). Individual differences in lexical processing at 18 months predict vocabulary growth in typically developing and late-talking toddlers. *Child Development*, *83*, 203–222. http://dx.doi.org/10.1111/j.1467-8624.2011.01692.x

Fernald, A., Perfors, A., & Marchman, V. A. (2006). Picking up speed in understanding: Speech processing efficiency and vocabulary growth across the second year. *Developmental Psychology*, *42*, 98–116. http://dx.doi.org/10.1037/0012-1649.42.1.98

Fusaroli, R., Weed, E., Fein, D., & Naigles, L. (2014, November). *Linguistic adaptation between mothers and children in ASD: A longitudinal perspective*. Paper presented at the Annual Meeting of the Psychonomic Society, Long Beach, CA.

Gentner, D. (1982). Why nouns are learned before verbs: Linguistic relativity vs. natural partitioning. In S. Kuczaj (Ed.), *Language development: Language, cognition, and culture* (pp. 301–334). Hillsdale, NJ: Erlbaum.

Gerken, L. A., & MacIntosh, B. J. (1993). The interplay of function morphemes and prosody in early language. *Developmental Psychology*, *29*, 448–457. http://dx.doi.org/10.1037/0012-1649.29.3.448

Gertner, Y., Fisher, C., & Eisengart, J. (2006). Learning words and rules: Abstract knowledge of word order in early sentence comprehension. *Psychological Science*, *17*, 684–691. http://dx.doi.org/10.1111/j.1467-9280.2006.01767.x

Golinkoff, R. M., Hirsh-Pasek, K., Bloom, L., Smith, L. B., Woodward, A., Akhtar, N., . . . Hollich, G. (2000). *Becoming a word learner: A debate on lexical acquisition*. http://dx.doi.org/10.1093/acprof:oso/9780195130324.001.0001

Golinkoff, R. M., Ma, W., Song, L., & Hirsh-Pasek, K. (2013). Twenty-five years using the intermodal preferential looking paradigm to study language acquisition: What have we learned? *Perspectives on Psychological Science*, *8*, 316–339. http://dx.doi.org/10.1177/1745691613484936

Golinkoff, R. M., Mervis, C. B., & Hirsh-Pasek, K. (1994). Early object labels: The case for a developmental lexical principles framework. *Journal of Child Language*, *21*, 125–155. http://dx.doi.org/10.1017/S0305000900008692

Goodwin, A., Fein, D., & Naigles, L. R. (2012). Comprehension of wh-questions precedes their production in typical development and autism spectrum disorders. *Autism Research*, *5*, 109–123. http://dx.doi.org/10.1002/aur.1220

Goodwin, A., Fein, D., & Naigles, L. R. (2015). The role of maternal input in the development of wh-question comprehension in autism and typical development. *Journal of Child Language*, *42*, 32–63. http://dx.doi.org/10.1017/S0305000913000524

Graham, S. A., & Poulin-Dubois, D. (1999). Infants' reliance on shape to generalize novel labels to animate and inanimate objects. *Journal of Child Language*, *26*, 295–320. http://dx.doi.org/10.1017/S0305000999003815

Hirsh-Pasek, K., & Golinkoff, R. (1996). *The origins of grammar: Evidence from language comprehension*. Cambridge, MA: MIT Press.

Hoff, E., & Naigles, L. (2002). How children use input to acquire a lexicon. *Child Development*, *73*, 418–433. http://dx.doi.org/10.1111/1467-8624.00415

Huttenlocher, J. (1974). The origins of language comprehension. In R. Solso (Ed.), *Theories of cognitive psychology* (pp. 331–368). New York, NY: Halsted Press, Winston-Wiley.

Huttenlocher, J., Vasilyeva, M., Cymerman, E., & Levine, S. (2002). Language input and child syntax. *Cognitive Psychology*, *45*, 337–374. http://dx.doi.org/10.1016/S0010-0285(02)00500-5

Jyotishi, M., Fein, D., & Naigles, L. R. (2015, May). *Some wh-questions really are hard for children with ASD to understand*. Poster presented at the 2015 International Meeting for Autism Research, Salt Lake City, UT.

Kjelgaard, M. M., & Tager-Flusberg, H. (2001). An investigation of language impairment in autism: Implications for genetic subgroups. *Language and Cognitive Processes*, *16*, 287–308. http://dx.doi.org/10.1080/01690960042000058

Klinger, L. G., & Dawson, G. (2001). Prototype formation in autism. *Development and Psychopathology*, *13*, 111–124. http://dx.doi.org/10.1017/S0954579401001080

Knaus, T. A., Silver, A. M., Lindgren, K. A., Hadjikhani, N., & Tager-Flusberg, H. (2008). fMRI activation during a language task in adolescents with ASD. *Journal of the International Neuropsychological Society*, *14*, 967–979.

Kuhl, P. K., Coffey-Corina, S., Padden, D., Munson, J., Estes, A., & Dawson, G. (2013). Brain responses to words in 2-year-olds with autism predict developmental outcomes at age 6. *PLoS ONE, 8*, e64967. http://dx.doi.org/10.1371/journal.pone.0064967

Landau, B., Smith, L. B., & Jones, S. S. (1988). The importance of shape in early lexical learning. *Cognitive Development, 3*, 299–321. http://dx.doi.org/10.1016/0885-2014(88)90014-7

Lord, C., & Risi, S. (2004). Trajectory of language development in autistic spectrum disorders. In M. Rice (Ed.), *Developmental language disorders: From phenotypes to etiologies* (pp. 7–29). Mahwah, NJ: Erlbaum.

Lord, C., Rutter, M., DiLavore, P., & Risi, S. (1999). *The Autism Diagnostic Observation Schedule—Generic.* Los Angeles, CA: Western Psychological Service.

Maratsos, M. (1998). The acquisition of grammar. In D. Kuhn & R. S. Siegler (Eds.), *Handbook of child psychology: Vol. 2. Cognition, perception, and language* (pp. 421–466). New York, NY: Wiley.

Marchman, V. A., & Fernald, A. (2008). Speed of word recognition and vocabulary knowledge in infancy predict cognitive and language outcomes in later childhood. *Developmental Science, 11*, F9–F16. http://dx.doi.org/10.1111/j.1467-7687.2008.00671.x

Markman, E. (1989). *Categorization and naming in children.* Cambridge, MA: MIT Press.

McDuffie, A., & Yoder, P. (2010). Types of parent verbal responsiveness that predict language in young children with autism spectrum disorder. *Journal of Speech, Language, and Hearing Research, 53*, 1026–1039. http://dx.doi.org/10.1044/1092-4388(2009/09-0023)

Minshew, N. J., Meyer, J., & Goldstein, G. (2002). Abstract reasoning in autism: A dissociation between concept formation and concept identification. *Neuropsychology, 16*, 327–334. http://dx.doi.org/10.1037/0894-4105.16.3.327

Mullen, E. M. (1995). *Mullen Scales of Early Learning.* Circle Pines, MN: American Guidance Service.

Mundy, P., Sigman, M., & Kasari, C. (1990). A longitudinal study of joint attention and language development in autistic children. *Journal of Autism and Developmental Disorders, 20*, 115–128. http://dx.doi.org/10.1007/BF02206861

Naigles, L. (1990). Children use syntax to learn verb meanings. *Journal of Child Language, 17*, 357–374. http://dx.doi.org/10.1017/S0305000900013817

Naigles, L. G., & Kako, E. T. (1993). First contact in verb acquisition: Defining a role for syntax. *Child Development, 64*, 1665–1687. http://dx.doi.org/10.2307/1131462

Naigles, L. R., & Chin, I. (2015). Language development in children with autism. In E. L. Bavin & L. R. Naigles (Eds.), *The Cambridge handbook of child language* (2nd ed., pp. 637–658). http://dx.doi.org/10.1055/s-0033-1353446

Naigles, L. R., Kelty, E., Jaffery, R., & Fein, D. (2011). Abstractness and continuity in the syntactic development of young children with autism. *Autism Research, 4*, 422–437. http://dx.doi.org/10.1002/aur.223

Naigles, L. R., & Tovar, A. T. (2012). Portable intermodal preferential looking (IPL): Investigating language comprehension in typically developing toddlers and young children with autism. *Journal of Visualized Experiments, 70*, e4331.

Norbury, C. F. (2005). Barking up the wrong tree? Lexical ambiguity resolution in children with language impairments and autistic spectrum disorders. *Journal of Experimental Child Psychology, 90*, 142–171. http://dx.doi.org/10.1016/j.jecp.2004.11.003

Park, C. J., Yelland, G. W., Taffe, J. R., & Gray, K. M. (2012). Morphological and syntactic skills in language samples of preschool-aged children with autism: Atypical development? *International Journal of Speech-Language Pathology, 14*, 95–108. http://dx.doi.org/10.3109/17549507.2011.645555

Park, J., Tek, S., Fein, D., & Naigles, L. (2011, November). *Early joint attention predicts children's subsequent performance on preferential looking tasks.* Paper presented at the Boston University Conference on Language Development, Boston, MA.

Perovic, A., Modyanova, N., & Wexler, K. (2013). Comprehension of reflexive and personal pronouns in children with autism: A syntactic or pragmatic deficit? *Applied Psycholinguistics, 34*, 813–835. http://dx.doi.org/10.1017/S0142716412000033

Piotroski, J., & Naigles, L. (2012). Preferential looking. In E. Hoff (Ed.), *Research methods in child language: A practical guide* (pp. 17–28). Malden, MA: Wiley-Blackwell.

Potrzeba, E., Fein, D., & Naigles, L. (2015). Investigating the shape bias in typically developing children and children with autism spectrum disorders. *Frontiers in Psychology: Cognition.* http://dx.doi.org/10.3389/fpsyg.2015.00446

Quine, W. (1960). *Word and object.* Cambridge, MA: MIT Press.

Radford, A. (1990). The syntax of nominal arguments in early child English. *Language Acquisition, 1*, 195–223.

Roberts, J. A., Rice, M. L., & Tager-Flusberg, H. (2004). Tense marking in children with autism. *Applied Psycholinguistics, 25*, 429–448. http://dx.doi.org/10.1017/S0142716404001201

Seidl, A., Hollich, G., & Jusczyk, P. (2003). Early understanding of subject and object wh-questions. *Infancy, 4*, 423–436. http://dx.doi.org/10.1207/S15327078IN0403_06

Shi, R. (2014). Functional morphemes and early language acquisition. *Child Development Perspectives, 8*, 6–11. http://dx.doi.org/10.1111/cdep.12052

Shulman, C., & Guberman, A. (2007). Acquisition of verb meaning through syntactic cues: A comparison of children with autism, children with specific language impairment (SLI) and children with typical language development (TLD). *Journal of Child Language, 34*, 411–423. http://dx.doi.org/10.1017/S0305000906007963

Siller, M., & Sigman, M. (2008). Modeling longitudinal change in the language abilities of children with autism: Parent behaviors and child characteristics as predictors of change. *Developmental Psychology, 44*, 1691–1704. http://dx.doi.org/10.1037/a0013771

Smith, L. B. (2000). Learning how to learn words: An associative crane. In R. M. Golinkoff, K. Hirsh-Pasek, L. Bloom, L. B. Smith, A. L. Woodward, N. Akhtar, . . . G. Hollich (Eds.), *Becoming a word learner: A debate on lexical acquisition* (pp. 51–80). http://dx.doi.org/10.1093/acprof:oso/9780195130324.003.003

Smith, L. B., Jones, S. S., Landau, B., Gershkoff-Stowe, L., & Samuelson, L. (2002). Object name learning provides on-the-job training for attention. *Psychological Science, 13*, 13–19. http://dx.doi.org/10.1111/1467-9280.00403

Snyder, W. (2007). *Child language: The parametric approach.* Oxford, England: Oxford University Press.

Stone, W. L., Coonrod, E. E., & Ousley, O. Y. (2000). Brief report: screening tool for autism in two-year-olds (STAT): Development and preliminary data. *Journal of Autism and Developmental Disorders, 30*, 607–612. http://dx.doi.org/10.1023/A:1005647629002

Stromswold, K. (1995). The acquisition of subject and nonsubject wh-questions. *Language Acquisition, 4*, 5–48. http://dx.doi.org/10.1080/10489223.1995.9671658

Swensen, L. D., Kelley, E., Fein, D., & Naigles, L. R. (2007). Processes of language acquisition in children with autism: Evidence from preferential looking. *Child Development, 78*, 542–557. http://dx.doi.org/10.1111/j.1467-8624.2007.01022.x

Tager-Flusberg, H. (1994). Dissociations in form and function in the acquisition of language by autistic children. In H. Tager-Flusberg (Ed.), *Constraints on language acquisition: Studies of atypical children* (pp. 175–194). Hillsdale, NJ: Erlbaum.

Tamis-LeMonda, C. S., Bornstein, M. H., & Baumwell, L. (2001). Maternal responsiveness and children's achievement of language milestones. *Child Development*, *72*, 748–767. http://dx.doi.org/10.1111/1467-8624.00313

Tek, S., Jaffery, G., Fein, D., & Naigles, L. R. (2008). Do children with autism spectrum disorders show a shape bias in word learning? *Autism Research*, *1*, 208–222. http://dx.doi.org/10.1002/aur.38

Tek, S., Mesite, L., Fein, D., & Naigles, L. (2014). Longitudinal analyses of expressive language development reveal two distinct language profiles among young children with autism spectrum disorders. *Journal of Autism and Developmental Disorders*, *44*, 75–89. http://dx.doi.org/10.1007/s10803-013-1853-4

Tovar, A. T., Fein, D., & Naigles, L. R. (2015). Grammatical aspect is a strength in the language comprehension of young children with autism spectrum disorder. *Journal of Speech, Language, and Hearing Research*, *58*, 301–310. http://dx.doi.org/10.1044/2014_JSLHR-L-13-0257

Verhoeven, J. S., Rommel, N., Prodi, E., Leemans, A., Zink, I., Vandewalle, E., . . . Sunaert, S. (2012). Is there a common neuroanatomical substrate of language deficit between autism spectrum disorder and specific language impairment? *Cereb Cortex*, *22*, 2263–2271.

Wagner, L., Swensen, L., & Naigles, L. (2009). Children's early productivity with verbal morphology. *Cognitive Development*, *24*, 223–239. http://dx.doi.org/10.1016/j.cogdev.2009.05.001

Waterhouse, L., & Fein, D. (1982). Language skills in developmentally disabled children. *Brain and Language*, *15*, 307–333. http://dx.doi.org/10.1016/0093-934X(82)90062-1

Waxman, S., Fu, X., Arunachalam, S., Leddon, E., Geraghty, K., & Song, H. J. (2013). Are nouns learned before verbs? Infants provide insight into a longstanding debate. *Child Development Perspectives*, *7*, 1–5. http://dx.doi.org/10.1111/cdep.12032

Weisleder, A., & Fernald, A. (2013). Talking to children matters: Early language experience strengthens processing and builds vocabulary. *Psychological Science*, *24*, 2143–2152. http://dx.doi.org/10.1177/0956797613488145

Williams, D., Botting, N., & Boucher, J. (2008). Language in autism and specific language impairment: Where are the links? *Psychological Bulletin*, *134*, 944–963. http://dx.doi.org/10.1037/a0013743

Yoshimura, Y., Kikuchi, M., Shitamichi, K., Ueno, S., Munesue, T., Ono, Y., . . . Minabe, Y. (2013). Atypical brain lateralisation in the auditory cortex and language performance in 3- to 7-year-old children with high-functioning autism spectrum disorder: A child-customised magnetoencephalography (MEG) study. *Molecular Autism*, *4*, 38.

Yuan, S., Fisher, C., & Snedeker, J. (2012). Counting the nouns: Simple structural cues to verb meaning. *Child Development*, *83*, 1382–1399. http://dx.doi.org/10.1111/j.1467-8624.2012.01783.x

Andrea McDuffie, Angela John Thurman,
Marie Moore Channell, and Leonard Abbeduto

4 Learning Words in a Social World: Impairments Associated With ASD and Fragile X Syndrome

Early word learning represents a foundational skill for the subsequent development of grammar and morphology (Bates & Goodman, 1997). Word learning, however, is a challenge for children with neurodevelopmental disorders, such as autism spectrum disorder (ASD). These early word-learning challenges contribute to a negative developmental cascade. In contrast, competence in the ability to understand and use spoken language contributes to more positive outcomes in adulthood (Gillespie-Lynch et al., 2012; Magiati, Tay, & Howlin, 2014). Language skills are central to living independently, maintaining employment, developing proficiency in activities of daily life, establishing friendships, and participating in leisure activities (Clegg, Hollis, Mawhood, & Rutter, 2005; Hartley et al., 2011). Examining the processes of word learning in young children with neurodevelopmental disorders can inform the development of more effective language intervention approaches, which over the life course can lead to improved adult outcomes.

A framework for studying the processes through which early word acquisition occurs or may be disrupted is provided by three theoretical approaches (Ambridge & Lieven, 2011, p. 61): the lexical principles, associative learning, and social-pragmatic accounts. According to the lexical principles approach, the acquisition of early vocabulary is guided by a set of constraints that restrict the child's possible hypotheses about how novel labels are mapped onto their meanings (Woodward, Markman, & Fitzsimmons, 1994). These constraints include the whole object assumption (i.e., new words refer to whole objects rather than to actions or object properties), the mutual exclusivity assumption (i.e., children prefer each object has but a single label), and the taxonomic assumption (i.e., objects are to be grouped together into categories; Markman, 1994). An associative learning approach, on the other hand, explains the acquisition of new words through a process of a cross-modal pairing between a novel label and a salient novel object. That is, word learning is the result of temporal contiguity between label and object and a resulting associative pairing.

In the lexical principles and associative learning accounts, word learning is largely a cognitive activity with no special status afforded to social information. Although proponents of social-pragmatic theory acknowledge the importance of the cognitive and conceptual skills that enable children to segment the speech stream (Saffran, Aslin, & Newport, 1996), deploy processes of attention and memory (Samuelson & Smith, 1998),

http://dx.doi.org/10.1037/15964-005
Innovative Investigations of Language in Autism Spectrum Disorder, L. R. Naigles (Editor)

and use principles to constrain the range of potential word meanings (Woodward, Markman, & Fitzsimmons, 1994), this account primarily emphasizes the child's ability to follow into, share, and understand the referential intentions of communicative partners (Akhtar & Tomasello, 2000). Thus, within social-pragmatic theory, the dynamic interplay between the child and the social world in which language is experienced is of fundamental importance to language learning in general and in early word learning in particular. The social-pragmatic account, therefore, is a particularly attractive framework within which to begin investigating the word-learning difficulties of children who also face challenges participating in social interaction.

Nonsyndromic ASD Versus Fragile X Syndrome

The behavioral characteristics associated with many neurodevelopmental disorders are especially likely to create barriers to accessing and using social-pragmatic information to facilitate efficient word learning. In the present chapter, we examine two such neurodevelopmental disorders: nonsyndromic ASD (i.e., children with ASD for whom a specific genetic etiology has not been identified) and fragile X syndrome (FXS), the leading inherited cause of intellectual disability and a common comorbid cause of ASD. Here we present experimental data on the role of the social environment in supporting early lexical development children with these disorders.

Nonsyndromic ASD is a neurodevelopmental disorder that impedes functioning across the lifespan and is characterized by a core impairment in social communication accompanied by the presence of repetitive and stereotyped behaviors (American Psychiatric Association, 2013); however, there is considerable variability in symptom presentation across individuals with nonsyndromic ASD. Even though nonsyndromic ASD is a behaviorally defined disorder, it is a highly heritable, multifactorial condition (Ronald & Hoekstra, 2011), resulting from a dynamic interplay among various genetic susceptibilities and environmental factors (Hertz-Picciotto et al., 2006).

In contrast, FXS is caused by the mutation of a single gene, *FMR1*, located on the X chromosome (Verkerk et al., 1991). The healthy allele of *FMR1* comprises five to 54 CGG repeats, whereas individuals with FXS have expansions exceeding 200 repeats, which is termed the *full mutation*. The full mutation leads to hypermethylation and transcriptional silencing of the *FMR1* gene such that its protein product, the fragile X mental retardation protein (FMRP), is reduced or absent (Oostra & Willemsen, 2009). FMRP regulates protein synthesis at the synapse; thus, this protein is critical for cognitive and behavioral development because it guides neuronal development and experience-dependent learning (Bassell & Warren, 2008). Females with the FXS full mutation are less severely affected than males, given the protective presence of an unaffected X chromosome (Mazzocco, 2000).

Virtually all males with the *FMR1* full mutation have cognitive delays, with approximately 85% having IQs between 40 and 55 (Hessl et al., 2009). Additionally, language delays are often more severe than would be expected based on nonverbal cognitive level (Abbeduto, Brady, & Kover, 2007), likely because of other phenotypic characteristics that negatively affect learning. For instance, the majority of males with FXS display hyperarousal and attentional difficulties (Scerif, Longhi, Cole, Karmiloff-Smith, & Cornish, 2012), anxiety and social withdrawal (Cordeiro, Ballinger, Hagerman, & Hessl, 2011), and other challenging behaviors (Symons, Clark, Hatton, Skinner, & Bailey, 2003) that are likely to negatively affect language learning.

Individuals with FXS often exhibit symptoms of ASD. As many as 90% of males with FXS display behaviors such as hand flapping, repetitive speech, and gaze aversion (Merenstein et al., 1996). Indeed, symptoms of ASD are frequent and severe enough that approximately 60% of males with FXS receive a comorbid diagnosis of ASD based on gold standard diagnostic criteria (Bailey et al., 1998; Demark, Feldman, & Holden, 2003; Hall, Lightbody, Hirt, Rezvani, & Reiss, 2010). Some shared biological substrates have been implicated between the two disorders, especially those involving abnormalities in inhibitory neural transmission mediated through the gamma-aminobutyric acid–ergic signaling system (Coghlan et al., 2012). Additionally, many ASD susceptibility genes that have been identified are controlled by FMRP, reinforcing potential links between the biology of FXS and nonsyndromic ASD (Iossifov et al., 2012).

Behavioral development, however, reflects a complex and continuous interplay of genetic, developmental, and experiential factors. This raises the possibility that clinically meaningful differences in behavioral symptoms and neurobiological substrates between FXS and nonsyndromic ASD are masked by the use of a categorical diagnosis of ASD (Abbeduto, McDuffie, & Thurman, 2014). Thus, much of our research has focused on understanding in a more nuanced manner the similarities and differences between these two disorders, especially with regard to the ways that social information is used by individuals with nonsyndromic ASD or FXS.

Delays in communication are an early emerging characteristic of both disorders (Abbeduto et al., 2007; De Giacomo & Fombonne, 1998) and continue to be problematic across the lifespan, at least for those individuals who have co-occurring intellectual disabilities (Hartley et al., 2011; Howlin, Savage, Moss, Tempier, & Rutter, 2014). Additionally, both disorders are characterized by challenges in responding appropriately to the social cues of interactive partners as well as by increased risk for the presence of maladaptive behaviors likely to negatively affect learning. The severity and profile of these challenges, however, appears to differ across the groups (e.g., McDuffie, Kover, Hagerman, & Abbeduto, 2013; Thurman, McDuffie, Hagerman, & Abbeduto, 2014).

In this chapter, we review four experimental studies in which we compared children with nonsyndromic ASD and children with FXS as they learned novel words in the context of interactive experimental tasks that varied in the types of social cues available to support word learning. Results from these studies provide insights into the ability of school-age boys with nonsyndromic ASD or FXS to use specific types of social cues from conversational partners during word learning. These studies provide data on similarities and differences in word-learning performance across the two disorders as well as on the child characteristics influencing the ability to use the social cues in word learning. We conclude the chapter with a brief discussion of the clinical implications of our research.

Word Learning in Nonsyndromic ASD and FXS

Broadly speaking, *fast-mapping* describes a word-learning process in which children rapidly infer a correspondence between a novel label and a speaker's intended referent. According to Rice and colleagues, experimental fast-mapping tasks can reveal the minimum input conditions necessary for children to establish initial understanding of a novel word (Rice, Buhr, & Nemeth, 1990). Thus, fast-mapping tasks have been widely used to identify the types of social, affective, and attentional cues that are necessary to support novel word learning in different groups of children. These types of tasks have both theoretical and clinical importance in that children with stronger fast-mapping skills should be more efficient at adding new words to their lexicons. Thus, understanding the developmental emergence of the ability to use different social and contextual cues to infer the speaker's referential intent has the potential to inform intervention approaches that seek to support vocabulary and language growth.

Associative Word Learning in FXS and ASD

At 12 months of age, typically developing (TD) children require redundant contextual cues presented in synchrony for word learning to occur. These cues, provided by the speaker, include increasing the salience of the novel object, ensuring temporal contiguity between seeing the object and hearing the label, labeling the object when it is the child's current focus of attention, providing multiple presentations of the novel label, extending the duration of exposure to the novel object, and presenting the object in the same location during teaching and testing (Hollich et al., 2000). At this stage of development, the word-learning process in TD children is so fragile that successful word learning requires "bludgeoning" children with a wide variety of converging environmental supports (Hollich et al., 2000, p. 15). In our lab, we extended this associative learning paradigm to two groups of chronological age-matched 6- to 10-year-old boys with nonsyndromic ASD or FXS and compared their performance with that of a group of younger TD children matched on nonverbal mental age (McDuffie et al., 2013). In this study, rather than comparing discrete categorical subgroups of individuals with FXS based on comorbid ASD status, severity of autism symptoms as measured by the Autism Diagnostic Observation Schedule (ADOS; Lord, Rutter, DiLavore, & Risi, 1999) was examined as a continuous correlate of task performance (Gotham, Pickles, & Lord, 2009). On a scale of 1 to 10, the mean ASD severity score for participants with FXS was 6.30 ($SD = 2.01$) and for participants with nonsyndromic ASD was 8.03 (*SD* = 1.40), with higher scores reflective of more severe symptoms of autism.

In this interactive task, which was based on a procedure developed by McDuffie and colleagues (McDuffie, Yoder, & Stone, 2006), a novel target and distractor object were presented to each participant during four separate trials. During the teaching phase of each trial, the target object was labeled five times with a CVCV nonsense word and the distractor object was talked about for an equivalent amount of time without labeling. Each novel object was presented individually and the examiner used a variety of attention-directing cues (e.g., head turns, gaze shifts, object movement, and pointing gestures) intended to direct and maintain the child's attention to the novel object while the examiner was labeling or talking about it. Word learning was then evaluated for each trial using a forced choice paradigm, during which the child was asked to give the examiner the previously labeled target object. Given that only a single object was labeled during a trial, this task is designed to evaluate the results of an associative learning process as the child is not required to use social-pragmatic cues to disambiguate the adult's intended referent. That is, the task provides an opportunity for the child to pair the nonsense label with only one of the novel objects. We designed this task to assess a baseline level of associative word learning against which performance on subsequent tasks that required a higher level of social inferencing could be compared.

In terms of the mean number of correct objects chosen during comprehension trials, results demonstrated that although performance by all groups was above chance levels, the TD boys outperformed the boys with nonsyndromic ASD and FXS, after controlling for nonverbal mental age. In addition, despite having lower levels of nonverbal cognition, the boys with FXS outperformed the boys with nonsyndromic ASD and had higher concurrent levels of receptive and expressive vocabulary as measured by standardized vocabulary tests. Finally, between-group differences were observed in the child factors associated with word learning: for boys with FXS, task performance was significantly associated with both receptive and expressive vocabulary as well as nonverbal cognition, whereas no significant associations between measured child characteristics and fast-mapping performance were observed for boys with nonsyndromic ASD.

In general, then, results from this study suggest that boys with FXS may be more likely than boys with nonsyndromic ASD to benefit from interactive word-learning contexts that are highly scaffolded by the communicative partner to provide an straightforward pairing between label and object and which, presumably, rely on associative learning processes. This finding is somewhat surprising because males with FXS display more severe cognitive impairments and higher rates of some types of challenging behaviors (e.g., inattention, anxiety) that could be expected to negatively affect associative learning relative to boys with nonsyndromic ASD. Yet these results suggest that boys with FXS may be more proficient at an associative learning task in which attention to a salient label-object pairing is supported by social cues from an interactive partner.

Measuring Visual Attention in FXS and ASD

A limitation of the McDuffie et al. (2013) study is that it was not possible to quantify the child's duration of visual attention to the novel object during teaching trials. Such data could provide converging evidence that the examiner's attention-directing cues and use of verbal labels did, in fact, influence how participants deployed their attention to the novel objects. In an attempt to more precisely evaluate how the social-pragmatic cues of pointing and object labeling affected word-learning performance for boys with nonsyndromic ASD or FXS, Benjamin et al. (2014) implemented an eye-tracking version of the McDuffie et al. (2013) fast-mapping paradigm. The mean ASD severity score for participants in the Benjamin et al. (2014) study was 6.36 ($SD = 2.59$) for participants with FXS and was 8.06 ($SD = 1.56$) for participants with nonsyndromic ASD, again with higher scores reflective of more severe symptoms of autism.

In this eye-tracking study, the stimuli were video-recorded presentations of an examiner labeling novel objects while looking and pointing at them. In contrast to previous findings for children with typically development or nonsyndromic ASD (McDuffie et al., 2006), Benjamin et al. (2014) failed to detect any significant within-group differences in gaze toward a target object as a function of the presence or absence of a verbal label during object presentation. This null result might indicate that the video-recorded stimuli were not as engaging as a live examiner and did not create as effective a context for responding to verbal labels as was observed for the interactive versions of the task.

Benjamin et al. (2014) did, however, observe between-group differences in performance. Participants with typical development and those with nonsyndromic ASD directed significantly more gaze to areas of interest (i.e., areas of the viewing field used for data analysis) containing the novel objects. In contrast, participants with FXS directed significantly more gaze to the area of interest containing the face. This latter finding is interesting because previous studies have documented gaze aversion in response to facial stimuli in individuals with FXS (e.g., Farzin, Rivera, & Hessl, 2009). Benjamin et al. (2014) also reported that all three groups of participants gazed at the novel objects significantly longer when object presentation was accompanied by a pointing gesture than when it was not, but duration of attention to the novel objects was influenced significantly more by pointing for participants with typical development and nonsyndromic ASD relative to FXS. The authors theorized that there may be a potential disruption in the ability of boys with FXS to disengage from the face to respond to pointing cues, which are expected to support word-learning performance. Finally, Benjamin et al. (2014) reported that duration of gaze to the target object was negatively related to ASD symptom severity for participants with non-syndromic ASD but not for participants with FXS; that is, for participants with non-syndromic ASD only, children who had less severe ASD symptomatology demonstrated longer durations of gaze to the target objects than children who had more severe ASD symptomatology. This finding provides an additional example of how symptoms of

ASD seem to have differential effects on social cognitive behaviors for boys with ASD relative to boys with FXS.

Taken together, therefore, results from McDuffie et al. (2013) and Benjamin et al. (2014) suggest that different learning processes or impairments may underlie the associative learning of novel words in children with nonsyndromic ASD and FXS. That is, for boys with FXS, but not boys with nonsyndromic ASD, task performance was related to performance on standardized measures of vocabulary ability (McDuffie et al., 2013), indicating that the same learning process that was measured in the fast-mapping task may also be involved in real-world vocabulary acquisition. Furthermore, it appears that severity of ASD symptomatology is negatively affecting the amount of time children with nonsyndromic ASD, but not FXS, spend looking at a target that is highlighted by social-pragmatic cues, such as pointing. However, it is important to recognize that overall levels of ASD symptomatology were lower in participants with FXS relative to participants with nonsyndromic ASD, offering an alternative explanation for observed between-group differences. Results across both studies suggest that the associative learning process involved in mapping a novel label to an object during word learning is more challenging for boys with nonsyndromic ASD than boys with FXS, and there may also be between-group differences in mechanisms involved in translating this initial fast mapping process into long-term learning. It is important to point out that neither of these studies evaluated associative learning between labels and objects in the absence of social cues as has been the paradigm implemented by some authors to assess associative learning processes in vocabulary acquisition (Schafer & Plunkett, 1998; Werker, Cohen, Lloyd, Casasola, & Stager, 1998; see also Naigles and Fein, Chapter 3, this volume). In both the McDuffie et al. (2013) and Benjamin et al. (2014) studies, the attention-directing signals that accompanied the temporal pairing between label and object were social in nature (i.e., delivered in an interactive context by an examiner), although some might argue that the interactive nature of the word-learning task was changed somewhat by having the cues presented via video recording in the Benjamin et al. (2014) study. Thus, although we argue that these two studies provide a baseline index of associative learning in children with two specific neurodevelopmental disorders, it can also be argued that the eye-tracking version of the task is not inherently social.

Discrepant Word Learning in FXS and ASD

Much of the language a very young child hears refers to the objects and actions that exist within his or her ongoing focus of attention. This situation occurs because adults typically "follow the child's lead" when interacting and communicating with developmentally young children. In fact, much early word learning takes place within the predictable context of frequently repeated interactive routines. Within these routines, caregivers use predictable and repetitive language that maps unambiguously onto the child's focus of attention (Bruner, 1985; Snow, 1989). As children grow into toddlerhood, social partners increasingly do not follow-into and talk exclusively about the child's current focus of attention (Harris, Jones, Brookes, & Grant, 1986). In such discrepant labeling contexts, social-pragmatic theory proposes that the child must become an active participant in disambiguating the objects and events the communicative partner intends to label. The speaker's direction of gaze toward the intended referent provides a particularly critical social cue that, when used efficiently by the child, decreases ambiguity and enables an accurate label-object pairing to be forged. By 18 months of age, TD toddlers have become reasonably proficient at word learning under conditions of discrepant labeling—that is, modifying their own attentional focus by following the adult's direction of gaze and mapping a novel word to the object on which the adult is focused (Baldwin, 1993).

Both nonsyndromic ASD and FXS are associated with atypical use of gaze in social contexts (Klin, Shultz, & Jones, 2015; Williams, Porter, & Langdon, 2014). Although the ability to use speaker direction of gaze to learn new words has been investigated in children with nonsyndromic ASD (Baron-Cohen, Baldwin, & Crowson, 1997; Leekam, Hunnisett, & Moore, 1998; Luyster & Lord, 2009), the ways in which gaze following affects language development for children with FXS are not well understood. In our lab, we adapted the Baron-Cohen et al. (1997) paradigm to examine the use of speaker direction of gaze during word learning by school-age children with FXS or nonsyndromic ASD, matched on chronological age and nonverbal cognition (both nonverbal IQ and cognitive growth scores) and younger TD boys matched on nonverbal growth scores (Benjamin et al., 2015). This matching strategy limits the effects of cognitive level in accounting for potential between-group differences in performance. The mean ASD severity score for participants with FXS was 5.17 ($SD = 2.09$) and for participants with nonsyndromic ASD was 8.29 ($SD = 1.41$), again indicating that, as a group, participants with FXS had lower levels of autism symptomatology than participants with ASD.

In the Benjamin et al. (2015) study, word learning was examined under two experimental conditions during which two potential object referents were available at the moment the novel label was provided. In the follow-in labeling condition, the object being labeled was the child's focus of attention. In the discrepant labeling condition, the object being labeled was the focus of the examiner's, but not the child's, attention. In both conditions, the novel label was not presented until the examiner ensured that the child was visually attending to his own object. Both objects were available during comprehension test probes along with two familiar objects included to assess the extent to which participants understood and could comply with task demands.

Regardless of condition, all participants showed high levels of correct performance on familiar-item test probes. In the follow-in labeling condition, all groups responded at above-chance levels and selected the child's object on comprehension probes more often than they selected the examiner's object. In the discrepant labeling condition, all groups responded at above-chance levels, but none of the groups selected the examiner's object more often than they selected their own object. In comparing levels of performance between conditions, however, boys with FXS showed significantly more correct choices during follow-in relative to discrepant labeling trials, whereas level of performance was similar across conditions for boys with nonsyndromic ASD and younger TD boys.

Benjamin et al. (2015) interpreted these findings as suggesting similarities across the groups, but also acknowledging that subtle differences may distinguish children with nonsyndromic ASD and FXS in the use of the speaker's gaze during word learning, even when matched on age and nonverbal cognitive ability. Given that boys with FXS showed significantly more correct choices during follow-in relative to discrepant labeling trials, the authors proposed that associative learning may be a relative strength for children with FXS, whereas their ability to use, monitor, and interpret eye gaze as a referential cue may be especially delayed, perhaps even more so than in children with ASD at similar cognitive levels.

Analysis of participant error patterns and trial type order effects also supported the interpretation of potential differences in learning processes across groups. Two types of errors were possible during this experimental task. First, a novel object error could occur if the child selected either the examiner's object during follow-in labeling trials or the child's object during discrepant labeling trials. Second, a familiar object error could occur if the child selected a familiar object during either experimental condition. Relative to boys with FXS or TD boys and regardless of experimental condition, boys with nonsyndromic ASD were significantly more likely to err by selecting a familiar object when the examiner requested the labeled novel object during comprehension probes. That is, rather than selecting the incorrect novel object when making an error, boys with nonsyndromic ASD were more than 10 times more likely relative to boys with FXS and over 6 times more likely relative to TD boys to err by selecting a familiar object. Finally, participants with nonsyndromic ASD were especially sensitive to context effects, maintaining the gaze following strategy that was "correct" for the initial trial of the experimental task (regardless of trial type) to guide their functional interpretation of "how" to play the game rather than actively using the examiner's actual gaze direction during each experimental trial type as a source of information.

Understanding the Speaker's Referential Intent

In addition to understanding the monitoring of adult direction of gaze, numerous experimental studies have focused on identifying the other types of social-pragmatic cues young children use while learning new words when temporal contiguity is not sufficient to support a correct association between the label and object. Tomasello and colleagues (Tomasello & Barton, 1994; Tomasello, Strosberg, & Akhtar, 1996) investigated whether children could use a social partner's emotional cues to inform their acquisition of a novel label for a target object. Tomasello and colleagues found that even very young word learners (18- and 24-month-olds) were able to use an adult's emotional reaction (e.g., surprise, disappointment) to correctly guide their label-object mappings and could do so even when that reaction was not synchronous with presentation of the novel label.

We used an adaptation of the Tomasello et al. (Tomasello & Barton, 1994; Tomasello et al., 1996) paradigms, which involved a search for a novel object in one of several opaque containers, to examine the child's ability to use an adult's positive (excitement) or negative (disappointment) emotional reaction to disambiguate the novel object that a speaker intends to label (Thurman et al., 2015). This paradigm is particularly useful because children with nonsyndromic ASD and those with FXS may demonstrate a continuum of impairment in the ability to notice, interpret, and respond to the emotional reactions of other people (Abbeduto, McDuffie, & Thurman, 2014; Constantino, 2011; Loesch et al., 2007). Participants with FXS and nonsyndromic ASD, who ranged in age from 4 to 10 years, were matched on chronological age, nonverbal IQ, and nonverbal cognitive growth scores, whereas younger TD participants were matched on nonverbal cognitive growth scores. Of the 32 participants with FXS included in this study, 23 met study criteria for a comorbid diagnosis of ASD; that is, they met diagnostic criteria for a diagnosis of ASD on the Autism Diagnostic Interview—Revised (ADI–R; Rutter, LeCouteur, & Lord, 2008) and achieved a calibrated severity of at least 4 on the ADOS. That being said, only two of the nine remaining participants with FXS failed to meet ASD criteria on either the ADOS or ADI–R, suggesting that symptoms of autism were present to some degree in most participants with FXS.

The examiner began each trial by announcing her intention to find a novel object (e.g., a "modi") by searching in a series of containers, each of which contained a different novel object. In the successful search condition, the target object was found in one of the four containers, and the examiner reacted with excitement upon locating the intended referent. For those containers in which the examiner did not find the intended object, the examiner reacted with disappointment as the distractor object was removed from its container. Importantly, the intended object was never found in the first container searched, thereby precluding participants from relying on temporal contiguity to inform successful word learning. In the unsuccessful search condition, the intended object was never found; thus, correct performance in the unsuccessful search condition required children to refrain from mapping the novel label to any of the objects retrieved from the containers. During comprehension probes for unsuccessful search trials, the child was required to make the inference that the previously heard label must map to a novel object not previously seen. For the successful search condition, the choices during comprehension probes included the intended novel object (i.e., the target), one previously seen object (i.e., the distractor), and two familiar objects. For the unsuccessful search condition, the choices included a previously unseen novel object (i.e., the target), a previously seen distractor object, and two familiar objects.

For both experimental conditions, participants in all three groups performed at greater-than-chance levels. For successful search trials, TD participants performed significantly better than did participants with nonsyndromic ASD, suggesting a particular difficulty for children with nonsyndromic ASD, even relative to nonverbal cognitive expectations, in using emotional reactions of excitement and disappointment to guide a label-object pairing. Also for successful search trials, participants with FXS performed significantly better than did participants with nonsyndromic ASD; however, these differences were no longer significant after controlling for ASD symptom severity. For unsuccessful search trials, participants with FXS performed significantly worse than both TD participants and participants with nonsyndromic ASD, after controlling for ASD symptom severity. When comparing within-group levels of performance on successful relative to unsuccessful trials, participants with FXS performed significantly better on successful trials, whereas no significant within-group differences were observed for participants with nonsyndromic ASD or typical development. In addition, unlike the TD participants, performance levels on the two trial types were not associated with one another for participants with nonsyndromic ASD or FXS, suggesting that word learning in these two contexts may rely on differing, and possibly unrelated, underlying processes.

When responding in error, participants with ASD were once again more likely than TD participants to select a familiar object rather than a novel distractor object. Differences were also found in the factors relating to word-learning performance between children with nonsyndromic ASD and children with FXS. When evaluating chronological age, nonverbal developmental level, social avoidance, and severity of ASD symptoms, no significant predictors of task performance on either the successful or unsuccessful search trials were identified for boys with FXS. In contrast, for participants with nonsyndromic ASD, nonverbal cognitive level and social avoidance emerged as significant and unique predictors of performance on successful search trials and ASD symptom severity emerged as a significant correlate of performance on the unsuccessful search trials. Thus, despite overlapping symptoms between the two disorders, the findings from the Thurman et al. (2015) study again point to differences in the way that children with FXS or nonsyndromic ASD use social cues to learn novel words.

Summary

Across the studies, by comparing between-group patterns of performance of children with FXS or nonsyndromic ASD as they acquire new vocabulary words under controlled experimental conditions, we have been able to gain insights into the similarities and differences across these two developmental disorders. With regard to the ability to form a quick initial pairing between a label and an object in instances in which the speaker uses multiple attention-directing cues to maintain the child's attention, it was not clear whether the FXS advantage in word learning would remain after controlling for differences in ASD symptom severity (McDuffie et al., 2013). When considering children's abilities to use speaker gaze or emotional reactions to disambiguate the novel object that the speaker intended to label, differences favoring the FXS group failed to remain after controlling for ASD symptom severity. In fact, the only between-group difference in overall performance observed after controlling for ASD symptom severity favored the males with nonsyndromic ASD in regard to the ability to use the emotional reaction of disappointment to infer the intended referent.

Recent studies have suggested that although the phenotypes of FXS and non-syndromic ASD are associated with difficulties navigating social interactions, there are differences in the developmental mechanisms underlying these difficulties (e.g., Thurman et al., 2014). The findings of our studies are consistent with this proposal. For example, McDuffie et al. (2013) observed that for boys with FXS, but not boys with nonsyndromic ASD, the ability to form a quick initial pairing between a label and an object in instances in which the speaker uses multiple attention-directing cues was related concurrently to nonverbal cognition and receptive and expressive vocabulary ability. In contrast, Thurman et al. (2015) found that for participants with nonsyndromic ASD, but not FXS, nonverbal cognitive level and social avoidance predicted the ability to use positive emotional reactions in word learning, and ASD symptom severity was associated with the ability to utilize negative emotional reactions.

Taken together, these findings provide additional evidence that there are important differences in the mechanisms underlying word learning between these two neurodevelopmental disorders and that these differences are reflective of important differences in the course of determinants of development. When we observe word learning differences, in essence, we are observing differences in the developmental outcomes of a complex interplay of genetic, developmental, and environmental factors. This is particularly apparent in comparisons of FXS and nonsyndromic ASD as a result of the etiological differences between these two conditions. However, it is our contention that in a multifactorial disorder like nonsyndromic ASD, it is vital to consider how differences in symptomatology and other phenotypic patterns influence the developmental trajectories of language learning.

Conclusion

In this chapter, we have highlighted recent findings from studies conceptualized within a social-pragmatic theoretical framework. Although it is unlikely that this account provides a complete explanation for typical or disordered development, it nonetheless provides a useful guide for examining word learning in children with neurodevelopmental disorders for whom navigating the social world is a challenge. The findings from the studies described, we believe, have important implications for research and clinical care of children with ASD or FXS, as well as those with other neurodevelopmental disorders. Our word-learning studies suggest that children with ASD and children with FXS are severely impaired in their ability to use the social-pragmatic cues typically available in the word-learning environment. One approach to intervention, of course, would be to try and improve attentional and motivational processes within the child so that he or she is more likely to use the social cues that are typically available. The social-pragmatic approach, however, suggests that another important avenue to improving language learning in these children would be to reorganize the environment to maximize the salience of social cues available to the child. Thus, intervention research must be focused not just on the child but on his or her environment. In the latter case, the task is to identify ways in which these environments can be structured or altered to provide more finely tuned interactions that support more efficient child learning. Such interventions could be designed to teach parents to continually adapt to their children's changing skills by helping them to attend to an ever-expanding range of social-pragmatic cues to word meaning. In short, although both nonsyndromic ASD and FXS have genetic etiologies, treating the concomitant impairments of these disorders requires understanding the ways in which affected individuals process social information as well as the nature of the social worlds that they inhabit.

Any efforts to improve the functioning of an individual with nonsyndromic ASD or FXS should include a plan for optimizing social information processing and organizing the interactive environment to maximally support learning relative to the individual's characteristics and ways of behaving. Thus, medications targeting core symptoms of ASD or FXS are likely to be more effective when combined with behavioral treatments that target social information processing and interaction in the social world. More generally, our findings and the tenets of a social-pragmatic theoretical approach remind us that a neurodevelopmental disorder reflects an alteration away from the normative in the ways in which the individual interacts with the world. Thus, the clinical challenge is to make those interactions more effective, which emphasizes accommodation to and support of, rather than simply remediation of, the affected individual.

References

Abbeduto, L., Brady, N., & Kover, S. T. (2007). Language development and fragile X syndrome: Profiles, syndrome-specificity, and within-syndrome differences. *Mental Retardation and Developmental Disabilities Research Reviews*, *13*, 36–46. http://dx.doi.org/10.1002/mrdd.20142

Abbeduto, L., McDuffie, A., & Thurman, A. J. (2014). The fragile X syndrome–autism comorbidity: What do we really know? *Frontiers in Genetics*, *5*, 355. http://dx.doi.org/10.3389/fgene.2014.00355

Akhtar, N., & Tomasello, M. (2000). The social nature of words and word learning. In R. Golinkoff & K. Hirsh-Pasek (Eds.), *Becoming a word learner: A debate on lexical acquisition* (pp. 115–135). http://dx.doi.org/10.1093/acprof:oso/9780195130324.003.005

Ambridge, B., & Lieven, E. V. (2011). *Child language acquisition: Contrasting theoretical approaches.* http://dx.doi.org/10.1017/CBO9780511975073

American Psychiatric Association. (2013). *Diagnostic and statistical manual of mental disorders* (5th ed.). Washington, DC: Author.

Bailey, D. B., Jr., Mesibov, G. B., Hatton, D. D., Clark, R. D., Roberts, J. E., & Mayhew, L. (1998). Autistic behavior in young boys with fragile X syndrome. *Journal of Autism and Developmental Disorders*, *28*, 499–508. http://dx.doi.org/10.1023/A:1026048027397

Baldwin, D. A. (1993). Infants' ability to consult the speaker for clues to word reference. *Journal of Child Language*, *20*, 395–418. http://dx.doi.org/10.1017/S0305000900008345

Baron-Cohen, S., Baldwin, D. A., & Crowson, M. (1997). Do children with autism use the speaker's direction of gaze strategy to crack the code of language? *Child Development*, *68*, 48–57. http://dx.doi.org/10.2307/1131924

Bassell, G. J., & Warren, S. T. (2008). Fragile X syndrome: Loss of local mRNA regulation alters synaptic development and function. *Neuron*, *60*, 201–214. http://dx.doi.org/10.1016/j.neuron.2008.10.004

Bates, E., & Goodman, J. (1997). On the inseparability of grammar from the lexicon: Evidence from acquisition, aphasia, and real time processing. *Language and Cognitive Processes*, *12*, 507–584. http://dx.doi.org/10.1080/016909697386628

Benjamin, D. P., Mastergeorge, A. M., McDuffie, A. S., Kover, S. T., Hagerman, R. J., & Abbeduto, L. (2014). Effects of labeling and pointing on object gaze in boys with fragile X syndrome: An eye-tracking study. *Research in Developmental Disabilities*, *35*, 2658–2672. http://dx.doi.org/10.1016/j.ridd.2014.06.021

Benjamin, D. P., McDuffie, A. S., Thurman, A. J., Kover, S. T., Mastergeorge, A. M., Hagerman, R. J., & Abbeduto, L. (2015). Effect of speaker gaze on word learning in fragile X syndrome: A comparison with nonsyndromic autism spectrum disorder. *Journal of Speech, Language, and Hearing Research*, *58*, 383–396. http://dx.doi.org/10.1044/2015_JSLHR-L-14-0136

Bruner, J. (1985). The role of interaction formats in language acquisition. In J. P. Forgas (Ed.), *Language and social situations* (pp. 31–46). http://dx.doi.org/10.1007/978-1-4612-5074-6_2

Clegg, J., Hollis, C., Mawhood, L., & Rutter, M. (2005). Developmental language disorders—A follow-up in later adult life: Cognitive, language and psychosocial outcomes. *Journal of Child Psychology and Psychiatry*, *46*, 128–149. http://dx.doi.org/10.1111/j.1469-7610.2004.00342.x

Coghlan, S., Horder, J., Inkster, B., Mendez, M. A., Murphy, D. G., & Nutt, D. J. (2012). GABA system dysfunction in autism and related disorders: From synapse to symptoms. *Neuroscience and Biobehavioral Reviews*, *36*, 2044–2055. http://dx.doi.org/10.1016/j.neubiorev.2012.07.005

Constantino, J. N. (2011). The quantitative nature of autistic social impairment. *Pediatric Research*, *69*, 55R–62R. http://dx.doi.org/10.1203/PDR.0b013e318212ec6e

Cordeiro, L., Ballinger, E., Hagerman, R., & Hessl, D. (2011). Clinical assessment of *DSM–IV* anxiety disorders in fragile X syndrome: Prevalence and characterization. *Journal of Neurodevelopmental Disorders*, *3*, 57–67. http://dx.doi.org/10.1007/s11689-010-9067-y

De Giacomo, A., & Fombonne, E. (1998). Parental recognition of developmental abnormalities in autism. *European Child & Adolescent Psychiatry*, *7*, 131–136. http://dx.doi.org/10.1007/s007870050058

Demark, J. L., Feldman, M. A., & Holden, J. J. (2003). Behavioral relationship between autism and fragile X syndrome. *American Journal on Mental Retardation*, *108*, 314–326. http://dx.doi.org/10.1352/0895-8017(2003)108<314:BRBAAF>2.0.CO;2

Farzin, F., Rivera, S. M., & Hessl, D. (2009). Brief report: Visual processing of faces in individuals with fragile X syndrome: An eye tracking study. *Journal of Autism and Developmental Disorders*, *39*, 946–952. http://dx.doi.org/10.1007/s10803-009-0744-1

Gillespie-Lynch, K., Sepeta, L., Wang, Y., Marshall, S., Gomez, L., Sigman, M., & Hutman, T. (2012). Early childhood predictors of the social competence of adults with autism. *Journal of Autism and Developmental Disorders*, *42*, 161–174. http://dx.doi.org/10.1007/s10803-011-1222-0

Gotham, K., Pickles, A., & Lord, C. (2009). Standardizing ADOS scores for a measure of severity in autism spectrum disorders. *Journal of Autism and Developmental Disorders*, *39*, 693–705. http://dx.doi.org/10.1007/s10803-008-0674-3

Hall, S. S., Lightbody, A. A., Hirt, M., Rezvani, A., & Reiss, A. L. (2010). Autism in fragile X syndrome: A category mistake? *Journal of the American Academy of Child & Adolescent Psychiatry*, *49*, 921–933. http://dx.doi.org/10.1016/j.jaac.2010.07.001

Harris, M., Jones, D., Brookes, S., & Grant, J. (1986). Relations between the nonverbal context of maternal speech and rate of language development. *British Journal of Developmental Psychology*, *4*, 261–268. http://dx.doi.org/10.1111/j.2044-835X.1986.tb01017.x

Hartley, S. L., Seltzer, M. M., Raspa, M., Olmstead, M., Bishop, E., & Bailey, D. B., Jr. (2011). Exploring the adult life of men and women with fragile X syndrome: Results from a national survey. *American Journal on Intellectual and Developmental Disabilities*, *116*, 16–35. http://dx.doi.org/10.1352/1944-7558-116.1.16

Hertz-Picciotto, I., Croen, L. A., Hansen, R., Jones, C. R., van de Water, J., & Pessah, I. N. (2006). The CHARGE study: An epidemiologic investigation of genetic and environmental factors contributing to autism. *Environmental Health Perspectives*, *114*, 1119–1125. http://dx.doi.org/10.1289/ehp.8483

Hessl, D., Nguyen, D. V., Green, C., Chavez, A., Tassone, F., Hagerman, R. J., . . . Hall, S. (2009). A solution to limitations of cognitive testing in children with intellectual disabilities: The case of fragile X syndrome. *Journal of Neurodevelopmental Disorders*, *1*, 33–45. http://dx.doi.org/10.1007/s11689-008-9001-8

Hollich, G. J., Hirsh-Pasek, K., Golinkoff, R. M., Brand, R. J., Brown, E., Chung, H. L., . . . Rocroi, C. (2000). Breaking the language barrier: An emergentist coalition model for the origins of word learning. *Monographs of the Society for Research in Child Development*, *65*, i–vi, 1–123.

Howlin, P., Savage, S., Moss, P., Tempier, A., & Rutter, M. (2014). Cognitive and language skills in adults with autism: A 40-year follow-up. *Journal of Child Psychology and Psychiatry*, *55*, 49–58. http://dx.doi.org/10.1111/jcpp.12115

Iossifov, I., Ronemus, M., Levy, D., Wang, Z., Hakker, I., Rosenbaum, J., . . . Wigler, M. (2012). De novo gene disruptions in children on the autistic spectrum. *Neuron*, *74*, 285–299. http://dx.doi.org/10.1016/j.neuron.2012.04.009

Klin, A., Shultz, S., & Jones, W. (2015). Social visual engagement in infants and toddlers with autism: Early developmental transitions and a model of pathogenesis. *Neuroscience and Biobehavioral Reviews*, *50*, 189–203.

Leekam, S. R., Hunnisett, E., & Moore, C. (1998). Targets and cues: Gaze-following in children with autism. *Journal of Child Psychology and Psychiatry*, *39*, 951–962. http://dx.doi.org/10.1111/1469-7610.00398

Loesch, D. Z., Bui, Q. M., Dissanayake, C., Clifford, S., Gould, E., Bulhak-Paterson, D., . . . Huggins, R. M. (2007). Molecular and cognitive predictors of the continuum of autistic behaviours in fragile X. *Neuroscience and Biobehavioral Reviews*, *31*, 315–326. http://dx.doi.org/10.1016/j.neubiorev.2006.09.007

Lord, C., Rutter, M., DiLavore, P., & Risi, S. (1999). *Autism Diagnostic Observation Schedule—WPS edition.* Los Angeles, CA: Western Psychological Services.

Luyster, R., & Lord, C. (2009). Word learning in children with autism spectrum disorders. *Developmental Psychology*, *45*, 1774–1786. http://dx.doi.org/10.1037/a0016223

Magiati, I., Tay, X. W., & Howlin, P. (2014). Cognitive, language, social and behavioural outcomes in adults with autism spectrum disorders: A systematic review of longitudinal follow-up studies in adulthood. *Clinical Psychology Review*, *34*, 73–86. http://dx.doi.org/10.1016/j.cpr.2013.11.002

Markman, E. M. (1994). Constraints on word meaning in early language acquisition. *Lingua*, *92*, 199–227. http://dx.doi.org/10.1016/0024-3841(94)90342-5

Mazzocco, M. M. (2000). Advances in research on the fragile X syndrome. *Mental Retardation and Developmental Disabilities Research Reviews*, *6*, 96–106. http://dx.doi.org/10.1002/1098-2779(2000)6:2<96::AID-MRDD3>3.0.CO;2-H

McDuffie, A., Kover, S. T., Hagerman, R., & Abbeduto, L. (2013). Investigating word learning in fragile X syndrome: A fast-mapping study. *Journal of Autism and Developmental Disorders*, *43*, 1676–1691. http://dx.doi.org/10.1007/s10803-012-1717-3

McDuffie, A., Yoder, P., & Stone, W. (2006). Fast-mapping in young children with autism spectrum disorders. *First Language*, *26*, 421–438. http://dx.doi.org/10.1177/0142723706067438

Merenstein, S. A., Sobesky, W. E., Taylor, A. K., Riddle, J. E., Tran, H. X., & Hagerman, R. J. (1996). Molecular-clinical correlations in males with an expanded *FMR1* mutation. *American Journal of Medical Genetics*, *64*, 388–394. http://dx.doi.org/10.1002/(SICI)1096-8628(19960809)64:2<388::AID-AJMG31>3.0.CO;2-9

Oostra, B. A., & Willemsen, R. (2009). *FMR1*: A gene with three faces. *Biochimica et Biophysica Acta*, *1790*, 467–477. http://dx.doi.org/10.1016/j.bbagen.2009.02.007

Rice, M. L., Buhr, J. C., & Nemeth, M. (1990). Fast mapping word-learning abilities of language-delayed preschoolers. *Journal of Speech & Hearing Disorders*, *55*, 33–42. http://dx.doi.org/10.1044/jshd.5501.33

Ronald, A., & Hoekstra, R. A. (2011). Autism spectrum disorders and autistic traits: A decade of new twin studies. *American Journal of Medical Genetics: Part B. Neuropsychiatric Genetics*, *156*, 255–274. http://dx.doi.org/10.1002/ajmg.b.31159

Rutter, M., LeCouteur, A., & Lord, C. (2008). *Autism Diagnostic Interview—Revised.* Los Angeles, CA: Western Psychological Services.

Saffran, J. R., Aslin, R. N., & Newport, E. L. (1996). Statistical learning by 8-month-old infants. *Science*, *274*, 1926–1928. http://dx.doi.org/10.1126/science.274.5294.1926

Samuelson, L. K., & Smith, L. B. (1998). Memory and attention make smart word learning: An alternative account of Akhtar, Carpenter, and Tomasello. *Child Development*, *69*, 94–104. http://dx.doi.org/10.1111/j.1467-8624.1998.tb06136.x

Scerif, G., Longhi, E., Cole, V., Karmiloff-Smith, A., & Cornish, K. (2012). Attention across modalities as a longitudinal predictor of early outcomes: The case of fragile X syndrome. *Journal of Child Psychology and Psychiatry*, *53*, 641–650. http://dx.doi.org/10.1111/j.1469-7610.2011.02515.x

Schafer, G., & Plunkett, K. (1998). Rapid word learning by fifteen-month-olds under tightly controlled conditions. *Child Development*, *69*, 309–320. http://dx.doi.org/10.1111/j.1467-8624.1998.tb06190.x

Snow, C. E. (1989). Understanding social interaction and language acquisition; sentences are not enough. In M. H. Bornstein & J. S. Bruner (Eds.), *Interaction in human development* (pp. 83–103). Mahwah, NJ: Erlbaum.

Symons, F. J., Clark, R. D., Hatton, D. D., Skinner, M., & Bailey, D. B., Jr. (2003). Self-injurious behavior in young boys with fragile X syndrome. *American Journal of Medical Genetics*, *118A*, 115–121. http://dx.doi.org/10.1002/ajmg.a.10078

Thurman, A. J., McDuffie, A., Hagerman, R., & Abbeduto, L. (2014). Psychiatric symptoms in boys with fragile X syndrome: A comparison with nonsyndromic autism spectrum disorder. *Research in Developmental Disabilities*, *35*, 1072–1086. http://dx.doi.org/10.1016/j.ridd.2014.01.032

Thurman, A. J., McDuffie, A., Kover, S. T., Hagerman, R., Channell, M. M., Mastergeorge, A., & Abbeduto, L. (2015). Use of emotional cues for lexical learning: A comparison of autism spectrum disorder and fragile X syndrome. *Journal of Autism and Developmental Disorders*, *45*, 1042–1061.

Tomasello, M., & Barton, M. E. (1994). Learning words in nonostensive contexts. *Developmental Psychology*, *30*, 639–650. http://dx.doi.org/10.1037/0012-1649.30.5.639

Tomasello, M., Strosberg, R., & Akhtar, N. (1996). Eighteen-month-old children learn words in nonostensive contexts. *Journal of Child Language*, *23*, 157–176. http://dx.doi.org/10.1017/S0305000900010138

Verkerk, A. J., Pieretti, M., Sutcliffe, J. S., Fu, Y. H., Kuhl, D. P., Pizzuti, A., . . . Warren, S. T. (1991). Identification of a gene (*FMR-1*) containing a CGG repeat coincident with a breakpoint cluster region exhibiting length variation in fragile X syndrome. *Cell*, *65*, 905–914. http://dx.doi.org/10.1016/0092-8674(91)90397-H

Werker, J. F., Cohen, L. B., Lloyd, V. L., Casasola, M., & Stager, C. L. (1998). Acquisition of word–object associations by 14-month-old infants. *Developmental Psychology*, *34*, 1289–1309. http://dx.doi.org/10.1037/0012-1649.34.6.1289

Williams, T. A., Porter, M. A., & Langdon, R. (2014). Social approach and emotion recognition in fragile X syndrome. *American Journal on Intellectual and Developmental Disabilities*, *119*, 133–150. http://dx.doi.org/10.1352/1944-7558-119.2.133

Woodward, A. L., Markman, E. M., & Fitzsimmons, C. M. (1994). Rapid word learning in 13-and 18-month-olds. *Developmental Psychology*, *30*, 553–566. http://dx.doi.org/10.1037/0012-1649.30.4.553

Aparna Nadig and Janet Bang

5 Parental Input to Children With ASD and Its Influence on Later Language

Language development is variable even in the typical case, but the majority of children begin to comprehend single words between the ages of 9 and 12 months and produce their first words between 12 and 15 months of age (MacArthur–Bates Communicative Development Inventories [MCDI]; Fenson et al., 2007). When evaluated as a group, toddlers with autism spectrum disorder (ASD) exhibit delays in early language development (e.g., Anderson et al., 2007; Weismer, Lord, & Esler, 2010). For example, whereas 50% of typically developing (TD) children label objects at 14 months, only 15% of children with ASD did so by 2 years of age (Luyster, Lopez, & Lord, 2007). In the context of this group-level delay, there is enormous individual variability in language skills among children with ASD. Kjelgaard and Tager-Flusberg (2001) found that by school age, approximately half of children with ASD had impaired language as assessed by standardized tests, a quarter had borderline skills within two standard deviations of the normal range, and the last quarter scored in the normal range or above. Notably, a minority of children with ASD perform as well as TD peers on standardized tests (Kjelgaard & Tager-Flusberg, 2001; Luyster et al., 2007). The first finding of delayed vocabulary as a group is commonly acknowledged, whereas the second point about variability within the autism spectrum has received relatively little attention in the fields of language development and developmental psychology.

In contemporary work, language development is often construed in an interactionist framework involving the dyadic interaction of *nature* and *nurture* components (Chapman, 2000). Much of what we know about language development and impairment in ASD falls on the nature side of the puzzle. ASD is a complex neurodevelopmental condition involving differences in genetics, in neural structure and function, and in learning mechanisms as well as attentional preferences, all of which in turn influence language development (Bourguignon, Nadig, & Valois, 2012). In many, but not all, cases of ASD, this results in early language delay. We also know of important nature-related predictors of better language outcomes in ASD: Nonverbal IQ and social communication skills (e.g., gestures, pointing to objects of interest) are strong predictors of concurrent and later language ability (Anderson et al., 2007; Luyster, Kadlec, Carter, & Tager-Flusberg, 2008; Thurm, Lord, Lee, & Newschaffer, 2007). School-age vocabulary skills have even been shown to predict linguistic functioning in adulthood (Mawhood, Howlin, & Rutter, 2000). Essentially, the more language children have the more they can learn, but beyond having the good fortune of coming equipped with

http://dx.doi.org/10.1037/15964-006
Innovative Investigations of Language in Autism Spectrum Disorder, L. R. Naigles (Editor)

high nonverbal IQ or strong social communication skills, what factors can shape the course of language learning in ASD?

In this chapter, we synthesize work on the nurture side of the puzzle. First, what does the language learning environment available to children with ASD, through their caregivers' language input, look like relative to that of TD children? Second, crucially, is there evidence that children with ASD are able to use language input to facilitate language development? If so, differences in input may help us explain part of the tremendous variability observed in trajectories of language development in this population.

We know from a wealth of evidence over the past 40 years that the nurture side of the puzzle, as indexed by more and varied language input, enhances TD language development, which in turn confers long-term linguistic and academic advantages. Hart and Risley (1995) reported extreme differences in amount of interaction and language input that children of different socioeconomic status receive. In their study, children from poorer backgrounds heard 30 million fewer words by age 3 than children with professional parents, and the latter had better academic outcomes at age 9 (Hart & Risley, 1995). Even among parents who have similar education levels, variation in the overall number of words parents speak has been shown to be related to their children's rate of vocabulary development (Huttenlocher, Haight, Bryk, Seltzer, & Lyons, 1991) and the speed of their later vocabulary processing (Hurtado, Marchman, & Fernald, 2008). Moreover, lexical richness as measured by the number of word types (different words) in the input and syntactic complexity as measured by MLU, are predictive of children's later vocabulary size (Hoff & Naigles, 2002). These findings reveal that children implicitly keep track of language input, and develop better language abilities when immersed in rich input environments. Recently, this body of research has been in the public spotlight, galvanizing campaigns in the United States that encourage parents to read, talk, and sing to their kids to "close the word gap" or decrease disparities normally experienced by underprivileged groups, for instance Providence Talks (http://www.providencetalks.org) and Too Small to Fail (http://toosmall.org).

There has been less attention paid to the nurture side of the language development puzzle in ASD. A historical reason for this is the psychoanalytic account of ASD, dominant in the mid-20th century, which inaccurately and tragically blamed parents for their children's autism (e.g., refrigerator mother theory; Bettelheim, 1967). Although sensitivity should be exercised in any reporting on parent behavior with respect to children with ASD, this legacy should not preclude the advancement of a line of research that has been fruitful in understanding the full scope of factors contributing to language development in TD children. Another reason there has been less research on the nurture side includes the simple fact that, especially under earlier diagnostic classifications, children with ASD had significant language delays and thus did not appear to benefit from language input in the same way as TD children. Finally, given that reduced early social attention is a defining feature of ASD, and that subgroups of young children with ASD show reduced attention to child-directed speech (Kuhl,

Coffey-Corina, Padden, & Dawson, 2005), learning from the input was not necessarily expected. However, the substantial individual differences in language development among children currently identified with ASD beg examination of nurture as well as nature contributions to language development. A clearer picture of the data that children with ASD have available to mine for language learning, as well as of specific relationships between aspects of the input and later language development, are essential for a comprehensive view of factors that contribute to language development in this population. This line of study also holds promise for improving language outcomes. For instance, if children with ASD are found to benefit from lexically and syntactically rich language input as TD children do, their language can be improved by exploiting the nurture side of the puzzle (e.g., strategically modifying the input they receive) in cases where nature does not pave the way for optimal language development (e.g., Yoder, Spruytenburg, Edwards, & Davies, 1995).

Before considering these questions, we raise the key methodological issue of matching criteria as it affects the interpretation of parental input data. Because children with ASD exhibit language delay as a group, if they are compared with same-age TD peers, they will have significantly lower language skills, especially at early stages of development. Parental input is sampled from situations of parent–child interaction that are inherently dyadic in nature; parents initiate topics and comments but also increasingly respond to their child's initiations and questions as the child's communicative repertoire grows. We know that parents tailor their input to their child's language level in multiple ways (Snow, 1995), for example, by adjusting syntactic complexity as measured by mean length of utterance (MLU; Konstantareas, Zajdeman, Homatidis, & McCabe, 1988), or the amount of acoustic modification used in infant-directed speech (Kitamura & Burnham, 2003). Unlike strangers, parents are perhaps especially skilled at language-level "tuning" as they have a privileged window on their child's comprehension abilities through ongoing interactions (Sokolov, 1993). The practice of matching groups on child language level, which dominates the literature, allows for an examination of how parental input to children with ASD versus typical development compares when the child's side of the exchange is controlled. In contrast, matching on child chronological age addresses the question of how the language delay present in the sample with ASD affects parental input at a given maturational point. These matching strategies provide complementary information on the language environment available to children with ASD, but the former teases apart whether any potential differences are due to ASD rather than its associated language delay. Another important way to examine whether differences are specific to ASD or shared with other language-delayed populations is to compare across children with ASD and those with non-ASD developmental delays. This is particularly informative because both chronological age and language level can be methodologically controlled at once.

In this chapter, we review evidence on parental input to children with ASD, moving from quantitative measures of linguistic features to qualitative measures of interaction. First, we examine *lexical and syntactic features* (e.g., number of utterances, MLU) in the input provided to children with ASD compared with TD children matched on language level. Second, we turn to work on *parental responsiveness*, or the tendency to provide verbal or gestural input in sync with the child's focus of attention, and how this compares across dyads including a child with ASD or a TD child. We also review findings on specific *functions of parental responsive utterances* and evaluate the impact these input features have on later child language in ASD. Finally, to provide a complete picture of the current state of the nurture side of the puzzle, we review findings on multiple *other aspects and contexts of parental input* where preliminary data is available. We conclude with a discussion of the pattern of striking similarities observed between groups for many of these features, what the differences point to, and how these findings inform our understanding of the nurture side of language development in ASD.

Lexical and Syntactic Features of Parental Input

Children are exposed to numerous features of spoken language in their language-learning environment. Some commonly examined features include measures of lexical information such as the number of utterances, number of word tokens, and number of word types, as well as grammatical information such as mean MLU and the use of *wh*-questions. This section reviews findings on lexical and grammatical input provided by parents to their children with ASD, compared with parents speaking to their children with TD, when dyads are matched on child language level (i.e., often vocabulary scores from parent-report measures or spoken vocabulary during the parent–child interaction). The mean age of children with ASD in these studies was approximately 40 to 50 months old, the mean age of TD children was approximately 20 to 30 months old, and sample sizes ranged from 10 to 24 children per group (one exception is Warren et al., 2010, who included 78 TD children). Additionally, studies have also matched groups on variables of child gender and socioeconomic status, usually as measured by level of maternal education. The large majority of these studies have examined parental input during parent–child free-play interactions (9–30 minutes) in the laboratory or at the family's home.

Number of Utterances and Lexical Features

Spoken language is divided into segments of speech termed *utterances*, which are delineated by a noticeable pause break or intonational markers such as rising pitch for questions. The total number of utterances provides a global measure of the quantity of parent talk. The large majority of studies have not found significant differences in the number of utterances spoken between parents of children with ASD and parents of TD children (Bang & Nadig, 2015; Goodwin, Fein, & Naigles, 2015; Watson, 1998, Wolchik & Harris, 1982; but see Wolchik, 1983).

When words are strung together, for example, "The black dog chews the bone," we can extract different types of lexical information. For instance, we can count the *word tokens* (the total number of words spoken, which is six in this case), the *word types* (the total number of different words spoken; five in this example), and the *lexical diversity* of the utterance (a measure of the number of words out of the total number of words, which would be five/six using a simple type/token ratio). We can also examine how parents use individual words. *Word frequency* refers to the number of times a word is spoken and *contextual diversity* refers to the number of unique words that appear before and after a target word (Hills, Maouene, Riordan, & Smith, 2010). For example, in the preceding phrase, the word frequency of *dog* is 1, and the contextual diversity of *dog* is 5 because there are two words before *dog* that each appear once (*the, black*) and three words after *dog* that each appear once (*chews, the, bone*).

Studies that have examined lexical features of parent input have not found significant differences between mothers of children with ASD and mothers of TD children with respect to word tokens, word types, or lexical diversity measures (Bang & Nadig, 2015; Slaughter, Peterson, & Mackintosh, 2007; Swensen, 2007; but see Warren et al., 2010, for a different perspective). Swensen (2007) found no significant differences between mothers of children with ASD and mothers of TD children on word types, noun types, and the percentage of different nouns. In the only study examining lexical features of parent input to children with ASD in a language other than English, Bang and Nadig (2015) matched English-speaking and French-speaking mother–child dyads with children with ASD or TD children. No significant differences were found between diagnostic groups in both English-speaking and French-speaking families during a free-play interaction on maternal word tokens, word types, and lexical diversity. Table 5.1 compares the 10 most frequent words in the corpora and demonstrates that mothers of children with ASD and mothers of TD children also used individual words similarly during the free-play interaction (Bang & Nadig, 2012). Figure 5.1 presents scatterplots of the contextual diversity values for individual words in our corpora spoken by mothers of children with ASD versus mothers of TD children. The plots demonstrate strong correlations between groups in both English and French; that is, the same words were spoken in few or many contexts across diagnostic groups. Current work in our lab aims to examine the influence of word frequency and contextual diversity on children's acquisition of individual words, as seen in typical development (Hills, Maouene, Riordan, & Smith, 2010; Huttenlocher et al., 1991).

Syntactic Features

We can also extract syntactic information from a speech sample. As previously observed for lexical features of the input, studies have unanimously found no significant

Tab. 5.1: Top 10 Most Frequent Words Spoken by Mothers to Children With ASD and TD Children

English speaking		French speaking	
ASD ($n = 11$)	**TD ($n = 11$)**	**ASD ($n = 9$)**	**TD ($n = 9$)**
you	**you**	**tu**	**tu**
it	**it**	**aller**	**ça**
go	**go**	**ça**	**aller**
what	**baby**	**faire**	**avoir**
that	**I**	**avoir**	**faire**
I	this	**je**	**lui/elle**
baby	**what**	**pas**	**je**
there	child's name	regarder	**pas**
her	**that**	**lui/elle**	mettre
put	not	bébé	petit

Note: Words in bold are shared between diagnostic groups within the respective language.
ASD = autism spectrum disorder; TD = typically developing.

differences between dyads with a child with ASD or a TD child with respect to parental MLU (Bang & Nadig, 2015; Goodwin et al., 2015; Swensen, Naigles, & Fein, 2007; Wolchik, 1983; Wolchik & Harris, 1982).

Another way syntactic complexity has been studied is through the analysis of the type of questions parents ask their children, specifically yes-or-no questions (e.g., "Do you have the train?") and wh-questions (e.g., who, what, when, where, why). Yes-or-no and wh-questions are syntactically advanced constructions because they (a) deviate from the standard word order of English (i.e., they are in the less frequent SOV order—subject, object, verb) and (b) highlight the use of auxiliary verbs that express tense and mood (e.g., do, can, and will). One study examined the use of yes-or-no questions during free play and found no differences between parents of children with and without ASD (Swensen, 2007); however, findings on wh-questions have been mixed. Whereas no significant differences were reported in early investigations of wh-questions (Wolchik, 1983; Wolchik & Harris, 1982), Goodwin et al. (2015; see also Naigles & Fein, Chapter 3, this volume) conducted a comprehensive examination of wh-question types and found that mothers of children with ASD produced a significantly lower percentage of wh-questions and less varied wh-questions than TD children. This discrepancy in findings may be linked to the particular constructions studied, for example, those that are simple and repetitive versus syntactically complex.

Finally, one study has examined parental input to different groups of children on the autism spectrum. Konstantareas et al. (1988) compared maternal input from mothers with high-functioning children with ASD with that of mothers of low-functioning children with ASD (language age approximately 12 months) matched on children's chronological age, gender, and socioeconomic status. No significant differences were

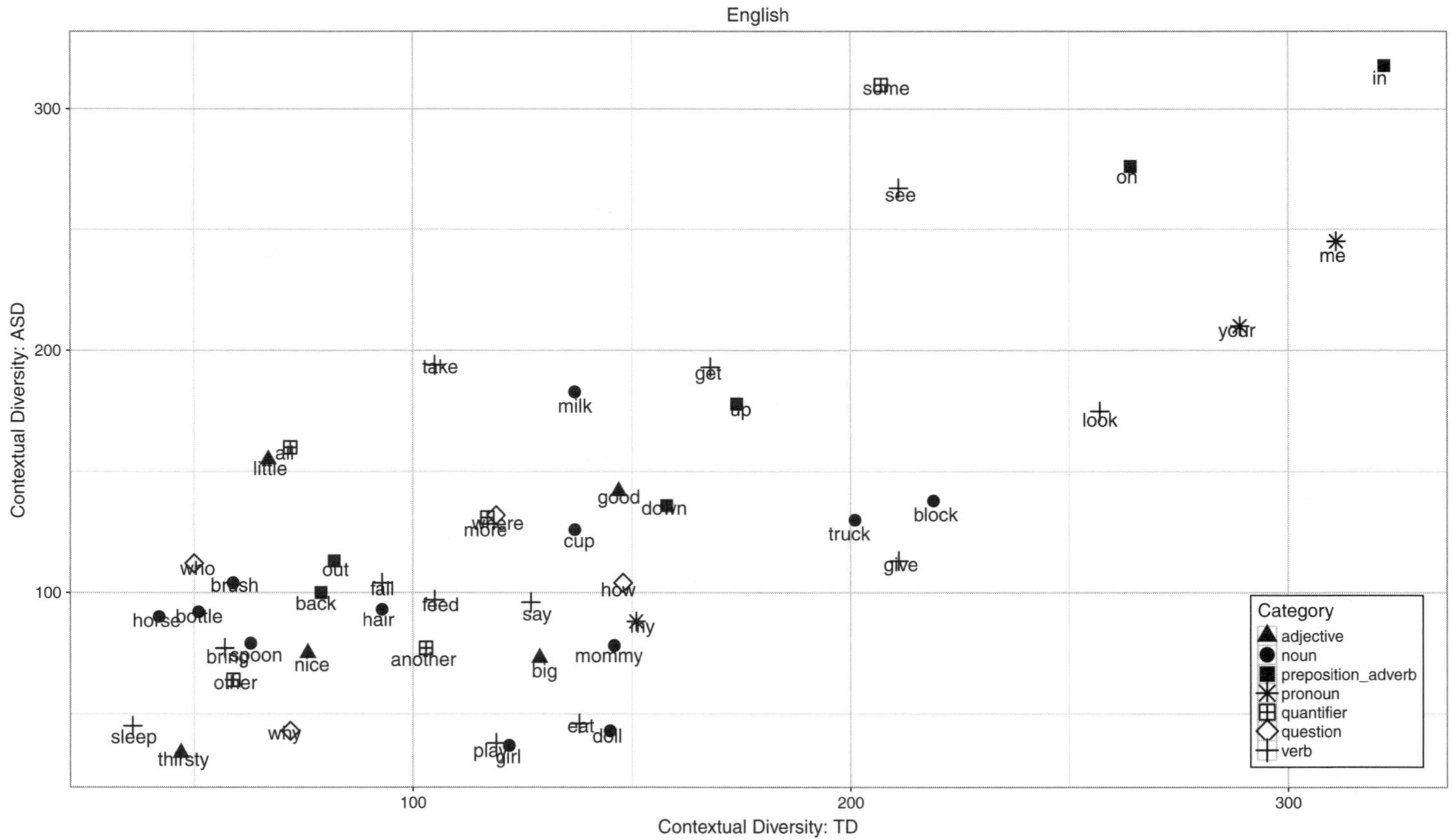

Fig. 5.1: The contextual diversity for individual words spoken in our corpora by mothers of children with ASD and TD children in English (first panel) and French (second panel). Following Hills et al. (2010), this was calculated within a window of five words before and five words after the target word, and analyses included words that (a) parents used during the parent–child interaction and (b) appear on the MacArthur–Bates Communicative Developmental Inventories (MCDI; Fenson et al., 2007). For presentation purposes, words with very high (i.e., values > 370) or low (i.e., values < 30) contextual diversity were not included. This figure demonstrates a strong positive correlation between diagnostic groups, which demonstrates that in both languages, mothers of children with ASD and mothers of TD children produced the same words in similar contexts.

(continues)

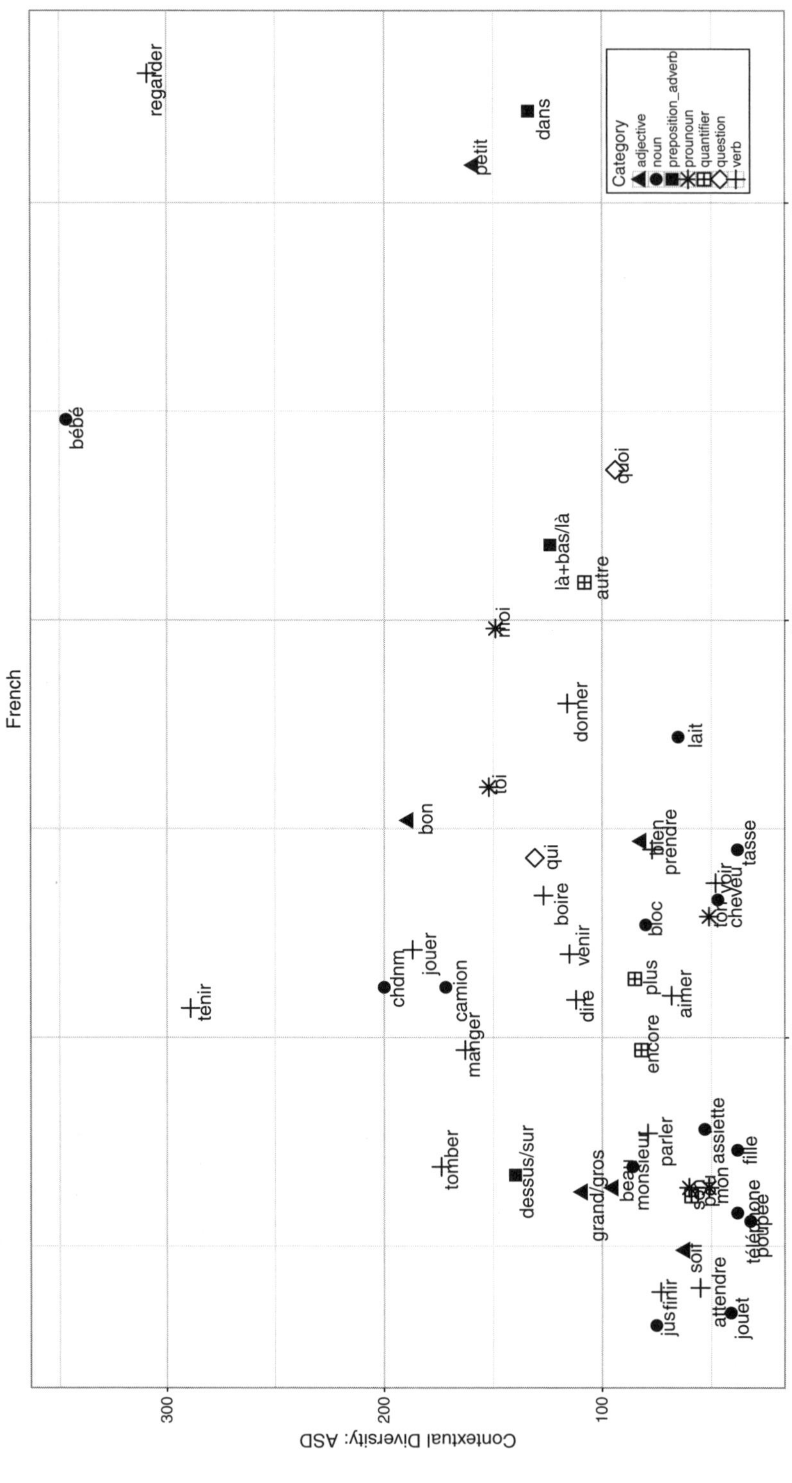

Fig. 5.1: (Continued)

found between groups on the number of utterances spoken by mothers, but, not surprisingly, mothers of high-functioning children produced more syntactically complex input (i.e., longer MLUs). This supports the idea that parents provide input that is calibrated to their children's language abilities, a point that will be returned to in the discussion.

In sum, a growing body of literature comparing parent input to children with ASD or to language-matched TD children demonstrates that parents produce strikingly similar linguistic environments in both cases, albeit at a substantial delay for most children with ASD because of their language proficiency. Other studies comparing parent–child dyads of children with ASD and children with either ASD or non-ASD developmental delays also did not find significant differences between groups when children were matched on language level (Cantwell, Baker, & Rutter, 1977; Venuti, de Falco, Esposito, Zaninelli, & Bornstein, 2012). Conversely, one area of possible difference between ASD and language-matched TD groups is in the use of wh-questions, which were decreased in input to children with ASD (Goodwin et al., 2015). Importantly the use of questions affects child syntactic development, as discussed later in this chapter and in Naigles and Fein (Chapter 3, this volume).

Impact of Lexical and Syntactic Features on Later Child Language

An overview of the linguistic input available to children with ASD presents a consistent picture that lexical and most syntactic features of maternal speech input studied to date are similar for children with ASD and TD children. However, even if the linguistic environment is rich with information, the critical next step is to assess whether children with ASD are able to use this information to support their later language, as has been demonstrated in TD children (e.g., Hoff & Naigles, 2002; Huttenlocher et al., 1991).

Frank, Allen, Stein, and Myers (1976) first reported a significant positive correlation between concurrent maternal and child MLU. Recent studies have shown that multiple features of the input are positively and significantly correlated with later child language. Warren and colleagues (2010) demonstrated significant positive correlations between input number of word tokens and children's later vocabulary production. Swensen (2007) explored multiple correlations (see preceding section for details on methodology) and found that the number of maternal noun types were positively and significantly correlated with child vocabulary production 4 months later as measured by number of word types and 8 months later as measured by the MCDI. Maternal use of yes-or-no questions was positively and significantly correlated with children's production of auxiliary verbs 4 months later. Partial correlations taking into account maternal IQ or child language abilities demonstrated similar relationships. These findings demonstrate a direct positive association in ASD between specific linguistic information in maternal input and children's later language production of related features.

Other studies using multiple regression have also demonstrated that after controlling for children's initial language abilities, maternal input features significantly account for variation in children's later language (Bang & Nadig, 2015; Goodwin et al., 2015). As discussed in more detail in Naigles and Fein (Chapter 3, this volume), Goodwin and colleagues (2015) found that for both ASD and TD groups, the percentage of input wh-questions with verbs positively contributed to children's later wh-comprehension over and above maternal (MLU) and child language abilities (word types). However, measures of specific types of wh-questions displayed divergent relationships across groups with respect to child language 1 year later.

To directly compare the relationship between maternal input features and later child language between children with ASD and TD children, Bang and Nadig (2015) used a hierarchical multiple regression model to investigate the contribution of maternal input MLU to children's vocabulary production 6 months later (as measured by the MCDI), over and above children's initial language abilities. Figure 5.2 visualizes the key finding that input MLU positively accounted for 8% of the variation in children's later vocabulary production. The finding that MLU was a positive predictor across both groups of children and a lack of a significant interaction between input MLU and diagnostic group indicates that this effect is not significantly different between groups, meaning that in both children with ASD and TD children, MLU contributed positively to their vocabulary development over 6 months.

To return to the goals of this review, we have established that on most quantitative measures of linguistic input, the language environment available to children with ASD is strikingly similar to that of TD children who are matched on language ability. Crucially, we also have evidence that children with ASD are able to make use of the linguistic input (e.g., word tokens, MLU, yes–no and wh-questions) to enhance their language development; this finding is of key clinical importance for improving language outcomes. Taken together, these conclusions suggest that the language delays observed in ASD do not stem from categorical differences on the nurture side of the puzzle, either with respect to differences in parental input nor on the nature side of the puzzle, to children's inability to make implicit use of the data in the input. However, significant relationships between linguistic input features and later child language do provide a partial nurture-related explanation for the tremendous variability observed in language development across children with ASD: variation in relevant parent input features. To complement findings on linguistic features, we now turn to research on parental responsiveness during parent–child interactions. Although quantitative measures of linguistic features were found to be quite similar across groups, qualitative measures of responsiveness may be more likely to be affected by the social impairments that characterize ASD.

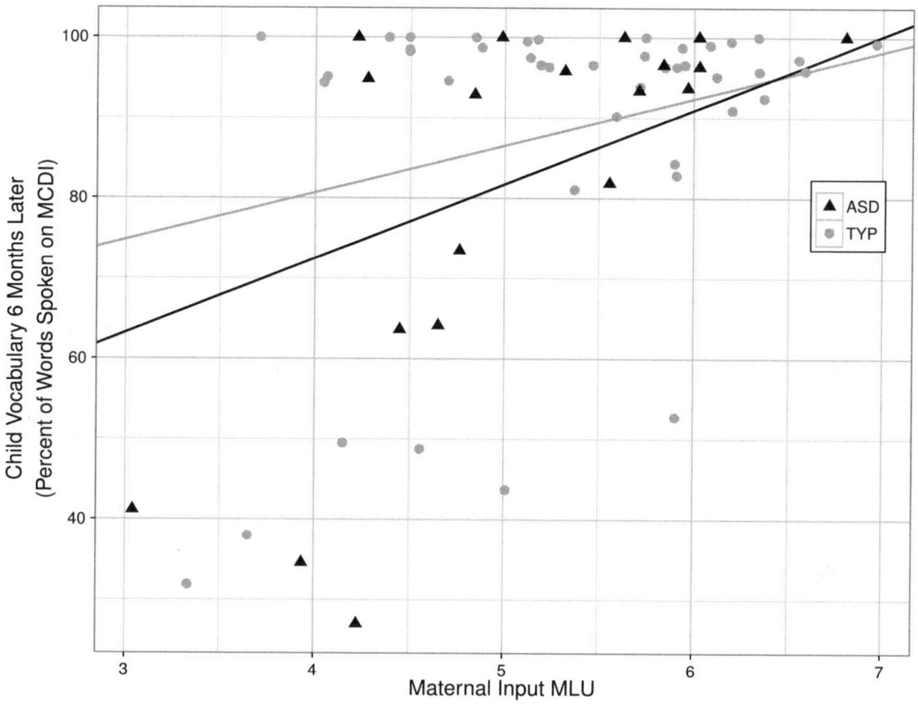

Fig. 5.2: Maternal input MLU and later child vocabulary. Depicts the raw data observed for each dyad: maternal input MLU and the respective child's T3% of words spoken on the MCDI. Regression lines depict the simple slopes for each diagnostic group calculated from the final regression model (Step 4), which holds all other predictors at their mean value. This figure demonstrates a positive linear relationship between input MLU and children's T3 productive vocabulary, which did not differ significantly between ASD and TYP groups. TYP = typically developing. From "Learning Language in Autism: Maternal Linguistic Input Contributes to Later Vocabulary," by J. Bang and A. Nadig, 2015, *Autism Research*, *8*, p. 220. Copyright 2015 by Wiley Online Publishing. Reprinted with permission.

Parental Responsiveness

Studies on typical development have reported on the linguistic benefits conferred by not only the quantity and content of parental speech but also the quality of how it is delivered (for a review, see Hoff & Naigles, 2002). Following the child's lead or following into a child's focus of attention (*parental responsiveness*) refers to parents' provision of verbal or gestural input contingent on the object or event currently holding their child's attention; importantly in these situations, the parent assumes the task of establishing joint attention. Children with ASD have difficulty tracking others' attention (e.g., Mundy, Sigman, & Kasari, 1990); consequently, following the child's attentional focus is a central component of many parent-training interventions (see McDuffie, Thurman, Channell, & Abbeduto, Chapter 4, this volume).

Comparisons between parents of children with ASD and parents of TD children reveal similar levels of parental verbal or gestural responsiveness (Bani Hani, Gonzalez-Barrero, & Nadig, 2013; Burns, 2012; Kasari, Sigman, Mundy, & Yirmiya, 1988; Siller & Sigman, 2002; Watson, 1998), and similar abilities to sustain periods of mutual engagement with their child (Adamson, Bakeman, Deckner, & Romski, 2009; Kasari et al., 1988). For example, Siller and Sigman (2002) found no significant group differences in mothers' verbal and gestural responsiveness, also referred to as maternal synchrony. Recent work from our lab replicated this basic finding. Burns (2012) found no group differences in parents' production of object labels that were synchronous with their child's focus of attention during play. In a different type of interaction, Bani Hani et al. (2013) investigated parental use of verbal and gestural cues when teaching children novel labels for objects. Again, no differences were found between groups in synchrony between parents' utterance of the label and children's attention to the object. Likewise, studies that compared children with ASD with children with non-ASD developmental delays did not find group differences (Adamson et al., 2009; Cantwell et al., 1977; Kasari et al., 1988; Siller & Sigman, 2002). However, a few specific differences have been observed. For instance, parents of children with ASD produce more out-of-focus utterances to guide their child's behavior (Watson, 1998), and parents of children with ASD provide more positive feedback than parents of TD children (Kasari et al., 1988) and parents of children with non-ASD developmental delays (Cantwell et al., 1977).

Overall, these findings indicate that parents interacting with their children with ASD are as verbally and gesturally responsive as parents interacting with TD children or children with other developmental delays but also provide significantly more positive remarks or behavioral guidance to their children. This suggests that parents of children with ASD may need to do extra work to structure and maintain the interaction to achieve the same level of engagement. The next section details how parental responsiveness measures are related to later child language.

Impact of Parental Responsiveness on Later Child Language

Siller and Sigman (2002) were the first to examine long-term effects of parental verbal and gestural responsiveness on child language at multiple time points in children with ASD. Although there were no significant associations with 1-year language gains, maternal synchrony for verbal utterances overall was significantly and positively correlated with language gain at 10 years. In another sample of children with ASD, Siller and Sigman (2008) used multilevel modeling analyses to reveal maternal synchrony measures of verbal and gestural responsiveness predicted children's rate of language growth over a period of 4 years. In both studies, these findings were independent of children's language and IQ scores, which suggests that these relationships were not spurious results driven by children's own level of functioning. These findings underscore the importance of parental responsiveness to support the later language of children with ASD; similar positive relationships have been found for sustained periods of engagement (Adamson et al., 2009). Notably, there is evidence that parent training programs are successful at increasing parent responsiveness (Roberts & Kaiser, 2011), indicating that it is possible to boost this consequential nurture factor. Researchers have also begun to tease apart the different functions served by parental responsive utterances and their specific contributions to children's later language (Haebig, McDuffie, & Weismer, 2013a, 2013b; McDuffie & Yoder, 2010; Rollins & Snow, 1998; see also McDuffie et al., Chapter 4, this volume).

Function of Parental Responsive Utterances

There are many ways to classify the function of responsive verbal utterances. For example, if a child is playing with a toy truck the parent could ask a question (e.g., "Where are you going with the truck?"), direct the child's language or behavior (i.e., *follow-in directives* such as "Push the truck to me!"), or comment on the child's attentional focus (i.e., *follow-in comments* such as "That's a bright red truck!"; Haebig et al., 2013a, 2013b; McDuffie & Yoder, 2010). Studies comparing the function of parental responsive utterances between parents of children with ASD and parents of TD children have again found no significant differences (Siller & Sigman, 2002; Wolchik, 1983; Wolchik & Harris, 1982). Walton and Ingersoll (2015) used a detailed microanalysis and found that follow-in directives more often preceded children's language than follow-in comments for both children with ASD and TD children.

As noted earlier for linguistic features, the few differences that have been found occur when comparing mothers of children with high-functioning versus low-functioning ASD (Konstantareas et al., 1988). Whereas mothers of high-functioning verbal children provided more questions, answers to children's questions, reinforcements of children's language, and language modeling (i.e., repetition, expansion, correction of child's language), mothers of low-functioning nonverbal children provided more directives and reinforcements of children's motor behavior.

These findings echo those of Kasari et al. (1988), who found that parents of high-functioning verbal children with ASD spent more time in mutual play and gave more positive feedback, and parents of low-functioning children with ASD provided more bids for attention, to initiate activities, and to hold them on task. These differences underscore once again how variability in child language ability and ensuing parental input inherently shapes their language environments, the nurture side of the puzzle.

Impact of Function of Parental Responsive Utterances on Later Child Language

Numerous studies have reported significant positive effects of follow-in comments, follow-in directives, and parent expansions on children's later language in ASD 6 months, 4 years, 10 years, and, strikingly, even up to 16 years later (McDuffie & Yoder, 2010; Siller & Sigman, 2002, 2008). Haebig and colleagues (2013a, 2013b) have also reported differences in the predictive power of follow-in comments versus follow-in directives for different subgroups of children with ASD. Whereas follow-in directives accounted for children's comprehension and production gains 1 year later (beyond follow-in comments and parent education levels), follow-in comments demonstrated a negative relationship (Haebig et al., 2013a). Further analyses revealed that a positive relationship was noted with follow-in comments for minimally verbal children (i.e., producing fewer than five words), whereas the verbally fluent children did not benefit from follow-in comments. A follow-up study showed that this pattern of findings continued to hold 3 years after the parent–child interaction data were collected (Haebig et al., 2013b).

The findings reviewed in this section demonstrate that, as for quantitative linguistic measures in the previous section, the quality of parental input as indexed by responsiveness has significant positive effects on later child language in ASD above and beyond child language and IQ. This adds another key player to the nurture side of the language development puzzle in ASD. An important future direction is to compare the impact of both quantitative and qualitative features longitudinally in the same sample of children with ASD, as well as to determine which functions of responsive utterances benefit which subgroups of children with ASD (Haebig et al., 2013a, 2013b). We now turn to preliminary findings from other domains that can contribute to the nurture side of the language development puzzle.

Other Aspects and Contexts of Parental Input

Diverse aspects of parental input to children with ASD have begun to be explored, from the acoustic modifications of child-directed speech to parental input in the context of storybook reading, including the production of internal state terms. We survey these findings in this section to paint as broad and complete a picture as possible of parental input to children with ASD and to outline productive areas for future work. In contrast to the evidence reviewed in the previous sections, a number of these studies report group differences as well as some points of similarity.

Acoustic Modification of Child-Directed Speech

In our lab, we examined the acoustic modification of child-directed speech to children with ASD using a book-reading task to elicit child-directed speech and an experimenter interview about the content of the books to elicit adult-directed speech from parents. Participants were parent–child dyads who either had a child with ASD (mean age 60 months) or a TD child (mean age 30 months) matched on child vocabulary level.

Individual words that a parent produced in both child- and adult-directed contexts were extracted from audio recordings of the session and analyzed for mean pitch, pitch range, and amplitude in each context. Parents in both groups demonstrated acoustic modifications characteristic of child-directed speech; they increased their pitch, pitch range, and amplitude on words spoken in the child-directed context and there were no significant group differences (Flores, Burack, & Nadig, 2011). Another group (Xu, Gilkerson, Richards, & Rosenberg, 2012) compared toddlers of the same age but different language levels and analyzed large samples of parental speech to children versus adults using ongoing recordings. These authors reported that parents of toddlers with ASD produced significantly longer vowel duration, louder vowel volume, and higher vowel pitch than parents of TD toddlers. This discrepancy in findings may be explained by different matching procedures across studies. In the Xu et al. (2012) study, the children with ASD had lower language levels than TD children, whereas in Flores et al. (2011) groups were matched on language level. Assuming that parents are sensitive to their child's language abilities when producing acoustic features of child-directed speech, it is not surprising that children at lower linguistic levels would receive more exaggerated child-directed speech than those at higher language levels. Future work should explore developmental changes in the production of child-directed speech to children with ASD in addition to confirming if differences observed are linked to child language ability rather than ASD per se.

Teaching Novel Labels

Bani Hani et al. (2013) found similar behaviors in parents' labeling of novel objects between parent–child dyads where there was a child with ASD versus a TD child matched on language level. The number of labels parents produced and number of nonverbal cues they used did not differ across groups. In addition, the number of episodes where multiple cues were produced in conjunction with the label was similar, as was the tendency to provide the first label when the object was already in the child's focus of attention (about 90% of episodes for both groups). Finally, the mean number and type of nonverbal cues used (e.g., gaze to object, showing, movement) was very similar across groups. Interestingly, parents of both groups provided more abundant cues when labeling for children who had lower language levels, suggesting they are sensitive to their child's comprehension needs. However, exact tactics differed by group, with parents of children with ASD repeating verbal labels to children with lower language levels, perhaps to gain their attention, whereas parents of TD children tended to use multiple nonverbal cues (e.g., gaze to object, showing, movement). These findings are consistent with the findings reviewed earlier in the chapter on similarities across groups in parental responsiveness during play interactions more generally.

Turn Taking

Warren and colleagues (2010) investigated language input from any adult in the environment to young children with ASD or to TD children who were similar in age (mean age approximately 30 months) using automated analyses of large samples of continuously recorded speech. Recordings were processed with LENA (Language ENvironment Analysis) software, which uses an algorithm to segment sounds based on acoustic features into speech-related (i.e., speech, singing) and non-speechlike (i.e., laughing, burping) as well as identifying speakers as children or adults. As would be expected given the language delay common in ASD, they found significantly fewer and shorter child vocalizations in the ASD group. With this background, there were also fewer conversational turns between adults and the child in the ASD group. Finally, the speech of TD children was more likely to take place in conversations than monologues, whereas the reverse was found for children with ASD. To further examine the back-and-forth nature of parent–child interactions over time, this group compared the social feedback loop between adults present in the language environment and children with ASD or TD children (Warlaumont, Richards, Gilkerson, & Oller, 2014). Specifically, they examined contingency of adults' responses to children's speech-related vocalizations and of children's responses back to the adult. More than 13,000 hours of the language environment was recorded from 106 families with TD children and 77 families with children with ASD matched on child chronological age, gender, and maternal education, but not child language ability. Warlaumont and colleagues (2014) replicated findings of fewer speech-related vocalizations by children with ASD relative to TD children but found a social feedback loop to be statistically present for both groups of children: Relative to chance, adult vocalizations were contingent to children's vocalizations, and children's vocalizations were more likely to be speech-related when an adult responded to the child's previous speech-related vocalization. However, the first contingency in the social feedback loop, that of adult responses to children, was significantly weaker for children with ASD than TD children.

This microanalysis is an important step toward understanding the reciprocity of parent–child interactions. The factors that lead to the weaker contingency observed in ASD are, however, an open question. Future work should examine the relative roles of parent versus child, as well as the specifics of their conversational contributions in establishing contingency. For example, the content of utterances, which was not analyzed in this impressively large but linguistically underspecified data set, are likely to be consequential. Additionally, although children's own vocalizations were statistically adjusted for, this does not provide the same control as matching groups on language ability. As discussed in the introduction, parents adapt to their child's language ability over time, thus comparison with TD children matched on language or a developmental delay group would provide a clearer understanding of whether the weaker contingency observed here is specific to ASD or if it characterizes interactions with children of lower language level more generally.

Parental Input in the Context of Shared Storybook Reading

In our lab, we have begun to examine the function of parent utterances in a context that is a particularly rich source of language input, shared storybook reading. Storybook reading differs from free-play interactions, in which most parental input data have been sampled, by being relatively more structured due to the presence of text and the goal of completing the book. We compared parental input to children with ASD (mean age approximately 50 months) or TD children (mean age 24 months) matched on receptive language. Parental speech was first categorized as reading of text or additional speech that was either story-related (e.g., labeling, responding to the child's questions, elaborating on the story) or non-story-related (e.g., managing behavior, getting the child's attention). Parents in both groups were similar in regard to proportion of speech that was read text or non-story-related utterances; however, significant differences were found in the use of story-related utterances. Specifically, parents of children with ASD produced significantly fewer story-related utterances: fewer questions, instances of labeling or requests for labels, and questions or statements relating the book to the child's own experience than did parents of TD children, resulting in a significantly lower total MLU (Smith & Nadig, 2012). Another analysis examined the types of questions parents produce during shared storybook reading found that parents of children with ASD asked fewer identifying questions (e.g., "Where is the mushroom man?") and yes–no questions (e.g., "Is mushroom man the pilot?") than did parents of TD children. Requests for labels (e.g., "What is this?") did not differ between groups (Gonzalez-Barrero & Nadig, 2013). Analyses in progress examine whether frequency of book reading in the home and parental education level contribute to the differences found. This initial evidence indicates a prominent number of differences in input provided in the context of shared storybook reading, relative to the global picture of nearly identical input provided to children with ASD in free play and less structured home environments. It is possible that focus on reading text rather than engaging in additional exchanges about the story is related to the strong interest in text and strength in decoding often observed in children with ASD, alongside poor reading comprehension (Huemer & Mann, 2010; Nation, Clarke, Wright, & Williams, 2006).

Production of Internal State Terms

Slaughter et al. (2007) examined parental input during shared picture book reading with a focus on internal state terms. Participants were 4- to 9-year-old children with ASD and TD children matched on receptive vocabulary. Mothers of children with ASD and those of TD children produced narratives of similar length, similar numbers of word tokens, and did not differ with respect to the mention of cognition, affect, or perception-attention terms. However mothers of children with ASD provided significantly fewer clarifications or elaborations of the cognition and affect terms they used.

That is, they were less likely to explicitly state the contents of characters' minds, include explanations of sources of knowledge, or note discrepancies either among different characters' mental states or between these and physical reality (Slaughter et al., 2007). In partial correlations controlling for verbal mental age, maternal education, and maternal verbosity, mention and clarification of cognition terms was associated with false belief performance in TD children, but only clarification of affect was related to false belief performance in the ASD group.

This suggests that parents are as likely to mention mental states in their speech to children with ASD; however, differences in the nurture environment emerge when it comes to elaborating on these mental states and working through their implications in real-life settings. It is likely that the social cognitive understanding of children with ASD would benefit from exposure to explicit explanations and elaborations of cognition and affect terms, as is the case for TD children, in parent interaction as well as language intervention.

Categories of Maternal Speech

Venuti et al. (2012) examined the functions of maternal utterances to Italian children with Down syndrome, ASD, or typical development of a similar developmental level (mean age approximately 25 months). Maternal speech during free-play sessions was classified into four categories: *information-salient*, that is propositional utterances that served to exchange information; *affect-salient*, which included emphatic and playful utterances; *child name*, involving use of the child's name or nickname to gain attention; and *other maternal speech*. Global similarities were found among mothers in the three groups, for instance, in the total amount of maternal speech, information-salient speech, other maternal speech, and the number of information-salient descriptions. Nevertheless, differences in interaction style were reflected in some significant differences between groups. Mothers of both developmentally disabled groups asked fewer questions and made fewer references to the environment but used more direct statements and references to their children's actions compared with mothers of TD children. A couple of diagnosis-specific effects emerged: Mothers of children with ASD called their name more often than did mothers of TD children, and mothers of children with Down syndrome used more affect-salient speech than TD children.

This study replicates the finding of similarities in overall quantity of utterances directed by parents to their children with ASD or TD in another language, Italian, and importantly adds an additional control group with Down syndrome. Questions posed to children once again surfaced as a source of group differences, as reported for both parent–child interaction and book-reading contexts; importantly, however, this study showed that questions were reduced in parental input to children with either disability and was not specific to ASD. Confirming the need to scaffold interaction with children with ASD, parents made more attentional bids (calling name) to children with ASD than other groups.

Discussion

In this chapter, we examined the nurture side of language development in ASD, that is, the language environment available to children by virtue of quantitative and qualitative aspects of their parents' linguistic and interactive behaviors surrounding language use. When children are matched on language ability, and thus the nature side of the puzzle is controlled for this factor, comparisons of parental input to children with ASD relative to children without ASD reveal many global similarities with a few emerging areas of difference. We found no evidence of group differences in parental input obtained during naturalistic free play with respect to lexical features (word tokens, word types, and lexical diversity), word-specific features (word frequency, contextual diversity), or syntactic complexity (MLU). The provision of similar linguistic environments to children with and without ASD has been demonstrated in French (Bang & Nadig, 2015) and Italian (Venuti et al., 2012), as well as English. Another domain of parental input that has been extensively examined is that of parental responsiveness, or the provision of verbal or gestural input contingent on the object or event currently holding the child's attention, as well as responsive utterances used for specific functions. The findings here largely echo those seen in areas of lexical and grammatical input: Parents of children with ASD are as responsive to their children's attention and comprehension needs as parents of children without ASD of the same language level. Given this evidence, we can rule out the possibility that the language delay observed in many but not all children with ASD stems from wholesale differences in nurture or the composition of the language input they receive.

Critically, however, children with ASD are receiving this similar input, commensurate to their language level, at a later point in maturation. This is due to the linguistic environment being inherently dyadic (i.e., the more a child initiates, the more opportunities an adult has to respond), combined with the fact that children with ASD are less socially interactive by definition (American Psychiatric Association, 2013), a nature-related factor. Consequently, when children with ASD (specifically, those who exhibit language delays) and TD children are compared at the same point in maturation, both child and parent or nurture sides of the interaction show reductions in, for example, child vocalizations, parent–child conversational turns, and reciprocal feedback loops (Warlaumont et al., 2014; Warren et al., 2010).

Having established that children with ASD have access to a rich language-learning environment, a critical next step is to examine whether they are able to use the data available to foster language development. The answer to this question is a resounding yes: Varied and complex lexical and syntactic input is significantly associated with better language 6 months (Bang & Nadig, 2015) and even up to 18 months

(Goodwin et al., 2015) later. Additionally, more responsive parental utterances and gestures are followed by positive language outcomes at 6 months (McDuffie & Yoder, 2010), 1 year (Haebig et al., 2013b; Siller & Sigman, 2002), 3 to 4 years (Haebig et al., 2013a; Siller & Sigman, 2008), and even up to 10 and 16 years (Siller & Sigman, 2002) later. One type of responsive utterance, follow-in comments, has been shown to specifically benefit children with minimal language abilities (i.e., fewer than 10 words; Haebig et al., 2013a, 2013b; McDuffie & Yoder, 2010). These findings demonstrate that although less studied than nature-related factors, nurture-related factors play a significant role in predicting language development and explaining variability among children with ASD, as they do for TD children. Further research is needed to explain how, or which, children with ASD are able to benefit from language input in these ways despite reductions in preferential attention to child-directed speech observed in subgroups of children with ASD (Kuhl et al., 2005).

Diverging from the many similarities noted earlier for more basic quantitative and qualitative measures of parental input to children with ASD, an area of difference that has been observed is a reduced number of certain types of questions in free-play settings (Goodwin et al., 2015; Venuti et al., 2012; but for nonsignificant differences, see Swensen, 2007; Wolchik, 1983; Wolchik & Harris, 1982), as well as during shared storybook reading (Gonzalez-Barrero & Nadig, 2013; Smith & Nadig, 2012). Children's language and social impairments appear to constrain the questions their parents pose to them, despite the fact that children with ASD in these studies were as linguistically able to respond to the questions as TD children. It seems the domain of questions may be especially sensitive to differences that emerge through the course of dyadic nature–nurture interaction, which may lead parents to have different communicative expectations of their children. Importantly, the same reduction in questions posed by parents was found for children with Down syndrome (Venuti et al., 2012), indicating that this is likely not an ASD-specific phenomenon. Future work is needed to understand causes and consequences of reduced questioning during interaction, as questions are a particularly rich source of linguistic information because they highlight words, auxiliaries, and constituent structure and serve the pragmatic functions of turn taking and learning about others' points of view. The benefits of incorporating dialogic reading strategies, which emphasize questioning, should be investigated for ASD interventions because they have been shown to improve language in other populations (e.g., Whitehurst et al., 1988). Another difference potentially linked to patterns of dyadic interaction is a reduced elaboration and explanation of cognitive and affective terms in speech to children with ASD relative to TD children (Slaughter et al., 2007). Other differences are likely to be uncovered as detailed investigations of input to children with ASD progress, it will be essential to investigate the same features in input to children with non-ASD developmental delays before concluding that any differences are ASD specific.

Related to dyadic interaction, numerous findings have showcased parents' sensitivity to the abilities of their children with ASD. For instance, language input was differentially adapted to child language (Cantwell, Baker, & Rutter, 1977; Konstantareas et al., 1988). Likewise, repeated labeling of novel objects (Bani Hani et al., 2013) and increased bids for attention and utterances to hold children on task (Kasari et al., 1988) were observed for children with ASD who had lower language relative to those with higher language abilities. These findings demonstrate that parents provide input that is calibrated to their children's abilities, arguing for the methodological practice of matching groups with respect to language rather than age when investigating parental input.

This body of work holds important implications for clinical practice, education, and families with children with ASD. It shows that, like children without ASD, children with ASD make use of the language they hear and benefit from lexically rich and syntactically complex input. Because children with ASD hear the greatest number of words during day-to-day activities and routines (Burgess, Audet, & Harjusola-Webb, 2013), caregivers should be encouraged to provide a rich language learning environment during these interactions. Other aspects of input that have repeatedly been shown to be positively related to long-term language gains are responsive utterances and gestures that follow into the children's attentional focus and create situations of joint engagement. Finally, this body of findings provides strong support for parent-implemented language interventions, which have been shown to have significant positive effects on receptive and expressive language skills in ASD (Roberts & Kaiser, 2011; see also McDuffie et al., Chapter 4, this volume).

References

Adamson, L. B., Bakeman, R., Deckner, D. F., & Romski, M. (2009). Joint engagement and the emergence of language in children with autism and Down syndrome. *Journal of Autism and Developmental Disorders, 39*, 84–96. http://dx.doi.org/10.1007/s10803-008-0601-7

American Psychiatric Association. (2013). *Diagnostic and statistical manual of mental disorders* (5th ed.). Washington, DC: Author.

Anderson, D. K., Lord, C., Risi, S., DiLavore, P. S., Shulman, C., Thurm, A., . . . Pickles, A. (2007). Patterns of growth in verbal abilities among children with autism spectrum disorder. *Journal of Consulting and Clinical Psychology, 75*, 594–604. http://dx.doi.org/10.1037/0022-006X.75.4.594

Bang, J., & Nadig, A. (2012, May). *A look at the input: Relationship between parental speech and children in autism and typical development.* Poster presented at the 11th Annual International Meeting for Autism Research, Toronto, Ontario, Canada.

Bang, J., & Nadig, A. (2015). Learning language in autism: Maternal linguistic input contributes to later vocabulary. *Autism Research, 8*, 214–223. http://dx.doi.org/10.1002/aur.1440

Bani Hani, H., Gonzalez-Barrero, A. M., & Nadig, A. S. (2013). Children's referential understanding of novel words and parent labeling behaviors: Similarities across children with and without autism spectrum disorders. *Journal of Child Language, 40*, 971–1002. http://dx.doi.org/10.1017/S0305000912000426

Bettelheim, B. (1967). *The empty fortress: Infantile autism and the birth of the self.* New York, NY: The Free Press.

Bourguignon, N., Nadig, A., & Valois, D. (2012). The biolinguistics of autism: Emergent perspectives. *Biolinguistics*, *6*, 124–165.

Burgess, S., Audet, L., & Harjusola-Webb, S. (2013). Quantitative and qualitative characteristics of the school and home language environments of preschool-aged children with ASD. *Journal of Communication Disorders*, *46*, 428–439. http://dx.doi.org/10.1016/j.jcomdis.2013.09.003

Burns, J. (2012). *Child play skills and parent verbal responsiveness: Effects on language growth in preschoolers with autism spectrum disorders and typical development* (Master's thesis). Available from escholarship@McGill.ca (PID No. 107883).

Cantwell, D. P., Baker, L., & Rutter, M. (1977). Families of autistic and dysphasic children. II. Mothers' speech to the children. *Journal of Autism & Childhood Schizophrenia*, *7*, 313–327. http://dx.doi.org/10.1007/BF01540390

Chapman, R. S. (2000). Children's language learning: An interactionist perspective. *Journal of Child Psychology and Psychiatry*, *41*, 33–54. http://dx.doi.org/10.1017/S0021963099004953

Fenson, L., Marchman, V. A., Thal, D. J., Dale, P. S., Reznick, J. S., & Bates, E. (2007). *MacArthur–Bates Communicative Development Inventories: User's guide and technical manual* (2nd ed.). Baltimore, MD: Brookes.

Flores, H., Burack, J., & Nadig, A. (2011, July). *Acoustic characteristics of maternal speech to young children with typical development and young children with autism.* Poster presented at the 12th International Congress for the Study of Child Language, Montreal, Quebec, Canada.

Frank, S. M., Allen, D. A., Stein, L., & Myers, B. (1976). Linguistic performance in vulnerable and autistic children and their mothers. *The American Journal of Psychiatry*, *133*, 909–915. http://dx.doi.org/10.1176/ajp.133.8.909

Gonzalez-Barrero, A., & Nadig, A. (2013, June). *Parental questions during shared storybook reading with children with autism spectrum disorders: Relationships with vocabulary growth.* Poster presented at the 2013 Child Language Seminar, Manchester, England.

Goodwin, A., Fein, D., & Naigles, L. (2015). The role of maternal input in the development of wh-question comprehension in autism and typical development. *Journal of Child Language*, *42*, 32–63. http://dx.doi.org/10.1017/S0305000913000524

Haebig, E., McDuffie, A., & Weismer, S. E. (2013a). Brief report: Parent verbal responsiveness and language development in toddlers on the autism spectrum. *Journal of Autism and Developmental Disorders*, *43*, 2218–2227. http://dx.doi.org/10.1007/s10803-013-1763-5

Haebig, E., McDuffie, A., & Weismer, S. E. (2013b). The contribution of two categories of parent verbal responsiveness to later language for toddlers and preschoolers on the autism spectrum. *American Journal of Speech-Language Pathology*, *22*, 57–70. http://dx.doi.org/10.1044/1058-0360(2012/11-0004)

Hart, B., & Risley, T. (1995). *Meaningful differences in the everyday experience of young American children.* Baltimore, MD: Brookes.

Hills, T. T., Maouene, J., Riordan, B., & Smith, L. B. (2010). The associative structure of language: Contextual diversity in early word learning. *Journal of Memory and Language*, *63*, 259–273. http://dx.doi.org/10.1016/j.jml.2010.06.002

Hoff, E., & Naigles, L. (2002). How children use input to acquire a lexicon. *Child Development*, *73*, 418–433. http://dx.doi.org/10.1111/1467-8624.00415

Huemer, S. V., & Mann, V. (2010). A comprehensive profile of decoding and comprehension in autism spectrum disorders. *Journal of Autism and Developmental Disorders*, *40*, 485–493. http://dx.doi.org/10.1007/s10803-009-0892-3

Hurtado, N., Marchman, V. A., & Fernald, A. (2008). Does input influence uptake? Links between maternal talk, processing speed and vocabulary size in Spanish-learning children. *Developmental Science*, 11, F31–F39.

Huttenlocher, J., Haight, W., Bryk, A., Seltzer, M., & Lyons, T. (1991). Early vocabulary growth: Relation to language input and gender. *Developmental Psychology*, *27*, 236–248. http://dx.doi.org/10.1037/0012-1649.27.2.236

Kasari, C., Sigman, M., Mundy, P., & Yirmiya, N. (1988). Caregiver interactions with autistic children. *Journal of Abnormal Child Psychology*, *16*, 45–56. http://dx.doi.org/10.1007/BF00910499

Kitamura, C., & Burnham, D. (2003). Pitch and communicative intent in mother's speech: Adjustments for age and sex in the first year. *Infancy*, *4*, 85–110. http://dx.doi.org/10.1207/S15327078IN0401_5

Kjelgaard, M. M., & Tager-Flusberg, H. (2001). An investigation of language impairment in autism: Implications for genetic subgroups. *Language and Cognitive Processes*, *16*, 287–308. http://dx.doi.org/10.1080/01690960042000058

Konstantareas, M. M., Zajdeman, H., Homatidis, S., & McCabe, A. (1988). Maternal speech to verbal and higher functioning versus nonverbal and lower functioning autistic children. *Journal of Autism and Developmental Disorders*, *18*, 647–656. http://dx.doi.org/10.1007/BF02211882

Kuhl, P. K., Coffey-Corina, S., Padden, D., & Dawson, G. (2005). Links between social and linguistic processing of speech in preschool children with autism: Behavioral and electrophysiological measures. *Developmental Science*, *8*, F1–F12. http://dx.doi.org/10.1111/j.1467-7687.2004.00384.x

Luyster, R. J., Kadlec, M. B., Carter, A., & Tager-Flusberg, H. (2008). Language assessment and development in toddlers with autism spectrum disorders. *Journal of Autism and Developmental Disorders*, *38*, 1426–1438.

Luyster, R. J., Lopez, K., & Lord, C. (2007). Characterizing communicative development in children referred for autism spectrum disorders using the MacArthur–Bates Communicative Development Inventory (CDI). *Journal of Child Language*, *34*, 623–654. http://dx.doi.org/10.1017/S0305000907008094

Mawhood, L., Howlin, P., & Rutter, M. (2000). Autism and developmental receptive language disorder—a comparative follow-up in early adult life. I: Cognitive and language outcomes. *Journal of Child Psychology and Psychiatry*, *41*, 547–559. http://dx.doi.org/10.1111/1469-7610.00642

McDuffie, A., & Yoder, P. (2010). Types of parent verbal responsiveness that predict language in young children with autism spectrum disorder. *Journal of Speech, Language, and Hearing Research*, *53*, 1026–1039. http://dx.doi.org/10.1044/1092-4388(2009/09-0023)

Mundy, P., Sigman, M., & Kasari, C. (1990). A longitudinal study of joint attention and language development in autistic children. *Journal of Autism and Developmental Disorders*, *20*, 115–128. http://dx.doi.org/10.1007/BF02206861

Nation, K., Clarke, P., Wright, B., & Williams, C. (2006). Patterns of reading ability in children with autism spectrum disorder. *Journal of Autism and Developmental Disorders*, *36*, 911–919. http://dx.doi.org/10.1007/s10803-006-0130-1

Roberts, M. Y., & Kaiser, A. P. (2011). The effectiveness of parent-implemented language interventions: A meta-analysis. *American Journal of Speech-Language Pathology*, *20*, 180–199. http://dx.doi.org/10.1044/1058-0360(2011/10-0055)

Rollins, P. R., & Snow, C. E. (1998). Shared attention and grammatical development in typical children and children with autism. *Journal of Child Language*, *25*, 653–673.

Siller, M., & Sigman, M. (2002). The behaviors of parents of children with autism predict the subsequent development of their children's communication. *Journal of Autism and Developmental Disorders*, *32*, 77–89. http://dx.doi.org/10.1023/A:1014884404276

Siller, M., & Sigman, M. (2008). Modeling longitudinal change in the language abilities of children with autism: Parent behaviors and child characteristics as predictors of change. *Developmental Psychology*, *44*, 1691–1704. http://dx.doi.org/10.1037/a0013771

Slaughter, V., Peterson, C. C., & Mackintosh, E. (2007). Mind what mother says: Narrative input and theory of mind in typical children and those on the autism spectrum. *Child Development*, *78*, 839–858. http://dx.doi.org/10.1111/j.1467-8624.2007.01036.x

Smith, S. C., & Nadig, A. (2012, May). *Parent–child shared storybook reading for children with autism spectrum disorders: A comparison with typical development and relationships with child language.* Poster presented at the 11th Annual International Meeting for Autism Research, Toronto, Ontario, Canada.

Snow, C. E. (1995). Issues in the study of input: Finetuning, universality, individual and developmental differences, and necessary causes. In P. Fletcher & B. MacWhinney (Eds.), *The handbook of child language* (pp. 180–193). Oxford, England: Blackwell Reference.

Sokolov, J. L. (1993). A local contingency analysis of the finetuning hypothesis. *Developmental Psychology*, *29*, 1008–1023. http://dx.doi.org/10.1037/0012-1649.29.6.1008

Swensen, L. D. (2007). *Exploring the effects of maternal input on the language of children with autism* (Doctoral dissertation). Available from ProQuest Dissertations and Theses (UMI No. 3286870)

Swensen, L. D., Naigles, L. R., & Fein, D. (2007). Does maternal input affect the language of children with Autism? In H. Caunt-Nulton, S. Kulatilake, & I. Woo (Eds.), *Proceedings of the 31st Annual Boston University Conference on Language Development* (pp. 609–619). Somerville, MA: Cascadilla Press.

Thurm, A., Lord, C., Lee, L. C., & Newschaffer, C. (2007). Predictors of language acquisition in preschool children with autism spectrum disorders. *Journal of Autism and Developmental Disorders*, *37*, 1721–1734. http://dx.doi.org/10.1007/s10803-006-0300-1

Venuti, P., de Falco, S., Esposito, G., Zaninelli, M., & Bornstein, M. H. (2012). Maternal functional speech to children: A comparison of autism spectrum disorder, Down syndrome, and typical development. *Research in Developmental Disabilities*, *33*, 506–517. http://dx.doi.org/10.1016/j.ridd.2011.10.018

Walton, K. M., & Ingersoll, B. R. (2015). The influence of maternal language responsiveness on the expressive speech production of children with autism spectrum disorders: A microanalysis of mother–child play interactions. *Autism*, *19*, 421–432. http://dx.doi.org/10.1177/1362361314523144

Warlaumont, A. S., Richards, J. A., Gilkerson, J., & Oller, D. K. (2014). A social feedback loop for speech development and its reduction in autism. *Psychological Science*, *25*, 1314–1324. http://dx.doi.org/10.1177/0956797614531023

Warren, S. F., Gilkerson, J., Richards, J. A., Oller, D. K., Xu, D., Yapanel, U., & Gray, S. (2010). What automated vocal analysis reveals about the vocal production and language learning environment of young children with autism. *Journal of Autism and Developmental Disorders, 40*, 555–569. http://dx.doi.org/10.1007/s10803-009-0902-5

Watson, L. R. (1998). Following the child's lead: Mothers' interactions with children with autism. *Journal of Autism and Developmental Disorders, 28*, 51–59. http://dx.doi.org/10.1023/A:1026063003289

Weismer, S. E., Lord, C., & Esler, A. (2010). Early language patterns of toddlers on the autism spectrum compared to toddlers with developmental delay. *Journal of Autism and Developmental Disorders, 40*, 1259–1273. http://dx.doi.org/10.1007/s10803-010-0983-1

Whitehurst, G. J., Falco, F. L., Lonigan, C. J., Fischel, J. E., DeBaryshe, B. D., Valez-Menchaca, M. C., & Caulfield, M. (1988). Accelerating language development through picture book reading. *Developmental Psychology, 24*, 552–559. http://dx.doi.org/10.1037/0012-1649.24.4.552

Wolchik, S. A. (1983). Language patterns of parents of young autistic and normal children. *Journal of Autism and Developmental Disorders, 13*, 167–180. http://dx.doi.org/10.1007/BF01531817

Wolchik, S. A., & Harris, S. L. (1982). Language environments of autistic and normal children matched for language age: A preliminary investigation. *Journal of Autism and Developmental Disorders, 12*, 43–55. http://dx.doi.org/10.1007/BF01531673

Xu, D., Gilkerson, J., Richards, J., & Rosenberg, S. (2012, May). *Unique acoustic characteristics of children with autism and their caregivers.* Paper presented at the 11th Annual International Meeting for Autism Research, Toronto, Ontario, Canada.

Yoder, P. J., Spruytenburg, H., Edwards, A., & Davies, B. (1995). Effect of verbal routine contexts and expansions on gains in the mean length of utterance in children with developmental delays. *Language, Speech, and Hearing Services in Schools, 26*, 21–32. http://dx.doi.org/10.1044/0161-1461.2601.21

Laurice Tuller, Sandrine Ferré, Philippe Prévost, Marie-Anne Barthez, Joëlle Malvy, and Frédérique Bonnet-Brilhault

6 The Effect of Computational Complexity on the Acquisition of French by Children With ASD

It is well known that most children with autism spectrum disorder (ASD) have difficulties with at least some aspects of language. Problems with language are among the first causes for concern in parents of children with ASD. In some children, language may be severely affected, either entirely absent or consisting of only a few words or phrases (Lord & Paul, 1997; Tager-Flusberg, 2006). Delay in the emergence of the first words and first sentences, compared with typically developing (TD) children, is also found in most children with autism (Grandgeorge et al., 2009; Howlin, 2003), and language regression or loss also occurs (Barger, Campbell, & McDonough, 2013).

However, little is known about the precise nature of language difficulties in ASD. In particular, although pragmatic competence has been widely examined, with a consensus that pragmatics is universally impaired in ASD, even in so-called optimal outcome children (Kelley, Paul, Fein, & Naigles, 2006), less attention has been paid to the formal aspects of language in children with ASD, especially in languages other than English. Several recent studies have aimed to address this shortcoming, comparing phonology and morphosyntax in children with ASD to children with those in children with specific language impairment (SLI), but these have mostly focused on high-functioning children (e.g., Durrleman & Zufferey, 2013; Eigsti & Bennetto, 2009; Terzi, Marinis, Kotsopoulou, & Konstantinos, 2014), thus leaving open the question of these aspects of language for the rest of the spectrum, which, by recent accounts, includes half of these children (Charman et al., 2011).

This chapter further compares the performance of children with ASD on formal aspects of language with that of children with SLI. The focus is on French, which has been underexplored in ASD research in this area, and the participants with ASD studied include children with both normal and impaired nonverbal cognition.

This research was supported by French National Research Agency Grant BLAN-0328-01. We are grateful to clinicians at autism centers at university teaching hospitals in Tours and in Brest: C. Barthélémy, M. Bataille, P. Dansart, E. Lemonnier, and J. Rozec. The comparison with specific language impairment was possible thanks to E. Sizaret, A.-G. Piller, and A. Galloux at the Language Reference Center of the children's hospital in Tours. We also thank the students and postdoctoral researchers involved in this study: S. Galés, E. Morin, M. Scheidnes, and R. Zebib.

http://dx.doi.org/10.1037/15964-007

Innovative Investigations of Language in Autism Spectrum Disorder, L. R. Naigles (Editor)

Background

One of the issues raised in research on the formal aspects of language in ASD is to what extent they compare with the characteristics of language of children with SLI (see, among others, Bishop, 2010; Kjelgaard & Tager-Flusberg, 2001; Riches, Loucas, Baird, Charman, & Simonoff, 2011; Tomblin, Bean, & McGregor, 2011) and thus whether study of language in ASD should consider two distinct profiles, children with language impairment and children with normal language (Tek, Mesite, Fein, & Naigles, 2014). SLI is a disorder affecting language development specifically in the absence of any primary disorder such as intellectual disability, auditory-perceptual impairment, obvious neurological dysfunction, or, indeed, ASD (as defined by the *Diagnostic and Statistical Manual of Mental Disorders, Fifth Edition*; American Psychiatric Association, 2013). Morphosyntax and phonology are two domains that are particularly affected in SLI, with children showing late language emergence and significant difficulties that often continue into adolescence and beyond (see, among others, Leonard, 1998; Rice, 2004; van der Lely, 1998). Some studies report morphosyntactic similarities between children with ASD and children with SLI. For instance, Roberts, Rice, and Tager-Flusberg (2004) found that, like children with SLI, English-speaking children with ASD struggle with tense marking in English, such as *–ed* and *–s*, often producing bare verb forms instead of inflected forms (see also Botting & Conti-Ramsden, 2003; Eigsti & Bennetto, 2009). Some scholars have suggested that phonology is not impaired in children with ASD but only delayed (Bartak, Rutter, & Cox, 1975; Bartolucci & Pierce, 1977). Other studies have found that a substantial proportion of children with ASD have impaired phonology compared with controls (Bishop et al., 2004; McCleery, Tully, Slevc, & Schreibman, 2006). Rapin, Dunn, Allen, Stevens, and Fein, (2009) reported that 23% of children with ASD show severe phonological deficits.

One aspect of SLI that has been attracting the attention of scholars in the past decade or so is the effect of computational complexity on language development. In morphosyntax, complexity has been proposed to depend on the number of syntactic operations involved in a derivation, essentially suggesting that the more operations involved, the more complex the derivation (Jakubowicz & Tuller, 2008; Prévost, Tuller, Scheidnes, Ferré, & Haiden, 2010). For example, the computation involved in the derivation of a sentence in which a constituent appears in a noncanonical position would be greater than that entailed in an identical sentence in which that constituent appears in its canonical position. Thus, sentences containing an object pronoun in languages such as French in which these elements appear in a special position to the immediate left of the verb (*Léa le voit*, literally “Lea him sees”) are more complex than those in which objects appear in the ordinary postverbal object position (*Léa voit Max*, “Lea sees Max”). Children (and adolescents) with SLI have been shown to have particular difficulties with specific constructions argued to entail complex derivations. Low performance on elicited production of pronoun object clitics is one of the hallmarks of impaired language in French-speaking children with SLI (Jakubowicz, Nash,

Rigaut, & Gérard, 1998; Paradis, 2004). Low rates of constructions containing a subordinate clause, such as a complement clause (e.g., *Léa sait que Max habite à Paris*; "Lea knows that Max lives in Paris") or a relative clause (e.g., *Léa a vu l'homme que le chien a mordu*; "Lea saw the man who the dog bit") have also been found to be characteristic of morphosyntactic impairment in SLI in French (Scheidnes, 2012; Tuller, Henry, Sizaret, & Barthez, 2012). In phonology, complexity increases with the presence of additional constituents in the syllable structure (such as branching onsets, e.g., /kl/ in *clown*; or codas, e.g., /l/ in *pale*). Children with SLI, including French-speaking children, have been found to have difficulties with syllable structure, particularly consonant clusters (Ferré, Tuller, Sizaret, & Barthez, 2012; Gallon, Harris, & van der Lely, 2007; Orsolini, Sechi, Maronato, Bonvino, & Corcelli, 2001) and the presence of consonants in coda position (Ferré, dos Santos, & de Almeida, 2015; Tamburelli & Jones, 2013). Increasing word length, which necessitates greater activation of phonological working memory, is also a well-known source of difficulties in children with SLI (Archibald & Gathercole, 2006; Thordardottir & Brandeker, 2013, among others).

Research exploring the effect of computational complexity on language in ASD has been comparatively sparse. Riches, Loucas, Baird, Charman, and Simonoff (2010) looked at performance on the production of English subject and object relatives in age-matched adolescents with SLI and adolescents with ASD (plus language impairment). The authors reported that both groups struggled with object relatives, which are more complex than subject relatives (see also Durrleman, Hippolyte, Zufferey, Iglesias, & Hadjikhani, 2015). However, the adolescents with SLI experienced even more difficulties than the adolescents with ASD, which Riches et al. attributed to impaired working memory. Working on similar populations, Riches et al. (2011) reported on the results of a nonword repetition task and found that the adolescents with SLI and those with ASD plus language impairment had difficulties with syllabic structure (see also Paul, Fuerst, Ramsay, Chawarska, & Klin, 2011) and that both groups produced phonemic substitutions. Bishop et al. (2004) also appealed to poor working memory, along with phonological processing deficits, to explain the poor performance of children with ASD on a nonword repetition task based on increasing word length.

Another aspect of our study will be to examine the impact of cognition on language development in ASD. Children with ASD vary in levels of cognitive development, and one question is to what extent their level of cognitive development affects their difficulties with language. In some studies, children with ASD have been found to have the same language skills as children of similar cognitive level (developing either typically or atypically; Howlin, 1984; Tager-Flusberg et al., 1990). In others, language has been found to develop independently of cognition in ASD (Eigsti, Bennetto, & Dadlani, 2007; Kjelgaard & Tager-Flusberg, 2001; Perovic, Modyanova, & Wexler, 2013). There appears to be generally little support for specific IQ profiles for children with ASD (Charman et al., 2011), although studies of very young children with ASD have shown there to be links between nonverbal IQ and gross language abilities (minimally verbal vs. high language level; Weismer & Kover, 2015). Overall, study of the links between measures of structural language complexity and nonverbal cognition has been exceedingly rare. In the case of SLI, low nonverbal cognition cannot, in principle, be the cause for language impairment, because by definition, children with SLI have *specific* difficulties with language despite normal cognitive development. Although normal nonverbal cognition is an integral part of the definition of SLI, a recent meta-analysis found that children with SLI score on average 10 IQ points below TD children across studies (Gallinat & Spaulding, 2014). However, it has not been established that nonverbal scores in children with SLI predict severity of language impairment, suggesting that nonverbal cognition does not have an effect on language impairment in these children (Leonard, 1998).

Participants With ASD and With SLI: Verbal and Nonverbal Characteristics

Our comparative ASD-SLI study explored structural language in two groups of 6- to 12-year-old children. After reporting on recruitment criteria and clinical characteristics of the children who participated in the study, we present here results from general language and nonverbal cognition tests which were administered to each child. These results allowed us to identify proportions of children with ASD who had deficits in language, nonverbal cognition, or both.

Characteristics of the Children With ASD and the Children With SLI

We assessed language and nonverbal cognition in 40 children aged 6 to 12, 20 children with ASD (16 boys and four girls; age: $M = 8.7$, $SD = 1.9$) and 20 age-matched children with SLI (12 boys and eight girls; age: $M = 8.7$, $SD = 1.5$). Children were recruited via university teaching hospital centers specialized, respectively, in either autism diagnosis or language and learning disability diagnosis. The 20 children with ASD had been diagnosed according to the *International Classification of Diseases* (10th revision) criteria via the Autism Diagnostic Interview—Revised (Rutter, LeCouteur, & Lord, 2003) and diagnosis was confirmed by the Autism Diagnostic Observation Schedule, module 2 or 3 (Lord et al., 1989). All children had a minimum mean length of utterance (MLU) of 2.5, an inclusionary criterion to ensure that language tests could be administered.

No inclusionary criterion was set for IQ because one of our goals was to look at the nature of formal language in verbal children across the spectrum, and this measure indeed varied. Available nonverbal IQ measures[1] for these children categorized half

1 The tests were the Wechsler Intelligence Scale for Children (WISC), Wechsler Preschool and Primary Scale of Intelligence, Kaufman Assessment Battery for Children, or Differential Scales of Intellectual Efficiency, depending on the child. One 6-year-old child, unable to complete an IQ test, tested normal on RPM and was thus included in the average nonverbal range group.

of them (10 of 20) in the average range (90–110) and four in the low average range (80–89); two had borderline performance (70–79), two scored in the mild intellectual disability range (55–69), and scored two in the moderate intellectual disability range (40–54).[2]

The 20 children with SLI were diagnosed following usual exclusionary criteria, and thus, notably, they had normal nonverbal levels and ASD had been ruled out by psychiatric examination. At the time of diagnosis, all of these children were deemed to be impaired in both phonology and syntax, a constellation commonly referred to in the French clinical setting as *phonologico-syntactic SLI*.

These two target groups of children were compared with population norms for standardized tests and to three groups of TD children for the experimental task and for analysis of spontaneous language samples, 14 TD 4-year-olds (TD-4), 12 TD 6-year-olds (TD-6), and 12 TD 8-year-olds (TD-8).

Standardized Language Evaluation

The children in the ASD and SLI groups were assessed in three areas—vocabulary, phonology, and morphosyntax—with tools commonly used to evaluate language by speech-language pathologists in France. Vocabulary was evaluated via a classical picture pointing task ELOLA (Batterie d'évaluation du langage oral de l'enfant aphasique; De Agostini et al., 1998), which is a French adaptation of the short form of the British Picture Vocabulary Scale (Dunn & Dunn, 1997). Phonology was evaluated via a word repetition task (Khomsi, Khomsi, Parbeau-Guéno, & Pasquet, 2007), which consists of prerecorded words of increasing length and phonological complexity, some of which are unfamiliar to children and thus serve as quasi-nonwords, according to the authors of the test. Morphosyntax was evaluated with a sentence completion test (Khomsi et al., 2007). For all three of these tests, raw scores were converted into *z* scores to take into account population norms.

Performance on the standardized tests was remarkably similar in the ASD and SLI groups for vocabulary ($M = -1.2$, $SD = 1.3$ and $M = -0.7$, $SD = 1.3$, respectively, with $U = 151$, $p = .283$) and for morphosyntax ($M = -2.0$, $SD = 1.5$ and $M = -1.9$, $SD = 1.0$, respectively, with $U = 192$, $p = .840$). Similar proportions of children displayed impaired performance in these two areas: In both the ASD and the SLI groups, roughly 40% of the children scored below –1 SD for vocabulary and 80% below that cutoff in morphosyntax, and approximately 60% in each group below –1.65 SD. For phonology, although all of the children

2 Our group did not include any children with nonverbal IQ performance in the above average range, which is not particularly surprising because such children are rare (see Charman et al., 2011). Our group also did not include any children with severe/profound intellectual disability (<40), probably a consequence of the fact that we excluded children with an MLU below 2.5. See the Morphosyntactic Complexity section later in the chapter.

Tab. 6.1: ASD-LN and ASD-LI: Age and Standardized Language Score Means

	Age, years (SD)	Vocabulary (SD)	Phonology (SD)	Morphosyntax (SD)
ASD-LN (*n* = 6), 5 M + 1 F	8;7 (2;2)	−0.1 (0.4)	−0.1 (0.6)	−0.5 (0.8)
ASD-LI (*n* = 14), 11 M + 3 F	8;7 (2;0)	−1.6 (1.3)	−5.7 (4.4)	−2.6 (1.2)
SLI (*n* = 20), 12 M + 8 F	8;7 (1;5)	−0.7 (1.3)	−7.9 (5.3)	−1.9 (1.0)

Note: ASD-LI = autism spectrum disorder (ASD) group with language impairment; ASD-LN = ASD group with normal language; F = female; M = male; SLI = specific language impairment group.

with SLI displayed severe impairment (with *z* scores below –1.65 and a group mean of –7.9, *SD* = 5.3), only slightly over 60% of children with ASD (*M* = –4.0, *SD* = 4.5) did, and *z* scores were significantly lower in the SLI group than in the ASD group ($U = 104.5$, $p = .009$).

Performance of the children with ASD on these standardized tests indicates that the majority of them have severe language difficulties in at least one area. Adopting a cutoff of –1.65 SD (5th percentile), one often used in clinical settings in France (Ramus et al., 2003), 14 of 20 (70%) had very low performance in at least one area. We dubbed this subgroup of children the ASD group with language impairment (ASD-LI) and the group of children with ASD who had no score below this threshold as the ASD group with normal language (ASD-LN). All 20 of the children in the SLI group, by this criterion, were language impaired, including some with impairment in one area only, as in the ASD-LI group (see Table 6.1).

Statistical analyses for ASD-LI–ASD-LN differences, although highly significant, are not reported because the ASD-LN group consisted of only six children. Comparisons of ASD-LI–SLI performance differences reached borderline statistical significance for vocabulary ($U = 72.5$, $p = .033$) but were not significant for either phonology ($U = 104.5$, $p = .217$) or morphosyntax ($U = 88$, $p = .071$).

Evaluation of Nonverbal Cognition

Nonverbal cognition was evaluated via Raven's Progressive Matrices (RPM) for all children, in both the ASD and the SLI groups, because the particular IQ test for which results were available varied from child to child.[3] As expected given the variability in nonverbal IQ scores of the children in the ASD group (described earlier), perfor-

3 It has consistently been found that children with ASD have significantly higher RPM scores compared with scores on IQ tests such as the WISC (Dawson, Soulières, Gernsbacher, & Mottron, 2007). This result has been interpreted as either representing an isolated skill or showing that in more global tests like the WISC, cognitive processing abilities are tested along with social learning (Charman et al., 2011). The latter view would mean that RPM scores might in fact constitute a more accurate indication of cognitive level in this population.

mance on RPM varied considerably, and the two were in fact correlated (r_s = .696, *p* = .001). The average midpoint percentile for the group was 38.1, and the *SD* was quite high (28.2), with scores ranging from 2.5 to 92.5, including eight children who were at or below the 10th percentile.[4] The average midpoint percentile for the SLI group was 43.0, and variability was also high in this group (*SD* = 29.1), which included four children with scores at or below the 10th percentile (but who had normal non-verbal IQ scores). The range of RPM scores (2.5–90) was nearly identical to that in the ASD group, and no significant difference was found in RPM performance in the two groups (*U* = 152.0, *p* = .201), despite the difference in group means.

Phonological Complexity

As seen in the preceding sections, there is evidence that phonological complexity related to syllable structure may be an important source of difficulty for children with SLI. The standardized task used to assess phonology in this study is made up of items selected according to two criteria: syllable length and phonological complexity. Although these criteria are not particularly well balanced, this task enjoys a reputation among clinicians for its ability to detect impairment in children. The task contains two parts. The first part (short version, presented here) is standardized for young children and contains 32 items of various complexity and/or length (from two to seven syllables with a mean of 2.7 syllables).

Children's responses were recorded and transcribed in the IPA by two trained experts. Each item was coded for identical repetition (1= *item succeeded*, 0 = *item failed*), the number of errors produced, together with the syllable position and error type, for example, substitution (/kask/ "cap">/kasp/, ANE, SLI), metathesis (/eklips/ "eclipse">/eklisp/, ROD,[5] ASD-LI) and omission (/aeʁopɔʁ/ "airport"> /aeopɔʁ/, QUL, SLI). Mean overall correct word production in the SLI and ASD-LI groups did not significantly differ (means of 20.3and 16.3, respectively, out of 32 items; *U* = 100.5, *p* = .165). The performance of the ASD-LI group also was much lower than that of the ASD-LN group (means of 20.4 vs. 29.7 items correct).

Turning to production of individual phonemes, the children in the ASD-LI and SLI groups behaved similarly for consonants (82% and 70%; *U* = 84.5, *p* = .052) and sonorants (77% and 62%; *U* = 94.5, *p* = .111), but they differed in production of /s/ (91% vs. 63%; *U* = 69, *p* = .009). Production of vocalic sounds (glides and vowels) was at least 80% correct in the two groups, which did not differ for either type of sound (for glides, 86% and 81%, *U* = 120.5, *p* = .484 and for vowels, 91% and 89%, *U* = 116.5, *p* = .408).

---

4 Because the French norms for RPM provide percentiles only and because some raw scores may fall between two percentiles, midpoint percentiles were calculated for each child.

5 A three-letter code (e.g., ROD, QUL) was used to identify participants.

Sonorants were the most difficult type of phoneme for children in the ASD-LI group (mean of 77%, compared with 99% in the ASD-LN group). The syllabic status of sonorants is in fact particular. These sounds are acquired late and have the particularity of being able to associate with specific syllable positions, such as a branching onset or a coda position. Because there was no correlation between production of sonorants and age in the ASD-LI group ($r_s = .461$, $p = .096$), we can suppose that the source of difficulty of children with language impairment lies much more in the syllable structure than in the phonemic status of sonorants.

Syllable structure configurations led to a large number of repetition errors in the ASD-LI group and the SLI group. Our questions are whether there are particular syllable structures indicative of language impairment and whether these are similar for children in these two groups. It appears that structures that were produced below the rate of 60% by the children in the SLI group were also those for which the children in the ASD-LI group had the most difficulties, despite the fact that the general mean for the structures most subject to error in the SLI group (49%) was much lower than in the ASD-LI group (79%).

Interestingly, the difficulties observed in the children with language impairment, both those in the ASD-LI and in the SLI groups, always involved phonological complexity. Similar (low) production rates were found for a consonant in a complex syllabic position, such as liquids in a final cluster (e.g., /tɛʁmomɛt**ʁ**/: 57% for the ASD-LI and 40% for the SLI; $U = 106$, $p = .204$) and in internal coda position (e.g., /ɔ**ʁ**lɔʒ/: 74% vs. 57%; $U = 109.5$, $p = .272$), and obstruents in internal coda position (e.g., /tʁa**k**tœʁ/: 60% vs. 55%; $U = 125.5$, $p = .595$). However, the difficulties observed in the children in the ASD-LI group were not always the same as in the SLI group. In particular, whereas the children in the ASD-LI group had little or no difficulty producing /s/ in final clusters, the children in the SLI group did (e.g., /ka**s**k/: 79% vs. 45%; $U = 78$, $p = .020$); the same was true for branching liquids in polysyllabic items (e.g., the second /ʁ/ in /ʁef**ʁ**iʒeratœʁ/: 71% vs. 35%; $U = 89$, $p = .039$), and /s/ in appendix position (e.g., /**s**pɛktakl/: 86% vs. 40%; $U = 76$, $p = .009$). In short, some syllabic configurations were the cause of difficulties in both the ASD-LI and SLI groups (consonants in coda position), but other areas were specific to the children with SLI.

A subsequent question was whether the groups of children used the same strategies to avoid complexity. Two types of strategies were favored in each group: phonemic substitution (e.g., /albɔm/ > /albɔl/ (HEG, ASD-LI) and omission (e.g., /sɔʁti/ > /sɔti/ (JOC, ASD-LI). Rates were high in both groups and did not differ (substitution: 49.4% for ASD-LI and 39.5% for SLI, $U = 91$, $p = .086$; omission 43.8% and 50.3%, $U = 112.5$, $p = .335$). Other types of errors were marginal (< 7%), for example, addition (/ɔʁlɔʒ/ > /ɔʁlɔʁʒ/, FLC, SLI) and metathesis (/eklips/ > /eklisp/ ROD, ASD-LI).

The performance of the children in the ASD-LN group contrasted with that found in the ASD-LI group. They performed at 92% for the production of obstruents in internal coda position and for the production of final liquids in a consonant cluster, and at 100% on the other structures. In fact, the most incorrectly produced phonemes for this group were those located at the beginning of long words, regardless of complexity at the syllable level.

Morphosyntactic Complexity

Morphosyntactic complexity was explored via measures from a task eliciting production of pronominal clitics and from analysis of spontaneous language samples. In Zebib, Tuller, Prévost, and Morin (2013), we looked at elicited production of wh-questions and found that the same 20 children with ASD resembled the age-matched children with SLI. Like the children with SLI, they used the structure entailing the least complex derivation available in French (wh-in situ, as in, for example, "Tu gares la voiture **où?**" Literally, "You park the car **where**?" rather than something such as "**Où** *est-ce que tu gares la voiture?*" meaning, "**Where** do you park the car?") significantly more often than TD 6-year-olds. The children with ASD avoided complex derivations in this task to a lesser degree than the children with SLI did. This result is interesting because the wh-question production task that was reported on was designed to determine which of several alternative *grammatical* wh-question strategies in French is used more frequently when the child is given a stimulus eliciting production of a wh-question; it remains to be seen whether these children with ASD, and in particular the children in the ASD-LI group, avoid complex morphosyntax in other contexts, using other methods.

Elicited Production of Pronominal Clitics

As mentioned earlier, elicited production of pronominal clitics in French is a task that has consistently distinguished children (and adolescents) with SLI from TD French-speaking children. Nonreflexive direct object clitics, henceforth *accusative clitics*, in particular, are not only slow to emerge in young TD children (Hamann, Rizzi, & Frauenfelder, 1996; Zesiger et al., 2010), they are omitted or substituted by full noun phrases in children with SLI (Chillier et al., 2001; Jakubowicz et al., 1998), leading to ungrammaticality (in the case of omission) or discourse infelicity (in the case of production of a full noun phrase). Different accounts for the specific difficulty inherent in the derivation of sentences with accusative clitics have been put forth (Chillier et al., 2001; Grüter, 2006; Tuller, Delage, Monjauze, Piller, & Barthez, 2011). These have in common the idea that the syntactic computation entailed in such derivations is greater than in sentences without accusative clitics due to the appearance of the clitic in a position other than the thematic object position (i.e., preverbal instead of postverbal).

We used a classical picture-prompt-with-question task to elicit production of nominative, reflexive, and accusative clitics. The task contains 32 items, each one eliciting a nominative clitic [*elle* in (1b) and (1b′)] and either an accusative clitic ($n = 16$), as in (1b), or a reflexive clitic ($n = 16$), as in (1b′). We focus here exclusively on third-person clitics;

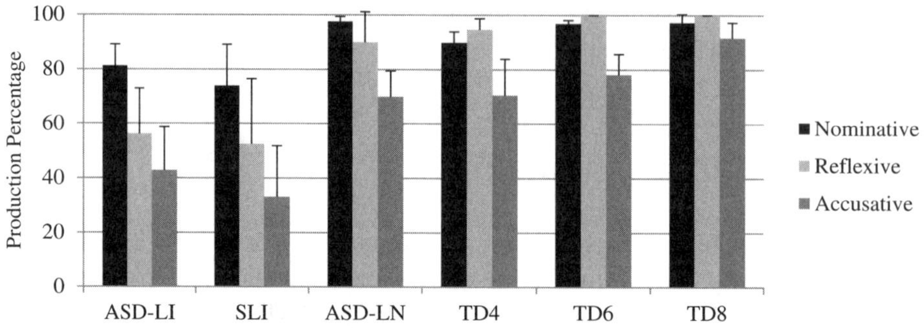

Fig. 6.1: Nominative, reflexive, and accusative clitic production rates: ASD-LI, SLI, ASD-LN, TD4, TD6, and TD8. ASD-LI = autism spectrum disorder (ASD) group with language impairment; ASD-LN = ASD group with normal language; SLI = specific language impairment; TD4, TD6, and TD8 = typically developing group, ages 4, 6, and 8 years, respectively.

expected responses are given in (1b) and in (1b′), and responses with object omission and a full noun phrase are given in (2a) and (2b), respectively.

1. *Experimenter*: a. Que fait Marie avec le chien?
what does Mary with the dog
"What's Mary doing to the dog?"
a′. Que fait Marie?
what does Mary
"What's Mary doing?"
Response: b. **Elle le** lave.
she ACC-Cl (3sm) washes
"She's washing it."
b′. **Elle se** lave
she REFL-Cl (3sm) washes
"She's washing herself."

2. a. Object omission (ungrammatical): Elle lave. "She's washing"
   b. Full noun phrase (discourse infelicitous): Elle lave le chien. "She's washing the dog"

Comparing rates for production of a clitic in nominative, reflexive, and accusative contexts (both correct clitic forms and clitic forms with incorrect gender), between the ASD and SLI groups,[6] Figure 6.1 shows that performance of the ASD-LN children in fact resembles that found in the groups of TD children, with nominative and reflexive clitics produced at basically equivalent rates, and accusative clitics slightly lower in the younger children (TD 4-year-olds; TD4). This contrasts with the performance of the ASD-LI group, which patterned nearly identically with the SLI group, with nominative clitics produced better than reflexive clitics and reflexive clitics better than accusative clitics.[7] The ASD-LI and SLI groups each performed significantly below even the TD4

6 All 20 children with SLI completed this task, but one child in the ASD-LN group (LUJ) did not because of an inability to cooperate. This child completed all other tasks reported in this chapter.

7 In the ASD-LI group, nominative clitics were significantly better produced than reflexive clitics ($Z = -2.665$, $p = .008$) and accusative clitics ($Z = -2.921$, $p = .016$).

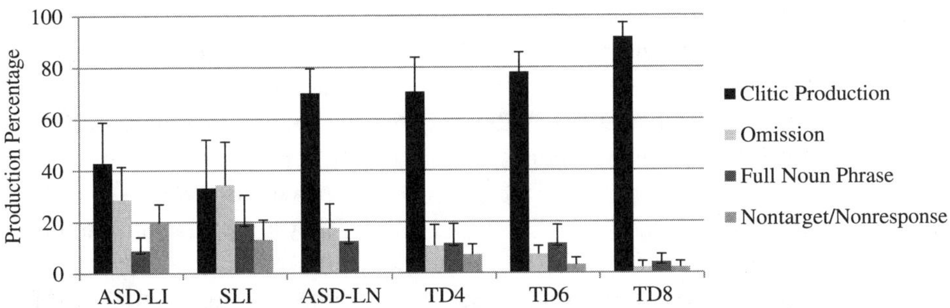

Fig. 6.2: Elicited production of accusative clitics: mean percentage of all response types. ASD-LI = autism spectrum disorder (ASD) group with language impairment; ASD-LN = ASD group with normal language; SLI = specific language impairment; TD4, TD6, and TD8 = typically developing group, ages 4, 6, and 8 years, respectively.

group for accusative clitics ($U = 64.5$, $p = .007$ and $U = 49.0$, $p = .024$, respectively) and well below the TD6 and TD8 groups, to which they are much closer in age (recall that the youngest children in the ASD and SLI groups were 6-year-olds, and the mean age in each group is 8;7).

Results have been reported recently suggesting that ASD-SLI similarities could be superficial and thus might disappear once error types are analyzed (Williams, Botting, & Boucher, 2008). Focusing on accusative clitics, which were the elements most subject to error and which have been proposed to constitute a robust marker of language impairment in French, responses other than clitic production consisted of object omission (see [2a]), full noun phrases (2b), and cases, labeled as *nontarget, nonresponse*). All groups produced both omission and full noun phrase responses, and although there was variation according to which of these strategies was used, omission was more frequent in the ASD-LI and SLI groups than in the TD groups (see Figure 6.2).[8]

The other type of nonclitic responses were those in which the child either did not supply a response (e.g., "I don't know") or in which the response given did not use the targeted (or related) verb (even after this was supplied with a second prompt), and thus the utterance did not contain an accusative clitic context (see Nontarget/ Nonresponse in Figure 6.2). The children in the ASD-LI group produced many non-target responses, as in (3), including some cases of echolalia (3b) and well as description of details of the drawing (3d). Although some of these nontarget responses would appear to be related to pragmatic impairment, nontarget (and nonresponses) were also found in the SLI group (and in the TD4 group).[9]

8 ASD-LI vs. TD4, $U = 55.5$, $p = .039$; SLI vs. TD4, $U = 85.0$, $p = .056$; ASD-LI vs. TD6, $U = 39.0$, $p = .020$; SLI vs. TD6, $U = 73.5$, $p = .070$; ASD-LI vs. TD8, $U = 24.0$, $p = .001$; SLI vs. TD8, $U = 51.0$, $p = .006$).

9 There were no responses of this type in the ASD-LN group, but recall that this group consisted of only five participants for this task (see Footnote 5).

3. Examples of nontarget responses (ASD-LI group)

a.	*Prompt:* Que fait le médecin avec le bébé? "What is doctor doing to the baby?"	*Expected response:* Il le pèse. "He's weighing him."
b.	Que fait le médecin avec le bébé?	(repetition of prompt; AUJ)
c.	Il faut voir comment il est lourd.	"We need to see how he's heavy." (ROD)
d.	Ils mettent des bougies	"They are getting out candles." (MAM)
e.	Il donne à manger un biberon.	"He's feeding a bottle." (WAE)
f.	Il pèse 100 kilos.	"He weighs 100 kilos." (BRR)

Although more children in the ASD-LI group produced at least one response of this type (11 of 14 = 79%), compared with the children in the SLI group (12 of 20 = 60%), the mean rates did not differ significantly between these groups (ASD-LI vs. SLI, $U = 98.0$, $p = .148$); the ASD-LI did produce significantly more of these responses than the TD4 ($U = 46.5$, $p = .016$), and this was not the case for the SLI group ($U = 110.5$ $p = .306$). In any event, eliminating these responses from all calculations would not have made the ASD-LI group more closely resemble the TD groups (as opposed to the SLI group).

Spontaneous Language Production Measures

Recent studies on spontaneous production in children with SLI have shown that these children tend to avoid constructions containing subordinate clauses, which involve numerous components of complexity, such as an increased number of dependencies between different elements in the sentence, the presence of an increased number of elements in the sentence, and an increased number of morphosyntactic operations (e.g., subject–verb agreement; Hamann, Tuller, Monjauze, Delage, & Henry, 2007; Scheidnes & Tuller, 2014). For example, in the sentence *Léa sait que Max habite à Paris* ("Lea knows that Max lives in Paris"), the main verb *sait* selects the embedded clause *que Max habite à Paris* and the mood of the embedded verb (indicative) depends on the selective properties of *savoir* ("know"). In addition, the sentence involves the overt complementizer *que* ("that"), and there are two subject–verb agreement operations, one in the main clause and one in the embedded clause. In sentences with a relative clause, such as *Léa a vu l'homme que le chien a mordu* ("Lea saw the man that the dog bit"), there is, in addition to subordination, a dependency between the head of the relative (*l'homme*) and the object position of the embedded verb *mordu*. It has also been reported that complex sentences produced by children with SLI tended to be more subject to error than those produced by age-matched TD children, as illustrated in (4) (from Hamann et al., 2007).

4. Et pis y a **une** (= un) sou qu'**il** est vraiment ron**de** (= rond) [Loris, age 6.9]
   "And, well, there is a coin that it is really round."

Spontaneous language samples lasting approximately 15 minutes were collected from each child. Exchanges between the child and the experimenter were initiated via a picture story, which the child was asked to tell (Khomsi & Nanty, 2001), followed by an open exchange on different themes, including an attempt to get the child to produce a narrative about a film, television show, book, or game. Each audio recording was transcribed and coded by at least two linguists via the Child Language Data Exchange System (MacWhinney, 2001), beginning at minute 5 until 60 utterances were reached. Spontaneous language samples from 17 of 20 children with ASD and 17 of 20 children with SLI were analyzable. The language in the samples obtained from three of the children with ASD (all from the ASD-LI group) was so sparse that analysis in terms of morphosyntactic measures would have been meaningless. Likewise, language samples of three of the children with SLI could not be analyzed, in this case because phonological deficits were so severe they were largely incomprehensible.

Each utterance was coded according to the types of clauses that it contained—namely, matrix clauses, coordinated clauses, complement clauses, adjunct clauses, and relative clauses. Moreover, each subordinate clause was coded for depth of embedding. Subordinate clauses which were not embedded in a matrix clause were coded as zero-level clauses [0], as in (5a). Subordinate clauses that were embedded in a matrix clause were labeled Level 1 clauses [1], as in (5b), clauses that were embedded within a Level 1 clause were coded Level 2 clauses [2], as in (5c), and so on (see Tuller et al., 2012).

5. a. [**That Max lives in Paris**] Level 0
   b. Lea knows [**that Max lives in Paris**] Level 1
   c. Lea knows [that everybody [thinks [**that Max lives in Paris**]]] Level 2

Use of subordination was examined via three measures: (a) rate of subordination (the total number of subordinate clauses over the total number of verbal utterances), (b) rate of complex utterances (the number of utterances containing a main clause and at least one embedded clause over the total number of verbal utterances), and (c) rate of deep embedding (the total number of clauses embedded at Level 2 or higher over the total number of subordinate clauses). The results on these measures are displayed in Table 6.2.

For both subordination and complex utterance rates, the performance of the ASD-LN group patterned with the TD children, in particular the TD6 group, and was higher than the performance of the ASD-LI and the SLI groups. Significant differences were found between the two language-impaired groups on the one hand, and the TD6 and TD8 groups on the other, for rate of subordination, but not for rate of complex utterances. Moreover, there was no difference between the children in the ASD-LI and SLI groups on either measure.

Deep embedding, which takes into account embedding within an embedded clause, was particularly low in the ASD-LI group, significantly lower than that found in all the other groups, including the SLI group ($U = 48$, $p = .033$; recall than no statistics were

Tab. 6.2: Means of Rate and Frequency of Subordination in Each Group

Group	Number of subordinate clauses (SD)	Rate of subordination (SD)	Number of complex utterances (SD)	Rate of complex utterances (SD)	Rate of deep embedding (SD)
ASD-LI	13.4 (7.7)	27.1%[a] (11.9)	9.3 (5.9)	18.4%[a] (9.4)	2.3%[a] (4.0)
SLI	12.9 (5.8)	28.4%[a] (13.6)	10.0 (4.0)	21.9%[a] (7.5)	10.0%[b] (9.7)
ASD-LN	17.2 (4.3)	32.0% (10.5)	13.8 (4.5)	25.7% (7.9)	8.3% (7.5)
TD4	14.0 (7.6)	29.8% (17.6)	11.0 (4.9)	23.1% (11.0)	11.2%[b] (10.2)
TD6	16.2 (6.3)	32.0%[b] (10.4)	13.0 (4.2)	25.9%[a] (8.5)	10.4%[b] (7.4)
TD8	18.6 (6)	36.3%[b] (11.6)	14.5 (4.8)	28.3%[a] (9.1)	12.4%[b] (6.8)

Note: Values with different superscripts within a particular column were significantly different ($p < .01$). Values with similar superscripts within a particular column were not significantly different. ASD-LI = autism spectrum disorder (ASD) group with language impairment; ASD-LN = ASD group with normal language; SLI = specific language impairment; TD4, TD6, and TD8 = typically developing group, ages 4, 6, and 8 years, respectively.

calculated for the ASD-LN children because of the small group size). Deep embedding was also less frequent in the SLI group than in the TD4 children and the TD8 children, albeit not statistically. Turning to the children with ASD and no language impairment, their performance was lower than that of the TD children, including the TD 4-year-olds. However, it is worth pointing out that the variability within each group was quite large. In particular, there were proportionally fewer children in the SLI group (11 of 17 = 65%) and the ASD-LI group (3 of 11 = 27.3%) who produced Level 2 embedding than in the ASD-LN group (4 of 5 = 80%). This suggests that some children with language impairment found it difficult to deal with (very) complex sentences. By comparison, the number (and percentage) of TD children who produced such utterances was 10 of 14 (71.4%) in the 4-year-olds, 10 of 12 (83.3%) in the 6-year-olds, and 11 of 12 (91.7%) in the 8-year-olds. So in terms of the ratio of children who produced deep embedding the ASD-LN group performed similarly to the TD6 group, which confirms the pattern observed so far.

Anticipating that more complex utterances should generate more errors in the children with language impairment, we compared the rate of erroneous verbal utterances in simple versus complex sentences (so monoclausals vs. multiclausals containing at least one error). Complex sentences led to more errors in all groups, including the TD children (although the proportion remained below 10% in the TD6 and TD8 children). Starting with simple utterances, the ASD-LN children produced fewer erroneous sentences than the two language-impaired groups, but they patterned more like the TD4 children (around 12% erroneous sentences) than the older TD children, for whom the error rate was below 1%. A similarly high error rate was found in simple utterances produced by the children with ASD-LI (27.2%) and the children with SLI (24.4%; $U = 100$, $p = .468$). In complex utterances, the error rate was once again highest in the ASD-LI children (50.6%) and the children with SLI (51.8%; $U = 90.5$, $p = .890$), but the performance of the ASD-LN children was not too far

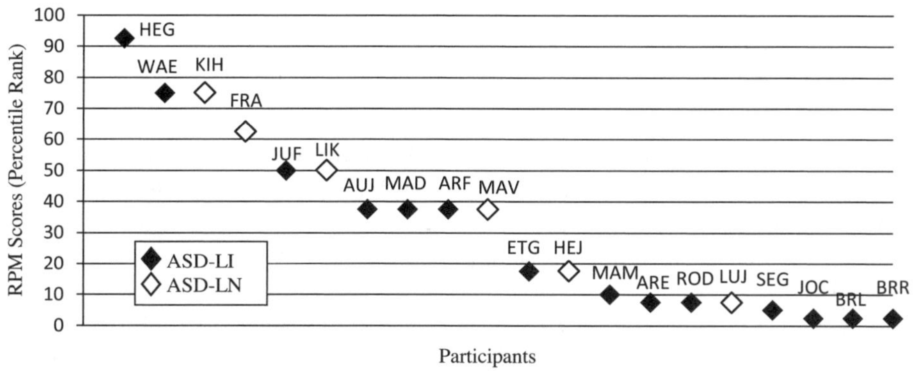

Fig. 6.3: Raven's Progressive Matrices (RPM) scores (percentile rank): autism spectrum disorder (ASD) group with language impairment (ASD-LI; $n = 14$) and ASD group with normal language (ASD-LN; $n = 6$). The three-letter codes identify individual participants.

below (41.5%). This rate was higher than what was found in the TD4 group (30.3%), suggesting that the children with ASD-LN, although they had much less difficulty producing complex utterances than the two language-impaired groups, as seen earlier, when they did produce such sentences, many of them made at least one error.

Nonverbal Cognition and Language Performance

Previous studies investigating whether language is affected by nonverbal cognition in children with ASD have yet to provide a (complete) answer to this question, in part because they have not looked specifically at structural aspects of language, and in particular formal language complexity (see the Background section earlier in the chapter), in relation to nonverbal cognition. The variability in nonverbal cognitive levels in the ASD group (see the Participants With ASD and With SLI: Verbal and Nonverbal Characteristics section earlier in the chapter) allowed us to explore the possible impact of nonverbal cognition on these children's language performance. Comparing, first of all, the ASD-LI group to the ASD-LN group, Figure 6.3 shows that both groups include children with scores above the 50th percentile and below the 10th percentile. Although the ASD-LI mean (27.5) was much lower than that of the ASD-LN (41.7), variability was high in both groups (*SDs* of 28.9 and 26.0, respectively).[10] Likewise, the ASD-LI group had lower performance on RPM compared with the SLI group ($M = 43.0$, $SD = 29.1$), although this difference did not reach significance ($U = 92.0$, $p = .090$).

Does nonverbal cognition determine the severity of language impairment for children in the ASD-LI group, and, more generally, in the ASD group as a whole, are

---

10 Statistical analysis was not performed because of the small number of children in the ASD-LN group ($n = 6$).

there links between nonverbal scores and language scores? To answer these questions, we calculated Spearman's rank correlation coefficients (r_s) between RPM scores and key language variables, within the ASD group, and within the ASD-LI group, compared with the SLI group.

Within the ASD group, no significant correlations were found between RPM and standardized language scores. Likewise, within the ASD-LI group, severity of language impairment in vocabulary, phonology or morphosyntax, as measured by global standardized scores, was not significantly linked with RPM. This was also true for the SLI group.

In general, the phonological measures were not correlated with RPM in any of the three groups. This is the case for global scores for identical word repetition on the phonology task, as for measures on phonemic productions (e.g., sonorants: ASD $r_s = .374, p = .104$; ASD-LI $r_s = .413, p = .142$; SLI $r_s = -.184, p = .437$) or on syllable structures (e.g., Final s + C cluster: ASD $r_s = -.019, p = .936$; ASD-LI $r_s = -.126, p = .666$; SLI $r_s = -.026, p = .910$).[11]

There were basically no significant correlations between measures of morphosyntactic complexity and RPM scores. In particular, the measures that distinguished the SLI and ASD-LI groups from the TD groups (but not from each other)—namely, accusative clitic production, accusative clitic omission, rate of subordination, and frequency of subordination did not correlate with RPM scores. It was not the case, for example, that children with higher RPM produced more accusative clitics or that children with lower RPM produced fewer embedded clauses, in any of the groups.[12]

Discussion

The objective of this chapter was to explore formal aspects of language in French-speaking children with ASD. We adopted a comparative approach with SLI because similarities between language difficulties in ASD and SLI have been reported in the literature (Kjelgaard & Tager-Flusberg, 2001; Rapin & Dunn, 2003; Roberts et al.,

---

11 Surprising correlations were found for three phonological measures in the ASD and ASD-LI groups but not in the SLI group (production of /s/: ASD $r_s = .516, p = .019$; ASD-LI $r_s = .516, p = .059$; appendix /s/: ASD $r_s = .495, p = .026$; ASD-LI $r_s = .562, p = .036$; and final liquids: ASD $r_s = .589, p = .006$; ASD-LI $r_s = .642, p = .013$). These results are not phonologically coherent, and when they are examined in detail, it appears that, with the exception of two children, the children with ASD produced the elements in question quite consistently. When these outliers are excluded, the significant correlations disappear, suggesting that what was originally found was not due to a real effect of nonverbal ability on phonological production in children with ASD.

12 The only measure of elicited production of pronominal clitics that was significantly correlated with RPM was the mean proportion of nontarget or nonresponses. In the ASD-LI group, children with lower nonverbal levels tended to produce more responses of this type (recall that no ASD-LN produced responses of this type). However, when one outlier is excluded (who had a RPM score of 2.5 and produced 50% nontarget or nonresponses), the correlation is no longer significant ($r_s = -.459, p = .115$).

2004; Tager-Flusberg, 2006). In particular, we looked at potential areas of difficulty from the perspective of derivational complexity, which poses difficulties to children with SLI, both in phonology and morphosyntax. These difficulties often result in the use of avoidance strategies and errors.

Comparison of a group of 20 children with ASD aged 6 to 12 and a group of 20 age-matched children with SLI on different standardized measures of vocabulary, phonology, and morphology revealed that although all the children with SLI had at least one *z* score below the pathology threshold of –1.65 *SD*, 14 of 20 children with ASD did and six did not. This suggests that not all of these children with ASD have language impairment, which echoes recent findings on young English-speaking children with ASD (Tek et al., 2014). This difference led us to split the ASD group in two subgroups, a group of children with language impairment (ASD-LI), and a group of children with normal language (ASD-LN). These two groups were compared with the children with SLI on various measures of complexity, including syllable structure, production of object clitics, and production of embedded clauses. For all of these measures, it was found that the children with ASD and language impairment, as identified via their results on the standardized tests, tended to perform similarly to the children with SLI, below what was observed in TD children aged 4 to 8 (when comparisons included such children). In contrast, the children with ASD-LN behaved differently from the children with ASD-LI, and their performance resembled that of TD children.

Phonology was examined via the children's performance on a standardized word repetition task. It was found that the children in the ASD-LI group (and the children with SLI) were particularly sensitive to consonants in syllable final position, notably liquids and obstruents in internal coda position. Both groups of language-impaired children were found to use the same strategies to avoid syllabic complexity, such as omission of a segment. These results confirm Riches et al.'s (2011) findings that syllabic structure is problematic for adolescents with ASD and language impairment (see also Paul et al., 2011, on very young children with ASD). It is also worth pointing out that despite the fact that most children in the ASD-LI group performed poorly on the word repetition task, some did not, and thus had no problems producing words with complex syllable structure. According to the results on the standardized tests, 12 children had *z* scores below the –1.65 *SD* threshold in both phonology and morphosyntax, two had low scores in phonology only, with *z* scores in morphosyntax above –1.65 *SD*, and two had low scores in morphosyntax only, with normal *z* scores on phonology. In addition to these two children, three others repeated words correctly over 84% of the time.[13] This raises the question of subtypes of language impairment, in both ASD-LI and SLI groups, and their relative frequency: It seems reasonable to conclude that, as in SLI, in ASD-LI, it may be the case that both morphosyntax and phonology may be affected

13 However, these children had low *z* scores on the word repetition task because of their age (over 8.6). This task is particularly sensitive to errors produced by older children because TD children make almost no errors by age 8.

in some children, whereas in other children, only morphosyntax (or only phonology) may be impaired. Our study lends support to the conclusion that phonology may be impaired in ASD; future studies must tackle the question of just how often this is the case.

In morphosyntax, we looked at production of pronominal clitics and clausal embedding. Pronominal clitics are particularly interesting to explore in children with ASD because avoidance of object clitics have been identified as a clinical marker of SLI (see Jakubowicz & Tuller, 2008). Our results on an elicited production task showed that object clitics did indeed pose difficulties to the children with ASD deemed to have language impairment. Their performance was similar to that of the children with SLI and lower than that of the TD children. In contrast, the children with ASD-LN tended to produce object clitics at rates comparable to the TD groups.[14] The similarity in performance on the production of object clitics by the children in the ASD-LI and SLI groups extends to the errors that were produced. In particular, both groups were found to omit the object clitic to a relatively large extent, although the children in the ASD-LI group tended to use slightly more nontarget responses than the children with SLI (but not significantly more so). In their study on production of present tense in English-speaking children with ASD, Roberts et al. (2004) found that despite similarly low production rates of *–s* in the children with ASD and the children with SLI, the two groups of children differed in terms of the errors that they committed. In particular, the children with ASD produced many more nontarget answers than the children with SLI (e.g., "What does a cowboy do?" "He's a hero" instead of, e.g., "He rides a horse"), which led Williams et al. (2008) to propose that the overlap between ASD and SLI is superficial and that different underlying deficits are involved, with impairment in ASD mainly affecting pragmatics. In our study, some children in the ASD-LI group used nontarget answers quite consistently, but some children with SLI used such answers as well, and with comparable proportions. It is therefore difficult to conclude that the performance of the children with ASD-LI in our elicitation task of pronominal clitics is evidence of a pragmatic deficit. Moreover, our experimental battery did not include evaluation of the children's pragmatic abilities, so we were unable to determine whether those children who used nontarget answers had (more severe) pragmatic deficits. Because pragmatics can play a role in the performance of children with ASD on language tasks (see Zebib et al., 2013), pragmatic skills should be evaluated in explo-

14 Terzi et al. (2014) reported that a group of high-functioning LN 5- to 8-year-old Greek-speaking children with ASD performed significantly lower than vocabulary-matched TD children specifically on object clitics and suggested that this might be due to difficulties in syntax-pragmatics or syntax-phonology interfaces. Their mean performance was 88.3%, considerably higher than the production rate of our French-speaking ASD-LI group (43%), making it doubtful that interface considerations alone could be responsible for the latter, although the performance of our ASD-LN group (70%) could conceivably be attributed to such factors.

rations of the language abilities of children with ASD (e.g., see chapters in this volume by Norbury [Chapter 1], Bavin & Baker [Chapter 2], and Eigsti & Schuh [Chapter 9]).

In spontaneous production, the ASD-LI group patterned once again with the SLI group on measures of clausal embedding, such as rate of subordination and rate of complex utterances, with lower performances compared with the children in the ASD-LN group and the TD children. The ASD-LI group and the SLI group also had similarly high levels of erroneous complex sentences. These results suggest that both groups of children had problems including elements of increasing complexity in their utterances: Either they tended to avoid embedding or when they attempted it, the result was the production of errors. In their study on repetition of complex sentences by adolescents with ASD and language impairment (mean age 15.3), Riches et al. (2010) also reported a significant impact of complexity on language production. The participants with ASD were found to have particular difficulties repeating object relative clauses, the most complex sentences of the repetition task used, compared with subject relative clauses, which are less complex. However, they also found that their comparative group of age-matched children with SLI had even more problems with object relatives than the adolescents with ASD, which was attributed to impaired working memory abilities in SLI. In our study, the SLI group did not perform worse than the children in the ASD-LI group on any measure of complexity, in either spontaneous production or elicited production of pronominal clitics. However, the two studies differed in two major respects: the age of the participants (our study involved younger subjects, mean age 8;7) and the language tasks that were used. It could be the case that sentence repetition, while tapping morphosyntactic competence, is particularly demanding in terms of memory capacities compared with elicited production of pronouns or spontaneous production.

The one measure on which the children in the ASD-LI and SLI groups were found to differ was deep embedding. The performance of the children in the ASD-LI group was particularly poor. Only two of 14 children in the ASD-LI group produced constructions involving deep embedding, compared with 11 of 17 children with SLI. This difference may be due to the fact that children in the ASD-LI group have even greater difficulties with derivational complexity than children with SLI. However, both groups of children displayed similar behavior on all the other morphosyntactic measures of complexity that we looked at. Another possibility is that some of the children in the ASD-LI group had difficulties sustaining a conversation due to general communication impairment. In some cases, it was extremely difficult to get these children talk about anything and produce utterances consisting of more than minimal information. This differed from the vast majority of the children with SLI, who seemed to have no problem engaging in a conversation. This suggests that the poor performance on deep embedding by the children in the ASD-LI group may not be a true reflection of their linguistic competence. At this point, it is important to reiterate that morphosyntactic abilities in children with ASD should be investigated from a variety of experimental perspectives, such as the ones mentioned earlier.

One of the goals of this study was to examine the impact of nonverbal cognition on performance for structural aspects of language in children with ASD. We thus included children with a wide range of nonverbal cognitive levels, as ascertained by nonverbal IQ scores. Using midpoint percentile scores for RPM as the common measure for nonverbal cognition, we compared the ASD-LI and ASD-LN subgroups with each to other, and we looked for correlations with language measures. The two ASD subgroups did not differ for RPM scores, suggesting that overall language impairment, as determined by standardized language scores, is not determined by nonverbal cognition. This result, however, must be interpreted with caution because scores in both groups were highly variable and because the ASD-LN group contained only six children. We therefore also looked at whether specific language scores were linked to RPM scores. For each of the relevant measures of phonological complexity and morphosyntactic complexity, no significant correlation was found either within the ASD-LI group or within the entire ASD group; this was also the case for the SLI group.

These results appear to contradict some previous studies showing links between nonverbal levels and language levels in children with ASD. These studies have shown, for example, that nonverbal cognition positively predicts later language abilities in children with ASD (Anderson et al., 2007; Weismer & Kover, 2015). It should be noted that these previous studies included children with ASD who had a full range of verbal abilities, including children with minimal or no language. For example, Weismer and Kover (2015) demonstrated that nonverbal cognition at age 2.5 years was a significant predictor of whether a child would remain minimally verbal at age 5.5 years as opposed to having high language proficiency (see also studies such as Kjelgaard & Tager-Flusberg, 2001, which found that children able to complete the CELF battery had significantly higher IQ scores than those who did not). Our study was quite different in nature. The central concern of ASD–SLI comparative studies is about the other children with ASD—those who are neither minimally verbal nor have high language proficiency. Our result regarding a lack of a link between nonverbal cognition and language is, in other words, a function of the fact that our study was devoted exclusively to verbal children who produced sentences (minimum MLU 2.5).

We also sought to explore links between nonverbal cognition and specific aspects of linguistic competence, the ability to manipulate formal aspects of language, and, in particular, measures of phonological and morphosyntactic complexity. This is in contrast to some of the nonverbal cognition-language links reported in previous studies, which are related to vocabulary measures (Kjelgaard & Tager-Flusberg, 2001) or to very general language measures such as those tested by the verbal subtests of intelligence tests (Anderson et al., 2007). In contrast, our result that formal language measures do not correlate with nonverbal cognition supports some of the results of studies that specifically looked at measures of complex language and nonverbal cognition. Condouris, Meyer, and Tager-Flusberg (2003) found that nonverbal IQ was not significantly correlated with MLU in spontaneous language samples in 44 English-speaking children aged 4 to 14. Roberts et al. (2004) found that correct production of the past tense in English-speaking children with ASD was no different in children with normal versus low nonverbal IQ, although a difference in error type was found such that children with low nonverbal levels tended to omit past tense marking on irregular verbs. In contrast to the latter result, omission of accusative clitics was not significantly correlated with nonverbal level in our study.

We believe that the jury is definitely still out regarding the impact of nonverbal cognition on language in verbal children with ASD. Our study appears to show that severity of language impairment is not determined by nonverbal cognition in these children, although these findings clearly need replicating in larger groups of children.

The major concern of this chapter has been the ASD-LI–SLI comparison: To what extent is impairment on formal aspects of language similar in these two groups? To make this comparison, we first of all separated out the children with ASD who had normal language performance in these areas. Perhaps because the children with ASD were recruited in hospital ASD centers, the proportion of the latter children was much lower (six of 20), making intergroup statistical comparisons including this group impossible. Although these children did perform quite differently from the ASD-LI children on all of the complexity measures, they sometimes patterned like the TD 4-year-olds, other times like TD 6-year-olds or TD 8-year-olds. Although replication of this study with ASD groups of equivalent size is needed, the current results suggest that at least some of the ASD-SLI similarities in language performance may be due to different underlying deficits (e.g., rates of deep embedding in spontaneous language), while others would appear to be of the same nature (e.g., specific deficits in phonological complexity). Whether observed similarities could be due to significant incidence of ASD-SLI comorbidity remains an open question (see Norbury, Chapter 1, this volume).

Overall, the results presented here reinforce some previous results on structural language in children with ASD, which have largely been restricted to English-speaking children. They also emphasize the importance of targeting complex language to advance our understanding of language abilities in ASD and their relation to nonverbal cognition.

References

American Psychiatric Association. (2013). *Diagnostic and statistical manual of mental disorders* (5th ed.). Washington, DC: Author.

Anderson, D. K., Lord, C., Risi, S., DiLavore, P. S., Shulman, C., Thurm, A., . . . Pickles, A. (2007). Patterns of growth in verbal abilities among children with autism spectrum disorder. *Journal of Consulting and Clinical Psychology*, *75*, 594–604. http://dx.doi.org/10.1037/0022-006X.75.4.594

Archibald, L. M. D., & Gathercole, S. E. (2006). Nonword repetition: A comparison of tests. *Journal of Speech, Language, and Hearing Research*, *49*, 970–983. http://dx.doi.org/10.1044/1092-4388(2006/070)

Barger, B. D., Campbell, J. M., & McDonough, J. D. (2013). Prevalence and onset of regression within autism spectrum disorders: A meta-analytic review. *Journal of Autism and Developmental Disorders*, *43*, 817–828. http://dx.doi.org/10.1007/s10803-012-1621-x

Bartak, L., Rutter, M., & Cox, A. (1975). A comparative study of infantile autism and specific developmental language disorder. I. The children. *British Journal of Psychiatry*, *126*, 127–145. http://dx.doi.org/10.1192/bjp.126.2.127

Bartolucci, G., & Pierce, S. J. (1977). A preliminary comparison of phonological development in autistic, normal, and mentally retarded subjects. *British Journal of Disorders of Communication*, *12*, 137–147. http://dx.doi.org/10.3109/13682827709011317

Bishop, D. V. (2010). Overlaps between autism and language impairment: Phenomimicry or shared etiology? *Behavior Genetics*, *40*, 618–629. http://dx.doi.org/10.1007/s10519-010-9381-x

Bishop, D. V., Maybery, M., Wong, D., Maley, A., Hill, W., & Hallmayer, J. (2004). Are phonological processing deficits part of the broad autism phenotype? *American Journal of Medical Genetics*, *128B*, 54–60. http://dx.doi.org/10.1002/ajmg.b.30039

Botting, N., & Conti-Ramsden, G. (2003). Autism, primary pragmatic difficulties, and specific language impairment: Can we distinguish them using psycholinguistic markers? *Developmental Medicine and Child Neurology*, *45*, 515–524. http://dx.doi.org/10.1111/j.1469-8749.2003.tb00951.x

Charman, T., Pickles, A., Simonoff, E., Chandler, S., Loucas, T., & Baird, G. (2011). IQ in children with autism spectrum disorders: Data from the Special Needs and Autism Project (SNAP). *Psychological Medicine*, *41*, 619–627. http://dx.doi.org/10.1017/S0033291710000991

Chillier, L., Arabatzi, M., Baranzini, L., Cronel-Ohayon, S., Deonna, T., Dubé, S., . . . Zesiger, P. (2001, December). The acquisition of French pronouns in normal children and in children with specific language impairment (SLI). *Proceedings of Early Lexicon Acquisition (ELA)* [CDRom], Lyon, France.

Condouris, K., Meyer, E., & Tager-Flusberg, H. (2003). The relationship between standardized measures of language and measures of spontaneous speech in children with autism. *American Journal of Speech-Language Pathology*, *12*, 349–358. http://dx.doi.org/10.1044/1058-0360(2003/080)

Dawson, M., Soulières, I., Gernsbacher, M. A., & Mottron, L. (2007). The level and nature of autistic intelligence. *Psychological Science*, *18*, 657–662. http://dx.doi.org/10.1111/j.1467-9280.2007.01954.x

De Agostini, M., Metz-Lutz, M.-N., Van Hout, A., Chavance, M., Deloche, G., Pavao-Martins, I., & Dellatolas, G. (1998). Batterie d'évaluation du langage oral de l'enfant aphasique (ELOLA): Standardisation française (4–12 ans) [Spoken language evaluation battery for children with aphasia: French language standardization (4–12 years)]. *Revue de Neuropsychologie*, *8*, 319–367.

Dunn, L. M., & Dunn, L. M. (1997). *Peabody Picture Vocabulary Test* (3rd ed.). Circle Pines, MN: American Guidance Service.

Durrleman, S., Hippolyte, L., Zufferey, S., Iglesias, K., & Hadjikhani, N. (2015). Complex syntax in autism spectrum disorders: A study of relative clauses. *International Journal of Language & Communication Disorders*, *50*, 260–267. http://dx.doi.org/10.1111/1460-6984.12130

Durrleman, S., & Zufferey, S. (2013). Investigating complex syntax in autism. In S. Stavrakaki, P. Konstantinopoulou, & M. Lalioti (Eds.), *Advances in language acquisition* (pp. 405–415). Cambridge, England: Cambridge Scholars.

Eigsti, I. M., & Bennetto, L. (2009). Grammaticality judgments in autism: Deviance or delay. *Journal of Child Language, 36*, 999–1021. http://dx.doi.org/10.1017/S0305000909009362

Eigsti, I. M., Bennetto, L., & Dadlani, M. B. (2007). Beyond pragmatics: Morphosyntactic development in autism. *Journal of Autism and Developmental Disorders, 37*, 1007–1023. http://dx.doi.org/10.1007/s10803-006-0239-2

Ferré, S., dos Santos, C., & de Almeida, L. (2015). Potential clinical markers for SLI in bilingual children. In E. Grillo & K. Jepson (Eds.), *Proceedings of the 39th Annual Boston University Conference on Language Development* (pp. 152–164). Somerville, MA: Cascadilla Press.

Ferré, S., Tuller, L., Sizaret, E. A., & Barthez, M.-A. (2012). Acquiring and avoiding phonological complexity in SLI vs. typical development of French: The case of consonant clusters. In P. Hoole, L. Bombien, M. Pouplier, C. Mooshammer, & B. Kühnert (Eds.), *Consonant clusters and structural complexity* (pp. 285–309). Berlin, Germany: De Gruyter.

Gallinat, E., & Spaulding, T. J. (2014). Differences in the performance of children with specific language impairment and their typically developing peers on nonverbal cognitive tests: A meta-analysis. *Journal of Speech, Language, and Hearing Research, 57*, 1363–1382. http://dx.doi.org/10.1044/2014_JSLHR-L-12-0363

Gallon, N., Harris, J., & van der Lely, H. (2007). Non-word repetition: An investigation of phonological complexity in children with Grammatical SLI. *Clinical Linguistics & Phonetics, 21*, 435–455. http://dx.doi.org/10.1080/02699200701299982

Grandgeorge, M., Hausberger, M., Tordjman, S., Deleau, M., Lazartigues, A., & Lemonnier, E. (2009). Environmental factors influence language development in children with autism spectrum disorders. *PLoS ONE, 4*, e4683. http://dx.doi.org/10.1371/journal.pone.0004683

Grüter, T. (2006). *Object clitics and null objects in the acquisition of French* (Unpublished doctoral dissertation). McGill University, Montreal, Quebec, Canada.

Hamann, C., Rizzi, L., & Frauenfelder, U. (1996). On the acquisition of the pronominal system in French. In H. Clahsen (Ed.), *Generative approaches to first and second language acquisition* (pp. 309–334). Amsterdam, The Netherlands: Benjamins.

Hamann, C., Tuller, L., Monjauze, C., Delage, H., & Henry, C. (2007). (Un)successful subordination in French-speaking children and adolescents with SLI. In H. Caunt-Nulton, S. Kulatilake, & I. Woo (Eds.), *Proceedings of the 31st Annual Boston University Conference on Language Development* (pp. 286–297). Somerville, MA: Cascadilla Press.

Howlin, P. (1984). The acquisition of grammatical morphemes in autistic children: A critique and replication of the findings of Bartolucci, Pierce, and Streiner, 1980. *Journal of Autism and Developmental Disorders, 14*, 127–136. http://dx.doi.org/10.1007/BF02409656

Howlin, P. (2003). Outcome in high-functioning adults with autism with and without early language delays: Implications for the differentiation between autism and Asperger syndrome. *Journal of Autism and Development Disorders, 33*, 3–13. http://dx.doi.org/10.1023/A:1022270118899

Jakubowicz, C., Nash, L., Rigaut, C., & Gérard, C.-L. (1998). Determiners and clitic pronouns in French-speaking children with SLI. *Language Acquisition, 7*, 113–160. http://dx.doi.org/10.1207/s15327817la0702-4_3

Jakubowicz, C., & Tuller, L. (2008). Specific language impairment in French. In D. Ayoun (Ed.), *Studies in French applied linguistics* (pp. 97–134). Amsterdam, The Netherlands: Benjamins.

Kelley, E., Paul, J. J., Fein, D., & Naigles, L. R. (2006). Residual language deficits in optimal outcome children with a history of autism. *Journal of Autism and Developmental Disorders, 36*, 807–828. http://dx.doi.org/10.1007/s10803-006-0111-4

Khomsi, A., Khomsi, J., Parbeau-Guéno, A., & Pasquet, F. (2007). *Bilan informatisé de langage oral au Cycle III et au collège (BILO3C)* [Computerized Schedule for Oral Language for Level III and for College]. Paris, France: Editions du CPA.

Khomsi, A., & Nanty, I. (2001). *Evaluation des Compétences Linguistiques au Collège (ECL–C)* [Evaluation of linguistic competency for college]. Paris, France: Editions du CPA.

Kjelgaard, M. M., & Tager-Flusberg, H. (2001). An investigation of language impairment in autism: Implications for genetic subgroups. *Language and Cognitive Processes*, *16*, 287–308. http://dx.doi.org/10.1080/01690960042000058

Leonard, L. B. (1998). *Children with specific language impairment.* Cambridge, MA: MIT Press.

Lord, C., & Paul, R. (1997). Language and communication in autism. In D. J. Cohen & P. R. Volkmar (Eds.), *Handbook of autism and pervasive developmental disorders* (pp. 195–225). New York, NY: Wiley.

Lord, C., Rutter, M., Goode, S., Heemsbergen, J., Jordan, H., Mawhood, L., & Schopler, E. (1989). Autism diagnostic observation schedule: A standardized observation of communicative and social behavior. *Journal of Autism and Developmental Disorders*, *19*, 185–212. http://dx.doi.org/10.1007/BF02211841

MacWhinney, B. (2001). *The CHILDES project: Tools for analyzing talk* (3rd ed.). Mahwah, NJ: Erlbaum.

McCleery, J. P., Tully, L., Slevc, L. R., & Schreibman, L. (2006). Consonant production patterns of young severely language-delayed children with autism. *Journal of Communication Disorders*, *39*, 217–231. http://dx.doi.org/10.1016/j.jcomdis.2005.12.002

Orsolini, M., Sechi, E., Maronato, C., Bonvino, E., & Corcelli, A. (2001). Nature of phonological delay in children with specific language impairment. *International Journal of Language & Communication Disorders*, *36*, 63–90. http://dx.doi.org/10.1080/13682820150217572

Paradis, J. (2004). The relevance of specific language impairment in understanding the role of transfer in second language acquisition. *Applied Psycholinguistics*, *25*, 67–82. http://dx.doi.org/10.1017/S0142716404001043

Paul, R., Fuerst, Y., Ramsay, G., Chawarska, K., & Klin, A. (2011). Out of the mouths of babes: Vocal production in infant siblings of children with ASD. *Journal of Child Psychology and Psychiatry*, *52*, 588–598. http://dx.doi.org/10.1111/j.1469-7610.2010.02332.x

Perovic, A., Modyanova, N., & Wexler, K. (2013). Comprehension of reflexive and personal pronouns in children with autism: A syntactic or pragmatic deficit? *Applied Psycholinguistics*, *34*, 813–835. http://dx.doi.org/10.1017/S0142716412000033

Prévost, P., Tuller, L., Scheidnes, M., Ferré, S., & Haiden, M. (2010). Computational complexity effects in the acquisition of wh-questions in child L2 French. In P. Guijarro-Fuentes & L. Domínguez (Eds.), *New directions in language acquisition: Romance languages in the generative perspective* (pp. 415–443). Newcastle upon Tyne, England: Cambridge Scholars.

Ramus, F., Rosen, S., Dakin, S. C., Day, B. L., Castellote, J. M., White, S., & Frith, U. (2003). Theories of developmental dyslexia: Insights from a multiple case study of dyslexic adults. *Brain: A Journal of Neurology*, *126*, 841–865. http://dx.doi.org/10.1093/brain/awg076

Rapin, I., & Dunn, M. (2003). Update on the language disorders of individuals on the autistic spectrum. *Brain & Development*, *25*, 166–172. http://dx.doi.org/10.1016/S0387-7604(02)00191-2

Rapin, I., Dunn, M. A., Allen, D. A., Stevens, M. C., & Fein, D. (2009). Subtypes of language disorders in school-age children with autism. *Developmental Neuropsychology*, *34*, 66–84 [correction appears in *Developmental Neuropsychology*, *34*, 223]. http://dx.doi.org/10.1080/87565640802564648

Rice, M. L. (2004). Growth models of developmental language disorders. In M. L. Rice & S. F. Warren (Eds.), *Developmental language disorders: From phenotypes to etiologies* (pp. 207–240). Mahwah, NJ: Erlbaum.

Riches, N. G., Loucas, T., Baird, G., Charman, T., & Simonoff, E. (2010). Sentence repetition in adolescents with specific language impairments and autism: An investigation of complex syntax. *International Journal of Language & Communication Disorders, 45*, 47–60. http://dx.doi.org/10.3109/13682820802647676

Riches, N. G., Loucas, T., Baird, G., Charman, T., & Simonoff, E. (2011). Non-word repetition in adolescents with specific language impairment and autism plus language impairments: A qualitative analysis. *Journal of Communication Disorders, 44*, 23–36. http://dx.doi.org/10.1016/j.jcomdis.2010.06.003

Roberts, J., Rice, M. L., & Tager-Flusberg, H. (2004). Tense marking in children with autism. *Applied Psycholinguistics, 25*, 429–448. http://dx.doi.org/10.1017/S0142716404001201

Rutter, M., Le Couteur, A., & Lord, C. (2003). *Autism Diagnostic Interview—Revised.* Los Angeles, CA: Western Psychological Services.

Scheidnes, M. (2012). *Development of child L2 French: What is typical?* (Unpublished doctoral dissertation). François Rabelais University, Tours, France.

Scheidnes, M., & Tuller, L. (2014). L2 children embed normally, but children with SLI do not. In J. Costa, A. Fiéis, M. J. Freitas, M. Lobo, & A. L. Santos (Eds.), *New directions in the acquisition of romance languages: Selected proceedings of the Romance Turn V* (pp. 261–284). Newcastle upon Tyne, England: Cambridge Scholars.

Tager-Flusberg, H. (2006). Defining language phenotypes in autism. *Clinical Neuroscience Research, 6*, 219–224. http://dx.doi.org/10.1016/j.cnr.2006.06.007

Tager-Flusberg, H., Calkins, S., Nolin, T., Baumberger, T., Anderson, M., & Chadwick-Dias, A. (1990). A longitudinal study of language acquisition in autistic and Down syndrome children. *Journal of Autism and Developmental Disorders, 20*, 1–21. http://dx.doi.org/10.1007/BF02206853

Tamburelli, M., & Jones, G. (2013). Investigating the relationship between nonword repetition performance and syllabic structure in typical and atypical language development. *Journal of Speech, Language, and Hearing Research, 56*, 708–720. http://dx.doi.org/10.1044/1092-4388(2012/11-0171)

Tek, S., Mesite, L., Fein, D., & Naigles, L. (2014). Longitudinal analyses of expressive language development reveal two distinct language profiles among young children with autism spectrum disorders. *Journal of Autism and Developmental Disorders, 44*, 75–89. http://dx.doi.org/10.1007/s10803-013-1853-4

Terzi, A., Marinis, T., Kotsopoulou, A., & Konstantinos, F. (2014). Grammatical abilities of Greek-speaking children with autism. *Language Acquisition, 21*, 4–44. http://dx.doi.org/10.1080/10489223.2013.855216

Thordardottir, E., & Brandeker, M. (2013). The effect of bilingual exposure versus language impairment on nonword repetition and sentence imitation scores. *Journal of Communication Disorders, 46*, 1–16. http://dx.doi.org/10.1016/j.jcomdis.2012.08.002

Tomblin, J. B., Bean, A., & McGregor, K. (2011). Specific language impairment. In D. G. Amaral, G. D. Dawson, & D. H. Geschwind (Eds.), *Autism spectrum disorders* (pp. 315–329). http://dx.doi.org/10.1093/med/9780195371826.003.0022

Tuller, L., Delage, H., Monjauze, C., Piller, A.-G., & Barthez, M.-A. (2011). Clitic pronoun production as a measure of typical language development in French: A comparative study of SLI, mild-to-moderate deafness and benign epilepsy of childhood with centrotemporal spikes. *Lingua*, *121*, 423–444. http://dx.doi.org/10.1016/j.lingua.2010.10.008

Tuller, L., Henry, C., Sizaret, E., & Barthez, M.-A. (2012). SLI at adolescence: Avoiding complexity. *Applied Psycholinguistics*, *33*, 161–184. http://dx.doi.org/10.1017/S0142716411000312

van der Lely, H. K. J. (1998). SLI in children: Movement, economy and deficits in the computational syntactic system. *Language Acquisition*, *7*, 161–192. http://dx.doi.org/10.1207/s15327817la0702-4_4

Weismer, E., & Kover, S. T. (2015). Preschool language variation, growth, and predictors in children on the autism spectrum. *Journal of Child Psychology and Psychiatry*, *56*, 1327–1337.

Williams, D., Botting, N., & Boucher, J. (2008). Language in autism and specific language impairment: Where are the links? *Psychological Bulletin*, *134*, 944–963. http://dx.doi.org/10.1037/a0013743

Zebib, R., Tuller, L., Prévost, P., & Morin, E. (2013). Formal language impairment in French-speaking children With ASD: A comparative ASD/SLI study. In S. Stavrakaki, X. Konstantinopoulou, & M. Lalioti (Eds.), *Proceedings of GALA 2011* (pp. 472–480). Newcastle upon Tyne, England: Cambridge Scholars.

Zesiger, P., Zesiger, L. C., Arabatzi, M., Baranzini, L., Cronel-Ohayon, S., Franck, J., . . . Rizzi, L. (2010). The acquisition of pronouns by French children: A parallel study of production and comprehension. *Applied Psycholinguistics*, *31*, 571–603. http://dx.doi.org/10.1017/S0142716410000147

Vikki Janke and Alexandra Perovic

7 Advanced Syntax and Primary Pragmatics in Children With ASD

Difficulties with communication are one of the defining characteristics of autism spectrum disorder (ASD), whereas language abilities vary. Language, however, encompasses a vast array of knowledge. Lexical knowledge includes, for example, the ability to comprehend and produce a single vocabulary item, such as the verb *kick*. To learn this word, the language-learning child must categorize it as a verb and work out its meaning (e.g., to strike out with a foot). If she wishes to use this verb to refer to a past event, this requires morphological knowledge, such that as a regular verb, it takes the suffix –*ed* in the past tense. However, to use this word in a sentence, the child must also understand its syntactic properties. *Kick*, for example, needs an object, as well as a subject. This rudimentary syntactic knowledge will prevent her from producing illicit sentences such as "*Kicked the ball" or "*He kicked" yet permit "He kicked the ball." On the basis of these simple examples, language appears to use literal knowledge and a predictable rule-based set of skills. However, if we return to the simple declarative, "He kicked the ball," we can see that a listener cannot lean on any aspect of linguistic knowledge mentioned so far to establish the reference of the pronoun. Lexical and morphological knowledge indicate that a singular male subject is intended, but that is all, and syntactic knowledge does not contribute anything in this respect. To recover the pronoun's reference (i.e., its antecedent), attendance to the context in which the sentence is uttered is required. When people go beyond so-called computational components of language to work out who is being referred to, they are using pragmatic knowledge. This pragmatic skill enables them to choose a referent based on the degree of context provided. Sometimes the referent will be unequivocally linked to one antecedent (perhaps only one person has been mentioned in the preceding discourse), but on other occasions, several possible referents might be available so the listener must make a decision, somehow attributing the contenders with different weights in terms of the likelihood of their being the intended referent.

The current study taps precisely into this skill. We compare examples of language (shown in examples 1 and 2 below), that might be expected to cause children with ASD difficulty. The difficulty is anticipated because the sentences call on either quite advanced syntactic knowledge, as in (1), or syntactic *and* pragmatic knowledge, as in (2), to work out who is being referred to in the bracketed clause. (1) and (2), for example, comprise a main clause and an embedded clause that lacks an overt subject. Additionally, (2) requires the use of contextual knowledge

http://dx.doi.org/10.1037/15964-008
Innovative Investigations of Language in Autism Spectrum Disorder, L. R. Naigles (Editor)

to resolve who is reading the book, that is, to assign a reference to the agent of the verb, "read."

1. Harry persuaded Hermione [to drink the potion]. Who drank the potion?
2. [Reading the book slowly] made the class sleepy. Who read the book?

Because the reference resolution in (2) is context mediated, it is an example of pragmatic processing. However, because it depends on a less complex set of inferences than for those used in irony interpretation, for example, it is often referred to as *primary pragmatics*. Primary pragmatics refers to the path to literal interpretations, such as in reference assignment or disambiguation, in which a person does not need to go beyond the truth conditions to arrive at the intended meaning (see Carston, 2002; de Villiers, Stainton, & Szatmari, 2007; Recanati, 2004). Our focus on this less complex stage of pragmatic processing will enable us to identify pragmatic strengths in this population.

Having introduced some of the fundamental building blocks to linguistic knowledge, we can situate the topic of this chapter in relation to the two separate linguistic components: advanced syntax and primary pragmatics in children with ASD. In the next sections, we focus on one example of each of these with a view to drawing a comparison between the comprehension of typically developing (TD) children and children with ASD. The relevant examples belong to a set of constructions called *control constructions*, which is a term used for a heterogeneous set of sentences. All of them call on quite sophisticated syntactic knowledge, and some require primary pragmatic knowledge as well for the arguments (i.e., the subjects or objects) within them to be assigned a correct reference. It is rare to find a set of constructions that can track the step between syntax and pragmatics so neatly, which makes them particularly interesting for ASD. There is a great deal of literature on the more basic building blocks of language in ASD (Bartak, Rutter, & Cox, 1975; Bartolucci, Pierce, & Streiner, 1980; Eigsti & Bennetto, 2009; Eigsti, Bennetto, & Dadlani, 2007; Kjelgaard & Tager-Flusberg, 2001; Tovar, Fein, & Naigles, 2015; Walenski, Mostofsky, & Ullman, 2014; see also Naigles & Fein, Chapter 3, this volume; Naigles & Chin, 2015), whereas work on syntax is only recently receiving sustained attention (e.g., Goodwin, Fein, & Naigles, 2012; Janke & Perovic, 2015; Perovic, Modyanova, & Wexler, 2013a, 2013b; Riches, Loucas, Baird, Charman, & Simonoff, 2010). The results of these recent studies suggest that some examples of syntax do create acquisition problems for different subtypes within ASD and remind us of the vital importance of keeping the heterogeneity of this disorder at the forefront of any research.

Work on pragmatics in ASD has a much longer trajectory (Baron-Cohen, 1988; Happé, 1993; Norbury, 2005), yet most attention has been focused on deficits in initiating and maintaining conversational interactions (see Boucher, 2009; Tager-Flusberg & Anderson, 1991) as well as understanding and use of figurative language, which calls on quite an advanced set of pragmatic skills: on metaphor (e.g., Dennis,

Lazenby, & Lockyer, 2001; Norbury, 2005; for a comparison between metaphor and metonymy, see Rundblad & Annaz, 2010a, 2010b), irony (e.g., MacKay & Shaw, 2004; Martin & McDonald, 2004) and humor (e.g., Ozonoff & Miller, 1996; see also Whyte & Nelson, 2015, for findings from a standardized test involving instances of both figurative language and appropriate language use in social contexts). Deriving scalar implicatures has been reported not to be problematic, however (for comprehension of the quantifier *some*, see Pijnacker, Hagoort, Buitelaar, Teunisse, & Geurts, 2009; for the scalar term *or*, see Chevallier, Wilson, Happé, & Noveck, 2010). If the distinction between primary and secondary pragmatics is pertinent to ASD, as argued by de Villiers, Stainton, and Szatmari (2007), the findings from the literature could be interpreted as if aspects of secondary pragmatic knowledge, such as figurative language,[1] or conversational implicatures, are more susceptible to deficiency in ASD than primary pragmatic knowledge. In this chapter, we extend and modify the existing profile by concentrating on the far less studied area of primary pragmatics. By looking at examples of control where the relevant argument's reference must be recovered pragmatically, our understanding of one of the first steps involved in pragmatic inference will be improved. An increased understanding of the earlier stages of pragmatics will make it possible to identify the point at which problems with contextual cues in ASD truly begin. Researchers and clinicians can then incorporate and build on the pragmatic strengths that exist in this population, perhaps thereby finding ways of rendering the more advanced examples of pragmatics less of a leap for the child.

In the next section, we explain what control constructions are, elaborating on the earlier examples introduced in (1) and (2), drawing a distinction between the syntactically regulated example (obligatory control) and its pragmatically regulated counterpart (nonobligatory control). With their properties clear, we move on to the interpretative issues they present and build on recent research on obligatory control in high-functioning children with ASD (Janke & Perovic, 2015). This leads to the innovation of the current study in which we compare the referent choice of TD children and children with ASD in three examples of control under three conditions: one in which the critical sentences are presented in isolation (no prime), a second in which a topic of discourse is weakly established before the critical sentences (weak prime), and a third in which a topic is strongly established before the critical sentences (strong prime). Our aim is to draw a comparison between our two populations' attention to pragmatic cues. Specifically, we wish to find the point at which their choice of referent in control constructions is affected by cues that prime particular arguments in those sentences. If this aspect of pragmatics is intact in our children with ASD, we expect no significant difference between our two populations.

---

1 See Carston (2007) for arguments that metaphor should be seen as belonging to primary rather than secondary pragmatic knowledge.

Control

Control constructions in English vary widely in their linguistic properties; however, they are all made up of at least a main clause and an embedded clause. The embedded clause, which is nonfinite (i.e., the verb inside it occurs in its gerund *–ing* form) or infinitival (the relevant verb is in its bare form preceded by *to*), has an understood, yet phonetically silent, subject. In the literature, this unpronounced subject is often called an empty category (*ec*), which is the term we adopt here in our examples. The *ec*'s reference can be recovered from a number of sources. Sometimes there is no choice, and its reference is restricted to a particular antecedent in the main clause. This may be the subject, as in (3a), or the object, as in (3b). The control relation is between the antecedent in the main clause (underlined), and the understood subject in the embedded clause, where the former "controls" the interpretation of the latter. When the interpretation of the *ec* is restricted to a designated argument in the main clause, the control relation is called obligatory. Thus the sentences in (3) are examples of obligatory control (i.e., *Harry* is the only candidate for feeding the owl, and *Hermione* for drinking the potion).

3. a. Harry tried [*ec* to feed the owl].
   b. Harry persuaded Hermione [*ec* to drink the potion].

In other types of control, the reference of the *ec* exhibits flexibility in its interpretation in that its reference can be linked to one of several arguments in the main clause. In (4a), for example, either the subject or the object can be understood as the agent in the embedded clause, even though people often demonstrate a strong preference for one (usually the object) over the other in the absence of any guiding context (see Janke, 2013).[2] Because of the possibility of a "long-distance" reading of the *ec*, namely, that an object reading may be skipped in favor of the "farther away" subject reading, this type of control is called long-distance control.

4. a. Harry said to Luna that [[*ec* flying the broom upside down] was a great trick].

There are also examples of control where the choice of the *ec*'s referent is between a sentence-internal referent or an unmentioned sentence-external one. In (4b), the most easily inferred agent of *read* in the bracketed verbal gerund is *the class*, the members of which are engaged in a collective reading activity. This is called a sentence-internal

2 In this example, there are other options in terms of referent choice, namely, both the subject and the object, someone else, or an arbitrary one, where the *ec* is interpreted generically. These possibilities are not discussed here because the experiment we conduct focuses only on the interpretation in which a choice between the subject and the object needs to be made. We return to how this is achieved later.

referent reading. Given sufficient context, however, we could also infer an unmentioned agent, such as an unfortunate pupil, picked out by the teacher to read aloud to the rest of the class, which would be a sentence-external referent reading. This type of control is a controlled verbal-gerund subject.

4. b. [*ec* Reading the book slowly] made the class sleepy.

There are further differences between and within these constructions, as well as many more types of control, but on the basis of the three illustrated here, we can separate them into two main categories: those whose interpretations are constrained structurally and those who are not. The labels used to describe these categories are obligatory control (OC), represented by (3a and 3b) and nonobligatory control (NOC), as in (4a) and (4b). This demarcation captures the fact that in the first group, the reference of the *ec* is linked to a designated controller, whereas in the second, there is a choice to be made with respect to reference assignment, where pragmatic factors regulate that choice.

One of the key pragmatic factors determining the choice of referent in NOC is topichood. The topic of a sentence is informally described by the concept of *aboutness* (see Reinhart, 1981). In English, the topic often coincides with the subject (Givón, 1983; Reinhart, 1981). Thus in (5), "John" is the preferred topic.

5. John met Peter at the library.

However, topic is a discourse-based notion rather than a grammatically based one, and as such, new discourse can shift the topic to another argument. One way of doing this is to precede the critical sentence with one that promises to introduce a new topic in the forthcoming discourse, as in (6).

6. This story is about Peter. John met Peter at the library.

The topic-led interpretation of the *ec* in NOC constructions can be further demonstrated by switching or introducing new topics with increasing degrees of strength (see Bresnan, 1982).

Note what happens to the interpretation of our original example in (4b), if a forthcoming topic is weakly established, as in (7), or strongly established, as in (8).

7. This story is about Ron. *ec* Reading the book slowly made the class sleepy.
8. Ron is learning a new poem. Ron says each word bit by bit. *ec* Reading the book slowly made the class sleepy.

The degree of interpretative shift is linked to the strength of the pragmatic lead, where the weakly established topic in (7) has less of an effect than the strongly established one in (8). We refer to the former as a weak prime and the latter as a strong prime. The same effect is visible in long-distance control. Depending on a person's original preference in the baseline example in (4), this initial preference can gradually be switched by priming whichever of the arguments was their least preferred choice, as in (9) and (10).

9. This story is about Harry/Luna. Harry said to Luna that *ec* flying the broom upside down was a great trick.
10. Harry/Luna is testing his/her flying skills. Harry/Luna takes off in the air. Harry said to Luna that *ec* flying the broom upside down was a great trick.

Note that neither a weak or strong prime can interfere with judgments of OC because this relation is set within the grammar. In (11) and (12), the antecedent of the *ec* remains resolutely the object, namely, "Ron":

11. This story is about Hermione. Hermione persuaded Ron *ec* to bake the cake.
12. Hermione is having a party. Hermione makes all the party food. Hermione persuaded Ron *ec* to bake the cake.

The introduction of weak and strong topic primes provides a good way of testing whether children's acquisition of OC is complete. Once fully developed, their grammar should not permit a subject referent for this example, no matter how strong the contextual cue. To our knowledge, there is no work that has looked at the referent choices made by children with ASD in NOC under any conditions. Our interest is whether children with ASD will make similar topic-based choices to children without ASD. In the next subsection, we summarize briefly what is known about OC in children with ASD. This previous research on OC serves as a precursor to the current investigation into primary pragmatics in this population. Once we have established that their underlying syntax is intact, we can progress to a consideration of primary pragmatics, confident that any problems observed are not due to an impoverished syntax.

Control in Typical Development and ASD

TD children start producing OC structures at around age 3 years (see Broihier & Wexler, 1995; Guasti, 2002; Sherman & Lust, 1993). Despite this early production, comprehension is not adult-like for a few more years because some children continue to accept an illicit referent in OC environments (see Broihier & Wexler, 1995; Eisenberg & Cairns, 1994; Lust, Solan, Flynn, Cross, & Schuetz, 1986; Cairns, McDaniel, Hsu, & Rapp, 1994; Tavakolian, 1978).

Building on this literature with TD children, Janke and Perovic (2015) conducted a first study on the comprehension of OC in high-functioning children with ASD (HFA).

They focused on examples of subject- and object-oriented OC, similar to those introduced in (3), with a view to assessing whether children (aged between 7 and 16 years) would permit illicit referents in single-complement subject control, as in (13a) or object control, as in (13b).

13. a. Homer tried [*ec* to wash Bart].
    b. Marge persuaded Homer [*ec* to drive the car].

The results showed that the children performed excellently on these types of grammatically regulated control as well as the fillers, and there were no significant differences between these conditions or between the ASD group and two TD groups, one matched on nonverbal MA to the ASD group and the other on verbal MA. The results of this first study demonstrated that canonical OC, as an example of complex syntax, is right on track in children with ASD who are further classified as HFA.

There is far less acquisition literature on NOC in TD children (see Adler, 2006; Goodluck, 1987; Tavakolian, 1978). Adler (2006) investigated verbal gerund subject control, as introduced in (4b), in TD children, aged 3 to 6 years. She found that, contrary to adults, who base their interpretations of these on the topic of discourse, very young children are strongly biased toward the external referent. This is in line with early literature on the acquisition of similar constructions, which indicates that children aged 5 to 6 years opt more frequently for an external referent than a sentence-internal one (Goodluck, 1987), a pattern that might indicate an immature grammar which has not yet restricted them to the sentence-internal referent, namely, the topic in the sentence. The TD children in our current investigation are much older (mean age 9.5 years), so we anticipated an effect of topic against which to compare the children with ASD (see Janke, in press).

In the next section, we turn to this first study, testing both OC and NOC in children with ASD, where we examine their interpretation of three examples of control under different amounts of discourse pressure: object control (OC), shown in (3b); controlled verbal gerund subjects (VGS), as in (4b); and long-distance control (LDC), illustrated in (4a). Specifically, we investigate the influence of topic on their interpretations of these constructions and compare their choices with those of a group of 14 nonverbal and verbal MA-matched TD children. The children will be presented with the constructions in three conditions: no prime, weak prime (weakly established topic), and strong prime (strongly established topic). We have seen that children with ASD are generally reported as having deficient pragmatics. In this experiment, we demonstrate that one example of pragmatic knowledge in children with ASD is fully functioning. To anticipate, just like the TD children against whom they are matched, children with ASD are guided by the discourse topic to recover the reference of the null subject. Interestingly, they also know when to ignore it. When the pragmatic cues used to manipulate interpretation of the NOC constructions are applied to OC, the children's grammar constrains them and they are not steered away from the

Tab. 7.1: Ages and Mean Scores (Standard Deviations) on Standardized Tests of Language and Cognition

Group	ASD ($n = 14$)	TD ($n = 14$)
Age in months	160.14 (16.08)	115.93 (25.54)
Age range in months	140–197	69–157
KBIT Matrices RS	**27.86 (5.33)**	**27.50 (6.57)**
KBIT Matrices SS	91.71 (15.26)	108.21 (14.63)
BPVS–II RS	**93.64 (17.09)**	**102.50 (20.08)**
BPVS–II SS	78.70 (14.67)	110.79 (13.26)
TROG–2 RS	13.21 (2.97)	
TROG–2 SS	83 (13.56)	

Note: The scores for the measures on which participants with autism were matched to controls are in bold. ASD = autism spectrum disorder; TD = typically developing; BPVS–II = British Picture Vocabulary Scales—Second Edition; KBIT = Kaufman Brief Intelligence Test; RS = raw score; SS = standard score; TROG–2 = Test of Reception of Grammar—Second Edition.

structurally determined antecedent. As such, it can be argued that this aspect of their grammar is adult-like.

Discourse Effects on OC and NOC in HFA

Participants

Twenty-eight[3] children took part in the study: 14 children[4] clinically diagnosed with ASD (all boys) aged between 11.6 and 16.4 ($M = 13.34$) and 14 younger TD controls (4 girls), aged 5.7 to 13.8 ($M = 9.66$). Children with ASD all attended one of two specialist schools for children with ASD in London and Kent. The formal diagnosis of ASD, which was an entry requirement to the schools, was made on the basis of the *Diagnostic and Statistical Manual of Mental Disorders* (fourth ed., text rev.; American Psychiatric Association, 2000) or the *International Classification of Diseases* (10th rev.; World Health Organization, 1992). None had any hearing impairments or any accompanying neurological or genetic deficits. Details of their scores on measures of verbal and nonverbal abilities are given in Table 7.1. Their nonverbal IQ, as measured on the Matrices subtest of the Kaufman Brief Intelligence Test (KBIT) ranged between 70 and 111, $M = 91.71$ ($SD = 15.26$;

3 An additional four children with ASD were recruited, but three were excluded for failing to meet the threshold of 70 on nonverbal IQ, and for one child, no suitable match on nonverbal MA was found.
4 Five of these children also took part in Janke & Perovic (2015) in their previous academic year at school, where they were tested on a different picture-selection task (using completely different drawings, e.g., the Simpson family) tapping into binding and obligatory control.

to be classified as HFA, we include only children whose nonverbal IQ was 70 and higher, see, e.g., Howlin, 2003). Their scores on standardized tests of verbal abilities were more heterogeneous, in line with the literature (e.g., Kjelgaard & Tager-Flusberg, 2001): On British Picture Vocabulary Scales–2 (BPVS–2), they ranged from 54 to 105, $M = 78.79$ ($SD = 14.67$), and on Test of Reception of Grammar–2 (TROG) from 55 to 106, $M = 83$ ($SD = 13.56$). Typical controls with no known developmental delays or hearing impairments were recruited from schools in greater London. They were matched to the children with ASD on nonverbal MA (no statistically significant differences between groups on raw scores of the Matrices subtest on the KBIT, $p = .517$) and verbal MA (no statistically significant differences between groups on raw scores on BPVS–2, $p = .322$).

Task

We used a two-choice picture-selection task, a method widely used in the literature with school-age TD children and children with developmental disorders with and without intellectual impairment (e.g., Perovic et al., 2013a; Ring & Clahsen, 2005). Four examples of control were included in the experiment, but here we report on the three introduced earlier, OC, LDC, and VGS. From the two pictures, children were asked to choose the one that best matched the sentence they heard. Item presentation was randomized automatically for each participant, and location of the correct picture balanced throughout (left or right). Task demands were reduced by limiting characters to four from the Harry Potter series (Harry, Ron, Hermione, and Luna), recognizable to children of all ages. Children were nevertheless familiarized with them during the introductory session. Two filler conditions, one using an embedded sentence and the other a simple SVO sentence preceded by a strong prime, were also included. Each construction included six trials in each condition. Thus, the OC and VGS constructions in three conditions (no prime, weak prime, and strong prime), the LDC in five conditions (no prime, weak prime of object, weak prime of subject, strong prime of object, and strong prime of subject), plus the two filler conditions translated into 78 trials in total. The stimuli were presented on a laptop computer and randomized by a computer program, over three testing sessions, within 7 to 10 days of each other.

Sentence Types

(Object Control) Hermione persuaded Ron to bake the cake.

The OC construction used pictures in which the character represented by the matrix object engaged in an action while the character represented by the matrix subject stood by. The foil depicted the matrix subject engaging in the action. For the preceding example sentence, the corresponding picture showed "Ron" baking the cake, with "Hermione" standing next to him, whereas the foil showed "Hermione" baking the cake, with "Ron" standing next to her.

(Verbal Gerund Subject) Reading the book slowly made Hermione sleepy.

The VGS pictures showed the sentence-internal referent engaged in an action, with the sentence-external character next to him or her. The alternative picture depicted the sentence-external referent engaging in the action instead. To clarify, in the preceding example, the picture corresponding to an interpretation in which "Hermione" is reading, showed "Ron" and "Hermione" sitting on the sofa, with "Hermione" holding a book having fallen asleep, whereas the picture corresponding to the interpretation in which "Ron" is reading, showed "Ron" holding the book, with "Hermione" having fallen asleep next to him.

(Long-Distance Control) Harry said to Luna that flying the broom upside down was a great trick.

LDC had one picture in which the character represented by the matrix object engaged in an action, while the matrix subject stood by, and a second, where the characters' actions were reversed. In the example sentence above, the picture corresponding to "Harry" being the agent of *fly* had "Harry" flying the broomstick, with "Luna" standing by, whereas the picture corresponding to "Luna" as the agent of *fly*, had "Luna" flying and "Harry" standing by.

These same pictures were used for all three conditions: no prime; weak prime, in which a topic is introduced before the critical sentence, as shown in (7), (9), and (11); and strong prime, in which a topic is introduced and then reinforced before the critical sentence, as illustrated in (8), (10), and (12).

Results

Each experimental condition included three different verbs × two repetitions, amounting to six trials in each one. For OC and LDC, the responses were summed up according to the number of times the object was chosen as the referent, which gave a 7-point scale, ranging from 0 to 6. Comparisons focused on the degree to which the children's initial preferences for the subject or object could be altered as a function of the primes. For VGS, responses were summed according to the number of times the internal referent was chosen. This also gave a 7-point scale ranging from 0 to 6. These comparisons focused on the degree to which their initial preferences for the internal–external referent could be altered as a function of the primes. Both groups scored at ceiling on the two filler conditions (embedded subject–verb–object [SVO] and SVO preceded by a strong prime), which were excluded from further analysis.

Obligatory Control

We first looked at both groups' object responses in OC across the three conditions: no prime, weak prime, and strong prime. The medians for both groups' preference for the

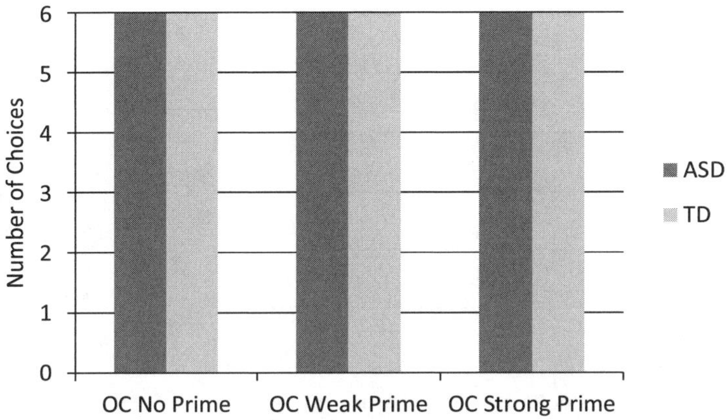

Fig. 7.1: Median number of object choices in obligatory control (OC). ASD = children with autism spectrum disorder; TD = typically developing children.

matrix object as the antecedent of the *ec* in the infinitival complement were uniform in all three conditions: 6, 6, 6 (the only appropriate answer in this condition). Two Friedman's tests conducted on the TD group's responses to OC across the three conditions and the ASD group's responses across the three conditions were not significant, demonstrating that neither of the groups was affected by either of the primes. Figure 7.1 illustrates the uniformity of the children's responses across the three conditions.

Verbal Gerund Subjects

Comparisons on TD children's responses to VGS revealed an effect of the primes on referent choice. Their preference for the internal referent in the baseline condition switched to the external referent in both the weak and strong prime conditions (*Mdn*s: 4, 0, 0). A Friedman test conducted on their scores across the three conditions was significant ($p < .001$). Three Wilcoxon tests (Bonferroni adjusted) compared responses in the no prime condition versus the weak prime condition, the no prime condition versus the strong prime condition, and the weak prime condition versus the strong prime condition. The first two were significant ($p < .001$ and $p < .001$), and the last was not. This showed that both the weak primes and the strong primes swayed TD children's interpretations toward the topic. The absence of a difference between the weak and strong primes can be sourced to the strength of the weak prime, rendering the strong prime effect undetectable.

The same comparisons were conducted on the ASD group. In the baseline condition in which there was no prime, children with ASD were split between choosing the internal or external referent. The addition of the weak and strong prime, however, steered them unequivocally toward the external referent, as indicated by the median

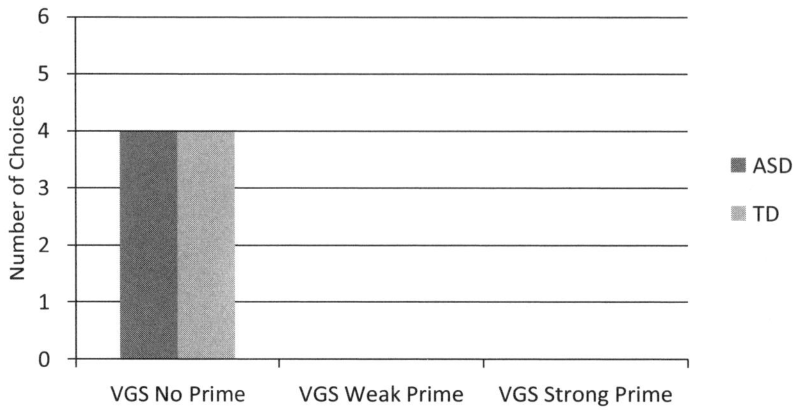

Fig. 7.2: Median number of internal referent choices in verbal gerund subjects (VGS). ASD = children with autism spectrum disorder; TD = typically developing children.

values, which, like the TD children, were 4, 0, 0. The Friedman test conducted on their scores across the three conditions was significant (p = .003). Three Wilcoxon tests compared responses in the no prime condition versus the weak prime condition, the no prime condition versus the strong prime condition, and the weak prime condition versus the strong prime condition. The first two were significant (p = .006 and p = .004) and, as with the TD group, the last was not, which showed that both the weak and the strong primes guided children with ASD to the topic. These results across both groups are displayed in Figure 7.2.

Long-Distance Control

The focus of LDC was again the number of object-oriented interpretations across the three conditions. We first compared TD children's object responses in the no prime condition, the weak-prime-object condition and the strong-prime-object condition. As expected, TD children demonstrated a strong preference for the object in the baseline condition, which made the effect of topic less detectable (*Mdns*: 5, 5, 6); this was confirmed by a Friedman test, which did not reach significance. We then compared TD children's object responses in the no prime condition, the weak-prime-*subject* condition and the strong-prime-*subject* condition. If a prime effect were to be visible, it was predicted to be in this condition, given the children's preference for an object-oriented reading in the baseline condition. The medians indicated an effect of the strong prime (*Mdns*: 5, 5, 2), which was supported by a Friedman test (p = .006). Two Wilcoxon tests were conducted to confirm that the source of the significance came from the strong-prime-*subject* condition. The comparison between the no prime condition and the weak-prime-*subject* condition was not significant, whereas for the comparison between the no prime condition and the strong-prime-*subject* condition was ($p = .009$). Thus, although the weak prime of the subject did not cause the children to veer away from their baseline preference of the object, the strong prime did.

Our comparisons of the ASD group proceeded in the same way. We first compared children with ASD's object responses in the no prime condition, the weak-prime-object condition and the strong-prime-object condition. Children with ASD also demonstrated a preference for the object in the baseline condition (*Mdns*: 4, 5, 6), yet an effect of the strong prime could still be detected by a Friedman test ($p = .001$). Three Wilcoxon tests were conducted to test the difference between the no prime condition and the weak prime of the object, the no prime condition and the strong prime of the object, and the weak and strong prime conditions. The first was not significant, but the latter two were ($p = .007$ and $p = .01$, respectively). This demonstrates that although the weak prime of the object had no effect on choice, the strong priming of the object did. The significance of this, relative to the nonsignificance of it for TD children, can be sourced to the difference between the two group's baseline interpretations: TD children preferred the object in the baseline condition to a greater degree than children with ASD, who were more varied in their subject- and object-oriented interpretations in the baseline. We then compared the object responses of our participants with ASD in the no prime condition, the weak-prime-subject condition, and the strong-prime-subject condition. The medians suggested a marginal move toward the topic (*Mdns*: 4, 3, 3), but a Friedman test was not significant. These results are displayed in Figure 7.3.

Discussion

The current study used a topic-based experiment to gain an initial insight into the reference assignment strategies in control of high-functioning children with ASD. We concentrated on three examples (object control, verbal-gerund-subject control, and long-distance control) and tested 28 children's interpretations of the *ec* under different strengths of discourse pressure. The main questions were whether their choices were affected by pragmatic leads and, if they were, whether they differed from TD children in terms of the strength of cue necessary before a significant shift in interpretation became visible. The results showed that contextual cues did not interfere with judgment on OC in either group. The results on NOC revealed different effects for control type but not for group. That is, both the weak and strong primes affected referent choice for the *ec* in VGS for both groups of children, but only the strong prime could affect their referent choice in LDC. We now consider these results in this order, establishing how they build on existing literature and the implications they have for the grammatical and pragmatic profile of children with ASD.

The results on OC are interesting in several respects. First, our ASD group performed excellently in the condition without any prime. We have thus supported the previous

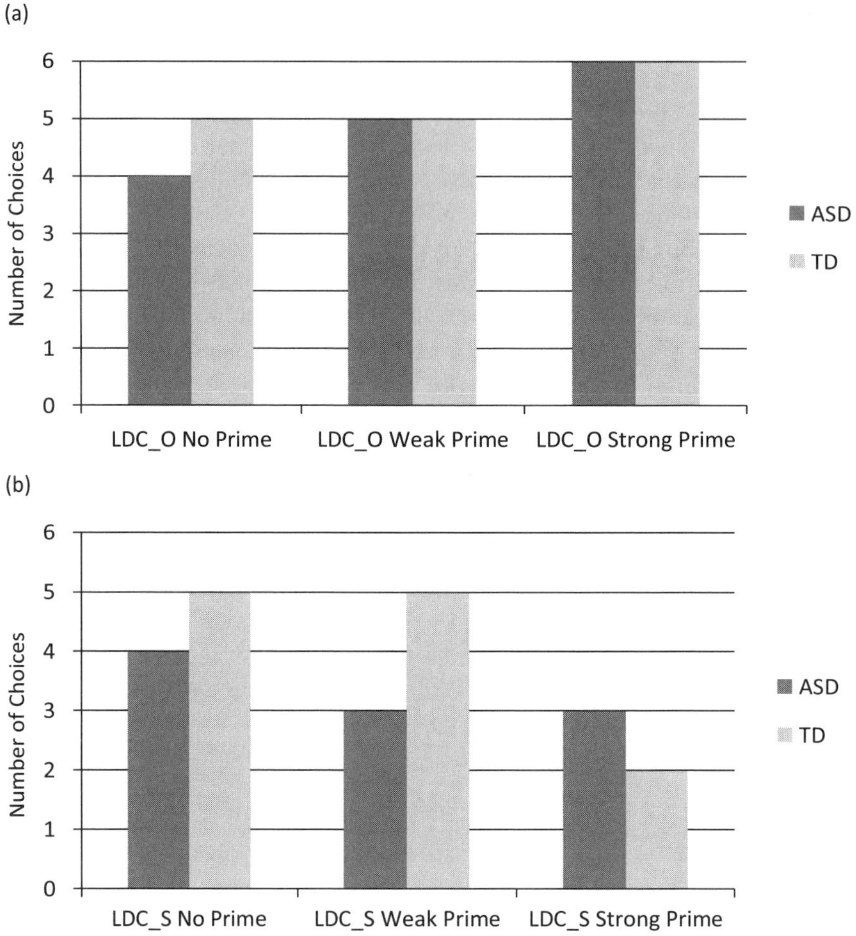

Fig. 7.3: (a) Median number of object choices in long-distance control (LDC) when object (O) is primed. (b) Median number of object choices in long-distance control (LDC) when subject (S) is primed. ASD = children with autism spectrum disorder; TD = typically developing children.

findings of Janke and Perovic (2015), which tested single-complement subject control (i.e., with *try*) and object control (i.e., with *persuade*) and found the constructions to be intact. Given the absence of any other literature on this example of advanced syntax in this population, our ability to replicate the absence of problems with OC in our current ASD group is important. We can now be more confident that OC is an example of complex syntax with which high-functioning children with ASD do not have difficulties. This forms an important contribution to the growing profile of syntactically based reference assignment in ASD. Work conducted by Perovic et al. (2013b), for example, has indicated that reference assignment in reflexive binding (i.e., "Bart washed himself") also seems unaffected in high-functioning children with

ASD, where children comprehend that the reflexive, *himself*, is obligatorily linked to the most local referent, namely, *Bart*. This is in contrast to pronominal binding (i.e., "Bart washed him"), which goes beyond purely syntactic knowledge and was found to be more problematic for these children. Children with HFA were apt to accept illicit readings in which *him* and *Bart* co-refer. In contrast, children with ASD who were low functioning struggled with both constructions.

An addition in the current study was the inclusion of two priming conditions, which further corroborate that this aspect of syntax is adult-like in our population. Recall that young TD children may produce OC structures early, but their acquisition was shown not to be complete by comprehension studies that tested whether they would permit illicit referents. Specifically, for a few years after their first productions, some TD children permit incorrect referents in OC when prompted by a contextual cue. When children no longer allow their reference choices to be guided by the context in structures that are grammatically determined, this is a good indication that their grammar has converged with adult grammar for this construction. Our TD and HFA groups' consistent object-oriented interpretation of OC across all three conditions suggests that both groups of children have reached this point. In addition, the ASD group's 100% correct scores on the filler conditions, one of which also primed an illicit referent, buttress the demarcation they have drawn between grammatically and pragmatically determined reference relations. This argument of course depends on the children with ASD using the contextual cues in environments where they are warranted. As we now turn to NOC, we will see that they do.

In the VGS construction, the baseline condition has one referent, and this is sentence-internal. This referent, then, is also the topic of the sentence, rendering it, all else being equal, the preferred referent for the *ec*. In this particular task, however, where children are shown two pictures, a sentence-external referent is visually represented in the alternative picture. That is, for the trial "Pouring the water quickly made Luna wet," the children are shown one picture in which Luna is pouring the water, making herself wet with Harry standing next to her, and an alternative one in which Harry is pouring water and making Luna wet. This introduces a visual prompt absent from the sentence when seen or read out in isolation, and this was shown to influence both groups' choice of referent in the baseline condition. Contrary to adults, the majority of whom opt for the sentence-internal referent when reading the sentence without an accompanying picture, the children were split between an internal and external referent choice in this condition. Recall that the medians for an internal referent reading for both the TD and ASD group were 4, where the range was from 0 to 6. The introduction of the weak prime, however, which introduced the external referent as the topic, reduced the medians in both the TD and ASD group to 0, a drop that was significant for both groups. This indicates that for TD children and children with ASD alike, a weakly established topic was a sufficiently strong cue to guide away from the sentence-internal referent to the sentence-external one: The topic decided the referent. Unsurprisingly, the strong prime, in which the topic was strongly established, also switched referent choice definitively. At this point, then, we have shown one example of NOC, whose *ec*'s referent is topic-led in adult grammars (see Adler, 2006; Bresnan, 1982; Janke, 2007), to be topic-led in our group of children with ASD as well as the younger TD group against whom they were matched. If we contrast this result with our observations for OC, we now have evidence of their applying this discourse rule selectively and appropriately.

The second type of NOC we tested was long-distance control (LDC), which was also expected to exude discourse effects. However, there were properties that distinguished LDC from VGS, which might have interacted with the topic primes. In particular, in LDC, there are two arguments in the main clause that could serve as the antecedent for the *ec* in the embedded clause, as in (14), whereas in VGS control (15), there was only one.

14. Harry said to Luna that [(*ec* flying the broomstick upside down) was a great trick].
15. [*ec* Pouring the water slowly] made Luna wet.

The availability of two arguments in LDC introduces some new factors that might influence referent preference. The two arguments serve different syntactic functions, for example, where one is the subject and one is the object. Subjects are more frequently associated with topichood, so the subject's potential topic status might give it precedence for some in the baseline condition and compete with the experimentally induced pragmatic leads in the primed conditions. Alternatively, the object is linearly (but not structurally) more local to the *ec*, which might be a contributory factor. Linear distance is relevant to the interpretation of other pragmatically regulated elements such as overt pronouns. This can be seen in (16), where there is a strong preference for the pronoun in the third sentence to refer to the last mentioned argument, namely, "Ron," as demonstrated by the less felicitous (17a) compared with (17b).

16. Harry looked at Ron. He had tripped over the fence.
17. a. Harry looked at Ron. #He had tripped over the fence, and so had Ron.[5]
    b. Harry looked at Ron. He had tripped over the fence, and so had Harry.

Given that there are some similarities between discourse-mediated pronouns and the *ec* in NOC, linear distance might be another factor influencing referent choice, independent of topichood.

The results in LDC revealed topic effects for both groups, but only in the strong prime condition. TD children strongly preferred the object as the referent for the *ec* in the baseline condition, a fact that made the priming of the object fruitless. For this group, it was the priming of the subject that tested for the effect of topic on interpreta-

5 The hashtag (#) symbol indicates when an interpretation is semantically anomalous.

tion. These were significant only in the strong prime condition. For the ASD group, a slightly different pattern was observed. Although they, too, exhibited a preference for the object in the baseline condition, the strong priming of the object was significant. In contrast to the TD group, the strong priming of the subject did not yield a significant shift. There are a number of possible reasons for this. First, more children with ASD opted for a subject interpretation in the baseline than did the TD children, which might have contributed to masking the effect of the prime (as with the object prime for the TD children). Another possibility is that those children with ASD who preferred an object reading to begin with were reluctant to switch to a less local referent. In contrast, those who preferred a subject reading to begin with found it easier to be guided by the topic to the more local referent. This is an interesting issue, but one we leave for future research. What this second example of NOC has demonstrated, however, is that children with ASD required the same strength of pragmatic cue as their TD counterparts before switching from their initial interpretations, a finding that points to the children using this area of primary pragmatics in the same way as each other. In OC, when the TD children ignored the pragmatic cue, so did the ASD group. In VGS, when the TD children were guided by both cues, so were the children with ASD. Finally, when the TD children discerned between the two strengths of prime, ignoring the weak one but using the strong one, so did the children with ASD.

The broader relevance of this study is that it has focused on the point at which syntax and pragmatics meet, thereby isolating the first steps of pragmatic processing. It is an important addition to the aforementioned studies that have examined more complex examples of pragmatics, where the gap between what has been said and what is intended is much larger. We have demonstrated that one of the smaller inferential stages involved in pragmatic processing is intact, a skill that might be exploited for the more complex cases.

Conclusion

In this chapter, we have focused on an example of advanced syntax and an example of primary pragmatics (obligatory and nonobligatory control) to compare reference assignment in two language domains. We first showed that the performance of children with ASD on OC was flawless. This affirmative result substantiates our claim that certain complex syntactic dependencies are intact: The children understand the obligatory, structurally determined local relation between an antecedent and its dependent. These results contribute to current debate about which examples of advanced syntax are preserved in this population and which cause difficulty.

We then showed that the children's pragmatically mediated reference resolution with two examples of NOC patterned precisely with those of TD children. This will complement research on communicative ability in ASD so far, which, focusing extensively on the social requirements of communication (e.g., conversational turn-taking and reciprocity) and also advanced areas of pragmatics (e.g., that employed in figurative language), has reported major impairments. By tapping into children with ASD's comprehension in this far less charted domain, we hope a more precise profile of pragmatic ability will become possible. Viewed in the context of the few other studies on primary pragmatics (Chevallier et al., 2010; de Villiers et al., 2007; Pijnacker et al., 2009), a more positive picture is emerging. There are areas of pragmatics in which children with ASD excel—and these areas might just provide the stepping-stones to more complex pragmatic milestones.

References

Adler, A. (2006). *Syntax and discourse in the acquisition of adjunct control* (Doctoral dissertation). Massachusetts Institute of Technology, Cambridge, MA. Retrieved from https://dspace.mit.edu/handle/1721.1/37417

American Psychiatric Association. (2000). *Diagnostic and statistical manual of mental disorders* (4th ed., text rev.). Washington, DC: Author.

Baron-Cohen, S. (1988). Social and pragmatic deficits in autism: Cognitive or affective? *Journal of Autism and Developmental Disorders*, *18*, 379–402. http://dx.doi.org/10.1007/BF02212194

Bartak, L., Rutter, M., & Cox, A. (1975). A comparative study of infantile autism and specific developmental receptive language disorder. *The British Journal of Psychiatry*, *126*, 127–145.

Bartolucci, G., Pierce, S., & Streiner, D. (1980). Cross-sectional studies of grammatical morphemes in autistic and mentally retarded children. *Journal of Autism and Developmental Disorders*, *10*, 39–50.

Boucher, J. (2009). *The autistic spectrum: Characteristics, causes and practical issues*. Thousand Oaks, CA: Sage.

Bresnan, J. (1982). Control and complementation. *Linguistic Inquiry*, *13*, 343–434.

Broihier, K., & Wexler, K. (1995). Children's acquisition of control in temporal adjuncts. In C. Schutze, J. Ganger, & K. Broihier (Eds.), *MIT Working Papers in Linguistics, 26*. Cambridge, MA: MIT Press.

Cairns, H., McDaniel, D., Hsu, J., & Rapp, M. (1994). A longitudinal study of principles of control and pronominal reference in child English. *Language*, *70*, 260–288.

Carston, R. (2002). *Thoughts and utterances*. http://dx.doi.org/10.1002/9780470754603

Carston, R. (2007). How many pragmatic systems are there? In M. J. Frapolli (Ed.), *Saying, meaning, referring: Essays on the philosophy of Francois Recanati* (pp. 18–48). London, England: Palgrave Macmillan.

Chevallier, C., Wilson, D., Happé, F., & Noveck, I. (2010). Scalar inferences in autism spectrum disorders. *Journal of Autism and Developmental Disorders*, *40*, 1104–1117. http://dx.doi.org/10.1007/s10803-010-0960-8

Dennis, M., Lazenby, A. L., & Lockyer, L. (2001). Inferential language in high-function children with autism. *Journal of Autism and Developmental Disorders*, *31*, 47–54. http://dx.doi.org/10.1023/A:1005661613288

de Villiers, J., Stainton, R., & Szatmari, P. (2007). Pragmatic abilities in autism spectrum disorder: A case study in philosophical and the empirical. *Midwest Studies in Philosophy*, *31*, 292–317.

Eigsti, I.-M., & Bennetto, L. (2009). Grammaticality judgments in autism: Deviance or delay. *Journal of Child Language*, *36*, 999–1021. http://dx.doi.org/10.1017/S0305000909009362

Eigsti, I.-M., Bennetto, L., & Dadlani, M. B. (2007). Beyond pragmatics: Morphosyntactic development in autism. *Journal of Autism and Developmental Disorders*, *37*, 1007–1023. http://dx.doi.org/10.1007/s10803-006-0239-2

Eisenberg, S. L., & Cairns, H. S. (1994). The development of infinitives from three to five. *Journal of Child Language*, *21*, 713–734. http://dx.doi.org/10.1017/S0305000900009521

Givón, T. (Ed.). (1983). *Topic continuity in discourse: A quantitative cross-language study.* Amsterdam, The Netherlands: Benjamins.

Goodluck, H. (1987). Children's interpretations of pronouns and null NPs: An alternative view. In B. Lust (Ed.), *Studies in the acquisition of anaphora* (Vol. 2, pp. 247–269). http://dx.doi.org/10.1007/978-94-009-3387-3_11

Goodwin, A., Fein, D., & Naigles, L. R. (2012). Comprehension of wh-questions precedes their production in typical development and autism spectrum disorders. *Autism Research*, *5*, 109–123. http://dx.doi.org/10.1002/aur.1220

Guasti, M. T. (2002). *Language acquisition: The growth of grammar.* Cambridge, MA: MIT Press.

Happé, F. G. E. (1993). Communicative competence and theory of mind in autism: A test of relevance theory. *Cognition*, *48*, 101–119. http://dx.doi.org/10.1016/0010-0277(93)90026-R

Howlin, P. (2003). Outcome in high-functioning adults with autism with and without early language delays: Implications for the differentiation between autism and Asperger syndrome. *Journal of Autism and Developmental Disorders*, *33*, 3–13. http://dx.doi.org/10.1023/A:1022270118899

Janke, V. (2007). *Control without PRO.* Doctoral dissertation, University College London, London, England.

Janke, V. (2013). The distribution of NOC and its + human restriction. In M. Kolokonte & V. Janke (Eds.), *Interfaces in language III* (pp. 121–157). Newcastle upon Tyne, England: Cambridge Scholars.

Janke, V. (in press). Pragmatic leads and null subjects: When children consult leads and when they do not. *Proceedings of the 40th annual Boston University Conference on Language Development.* Somerville, MA: Cascadilla Press.

Janke, V., & Perovic, A. (2015). Intact grammar in HFA? Evidence from control and binding. *Lingua*, *164*, 68–86. http://dx.doi.org/10.1016/j.lingua.2015.06.009

Kjelgaard, M. M., & Tager-Flusberg, H. (2001). An investigation of language impairment in autism: Implications for genetic subgroups. *Language and Cognitive Processes*, *16*, 287–308. http://dx.doi.org/10.1080/01690960042000058

Lust, B., Solan, L., Flynn, S., Cross, C., & Schuetz, E. (1986). A comparison on null and pronoun anaphora in first language acquisition. In B. Lust (Ed.), *Studies in the acquisition of anaphora* (Vol. 2, pp. 245–277). http://dx.doi.org/10.1007/978-94-009-4548-7_7

MacKay, G., & Shaw, A. (2004). A comparative study of figurative language in children with autistic spectrum disorders. *Child Language Teaching and Therapy*, *20*, 13–32. http://dx.doi.org/10.1191/0265659004ct261oa

Martin, I., & McDonald, S. (2004). An exploration of causes of non-literal language problems in individuals with Asperger syndrome. *Journal of Autism and Developmental Disorders*, *34*, 311–328. http://dx.doi.org/10.1023/B:JADD.0000029553.52889.15

Naigles, L. R., & Chin, I. (2015). Language development in children with autism. In E. L. Bavin & L. R. Naigles (Eds.), *The Cambridge handbook of child language* (2nd ed., pp. 637–658). http://dx.doi.org/10.1017/CBO9781316095829.029

Norbury, C. (2005). The relationship between theory of mind and metaphor: Evidence from children with language impairment and autistic spectrum disorder. *British Journal of Developmental Psychology*, *23*, 383–399. http://dx.doi.org/10.1348/026151005X26732

Ozonoff, S., & Miller, J. N. (1996). An exploration of right-hemisphere contributions to the pragmatic impairments of autism. *Brain and Language*, *52*, 411–434. http://dx.doi.org/10.1006/brln.1996.0022

Perovic, A., Modyanova, N., & Wexler, K. (2013a). Comparisons of grammar in neuro-developmental disorders: The case of binding in Williams syndrome and autism with and without language impairment. *Language Acquisition*, *20*, 133–154. http://dx.doi.org/10.1080/10489223.2013.766742

Perovic, A., Modyanova, N., & Wexler, K. (2013b). Comprehension of reflexive and personal pronouns in children with autism: A syntactic or pragmatic deficit? *Applied Psycholinguistics*, *34*, 813–835. http://dx.doi.org/10.1017/S0142716412000033

Pijnacker, J., Hagoort, P., Buitelaar, J., Teunisse, J. P., & Geurts, B. (2009). Pragmatic inferences in high-functioning adults with autism and Asperger syndrome. *Journal of Autism and Developmental Disorders*, *39*, 607–618. http://dx.doi.org/10.1007/s10803-008-0661-8

Recanati, F. (2004). *Literal meaning*. Cambridge, England: Cambridge University Press.

Reinhart, T. (1981). Pragmatics and linguistics: An analysis of sentence topics. *Philosophica*, *27*, 53–94.

Riches, N. G., Loucas, T., Baird, G., Charman, T., & Simonoff, E. (2010). Sentence repetition in adolescents with specific language impairments and autism: An investigation of complex syntax. *International Journal of Language & Communication Disorders*, *45*, 47–60. http://dx.doi.org/10.3109/13682820802647676

Ring, M., & Clahsen, H. (2005). Distinct patterns of language impairment in Down's syndrome and Williams syndrome: The case of syntactic chains. *Journal of Neurolinguistics*, *18*, 479–501. http://dx.doi.org/10.1016/j.jneuroling.2005.06.002

Rundblad, G., & Annaz, D. (2010a). The atypical development of metaphor and metonymy comprehension in children with autism. *Autism*, *14*, 29–46. http://dx.doi.org/10.1177/1362361309340667

Rundblad, G., & Annaz, D. (2010b). Development of metaphor and metonymy comprehension: Receptive vocabulary and conceptual knowledge. *British Journal of Developmental Psychology*, *28*, 547–563. http://dx.doi.org/10.1348/026151009X454373

Sherman, J. C., & Lust, B. (1993). Children are in control. *Cognition*, *46*, 1–51. http://dx.doi.org/10.1016/0010-0277(93)90021-M

Tager-Flusberg, H., & Anderson, M. (1991). The development of contingent discourse ability in autistic children. *Journal of Child Psychology and Psychiatry*, *32*, 1123–1134. http://dx.doi.org/10.1111/j.1469-7610.1991.tb00353.x

Tavakolian, S. L. (1978). Children's comprehension of pronominal subjects and missing subjects in complicated sentences. In H. Goodluck & L. Solan (Eds.), *Papers in the structure and development of child language* (UMASS Occasional Papers in Linguistics, Vol. 4, pp. 145–152). Amherst: University of Massachusetts.

Tovar, A. T., Fein, D., & Naigles, L. R. (2015). Grammatical aspect is a strength in the language comprehension of young children with autism spectrum disorder. *Journal of Speech, Language, and Hearing Research*, *58*, 301–310. http://dx.doi.org/10.1044/2014_JSLHR-L-13-0257

Walenski, M., Mostofsky, S. H., & Ullman, M. T. (2014). Inflectional morphology in high-functioning autism: Evidence for speeded grammatical processing. *Research in Autism Spectrum Disorders, 8*, 1607–1621. http://dx.doi.org/10.1016/j.rasd.2014.08.009

Whyte, E. M., & Nelson, K. E. (2015). Trajectories of pragmatic and nonliteral language development in children with autism spectrum disorders. *Journal of Communication Disorders, 54*, 2–14. http://dx.doi.org/10.1016/j.jcomdis.2015.01.001

World Health Organization. (1992). *The ICD–10 classification of mental and behavioural disorders: Clinical descriptions and diagnostic guidelines*. Geneva, Switzerland: Author.

Stephanie Durrleman-Tame, Morgane Burnel, and Anne Reboul

8 Connections Among Complementation Sentences, Executive Functioning, and Theory of Mind in Autism

The ability to impute mental states to others and to predict their behavior based on this knowledge is referred to as *theory of mind* or ToM (Premack & Woodruff, 1978). A classic method for evaluating ToM is the false belief (FB) task, such as the Sally and Anne paradigm, in which children are asked to predict where a character, Sally, will first look for an object that was moved to a new location (by Anne) in her absence (Baron-Cohen, Leslie, & Frith, 1985). To succeed, children must grasp that a belief (namely, Sally's) does not necessarily correspond to reality but rather to representations that may be true or false (Dennett, 1978). Success at FB tasks is achieved by typically developing (TD) children around 4 to 5 years of age (Wellman, Cross, & Watson, 2001), whereas children with autism spectrum disorder (ASD) of higher nonverbal mental age still fail at this task (Yirmiya, Erel, Shaked, & Solomonica-Levi, 1998). This has led some researchers to suggest that communicative and social difficulties associated with this population are the result of a core mentalizing deficit (Frith, 2001; Frith, Morton, & Leslie, 1991).

Crucially, however, in every study assessing FB in children with ASD, a proportion of participants pass, ranging from a minority (e.g., 20%, as in Baron-Cohen, Leslie, & Frith, 1985) to a majority (e.g., 60%, as in Prior, Dahlstrom, & Squires, 1990). If ToM is a core deficit of the population, what allows a subset of children with autism to be successful at ToM tasks? One proposal in the literature is that this subset of ToM passers applies compensatory, verbally mediated strategies when figuring out the correct responses, thus camouflaging their attenuated ToM (Bowler, 1992; Happé, 1995). This proposal finds support in the observation that language abilities and success at basic ToM tasks have been shown to be linked both in TD children (e.g., Astington & Jenkins, 1999) as well as in children with autism, with the latter group requiring more advanced language abilities than the former to pass (Happé, 1995).

This work was supported by the Swiss NSF (PA00P1_136355) to S. Durrleman. Many thanks to Professor Pierre Fourneret and Dr. Sandrine Sonie of the Centre de Ressources en Autisme Rhone Alpes, to the schools and institutions (in Grenoble, Lyon, and Geneva), and to the children for their invaluable participation.

http://dx.doi.org/10.1037/15964-009
Innovative Investigations of Language in Autism Spectrum Disorder, L. R. Naigles (Editor)

The Role of Complementation in ToM

The notion that children with autism may rely more heavily on verbalizing for ToM representation has fueled research investigating which particular component of linguistic competency may impact FB task success the most, with certain authors highlighting the privileged role of grammar (Fisher, Happé, & Dunn, 2005) and, more specifically, complementation (Lind & Bowler, 2009[1]; Tager-Flusberg, 2000; Tager-Flusberg & Joseph, 2005). Indeed, the semantic and syntactic properties of complement clauses render them ideal tools for reasoning about other minds (de Villiers, 1995, 2000; de Villiers & de Villiers, 2000). Consider this sentence as an illustration: *Some researchers believe that <u>mastery of complementation influences ToM performance</u>*. This sentence is true once some researchers entertain the belief expressed in the italicized complement clause, independently of whether mastery of complementation influences ToM performance. The truth-value of the complement clause is thus crucially evaluated with respect to the mental worlds of the researchers in question (Lewis, 1986), which may be separate from our own mental world and may conflict with reality. These semantic and syntactic characteristics of complements explain why they are ideal for representing contradictions between mental states and reality and thus may serve as a keystone for explicitly reasoning about FBs and other minds (de Villiers & Pyers, 2002).

Children with ASD have been reported to produce few sentential complements in their spontaneous speech (Durrleman & Zufferey, 2013; Yi, Fan, Zhao, Huang, Li, & Zou, 2013), and their performance on complements of verbs of communication (although not of verbs of cognition) correlates with their performance on FB tasks (Lind & Bowler, 2009; Tager-Flusberg, 2000; Tager-Flusberg & Joseph, 2005). This has been interpreted to suggest that mastery of complementation facilitates ToM task performance in ASD, with children on the spectrum plausibly bootstrapping their FB understanding through speaking about what people say rather than about what they think (Tager-Flusberg & Joseph, 2005). However, it is still to be determined whether the link found between complementation and FB performance is the result of an experimental confound between the tasks involved, namely, their reliance on similar levels of verbal skills—and whether the impact of complementation on FB performance is privileged compared with executive function (EF), which is also claimed to be related to ToM success (e.g., Pellicano, 2007).

1 It is worth noting that there is considerable debate regarding which component of language most affects theory of mind in typical development—that is to say, whether it is more general language abilities or more specifically the competency with complementation (for a review, see Farrar, Lee, Cho, Tamargo, & Seung, 2013).

Experimental Confounds in ToM and Complementation Tasks

A limitation to date of studies highlighting the relationship between FB and complementation is their use of FB tasks, which are themselves reliant on advanced linguistic competency. For example, the tasks employed require parsing of the past tense and wh-questions, two grammatical features that can pose problems for children on the autistic spectrum (Goodwin, Fein, & Naigles, 2012; J. Roberts, Rice, & Tager-Flusberg, 2004; Zebib, Tuller, Prévost, & Morin, 2013). Moreover, these grammatical features were also present in the tasks used to assess complements; therefore, the relationship reported between success on the FB and complement tasks may arguably result from a reliance on similar levels of language ability. This underlying experimental confound renders it impossible to conclude that there is a functional link between ToM and complementation in ASD.

Role of Executive Function in ToM

Executive function (EF) is an umbrella term referring to processes responsible for self-control, such as planning, decision making, working memory, cognitive flexibility, impulse control, and inhibition (Rabbitt, 1997; A. Roberts, Robbins, & Weiskrantz, 1998). Some of these processes—in particular, memory and inhibition—may play a role in FB success. Indeed, for participants to reply accurately during a FB task, they need to both remember the sequence of events in the FB story and suppress a natural tendency to point to where they know the object in question is located and point instead to where they know the object is not found. Weaknesses in inhibition thus potentially explain links between EF and ToM tasks in both TD (Hughes, 1998; Perner & Lang, 1999; Sabbagh, Moses, & Shiverick, 2006) and ASD groups (Ozonoff & Jensen, 1999; Ozonoff, Pennington, & Rogers, 1991; Pellicano, 2007). Indeed EF deficits are attested in ASD (Booth, Charlton, Hughes, & Happé, 2003; Ozonoff & Jensen, 1999; Prior & Hoffmann, 1990), including difficulty with pointing to an empty box rather than a box where a desired object is located (Hughes & Russell, 1993). The conclusion that EF impacts ToM rather than vice versa is upheld by studies showing that it is possible to predict future ToM performance from executive abilities, while ToM performance does not predict future executive performance, for either TD children (Carlson, Mandell, & Williams, 2004; Carlson, Moses, & Breton, 2002; Flynn, 2007; Hughes, 1998) or children with ASD (Fisher & Happé, 2005).

In sum, both EF and complementation have been claimed to influence ToM performance in both ASD and TD groups, which raises the question: Does one play a more crucial role than the other? A longitudinal study (Chen, 2013) investigating the contributory roles of EF and complements on ToM assessed TD children aged 3 to 6 at

1-year intervals showed that although their inhibition skills better predicted FB performance at Time 1 than at Time 2, the comprehension of complement clauses predicted FB performance equally well at both time points. These results suggest that in TD children inhibition is less important to ToM development than complementation; however, the question remains unexplored to date for children with ASD.

Research Aims and Predictions

This chapter explores the impact of complementation on ToM performance in ASD, with the aim of clarifying how this impact compares with that of EF, and whether this impact is observable not only when ToM is assessed verbally but also when it is assessed nonverbally. If complementation plays a privileged role in ToM, correlations should be more clearly established between complements and ToM than between EF and ToM. This is tested in Study 1 (Durrleman & Franck, 2015). If complementation is linked to general ToM reasoning, correlations should arise not only between complements and verbal ToM but also between complements and nonverbal ToM. This is tested in Study 2 (Durrleman et al., 2015).

Study 1: Relations Among Sentence Complements, ToM, and EF

Participants

This study included 17 French-speaking children with ASD, with or without intellectual disability (aged 6–16 years, mean age 9;2) and 17 younger TD peers (4–9 years, mean age 7;6). All children had to be able to produce and understand simple sentences of at least three words for inclusion. The two groups were of similar nonverbal mental age as measured by the Raven's Progressive Matrices ($M = 24$). Participants with ASD were recruited through parent associations and psychologists in Geneva and the suburbs and were diagnosed by a specialist as meeting *Diagnostic and Statistical Manual of Mental Disorders* (fourth edition; *DSM–IV*; American Psychiatric Association, 1994) criteria for an ASD. TD participants were recruited from a primary school in Geneva, Switzerland.

Materials and Procedure

For our ASD sample, we administered three standardized tasks: one of nonverbal intelligence (Raven's Progressive Matrices; Raven, Court, & Raven, 1998), one of vocabulary (Echelle de Vocabulaire en Images Peabody [EVIP]; Dunn, Thériault-Whalen, & Dunn, 1993), and one of morphosyntax (Production d'Enoncés du Bilan Informatisé de Langage Oral [Prod-E BILO]; Khomsi, Khomsi, Parbeau-Guéno, & Pasquet, 2007). All participants were also presented with experimental tasks assessing complementation, EF, and ToM, which were purposefully computerized because this mode is reported to improve the participation of children with ASD (Ozonoff, 1995; Ozonoff & Strayer, 2001).

Complement Clause Task

The task assessing complement sentences with verbs of communication (Durrleman & Franck, 2015) avoided linguistic structures such as interrogatives or the use of the past tense, which as explained may pose problems for children with ASD. It involved a sentence–picture matching procedure. Children were instructed to listen to prerecorded sentences and then to select one picture out of two appearing on a computer screen. The task contained three phases: warm-up, control condition, and test condition.

The warm-up phase ensured that participants recognized characters, speech, and thought bubbles and were precise at pointing. All children performed at ceiling when having to recognize the four characters ("Marie," "Thomas," "La soeur de Marie"/"The sister of Mary," and "Le frère de Thomas"/"The brother of Thomas") on the basis of simple instructions ("Montre-moi le frère de Marie"/"Show me the brother of Mary").

In the control condition, the sentence heard contained a simple noun subject as in "Marie dit que la fille joue du piano" ("Marie says that the girl is playing the piano"; see Figure 8.1a). The child then had to point to the left or the right of the picture on the screen, as shown in Figure 8.1a. Success at this phase alone does not necessarily depend on the correct parsing of the syntactic dependencies of the sentence. Indeed, it may be based on the partial parsing of the subordinate clause, which is identical to one of the prerecorded sentences depicting the picture ("La fille joue du piano"/"The girl is playing the piano"). This condition served nonetheless to ensure that participants were able to focus their attention on the parsing of the subordinate clause, which in the critical test condition had to be linked syntactically to the correct nominal in the main clause.

In the test condition, the child again heard two prerecorded declarative sentences depicting the contents of speech bubbles (although this time there were two different voices corresponding either to a male or a female character), followed by a complement clause. The subject of the complement clause in this condition was a complex subject such as "Mary's brother," which in French translates word-for-word as "The brother of Mary" ("Le frère de Marie"). For example, children heard "Le frère de Marie dit que la fille joue au football" ("The brother of Mary says that the girl is

(a)

(b)

Fig. 8.1: (a) Picture from the control condition for complements of communication verbs. (b) Picture from the test condition for complements of communication verbs. From "Exploring Links Between Language and Cognition in Autism Spectrum Disorders: Complement Sentences, False Belief, and Executive Functioning," by S. Durrleman and J. Franck, 2015, *Journal of Communication Disorders*, *54*, pp. 19–20. Copyright 2015 by Elsevier, Inc. Reprinted with permission.

playing football") and had to point to the relevant picture on the computer screen (see Figure 8.1b). More precisely, they had to know that it is *le frère* ("the brother") who is the subject of the verb *dire* ("say") and not "Marie," which is linearly closer to the verb. Success at this condition thus depends on the child's ability to correctly analyze the syntactic relationships involved in the sentence, by relating the correct nominal to the verb *dire* ("say"), which selects a complement clause. Given that the control condition primed children to focus on the complement and the test phase required children to select the accurate nominal in the main clause to link the complement to, the two conditions together tap into children's parsing of complementation sentences.

EF Task

EF was assessed via an adapted, computerized version of the Dimensional Change Card-Sorting Task (Diamond & Kirkham, 2005). This task requires children to sort images appearing on the computer screen into one of two boxes: the one on the left with a blue car on its front or the one on the right with a red teddy bear on its front. Children were told that they would play a game of sorting according to either shape or colour. Stimuli to be sorted were either identical to that on the front of the box or incongruent along one dimension, that is to say color or shape.

The task contained three blocks: Block 1 requiring sorting according to color, Block 2 requiring sorting according to shape, and Block 3 where the sorting criterion varied across items and was announced by a computer voice just before the object was presented ("color!" or "shape!"). Perceptual inhibition was assessed in Blocks 1 and 2 by contrasting the conflict condition in which the shape of the object to be sorted mismatched that of the object represented on the box to the no conflict condition in which both the color and the shape of the object to be sorted matched that of the object on the box. Hence, in the conflict condition, the children need to inhibit perceptual information present in the stimulus. A score of perceptual inhibition was obtained by subtracting performance in the conflict condition (12 items) from performance in the no conflict condition (12 items). Rule inhibition was assessed by contrasting performance on the last two conflict items in Block 1 to performance on the first two conflict items in Block 2, which involved a change in the sorting criterion. Flexible rule switching was assessed in the third block by subtracting performance with items in the switch condition (12 items) from items in the no switch condition (12 items). The stimuli of all three blocks were presented in a pseudo-random order. Before each test block, a practice block of eight items familiarized the participant with the procedure and feedback (correct or incorrect) was provided. Feedback was not given during the three subsequent test blocks tapping into the cognitive control components described later.

ToM Task

The ToM assessment was composed of four FB tasks. The experimenter used dolls while telling these four stories, always involving Protagonist B transferring an object from one location to another during the absence of Protagonist A. When Protagonist A returned, the child was asked three questions, two of which were control conditions (Reality: Where is the [object] now? Memory: Where was the [object] at the beginning?), and one of which was the test question targeting FB attribution (Where will A look for the [object] first?). Note that for the FB condition we decided to add the term *en premier* ("first") at the end of the question because it has been shown to improve TD children's performance on the task (Surian & Leslie, 1999). This task was composed of eight control questions (four reality questions and four memory questions) and four test FB questions.

Results

Complement Clause and ToM Performance

Figure 8.2 shows that both ASD and TD groups performed well in the control conditions of the complement task. The TD group continued to show good performance in the test condition, whereas the performance of the group with ASD decreased somewhat. Results showed a significant difference between the control and test conditions in both ASD and TD groups. Comparisons between groups showed no difference between them in the control condition and no difference in the test condition ($t < 1$). The difference in the corrected score for the test condition also failed to reach the significance level.

Figure 8.2 also reveals that the ASD group showed significantly poorer performance in the FB condition compared with the reality condition, $t(16) = 2.40$, $p < .05$, $d = .76$, and to the memory condition, $t(16) = 2.09$, $p = .053$, $d = 0.61$. The latter two conditions did not differ ($t < 1$). TD children showed no significant difference between the FB condition and the reality condition, $t(16) = 1.77$, $p = .10$, $d = .39$; the FB and the memory condition ($t < 1$); and the reality and memory conditions, $t(16) = 1.43$, $p = .17$, $d = .26$. Comparisons across groups showed significantly poorer performance in ASD in the FB condition, $t(28.85) = 2.93$, $p < .05$, $d = .94$, whereas the difference in the reality and memory conditions did not reach statistical significance levels, $t(20.82) = 1.83$, $p = .08$, $d = .61$ and $t(21.42) = 1.71$, $p = .10$, $d = .62$), respectively.

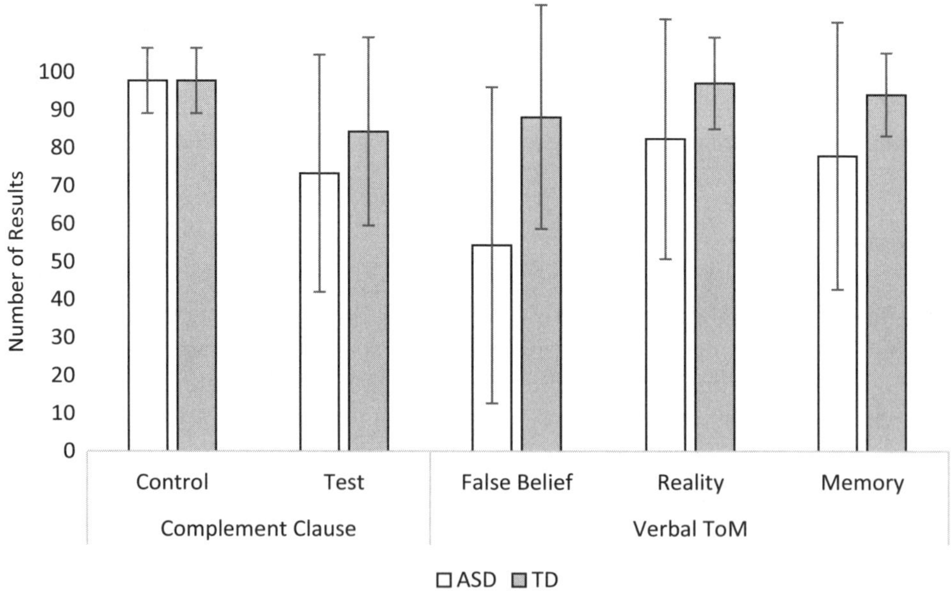

Fig. 8.2: Results for complement clauses and theory of mind (ToM).

Complements and ToM Comparison

Correlations were conducted on the overall group of children and showed a significant correlation between the FB task and the complement task, $r(24) = .54$, $p = .005$.

Given the considerable variability in performance within the ToM task by the ASD group, we further explored through correlational analyses whether more general syntax and lexical abilities as measured by the BILO and EVIP accounted for their performance in ToM. Performance in the FB condition of the ToM task showed no significant correlation with scores on the EVIP nor with those on the BILO.

EF Results

The two groups did not differ in their sensitivity to rule inhibition or to rule switching ($t < 1$) and thus had a similar level of EF (for more details, see Durrleman & Franck, 2015).

EF and ToM Comparison

For the two groups, correlations run with the score at the Raven's Progressive Matrices as control showed no significant correlation with any EF index—perceptual inhibition, rule inhibition, nor flexible rule switching.

Discussion

This first study set out to determine how the role played by complementation in ToM success compares with the role played by EF. The performance of the children with ASD tested for complementation and EF was similar to the performance by younger TD peers functioning at a similar cognitive level and as such indicates a delay in the development of these abilities. FB attribution in ASD was significantly worse than in the children matched on nonverbal IQ, however, confirming the often-reported ToM deficit in ASD. Our results also replicated a relation between complement sentence and ToM performance, whereas links did not emerge between EF and ToM. Still, on the basis of our correlational results alone, we cannot conclude that this link between complements and ToM is a causal one, with complementation being a precursor of ToM. Nonetheless, our findings are compatible with this view, which is empirically supported by previous longitudinal work showing that performance on complements predicts later FB performance in both TD (e.g., de Villiers & Pyers, 2002) and ASD (e.g., Tager-Flusberg & Joseph, 2005). The fact that variability in general language abilities did not account for the complement sentences and verbal FB relationship further suggests that this link is a selective one. In light of all these considerations, we can conclude that complementation seems to play a privileged role in ToM performance in ASD.

Study 2: Relations Among Sentence Complements, Verbal ToM, and Nonverbal ToM

We have seen that the link found between complementation and ToM holds even when other cognitive capacities do not show such a relationship. However, it is still an open question whether complementation is a key ingredient in ToM reasoning or whether the level of linguistic sophistication presupposed by complementation is also presupposed by verbal ToM tasks. If complementation is involved in ToM reasoning, we expect correlations between measures of complements and nonverbal measures of ToM.

Participants

Participants included 34 native French speakers with ASD, aged 6;9 to 14;4 years (mean age 10;6), recruited through the Centre de Ressources Autisme Rhône-Alpes of the Centre Hospitalier Le Vinatier and the Hôpital Saint Jean de Dieu in Lyon, France. They had all been diagnosed with ASD by a qualified clinician according to *DSM–IV—Text Revision* criteria (American Psychiatric Association, 2000) as well as the Autism Diagnostic Observation Schedule—Generic (Lord et al., 2000), the Autism Diagnostic Interview—Revised (Rutter, LeCouteur, & Lord, 2003), or both. The average mental age of our ASD sample was 8;9 years, and they were all enrolled in intensive therapeutic educational programs. Controls were 24 TD children (5;4 to 11;8 mean age 8;2), recruited from local French schools and day-care centers of similar nonverbal mental age to that of the ASD group as measured by the Leiter International Performance Scale—Revised (Roid & Miller, 1997). All children were able to produce and understand simple sentences of at least three words.

Materials and Procedure

Subjects were administered standardized tasks measuring nonverbal abilities (Leiter International Performance Scale—Revised), as well as global morphosyntax (BILO; Khomsi et al., 2007). The TD children had numerically but not significantly higher mean scores than the children with ASD for mental age, $\chi 2(1) = 0.08$, $p = .78$, and for morphosyntax, $\chi 2(1) = 3.31$, $p = .07$.

Complement Clause Task

The complement sentences task was a French adaptation of the experiment by de Villiers and Pyers (2002). This task included 10 stories of two lines, which were read by the experimenter while pointing to two illustrative photographs on a computer screen. Stories contained a complement embedded under a tensed communication verb (*dire*/"say"). Given that difficulties with past tense are reported for children with ASD (Roberts et al., 2004), we modified the original task to use only the present tense. Compare 1 with 2:

1. "The teacher said the girl had a bug in her hair" (experimenter points to the first picture). "But look, it was only a leaf" (experimenter points to the second picture). "What did she say the girl had in her hair" (experimenter points back to the first)?
2. *La maîtresse dit que la fille a un insecte dans les cheveux* (experimenter points to the first picture). *Mais en fait, c'est une feuille* (experimenter points to the second picture). *Qu'est-ce qu'elle dit que la fille a dans les cheveux* (experimenter points back to the first)?
   "The teacher says that the girl has a bug in her hair. But really, it's just a leaf. What does she say that the girl has in her hair?"

Each correct response to the test question yielded 1 point, amounting to a maximum score of 10 points. Responses were counted as accurate once the participant was able to produce the embedded (false) complement of the verb of communication.

Verbal ToM Task

Verbal ToM measures were composed of two unexpected transfer tasks, one acted out with dolls, as in Study 1, with an accompanying narrative, and one presented in the form of a story told while referring to pictures in a book (see the ToM storybook, sixth story; Serra, Loth, van Geert, Hurkens, & Minderaa, 2002). In the latter, a character named Simon puts his new rollerblades in a toy chest and goes out. His sister, Lucie, then arrives and removes these from the toy chest to place them in a box. Upon Simon's return, children are asked the FB question: "Where is Simon going to look for his rollerblades?" In addition, a control (reality) question is asked (i.e., "Where are the rollerblades really?"). For both FB measures, accurate FB replies scored 1 point and inaccurate ones zero and were only calculated for children who replied accurately to the control question(s).

Nonverbal ToM Task

The nonverbal assessment of ToM, in contrast to the verbal tasks, did not involve a narrative being told followed by questions to be answered. Instead, this task, an

Fig. 8.3: Illustration of (a) the mechanical condition of the nonverbal theory of mind (ToM) task and (b) the intentional condition of the nonverbal ToM task. From "Picture Sequencing Test," 2016, Autism Research Centre, University of Cambridge, Cambridge, United Kingdom. Copyright 2016 by Autism Research Centre. Reprinted with permission.

adaptation of a picture-sequencing task (Baron-Cohen, Leslie, & Frith, 1986), required children to arrange pictures to illustrate a story composed of four cards. The experimenter always commenced by placing the first card down in a frame composed of four empty squares; the child then had to sort the remaining three cards. The only verbal instruction provided was "Put into order." In our adapted version, two types of events were depicted: mechanical and intentional (Figures 8.3a and 8.3b, respectively). The mechanical, control condition depicted cause-and-effect occurrences and served to ensure that children were capable of producing sequences to tell a story. The intentional, test condition involved FB attribution to arrive at the accurate sequence. Scoring was conducted following Baron-Cohen and colleagues (1986), which yielded 2 points for a fully correct sequence, 1 point for partially correct sequences with the last picture accurately placed at the end, or 0 points for other responses. This amounted to a maximum score of 6 points for each condition.

Results

Complements and ToM Performance

The TD group performed significantly better than the ASD group for the complement task, $\chi 2(1) = 6.55$, $p < .05$. Concerning the verbal ToM results, although TD children performed better than children with ASD, this difference did not reach significance, $\chi2(1) = 3.04$, $p = .08$.

Concerning the nonverbal ToM results, performance between the groups did not differ significantly for the mechanical, $\chi2(1) = 0.26$, $p = .61$, and intentional, $\chi2(1) = 1.82$, $p = .18$, conditions. Tests showed significantly better performance on mechanical sequences than intentional ones, for both ASD, $\chi2(1) = 13.95$, $p < .05$, and TD groups, $\chi2(1) = 4.13$, $p < .05$. As with the verbal ToM task, both groups performed similarly on the nonverbal ToM task, $\chi2(1) = 2.20$, $p = .14$.

Complements and ToM Comparisons

We then examined the relationship between FB performance and knowledge of complement sentences compared with other aspects of language for the two groups separately, with the scores of the FB conditions of the ToM tasks as the dependent measures and nonverbal IQ and morphosyntax entered separately.

For TD children, partial correlations controlling for nonverbal mental age revealed significant correlations between verbal ToM and comprehension of complement sentences, $\tau(21) = 0.37$, $p < .05$. In addition, the correlation between verbal ToM and complements was still present when controlling for general morphosyntax, $\tau(21) = 0.47$, $p < .05$. Although a significant correlation also emerged between nonverbal ToM and general morphosyntax, $\tau(23) = 0.34$, $p < .05$, this correlation became marginal once mental age was controlled for, $\tau(23) = 0.28$, $p = .06$. No correlation was found between nonverbal ToM and complements, $\tau(23) = 0.19$, $p = .30$.

For children with ASD, partial correlations controlling for mental age revealed significant correlations between verbal ToM and morphosyntax and complement clauses, $\tau(21) = 0.52$, $p < .05$, and $\tau(21) = 0.41$, $p < .05$, respectively. In addition, the correlation between verbal ToM and complements was still present when controlling for general morphosyntax, $\tau(21) = 0.33$, $p < .05$. After mental age was controlled, a significant correlation between complementation and nonverbal ToM was also observed, $\tau(31) = 0.31$, $p < .05$. Furthermore, the correlation between nonverbal ToM and communication complements persisted after controlling for general morphosyntax, $\tau(31) = 0.32$, $p < .05$.

Discussion

With this study, we aimed to determine whether knowledge of sentential complements influences ToM when assessed not only verbally but also nonverbally. Regarding performance at complements, our group with ASD was below that of TD peers, contrasting with previous reports (Lind & Bowler, 2009). As for verbal and nonverbal FB, the group with ASD performed similarly to TD controls. The good performance of our ASD sample for ToM could be related to various characteristics of our sample, such as having an average mental age of 8;9 years and having received intensive therapeutic interventions for years before testing. Indeed, children with ASD have previously shown good performance in tasks such as ours when around the mental age of 9 years, with the youngest passing such tests being 5;5 years (Happé, 1995). It is worth noting that this is still later than TD children, who tend to succeed before 5 years (Flavell, 1999; Hogrefe, Wimmer, & Perner, 1986). As such, the mindreading skills of our sample with ASD may have had time to catch up by the time they were tested. Also, the therapeutic interventions they had been receiving may well have played into their improved FB performance, as certain training studies have been reported to show positive effects (Paynter & Peterson, 2013; Wellman et al., 2002).

The verbal ToM–complement relationship was observed in both TD and ASD groups after partialling out the effect of mental age and general morphosyntactic abilities. This result is consistent with previous reports for TD children (de Villiers & Pyers, 1997; Tager-Flusberg, 1997, 2000) and children with ASD (Lind & Bowler, 2009; Tager-Flusberg & Joseph, 2005), and has been interpreted to suggest a privileged relation between structures that allow for the embedding of a false proposition and verbal FB attribution. This is because such propositions would invite us to entertain the possibly false worlds of others and as such be the ideal tool for representing the beliefs of others and judging their truth and falsity (de Villiers, 2000, 2007). However, recall that another possible interpretation is that this link stems from an underlying similarity of the tasks assessing ToM and complements, namely, their reliance on the parsing of complex linguistic structures such as interrogatives (i.e., "What does the woman say is in the bathtub?" is in the complement task, and "Where will Sally look for her marble?" is in the FB task).

With the low-verbal ToM task, we explored whether the ToM-complement link would remain in the absence of this experimental confound. The link did not emerge in the TD group; however, it was evident in the ASD group, even after partialling out the effects of general morphosyntax. This difference between the ASD and TD groups could suggest that while the TD children used nonverbal and implicit strategies, the children with ASD relied predominantly on an internal monologue involving an explicit linguistic rehearsal of the reasoning: "She did not see or say that the sweet was eaten, so she can't expect it to not be there and she is surprised." This is consistent with previous hypotheses suggesting that individuals with ASD who succeed at FB are using verbal compensatory strategies (Happé, 1995; Lind & Bowler, 2009; Tager-Flusberg, 2000; Tager-Flusberg & Joseph, 2005). The current study thus suggests that individuals with ASD may rely more specifically on competency in complementation than other populations for FB reasoning. Their reliance plausibly stems from an underlying difficulty in this domain, but one that can be overcome with the correct compensatory mechanisms. An analogy may be made with individuals with an intuitive sense of spatial orientation as opposed to individuals who have a weakness in this domain. For the latter group, compensatory mechanisms become crucial when getting from A to B. The preferred strategy may be a visual one (e.g., a map) or a verbal one (e.g., an internal monologue of the sort: "First I have to go straight and then three roads down I'll take the first left, and after that the third street right"). A similar phenomenon may be at stake in children with autism when faced with a mental state attribution task. In such instances, they would turn to explicitly reasoning through the representation of subjective truth by means of embedded sentences: for example, "Even if the marble is in the basket she says (to herself) that the marble is in the box."

Conclusion

Reasoning about the content of mental states, an important step in ToM, is challenging for children with ASD and potentially explains various social and communicative impairments associated with their condition. A subset of children on the spectrum nevertheless succeeds on ToM tasks. It has been argued that this success is a result of their transposing ToM into language, the way that some individuals with limited spatial skills transpose a map into verbal directions. The linguistic tool par excellence hypothesized to assist them is the complement clause (Tager-Flusberg, 2000; Tager-Flusberg & Joseph, 2005; Lind & Bowler, 2009). Still, methodological confounds between tasks used in these studies make it difficult to discern the relationship between complements and ToM. It has also been argued that certain EFs influence FB performance, such as the holding information in working memory and the inhibition of a prepotent response (Ozonoff & Jensen, 1999; Ozonoff, Pennington, & Rogers, 1991; Pellicano, 2007). More research is thus necessary to ascertain whether complements or EF skills are related in a special way to ToM in ASD.

This chapter has presented two studies providing evidence in favor of the view that complement sentences show a privileged link with ToM success as measured by FB tasks. The first study indicated that this link is privileged compared with another cognitive tool, namely, EF. Indeed, despite controlling for nonverbal IQ, the FB–complementation connection surfaced, but no such connection surfaced between FB and EF or between FB and general language measures. Although it is possible that a connection between ToM and EF or general language could well have surfaced if the sample size had been larger, the fact that a ToM–complementation connection surfaced despite this limitation still argues in favor of its special status. The second study showed that links between complementation and ToM carry over to nonverbal ToM performance in ASD, independent of mental age and general grammatical abilities. Taken together with previous longitudinal work revealing that complementation skills in TD and ASD are a significant predictor of concurrent and later FB task success, but not vice versa (de Villiers & Pyers, 2002; Tager-Flusberg & Joseph, 2005), our studies suggest that mastery of complementation provides a crucial tool for FB representation in ASD, in line with the hypothesis of linguistic determinism (de Villiers, 1995, 2000;

de Villiers & de Villiers, 2000). Children with ASD thus seem to use complementation as a way to compensate their difficulties in ToM.

Further research is needed to explore whether and how these findings may help to fine-tune clinical interventions targeting ToM remediation in ASD, for example, through the coaching of complement sentences, along the lines of that which has been shown by training studies conducted with TD children (Hale & Tager-Flusberg, 2003; Lohmann & Tomasello, 2003). Moreover, one might ask whether the observed links between complementation and ToM are limited to FB tasks or if they can be found in other ToM tasks mastered at different points in development. Other tasks assessing intermediate steps in mental state understanding are mastered by children in a specific order between the ages of 3 and 5 years (Wellman & Liu, 2004), namely, the understanding of (a) diverse desires, (b) diverse beliefs, (c) perceptual access to knowledge, (d) FB, and (e) hidden emotion. Complementation, in addition to assisting with FB, might also assist with understanding that someone who has not seen inside a box is ignorant with respect to its contents (i.e., diverse beliefs or perceptual access to knowledge). An intuitive argument could be that embedding allows children to represent that "He doesn't know/believe *that the box contains a toy.*" On the other hand, it is less clear how it could explain hidden emotion or diverse desires. The different tasks may also have different executive demands and could require different amounts of executive control or flexibility. These could be interesting points to study to better understand what is useful for different aspects of ToM development and to propose adapted training to children with ASD, fine-tuned to their stage of development.

Finally, studies devoted to pragmatic abilities (implicatures, metaphor, irony) in individuals with ASD have shown that their performances are variable but that success seems correlated both to ToM performance and to verbal IQ (see, e.g., Chevallier, Wilson, Happé, & Noveck, 2010; Happé, 1993; Pijnacker, Hagoort, Buitelaar, Teunisse, & Geurts, 2009). This suggests that investigating more precisely the relevant linguistic factors, including complementation, would be an interesting area of study, with the aim of enhancing communication for individuals with ASD.

References

American Psychiatric Association. (1994). *Diagnostic and statistical manual of mental disorders* (4th ed.). Washington, DC: Author.

American Psychiatric Association. (2000). *Diagnostic and statistical manual of mental disorders* (4th ed., text rev.). Washington, DC: Author.

Astington, J. W., & Jenkins, J. M. (1999). A longitudinal study of the relation between language and theory-of-mind development. *Developmental Psychology*, *35*, 1311–1320. http://dx.doi.org/10.1037/0012-1649.35.5.1311

Baron-Cohen, S., Leslie, A. M., & Frith, U. (1985). Does the autistic child have a "theory of mind"? *Cognition*, *21*, 37–46. http://dx.doi.org/10.1016/0010-0277(85)90022-8

Baron-Cohen, S., Leslie, A. M., & Frith, U. (1986). Mechanical, behavioural and intentional understanding of picture stories in autistic children. *British Journal of Developmental Psychology*, *4*, 113–125. http://dx.doi.org/10.1111/j.2044-835X.1986.tb01003.x

Booth, R., Charlton, R., Hughes, C., & Happé, F. (2003). Disentangling weak coherence and executive dysfunction: Planning drawing in autism and attention-deficit/hyperactivity disorder. *Philosophical Transactions of the Royal Society of London: Series B. Biological Sciences*, *358*, 387–392. http://dx.doi.org/10.1098/rstb.2002.1204

Bowler, D. M. (1992). “Theory of mind” in Asperger's syndrome. *Journal of Child Psychology and Psychiatry*, *33*, 877–893. http://dx.doi.org/10.1111/j.1469-7610.1992.tb01962.x

Carlson, S. M., Mandell, D. J., & Williams, L. (2004). Executive function and theory of mind: Stability and prediction from ages 2 to 3. *Developmental Psychology*, *40*, 1105–1122. http://dx.doi.org/10.1037/0012-1649.40.6.1105

Carlson, S. M., Moses, L. J., & Breton, C. (2002). How specific is the relation between executive function and theory of mind? Contributions of inhibitory control and working memory. *Infant and Child Development*, *11*, 73–92. http://dx.doi.org/10.1002/icd.298

Chen, M. (2013). *Language, inhibitory control and false belief reasoning: A longitudinal study* (Honors thesis). Smith College, Northampton, MA. Retrieved from http://scholarworks.smith.edu/theses/147

Chevallier, C., Wilson, D., Happé, F., & Noveck, I. (2010). Scalar inferences in autism spectrum disorders. *Journal of Autism and Developmental Disorders*, *40*, 1104–1117. http://dx.doi.org/10.1007/s10803-010-0960-8

de Villiers, J. G. (1995, March). *Steps in the mastery of sentence complements.* Presented at the Biennial Meeting of the Society for Research in Child Development, Indianapolis, IN.

de Villiers, J. G. (2000). Language and theory of mind: What are the developmental relationships? In S. Baron-Cohen, H. Tager-Flusberg, & D. J. Cohen (Eds.), *Understanding other minds: Perspectives from developmental cognitive neuroscience* (2nd ed., pp. 83–123). New York, NY: Oxford University Press.

de Villiers, J. G. (2007). The interface of language and theory of mind. *Lingua*, *117*, 1858–1878.

de Villiers, J. G., & de Villiers, P. A. (2000). Linguistic determinism and the understanding of false beliefs. In P. Mitchell & K. Riggs (Eds.), *Children's reasoning and the mind* (pp. 189–226). Hove, England: Psychology Press.

de Villiers, J. G., & Pyers, J. (1997). Complementing cognition: The relationship between language and theory of mind. In *Proceedings of the 21st Annual Boston University Conference on Language Development* (pp. 136–147). Somerville, MA: Cascadilla Press.

de Villiers, J. G., & Pyers, J. (2002). Complements to cognition: A longitudinal study of the relationship between complex syntax and false belief understanding. *Cognitive Development*, *17*, 1037–1060. http://dx.doi.org/10.1016/S0885-2014(02)00073-4

Dennett, D. C. (1978). Beliefs about beliefs. *Behavioral and Brain Sciences*, *1*, 568–570. http://dx.doi.org/10.1017/S0140525X00076664

Diamond, A., & Kirkham, N. (2005). Not quite as grown-up as we like to think: Parallels between cognition in childhood and adulthood. *Psychological Science*, *16*, 291–297. http://dx.doi.org/10.1111/j.0956-7976.2005.01530.x

Dunn, L., Thériault-Whalen, C., & Dunn, L. (1993). *Échelle de vocabulaire en images Peabody: Adaptation française du Peabody Picture Vocabulary Test—Revised* [Peabody Picture Vocabulary Scale: French adaptation of the Peabody Picture Vocabulary Test—Revised]. Toronto, Ontario, Canada: PsyCan.

Durrleman, S., Burnel, M., Reboul, A., Thommen, E., Foudon, N., Sonié, S., & Fourneret, P. (2015). The language cognition interface in autism spectrum disorders: Complement sentences and false belief reasoning. *Research in Autism Spectrum Disorders*, *21*, 109–120. http://www.sciencedirect.com/science/article/pii/S1750946715001427

Durrleman, S., & Franck, J. (2015). Exploring links between language and cognition in autism spectrum disorders: Complement sentences, false belief, and executive functioning. *Journal of Communication Disorders*, *54*, 15–31. http://www.sciencedirect.com/science/article/pii/S0021992414001051

Durrleman, S., & Zufferey, S. (2013). Investigating complex syntax in autism. In S. Stavrakaki, P. Konstantinopoulou, & M. Lalioti (Eds.), *Advances in language acquisition* (pp. 405–415). Newcastle upon Tyne, England: Cambridge Scholars.

Farrar, M. J., Lee, H., Cho, Y. H., Tamargo, J., & Seung, H. (2013). Language and false belief in Korean-speaking and English-speaking children. *Cognitive Development*, *28*, 209–221. http://dx.doi.org/10.1016/j.cogdev.2013.01.010

Fisher, N., & Happé, F. (2005). A training study of theory of mind and executive function in children with autistic spectrum disorders. *Journal of Autism and Developmental Disorders*, *35*, 757–771. http://dx.doi.org/10.1007/s10803-005-0022-9

Fisher, N., Happé, F., & Dunn, J. (2005). The relationship between vocabulary, grammar, and false belief task performance in children with autistic spectrum disorders and children with moderate learning difficulties. *Journal of Child Psychology and Psychiatry*, *46*, 409–419. http://dx.doi.org/10.1111/j.1469-7610.2004.00371.x

Flavell, J. H. (1999). Cognitive development: Children's knowledge about the mind. *Annual Review of Psychology*, *50*, 21–45. http://dx.doi.org/10.1146/annurev.psych.50.1.21

Flynn, E. (2007). The role of inhibitory control in false belief understanding. *Infant and Child Development*, *16*, 53–69. http://dx.doi.org/10.1002/icd.500

Frith, U. (2001). Mind blindness and the brain in autism. *Neuron*, *32*, 969–979. http://dx.doi.org/10.1016/S0896-6273(01)00552-9

Frith, U., Morton, J., & Leslie, A. M. (1991). The cognitive basis of a biological disorder: Autism. *Trends in Neurosciences*, *14*, 433–438. http://dx.doi.org/10.1016/0166-2236(91)90041-R

Goodwin, A., Fein, D., & Naigles, L. R. (2012). Comprehension of wh-questions precedes their production in typical development and autism spectrum disorders. *Autism Research*, *5*, 109–123. http://dx.doi.org/10.1002/aur.1220

Hale, C. M., & Tager-Flusberg, H. (2003). The influence of language on theory of mind: A training study. *Developmental Science*, *6*, 346–359.

Happé, F. G. (1993). Communicative competence and theory of mind in autism: A test of relevance theory. *Cognition*, *48*, 101–119.

Happé, F. G. (1995). The role of age and verbal ability in the theory of mind task performance of subjects with autism. *Child Development*, *66*, 843–855. http://dx.doi.org/10.2307/1131954

Hogrefe, G., Wimmer, H., & Perner, J. (1986). Ignorance versus false belief: A developmental lag in attribution of epistemic states. *Child Development*, *57*, 567–582. http://dx.doi.org/10.2307/1130337

Hughes, C. (1998). Executive function in preschoolers: Links with theory of mind and verbal ability. *British Journal of Developmental Psychology*, *16*, 233–253. http://dx.doi.org/10.1111/j.2044-835X.1998.tb00921.x

Hughes, C., & Russell, J. (1993). Autistic children's difficulty with mental disengagement from an object: Its implications for theories of autism. *Developmental Psychology*, *29*, 498–510. http://dx.doi.org/10.1037/0012-1649.29.3.498

Khomsi, A., Khomsi, J., Parbeau-Guéno, A., & Pasquet, F. (2007). *Bilan informatisé de langage oral au Cycle III et au collège (BILO3C)* [Computerized oral language assessment in Cycle 3 and college]. Paris, France: Editions du CPA.

Lewis, D. K. (1986). *On the plurality of worlds* (Vol. 322). Oxford, England: Blackwell.

Lind, S. E., & Bowler, D. M. (2009). Language and theory of mind in autism spectrum disorder: The relationship between complement syntax and false belief task performance. *Journal of Autism and Developmental Disorders*, *39*, 929–937. http://dx.doi.org/10.1007/s10803-009-0702-y

Lohmann, H., & Tomasello, M. (2003). The role of language in the development of false belief understanding: A training study. *Child Development*, *74*, 1130–1144. http://dx.doi.org/10.1111/1467-8624.00597

Lord, C., Risi, S., Lambrecht, L., Cook, E. H., Jr., Leventhal, B. L., DiLavore, P. C., . . . Rutter, M. (2000). The autism diagnostic observation schedule-generic: A standard measure of social and communicative deficits associated with the spectrum of autism. *Journal of Autism Developmental Disorders*, *30*, 205–223.

Ozonoff, S. (1995). Executive functions in autism. In E. M. G. B. Schopler (Ed.), *Learning and cognition in autism* (pp. 199–219). http://dx.doi.org/10.1007/978-1-4899-1286-2_11

Ozonoff, S., & Jensen, J. (1999). Brief report: Specific executive function profiles in three neuro developmental disorders. *Journal of Autism and Developmental Disorders*, *29*, 171–177. http://dx.doi.org/10.1023/A:1023052913110

Ozonoff, S., Pennington, B. F., & Rogers, S. J. (1991). Executive function deficits in high-functioning autistic individuals: Relationship to theory of mind. *Journal of Child Psychology and Psychiatry*, *32*, 1081–1105. http://dx.doi.org/10.1111/j.1469-7610.1991.tb00351.x

Ozonoff, S., & Strayer, D. L. (2001). Further evidence of intact working memory in autism. *Journal of Autism and Developmental Disorders*, *31*, 257–263. http://dx.doi.org/10.1023/A:1010794902139

Paynter, J., & Peterson, C. C. (2013). Further evidence of benefits of thought-bubble training for theory of mind development in children with autism spectrum disorders. *Research in Autism Spectrum Disorders*, *7*, 344–348. http://dx.doi.org/10.1016/j.rasd.2012.10.001

Pellicano, E. (2007). Links between theory of mind and executive function in young children with autism: Clues to developmental primacy. *Developmental Psychology*, *43*, 974–990. http://dx.doi.org/10.1037/0012-1649.43.4.974

Perner, J., & Lang, B. (1999). Development of theory of mind and executive control. *Trends in Cognitive Sciences*, *3*, 337–344. http://dx.doi.org/10.1016/S1364-6613(99)01362-5

Pijnacker, J., Hagoort, P., Buitelaar, J., Teunisse, J.-P., & Geurts, B. (2009). Pragmatic inferences in high-functioning adults with autism and Asperger syndrome. *Journal of Autism and Developmental Disorders*, *39*, 607–618. http://dx.doi.org/10.1007/s10803-008-0661-8

Premack, D., & Woodruff, G. (1978). Does the chimpanzee have a theory of mind? *Behavioral and Brain Sciences*, *1*, 515–526. http://dx.doi.org/10.1017/S0140525X00076512

Prior, M., Dahlstrom, B., & Squires, T. L. (1990). Autistic children's knowledge of thinking and feeling states in other people. *Journal of Child Psychology and Psychiatry*, *31*, 587–601. http://dx.doi.org/10.1111/j.1469-7610.1990.tb00799.x

Prior, M., & Hoffmann, W. (1990). Brief report: Neuropsychological testing of autistic children through an exploration with frontal lobe tests. *Journal of Autism and Developmental Disorders*, *20*, 581–590. http://dx.doi.org/10.1007/BF02216063

Rabbitt, P. (1997). *Methodology of frontal and executive function.* Hove, England: Psychology Press.

Raven, J. C., Court, J. H., & Raven, J. (1998). *Progressive matrices standard (PM38)*. Montreuil, France: Éditions du Centre de Psychologie Appliquée.

Roberts, A. C., Robbins, T. W., & Weiskrantz, L. (1998). *The prefrontal cortex: Executive and cognitive functions*. http://dx.doi.org/10.1093/acprof:oso/9780198524410.001.0001

Roberts, J., Rice, M., & Tager-Flusberg, H. (2004). Tense marking in children with autism. *Applied Psycholinguistics*, *25*, 429–448. http://dx.doi.org/10.1017/S0142716404001201

Roid, G. H., & Miller, L. J. (1997). *Leiter International Performance Scale—Revised: Examiners manual*. Wood Dale, IL: Stoelting.

Rutter, M., LeCouteur, A., & Lord, C. (2003). *Autism Diagnostic Interview*. Los Angeles, CA: Western Psychological Services.

Sabbagh, M. A., Moses, L. J., & Shiverick, S. (2006). Executive functioning and preschoolers' understanding of false beliefs, false photographs, and false signs. *Child Development*, *77*, 1034–1049. http://dx.doi.org/10.1111/j.1467-8624.2006.00917.x

Serra, M., Loth, F. L., van Geert, P. L. C., Hurkens, E., & Minderaa, R. B. (2002). Theory of mind in children with "lesser variants" of autism: A longitudinal study. *Journal of Child Psychology and Psychiatry*, *43*, 885–900. http://dx.doi.org/10.1111/1469-7610.00104

Surian, L., & Leslie, A. M. (1999). Competence and performance in false belief understanding: A comparison of autistic and 3-year-old children. *British Journal of Developmental Psychology*, *17*, 141–155. http://dx.doi.org/10.1348/026151099165203

Tager-Flusberg, H. (1997). Language acquisition and theory of mind: Contributions from the study of autism. In L. B. Adamson & M. A. Romski (Eds.), *Research on communication and language disorders: Contributions to theories of language development* (pp. 133–158). Baltimore, MD: Brookes.

Tager-Flusberg, H. (2000). Language and understanding minds: Connections in autism. In S. Baron-Cohen, H. Tager-Flusberg, & D. J. Cohen (Eds.), *Understanding other minds: Perspectives from developmental cognitive neuroscience*. (2nd ed., pp. 124–149). Oxford, England: Oxford University Press.

Tager-Flusberg, H., & Joseph, R. M. (2005). How language facilitates the acquisition of false-belief understanding in children with autism. In J. W. Astington & J. A. Baird (Eds.), *Why language matters for theory of mind* (pp. 298–318). http://dx.doi.org/10.1093/acprof:oso/9780195159912.003.0014

Wellman, H. M., Baron-Cohen, S., Caswell, R., Gomez, J. C., Swettenham, J., Toye, E., & Lagattuta, K. (2002). Thought-bubbles help children with autism acquire an alternative to a theory of mind. *Autism*, *6*, 343–363. http://dx.doi.org/10.1177/1362361302006004003

Wellman, H. M., Cross, D., & Watson, J. (2001). Meta-analysis of theory-of-mind development: The truth about false belief. *Child Development*, *72*, 655–684. http://dx.doi.org/10.1111/1467-8624.00304

Wellman, H. M., & Liu, D. (2004). Scaling of theory-of-mind tasks. *Child Development*, *75*, 523–541. http://dx.doi.org/10.1111/j.1467-8624.2004.00691.x

Yi, L., Fan, Y., Zhao, J., Huang, D., Li, Y., & Zou, X. (2013). Atypical understanding of mental terms in Chinese-speaking children with autism spectrum disorder. *Research in Autism Spectrum Disorders*, *7*, 1411–1417. http://dx.doi.org/10.1016/j.rasd.2013.08.009

Yirmiya, N., Erel, O., Shaked, M., & Solomonica-Levi, D. (1998). Meta-analyses comparing theory of mind abilities of individuals with autism, individuals with mental retardation, and normally developing individuals. *Psychological Bulletin*, *124*, 283–307. http://dx.doi.org/10.1037/0033-2909.124.3.283

Zebib, R., Tuller, L., Prévost, P., & Morin, E. (2013). Formal language impairment in French-speaking children with ASD: A comparative ASD/SLI study. In S. Stavrakaki, P. Konstantinopoulou, & M. Lalioti (Eds.), *Advances in language acquisition* (pp. 472–480). Newcastle upon Tyne, England: Cambridge Scholars.

Inge-Marie Eigsti and Jillian M. Schuh

9 Language Acquisition in ASD: Beyond Standardized Language Measures

Autism spectrum disorder (ASD) is characterized by impairments in social interactions, language and communication, and the presence of repetitive interests and behaviors. The bulk of empirical research in the past decade has emphasized the social nature of language deficits, a logical focus given the centrality of social interaction to the role of language. The current chapter presents an alternative focus, drawing on detailed evidence that low-level, nonsocial cognitive processes place significant constraints on language acquisition and processing in ASD. Although these constraints lead to both subtle and dramatic communication impairments in ASD, they often require the use of tools and methods that go beyond standardized tests and measures.

First, we offer some perspective on the current understanding of communication and language in ASD. It is critical to note that the *Diagnostic and Statistical Manual of Mental Disorders* (*DSM*) diagnostic system, used in essentially all U.S. research on ASD (and closely tied to the World Health Organization's *International Classification of Diseases* diagnostic system) recently underwent substantial revisions with regard to the diagnostic criteria for ASD. Specifically, the previous version, *DSM–IV–TR* (4th ed., text revision; American Psychiatric Association, 2000), specified three primary domains of impairment for ASD: (a) difficulties in social relatedness and reciprocity, (b) difficulties in language and communication, and (c) the presence of repetitive behaviors and stereotyped interests. In contrast, the fifth edition of the *DSM* (*DSM–5*; American Psychiatric Association, 2013), specified major changes to the ASD diagnosis. First, the distinct diagnoses of autistic disorder, pervasive developmental disorder—not otherwise specified, Asperger's disorder, Rett's disorder, and childhood disintegrative disorder were collapsed into just two: autism spectrum disorder and social (pragmatic) communication disorder (with the latter falling under "Communication Disorders"). (The rationale for these changes, the relevant empirical literature, and the likely effects on public health, are beyond the scope of this chapter; see Volkmar & McPartland, 2014.)

In the current diagnostic system, there are just two domains of impairment in ASD: (a) difficulties in social communication and interaction, including impairments in social-emotional reciprocity, in nonverbal communicative behaviors used for social

We gratefully acknowledge the helpful assistance of Daniel Mirman with data analysis, and Jim Magnuson's valuable insights. This work was possible through the generosity of our participants, who shared their time and energy.

http://dx.doi.org/10.1037/15964-010
Innovative Investigations of Language in Autism Spectrum Disorder, L. R. Naigles (Editor)

interaction, and in developing and maintaining relationships; and (b) the presence of restricted, repetitive behaviors, interests, and activities. The *DSM–5* diagnostic system removed "language and communication" as a primary domain of impairment in ASD. Why was this change made? One important motivation was that communication deficits are intimately related to social deficits; in fact, the *DSM* text suggests that they are manifestations of a "single set of symptoms" that can be present in different contexts. Although it is true that "language" has a strongly social component, psycholinguists have described many other nonsocial (or less social) processes that are highly relevant to language acquisition, comprehension, and production: statistical learning, phonological categorization, working memory, motor control, semantic organization, visuospatial processing, inhibition, cognitive control, and syntactic priming, to name a few; the list is long (Pickering & Garrod, 2013). This change in the diagnostic framework may serve to deemphasize research focused on the contributions of nonsocial processes to communication impairments. A second consequence of this change is to reduce the focus on structural aspects of language in ASD because deficits in language structure in ASD are seen as straightforward reflections of social differences. The exclusion of language and communication as a symptom domain of ASD has a third important ramification: From a clinical perspective, speech intervention and other language supports may be seen as ancillary or less critical for children with ASD.

There is an alternative to the current categorization scheme for mental illnesses and developmental disorders: the National Institute of Mental Health Research Domain Criteria (R-DOC), which conceptualize mental disorders as biological disorders involving brain circuits that implicate specific domains of cognition, emotion, or behavior (Insel, 2013). Under the R-DOC formulation, research is directed toward cognitive processes, including language, that may or may not be specific to a diagnosis but that can be linked to genetic, neurophysiological, or neuroanatomical, experiential, affective, or other broad domains. We may better understand the pathology of neurodevelopmental disorders by linking research at the *molecular* level (genetics), at the *neurofunctional* level (brain imaging), and at the *behavioral* level (symptomatology) by connecting complex behaviors to underlying genetic mechanisms. Indeed, language may be a highly tractable target for such efforts.

In the spirit of the R-DOC enterprise, the focus of the current chapter is to present recent research on nonsocial, low-level processes that influence language processing in high-functioning adolescents with ASD. We have used eye-tracking methodologies to study discourse—interaction via conversation—in ASD, and findings have led us to believe that limitations in working memory play a significant role in pragmatic impairments for these adolescents (Schuh, Eigsti, & Mirman, in press). Before discussing this empirical work, however, we provide a brief overview of language in ASD (see also Eigsti, de Marchena, Schuh, & Kelley, 2011; Naigles & Chin, 2015), including a discussion of research that motivated the *DSM* changes.

Language in ASD

While individuals with high-functioning ASD (typically defined as those with full-scale IQ scores > 78 or in the typical range) generally achieve fluent language skills, some 25% to 30% of affected individuals remain functionally nonverbal throughout the life span (Anderson, Liang, & Lord, 2014; Anderson et al., 2007). Of those who do acquire functional language, most exhibit significant delays in acquisition (Mitchell et al., 2006; Tager-Flusberg, Paul, & Lord, 2005), producing first words at age 24 months (12 months delayed) and first phrases at 48 months (18–24 months delayed; see also Grandgeorge et al., 2009). Although there is relatively little research on phonological development in ASD, findings suggest no deficits in sound categorization and production (Boucher, 1976, 2003). Similarly, individuals with ASD produce more neologisms than children with other developmental delays (Eigsti, Bennetto, & Dadlani, 2007; Volden & Lord, 1991) and show differences in some aspects of word learning such as the shape bias (Tek, Jaffery, Fein, & Naigles, 2008) and semantic priming (Kamio, Robins, Kelley, Swainson, & Fein, 2007). However, some aspects of word learning and semantic organization may be unimpaired (de Marchena, Eigsti, Worek, Ono, & Snedeker, 2011).

Turning to the combinatorial language domains of morphology and syntax, the literature is more complex. Some have suggested that there are distinct language subgroups in ASD, distinguished by the presence (autism-language impaired, or ALI) or absence (autism-language normal, or ALN) of morphosyntactic impairments (Kjelgaard & Tager-Flusberg, 2001; Rapin, 1996); these reports may have motivated, in part, the *DSM–5* diagnostic changes. The Kjelgaard and Tager-Flusberg (2001) study has been particularly influential because it detailed the possibility of an overlap between ASD and the disorder of specific language impairment (SLI), a possibility first discussed in the 1970s (Bartak, Rutter, & Cox, 1975, 1977). In this article, a group of 89 children aged 4 to 14 years completed an extensive battery of standardized language assessments: the Goldman–Fristoe Test of Articulation (Goldman & Fristoe, 1986), Peabody Picture Vocabulary Test (Dunn & Dunn, 1997), Expressive Vocabulary Test (Williams, 1997), Clinical Evaluation of Language Fundamentals (CELF; Semel, Wiig, & Secord, 1995), and the nonword repetition subtest from the NEPSY battery (Korkman, Kirk, & Kemp, 1997). Approximately 50% of the children were unable to complete the CELF, suggesting specific difficulty with language structure. Participants were divided into three groups on the basis of their CELF scores (normative, mildly delayed, and impaired). The authors claimed that the profile of performance across all measures for the impaired group seemed similar to profiles that would be expected for children with SLI. There are some significant challenges to the proposal that SLI and ASD may be overlapping diagnoses (or indeed may be distinct labels for the same symptoms), which are not discussed here (see Williams, Botting, & Boucher, 2008).

The study came to one important conclusion, based on the finding of intact performance on the CELF for a subset of participants ($n = 22$ of 89 total): ASD includes a group of children with "essentially normal" language skills, such that deficits in language skills are "not universal" in ASD. However, as the authors noted, performance on structured standardized tests reflects not only linguistic knowledge but multiple other factors (they list attentional factors, understanding the pragmatic demands of the task, and understanding task instructions; see Kjelgaard & Tager-Flusberg, 2001, p. 301). Certainly, responding on an item-by-item basis to the sequential probes of a standardized assessment, in a quiet room, with the opportunity to take as long as needed for each response, may draw on different skills than would participating in real dialogue or producing an extended monologue (e.g., telling a story). Although offline single-item syntactic queries have provided a strong foundation for our understanding of child language acquisition (indeed, this was the primary methodology in both linguistics and psycholinguistics for decades), recent work has drawn on a number of alternative methodologies to assess linguistic knowledge and language production skills in individuals with typical and atypical developmental histories.

A number of studies report that young children with ASD show not just delays but very different patterns of morphosyntactic development (Bartolucci, 1982; Eigsti et al., 2007; Rapin & Dunn, 2003), and these results are found to extend into early adolescence and with individuals with high-functioning ASD (Eigsti & Bennetto, 2009; Walenski, Mostofsky, & Ullman, 2014). These differences are more apparent in spontaneous language assessments, in narrative tasks (Norbury & Bishop, 2003; Norbury, Gemmell, & Paul, 2014), when using sensitive methodologies such as eye tracking (Norbury, 2014), and on tasks in which there are multiple demands on attention or other cognitive resources (e.g., Fitch, Fein, & Eigsti, 2015), as discussed later in the chapter. They may also be apparent with using statistical analyses such as Rasch analysis (also called intersubtest scatter analyses; Godber, Anderson, & Bell, 2000), which takes into account the pattern of responses (Eigsti et al., 2007; Lazenby et al., 2016).

In the domain of language pragmatics, findings universally demonstrate significant impairments for individuals with ASD of all ages and at all functional levels (Paul, 2007). They are evident early in development (Landa & Goldberg, 2005) and are characterized by fewer spontaneous bids for communication (Stone & Caro-Martinez, 1990), fewer purely social speech acts (Wetherby, 1986), fewer demonstrative gestures (Mundy, Sigman, Ungerer, & Sherman, 1987), and difficulty with turn taking (Loveland, Landry, Hughes, Hall, & McEvoy, 1988). Adolescents with ASD have difficulty comprehending nonliteral statements despite intact receptive language (Asberg, 2010), and show deficits in turn taking (Capps, Kehres, & Sigman, 1998), prosody (Eigsti, Schuh, Mencl, Schultz, & Paul, 2012; Paul, Augustyn, Klin, & Volkmar, 2005), comprehension of indirect requests and other such indirect language (Paul & Cohen, 1985; Rajendran, Mitchell, & Rickards, 2005; Uchiyama et al., 2006), and the production of conversational gestures, and their integration with speech (de Marchena & Eigsti, 2010; García-Pérez, Lee, & Hobson, 2007).

Prosody, an important component of pragmatic language skills, refers to the "melody of the voice." Important components of prosody include pitch, or the frequency of speech; amplitude or intensity; and rhythm and duration. Individuals with ASD, including those with strong verbal skills, consistently show differences in prosody, including (qualitatively) monotonic or machine-like prosody, deficits in the use of pitch and control of volume, deficiencies in vocal quality, and use of aberrant stress patterns (Ghaziuddin & Gerstein, 1996; Shriberg et al., 2001). These differences have tremendous clinical implications: They serve as one of the most significant barriers to social and vocational inclusion (Paul, Shriberg, et al., 2005) and are the primary contributors to an impression of "oddness" (Mesibov, 1992; Van Bourgondien & Woods, 1992). Furthermore, they are more resistant to remediation than any other language domain (DeMyer et al., 1973; Kanner, 1971; Rutter & Lockyer, 1967; Simmons & Baltaxe, 1975). A functional imaging study of prosody comprehension by our group reported group differences in prosody processing in ASD (Eigsti et al., 2012). Specifically, results suggested that a broader set of neural regions was recruited in ASD than in typical development; these regions may reflect heightened reliance on cognitive control, reading of intentions, attentional management, and visualization. This broader recruitment of executive and "mindreading" brain areas for a relative simple language-processing task may be interpreted to suggest that speakers with HFA have developed less automaticity in language processing.

Even highly subtle prosodic features show the influence of ASD symptomatology. Filled pauses, or "fillers," such as *uh* or *um*, are produced during a pause in speech; in place of a completely silent pause, fillers communicate discourse information. Offering time for speech planning and production, evidence suggests that fillers serve to hold the conversational floor (Maclay & Osgood, 1959), convey uncertainty (Brennan & Williams, 1995), and announce momentary delays for utterance planning (Clark & Fox Tree, 2002) and word finding (Goodwin & Goodwin, 1986). Interestingly, *uh* and *um* appear in complementary distribution and are produced in different grammatical contexts, suggesting that they may serve distinct functions; *uh* is produced more often within utterances, whereas *um* (the more marked form) is produced more often at utterance boundaries (Clark & Fox Tree, 2002). Evidence suggests that fillers, and particularly *um*, play a pragmatic role in language. Studies of filler production in ASD suggest that adults with ASD produce significantly fewer fillers relative to TD adults (Lake, Humphreys, & Cardy, 2011). Furthermore, a recent study reported that adolescents with ASD produced fillers, specifically *um*, less frequently than their TD peers; further, *um* production was correlated with ASD symptomatology, indexed via ADOS and SCQ scores (Irvine, Eigsti, & Fein, 2016). Analyses of spontaneous language production may serve to reveal individual differences that are not apparent on standardized assessments.

The research briefly reviewed here thus suggests a profile of generally intact phonology, mixed empirical findings for lexical and structural domains of language, and consistent pragmatic impairments. This profile has led many to conclude that it is the social aspects of language acquisition and processing in ASD that are impaired; this likely underlies the diagnostic changes in the *DSM–5*. Here, we propose an alternative possibility: That language impairments are central to the ASD diagnosis but may not be apparent in high-functioning individuals in their performance on untimed, highly structured, standardized language assessments. In support of this proposal, we describe findings from an eye-tracking study of language processing (Schuh et al., in press). These studies reveal an important role of working memory in language processing in ASD, and specifically, in pragmatics. The domain of pragmatics, because it is so generally impaired in ASD, provides the strongest test of whether nonsocial, low-level processes can affect the most social of language domains.

Eye Tracking Unmasks the Role of Working Memory in Language Processing

Referential Communication: Common Ground

Imagine a situation in which two colleagues are discussing a book that one of them is writing. The writer might say something like, "On the boat is where I get the most writing done." This person would only refer to this writing retreat with a definite article "the" if she knew that her colleague was aware that she had a boat; otherwise, she would more likely to say something like, "I recently inherited an old sailboat, and that is where I get the most writing done." As individuals engage in conversation, they develop and continuously update a representation of *common ground*; that is, "I know that my conversational partner knows *X*," where *X* represents information shared in the discourse so far (Clark, 1992; Glucksberg, Krauss, & Higgins, 1975; Krauss & Fussell, 1991). Common ground knowledge may encompass both long-held information, such as the fact that someone has a boat, or new information revealed during the course of a conversation, such as the fact that this boat has developed a small but worrying leak in the starboard hull. Common ground is incorporated seamlessly into conversations by most speakers and listeners and is nicely described by the Gricean conversational principle of *quantity*, which suggests that during discourse, speakers should be sufficiently informative while excluding information that is irrelevant or distracting; the maxim of *relation*, which suggests that speakers say things that are pertinent to the discussion; and the maxim of *manner*, which suggests that a speaker should be clear, brief, and orderly, avoiding obscurity and ambiguity (Grice, 1975).

One recent study examined common ground use in high-functioning youth with ASD compared with youth with typical development, matched on gender, age, receptive vocabulary, verbal IQ and nonverbal IQ (de Marchena & Eigsti, 2016). Participants told stories based on cartoon stimuli to a listener. The existence of common ground was experimentally manipulated such that participants told stories in one of two conditions: the *private* condition, in which information about the cartoon was known only to the participant, such that the listener and participant had no common ground; and the *shared* condition, in which the listener and participant shared knowledge about the cartoon and thus had common ground. Results indicated that while the TD group showed a significant drop in word count in the shared condition relative to the private condition, word count in the two conditions was equivalent within the ASD group. The degree of referential shortening was related to social skills in the ASD group.

Additional analyses suggested that this pragmatic skill may have been delayed, rather than absent altogether, for the ASD group. Interestingly, naive listeners were sensitive to condition differences; that is, they rated the "shared" stories in the shared condition as significantly harder to follow than those in the private condition. An analysis of discourse during these stories further revealed that when participants with ASD told stories in the shared condition, they were less likely to clarify or correct themselves when they stumbled during speech. One interpretation of this finding is that because they were aware that their partner already knew what they were talking about, they exerted less effort in explanation, resulting in stories that were harder for others to follow. A further implication of this work is, of course, that discourse analysis of narratives can be a highly informative approach to studying individual differences in language processing.

Individual Differences in Referential Communication

There are significant individual differences in the ability to monitor conversational (Harris, 1996) and visual (Farrant, Fletcher, & Maybery, 2006) perspective during communication. The ability to track common ground involves making inferences about the knowledge and perspective of conversational partners, or interlocutors; certainly, this ability could depend on theory of mind (ToM) skills (i.e., the ability to attribute mental states to others; Baron-Cohen, 1991). Referential communication also requires the ability to inhibit one's own perspective and to continuously update representations of the interlocutor's perspective; executive function abilities, including inhibition and working memory (WM), undergird the allocation of attentional and cognitive resources and may be relevant to these discourse processes.

A number of studies have reported that executive functions play an important role in referential communication. In adults, individual differences in WM are associated with the ability to access shared information (Horton & Gerrig, 2005a, 2005b), as is verbal inhibitory control (Brown-Schmidt, 2009; Rubin, Brown-Schmidt, Duff, Tranel, & Cohen, 2009). A study of children aged 3 to 5 years found an association between the ability to incorporate a partner's perspective and inhibitory control, but not WM (Nilsen & Graham, 2009); WM demands were relatively low, so findings may have been limited by floor effects. Both children and adults are found to be slower to integrate common ground information when WM demands increase, indicating that WM capacity constrains perspective taking (Schuh, Eigsti, Mirman, & Gustafson, 2009). By the mental age of 6 years, children are capable of accurately selecting a target object from a field of competing objects by drawing on common ground (Ackerman & Silver, 1990; Ackerman, Szymanski, & Silver, 1990; Nadig & Sedivy, 2002; Schuh, Mirman, & Eigsti, 2016).

Research on common ground in TD individuals often makes use of referential communication tasks (Clark, 1992; Clark & Wilkes-Gibbs, 1986; Epley, Morewedge, & Keysar, 2004; Hanna, Tanenhaus, & Trueswell, 2003; Keysar, Barr, Balin, & Brauner, 2000; Nadig & Sedivy, 2002). In these studies, a trained "partner" gives instructions to the participant; on critical trials, the instructions are temporarily ambiguous (e.g., Pick *the red one*). Listeners use common ground knowledge to resolve these ambiguities. Previous studies exploring the relationships among discourse ambiguity resolution, ToM abilities, and executive processes such as WM, have been correlational, comparing performance on one measure (e.g., WM) with performance on a discourse task. We conducted an eye-tracking study to determine whether individual differences in referential communication were driven by ToM versus WM constraints (Schuh et al., in press). Individuals with ASD have wide-ranging ToM and executive skills; the presence of significant variability along these dimensions allows one to detect correlations if they are present. We manipulated WM demands and discourse processes within a referential communication task.

Participants were 13 individuals with high-functioning ASD and 22 typically developing (TD) controls, aged 8 to 17. All participants had full-scale IQ scores of 80 or higher (Stanford–Binet, 5th edition; Roid, 2003), and structural language abilities in the normal range (CELF–4; Semel, Wiig, & Secord, 2003). Groups did not differ in chronological age, gender, IQ, or standardized language. Participants with ASD had significantly more impaired executive functioning, according to parent report on the Behavior Rating Inventory of Executive Function (Gioia, Isquith, Guy, & Kenworthy, 2000).

Common Ground Task

Participants played a cooperative referential computer game with a trained "partner." The game was adapted from Hanna and Tanenhaus (2004). Participants and partners worked at separate laptops, with an opaque barrier between them. Participants followed the partner's instructions to move colored shapes from a resource area to specific locations on a 16-square grid using the computer mouse; the goal was to match the partner's grid. When a shape was mentioned, it entered common ground. Trials contained "privileged" shapes, the existence of which was unknown to the partner; participants were told that these shapes had to be kept secret to prevent the partner from discovering the treasure too early. For critical trials, the privileged shapes were identical to the target shapes in common ground. Thus, in these critical trials, the display contained two identical shapes (e.g., two yellow squares): a target (the subject of the partner's instruction) and a competitor (the foil object). The partner instructed the participant to place a shape on top of the target shape (e.g., "Stack the red square on the yellow one"). This required the participant to consider which objects were known to the competitor when choosing the target. In *common ground* trials, the partner had already introduced the competing shape (i.e., both yellow squares, the competitor and target, were in common ground); as such, the instruction was ambiguous and required the participant to ask for more information. In contrast, for *privileged ground* trials, the competitor shape was a "secret," and thus the partner was ignorant of its existence; as such, the instructions were unambiguous (i.e., the partner could only be referring to the yellow square in common ground).

In addition, the study manipulated WM demands, by including only one privileged shape (low WM) or four privileged shapes (high WM). The number of objects on the screen and the number of the instructions that were given were held constant across trial types. Participants also completed four clinical assessments of verbal and nonverbal WM abilities (results are described in Schuh & Eigsti, 2012), and items from the NEPSY–II ToM subtest (Korkman, Kirk, & Kemp, 2007), to provide some external validity to support individual differences within the task in WM performance.

Behavioral accuracy (placing the correct shape in the correct location) was high for both groups, with no group difference. If results considered only these explicit, conscious responses, the conclusion would have been that participants performed similarly across groups, with greatest accuracy in the common, low WM load conditions.

In addition to explicit responding, however, analysis also monitored eye-movement patterns using a remote Eyelink eyetracker. These eye-tracking time course data were analyzed using Growth Curve Analysis (Mirman, Dixon, & Magnuson, 2008; Mirman, Yee, Blumstein, & Magnuson, 2011). Growth curve analysis (GCA) is a multilevel regression technique designed for analysis of time course data; it is particularly useful in the simultaneous analysis of both group-level effects (e.g., experimental manipulations) and individual-level effects (i.e., individual differences). GCA results indicated that both common ground and WM load influenced target fixation patterns. Specifically, participants were slower to fixate on the target when they had to consider the partner's perspective (when that perspective differed from their own), and when WM demands were greater. Furthermore, there were Group-by-Condition interactions that indicated that the ASD group was significantly more affected by both the common ground and WM manipulations.

Hierarchical linear regression analyses indicated that multiple factors contributed independent variance to eye-movement patterns, including symptom severity, as well as scores on the CELF language, PPVT, WM measures, and NEPSY ToM subtest. Individuals with high WM abilities seemed to exhibit more efficient referential communication. In contrast, these individual predictors were not associated with behavioral response accuracy. This strengthens the argument that language assessments relying entirely on offline explicit responses are likely to underestimate (or miss) group differences.

To illustrate the point, Figure 9.1 depicts the relationship between performance in the high-WM load, privileged ground condition (e.g., target fixation linear effect) and scores on the CELF Formulated Sentences subtest, $r(13) = -.58$, $p = .04$, for the

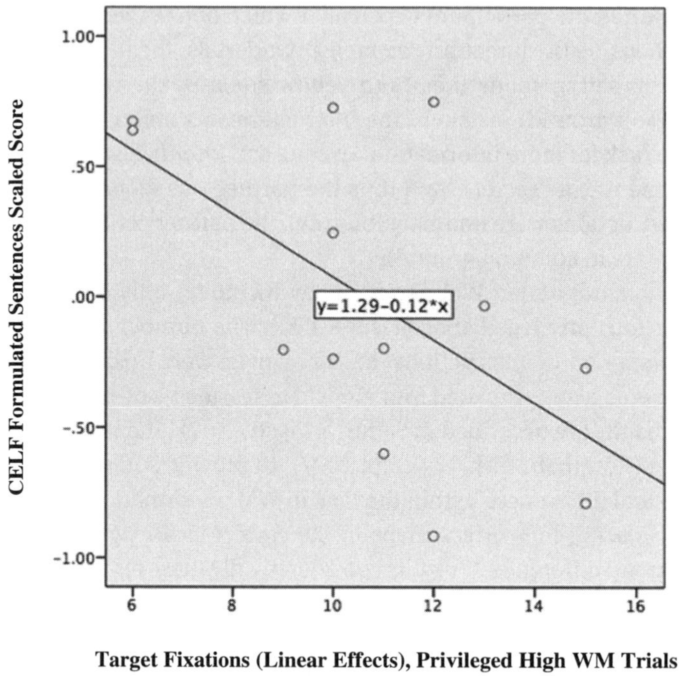

Fig. 9.1: Association between Clinical Evaluation of Language Fundamentals (CELF) Formulated Sentences subtest score and target fixations (linear effects) for the autism spectrum disorder group. WM = working memory.

ASD group. This test requires children to formulate meaningful grammatical spoken sentences, using given words (e.g., *house*, *car*, *or*, *when*) and a given picture; higher scores were associated with reduced linear effects.

These findings suggest that when maximally burdened by high WM load and the need to distinguish between privileged and common ground information, participants with better intrinsic WM abilities performed more efficiently in that they fixated more rapidly on the target shape. Autism severity, language ability, WM, and ToM abilities each contributed independently to this aspect of performance. Members of the ASD group had significantly worse executive skills, including WM, and they had a disproportionately larger difference in performance during high WM, privileged ground conditions; the significant predictors in the regression analysis indicate that individual differences in these dimensions contributed to the group differences in performance.

In summary, this study assessed the ability of individuals with ASD to represent common ground information during a structured referential communication (Tangram-style) task, and it also evaluated the role of WM and ToM in processing this common ground information. Accuracy of explicit, offline responses (i.e., clicking on specific shapes and moving them to specific locations) revealed few group differences and did not correlate with task-external measures of symptom severity, IQ, or WM. In contrast, online, nonconscious eye-movement data indicated that all participants were slower when required to integrate privileged information, and this difficulty increased under high WM demands. Across groups, eye-movement patterns were associated with both ToM and WM; within the ASD group, they also correlated with symptom severity, such that individuals with lower WM and ToM scores, and with greater symptomatology, were slower to fixate on the correct shape and more likely to fixate multiple other shapes. Differences in linear and quadratic effects for low versus high WM loads suggest that WM load modulated the ability to incorporate shared information; furthermore, the participants with greater WM impairment (i.e., individuals with ASD) were particularly influenced by WM demands.

Apparently social impairments in ASD can be strongly associated with WM impairments; for example, these eye-tracking results suggest that within-task WM factors influenced pragmatic performance for all participants and that participants with ASD had poorer WM abilities and were thus significantly more influenced by WM loads. These findings indicate that deficits in low-level, apparently nonsocial factors such WM can cascade up to exert influences on complex, high-level social discourse abilities.

Evidence From Other Domains

In this chapter, we have provided in-depth discussion of one specific nonsocial domain (working memory) that seems linked to a cascade of apparently social deficits. Our group and others have evidence of similar nonsocial, low-level deficits with significant consequences for language acquisition and language processing. For example, we and others have found that strengths in auditory perception (specifically, pitch discrimination) are associated with delays in language milestones (Bonnel et al., 2003; Eigsti & Fein, 2013). We have found that subtle timing differences in the coordination of gestures with speech have a significant negative effect on the clarity of communication (specifically, story quality) in youth with ASD (de Marchena & Eigsti, 2010). Across studies, the findings suggest that language and communication skills in ASD (and, by extension, in general) are susceptible to multiple influences, including those of an apparently nonsocial nature. This is true both during acquisition and also during online language processing in mature, fluent speakers.

This claim further emphasizes the need to go beyond offline, item-by-item standardized assessments of language abilities, which do not fully reveal the complexity of *in vivo* language and communication. The field of psycholinguistics and those who study language acquisition must increasingly tackle the challenge of using alternative methodologies to assess linguistic knowledge and language production skills in individuals with typical and atypical developmental histories.

Conclusion

In this chapter, we have selectively reviewed studies of language processing in ASD and presented detailed evidence from an eye-tracking study showing the effect of WM limitations on high-level communicative interactions. We proposed that examining the role of low-level processes such as WM, pitch discrimination, and motor planning, will illuminate the symptomatology of ASD. Furthermore, we proposed that deficits in language and social reciprocity reflect the operation of distinct mechanisms, rather than the manifestation of a simple set of symptoms present in differing contexts. Researchers wishing to probe language and communication deficits in ASD could refer to the R-DOC framework (Insel, 2013) as a guide to research on mental and developmental disorders. In the longer term, future diagnostic criteria for ASD may return to specifying incorporate impairments in language and communication as a specific domain of impairment, a change that would help to highlight the importance of nonsocial processes for development.

References

Ackerman, B. P., & Silver, D. (1990). Children's understanding of private keys in referential communication. *Journal of Experimental Child Psychology*, *50*, 217–242. http://dx.doi.org/10.1016/0022-0965(90)90040-F

Ackerman, B. P., Szymanski, J., & Silver, D. (1990). Children's use of the common ground in interpreting ambiguous referential utterances. *Developmental Psychology*, *26*, 234–245. http://dx.doi.org/10.1037/0012-1649.26.2.234

American Psychiatric Association. (2000). *Diagnostic and statistical manual of mental disorders* (4th ed., text rev.). Washington, DC: Author.

American Psychiatric Association. (2013). *Diagnostic and statistical manual of mental disorders* (5th ed.). Washington, DC: Author.

Anderson, D. K., Liang, J. W., & Lord, C. (2014). Predicting young adult outcome among more and less cognitively able individuals with autism spectrum disorders. *Journal of Child Psychology and Psychiatry*, *55*, 485–494. http://dx.doi.org/10.1111/jcpp.12178

Anderson, D. K., Lord, C., Risi, S., DiLavore, P. S., Shulman, C., Thurm, A., . . . Pickles, A. (2007). Patterns of growth in verbal abilities among children with autism spectrum disorder. *Journal of Consulting and Clinical Psychology*, *75*, 594–604. http://dx.doi.org/10.1037/0022-006X.75.4.594

Asberg, J. (2010). Patterns of language and discourse comprehension skills in school-aged children with autism spectrum disorders. *Scandinavian Journal of Psychology*, *51*, 534–539. http://dx.doi.org/10.1111/j.1467-9450.2010.00822.x

Baron-Cohen, S. (1991). The development of a theory of mind in autism: Deviance and delay? *Psychiatric Clinics of North America*, *14*, 33–51.

Bartak, L., Rutter, M., & Cox, A. (1975). A comparative study of infantile autism and specific development receptive language disorder. I. The children. *The British Journal of Psychiatry*, *126*, 127–145. http://dx.doi.org/10.1192/bjp.126.2.127

Bartak, L., Rutter, M., & Cox, A. (1977). A comparative study of infantile autism and specific developmental receptive language disorders. III. Discriminant function analysis. *Journal of Autism & Childhood Schizophrenia*, *7*, 383–396. http://dx.doi.org/10.1007/BF01540396

Bartolucci, G. (1982). Formal aspects of language in childhood autism. In J. Steffen (Ed.), *Autism and severe pathology: Advances in child behavior analysis and therapy* (Vol. 2, pp. 159–185). Lexington, MA: Lexington Books.

Bonnel, A., Mottron, L., Peretz, I., Trudel, M., Gallun, E., & Bonnel, A. M. (2003). Enhanced pitch sensitivity in individuals with autism: A signal detection analysis. *Journal of Cognitive Neuroscience*, *15*, 226–235. http://dx.doi.org/10.1162/089892903321208169

Boucher, J. (1976). Articulation in early childhood autism. *Journal of Autism & Childhood Schizophrenia*, *6*, 297–302. http://dx.doi.org/10.1007/BF01537907

Boucher, J. (2003). Language development in autism. *International Journal of Pediatric Otorhinolaryngology*, *67*(Suppl. 1), S159–S163. http://dx.doi.org/10.1016/j.ijporl.2003.08.016

Brennan, S. E., & Williams, M. (1995). The feeling of another's knowing: Prosody and filled pauses as cues to listeners about the metacognitive states of speakers. *Journal of Memory and Language*, *34*, 383–398. http://dx.doi.org/10.1006/jmla.1995.1017

Brown-Schmidt, S. (2009). The role of executive function in perspective taking during online language comprehension. *Psychonomic Bulletin & Review*, *16*, 893–900. http://dx.doi.org/10.3758/PBR.16.5.893

Capps, L., Kehres, J., & Sigman, M. (1998). Conversational abilities among children with autism and children with developmental delays. *Autism*, *2*, 325–344. http://dx.doi.org/10.1177/1362361398024002

Clark, H. H. (1992). *Arenas of language use.* Chicago, IL: University of Chicago Press.

Clark, H. H., & Fox Tree, J. E. (2002). Using uh and um in spontaneous speaking. *Cognition*, *84*, 73–111. http://dx.doi.org/10.1016/S0010-0277(02)00017-3

Clark, H. H., & Wilkes-Gibbs, D. (1986). Referring as a collaborative process. *Cognition*, *22*, 1–39. http://dx.doi.org/10.1016/0010-0277(86)90010-7

de Marchena, A., & Eigsti, I. M. (2010). Conversational gestures in autism spectrum disorders: Asynchrony but not decreased frequency. *Autism Research*, *3*, 311–322. http://dx.doi.org/10.1002/aur.159

de Marchena, A., & Eigsti, I. M. (2016). The art of common ground: Emergence of a complex pragmatic language skill in adolescents with autism spectrum disorders. *Journal of Child Language*, *43*, 43–80.

de Marchena, A., Eigsti, I. M., Worek, A., Ono, K. E., & Snedeker, J. (2011). Mutual exclusivity in autism spectrum disorders: Testing the pragmatic hypothesis. *Cognition*, *119*, 96–113. http://dx.doi.org/10.1016/j.cognition.2010.12.011

DeMyer, M. K., Barton, S., DeMyer, W. E., Norton, J. A., Allen, J., & Steele, R. (1973). Prognosis in autism: A follow-up study. *Journal of Autism & Childhood Schizophrenia*, *3*, 199–246. http://dx.doi.org/10.1007/BF01538281

Dunn, L. M., & Dunn, D. M. (1997). *Peabody Picture Vocabulary Test* (3rd ed.). Circle Pines, MN: American Guidance Service.

Eigsti, I. M., & Bennetto, L. (2009). Grammaticality judgments in autism spectrum disorders: Deviance or delay. *Journal of Child Language*, *19*, 1–23.

Eigsti, I. M., Bennetto, L., & Dadlani, M. B. (2007). Beyond pragmatics: Morphosyntactic development in autism. *Journal of Autism and Developmental Disorders*, *37*, 1007–1023. http://dx.doi.org/10.1007/s10803-006-0239-2

Eigsti, I. M., de Marchena, A. B., Schuh, J. M., & Kelley, E. (2011). Language acquisition in autism spectrum disorders: A developmental review. *Research in Autism Spectrum Disorders*, *5*, 681–691. http://dx.doi.org/10.1016/j.rasd.2010.09.001

Eigsti, I. M., & Fein, D. A. (2013). More is less: Pitch discrimination and language delays in children with optimal outcomes from autism. *Autism Research*, *6*, 605–613. http://dx.doi.org/10.1002/aur.1324

Eigsti, I. M., Schuh, J., Mencl, E., Schultz, R. T., & Paul, R. (2012). The neural underpinnings of prosody in autism. *Child Neuropsychology*, *18*, 600–617. http://dx.doi.org/10.1080/09297049.2011.639757

Epley, N., Morewedge, C. K., & Keysar, B. (2004). Perspective taking in children and adults: Equivalent egocentrism but differential correction. *Journal of Experimental Social Psychology*, *40*, 760–768. http://dx.doi.org/10.1016/j.jesp.2004.02.002

Farrant, B. M., Fletcher, J., & Maybery, M. T. (2006). Specific language impairment, theory of mind, and visual perspective taking: Evidence for simulation theory and the developmental role of language. *Child Development*, *77*, 1842–1853. http://dx.doi.org/10.1111/j.1467-8624.2006.00977.x

Fitch, A., Fein, D. A., & Eigsti, I. M. (2015). Detail and gestalt focus in individuals with optimal outcomes from autism spectrum disorders. *Journal of Autism and Developmental Disorders*, *45*, 1887–1896. http://dx.doi.org/10.1007/s10803-014-2347-8

García-Pérez, R. M., Lee, A., & Hobson, R. P. (2007). On intersubjective engagement in autism: A controlled study of nonverbal aspects of conversation. *Journal of Autism and Developmental Disorders*, *37*, 1310–1322. http://dx.doi.org/10.1007/s10803-006-0276-x

Ghaziuddin, M., & Gerstein, L. (1996). Pedantic speaking style differentiates Asperger syndrome from high-functioning autism. *Journal of Autism and Developmental Disorders*, *26*, 585–595. http://dx.doi.org/10.1007/BF02172348

Gioia, G. A., Isquith, P. K., Guy, S. C., & Kenworthy, L. (2000). *Behavior Rating Inventory of Executive Function*. Odessa, FL: Psychological Assessment Resources.

Glucksberg, S., Krauss, R. M., & Higgins, E. T. (1975). The development of referential communication skills. In F. E. Horowitz (Ed.), *Review of child development research* (Vol. 4, pp. 305–345). Chicago, IL: University of Chicago Press.

Godber, T., Anderson, V., & Bell, R. (2000). The measurement and diagnostic utility of intrasubtest scatter in pediatric neuropsychology. *Journal of Clinical Psychology*, *56*, 101–112. http://dx.doi.org/10.1002/(SICI)1097-4679(200001)56:1<101::AID-JCLP9>3.0.CO;2-J

Goldman, R., & Fristoe, M. (1986). *Goldman–Fristoe Test of Articulation*. Circle Pines, MN: American Guidance Service.

Goodwin, M. H., & Goodwin, C. (1986). Gesture and coparticipation in the activity of searching for a word. *Semiotica*, *62*, 51–75.

Grandgeorge, M., Hausberger, M., Tordjman, S., Deleau, M., Lazartigues, A., & Lemonnier, E. (2009). Environmental factors influence language development in children with autism spectrum disorders. *PLoS ONE*, *4*, e4683. http://dx.doi.org/10.1371/journal.pone.0004683

Grice, H. P. (1975). Logic and conversation. In P. Cole & J. L. Morgan (Eds.), *Speech acts* (pp. 41–58). New York, NY: Academic Press.

Hanna, J. E., & Tanenhaus, M. K. (2004). Pragmatic effects on reference resolution in a collaborative task: Evidence from eye movements. *Cognitive Science*, *28*, 105–115. http://dx.doi.org/10.1207/s15516709cog2801_5

Hanna, J. E., Tanenhaus, M. K., & Trueswell, J. C. (2003). The effects of common ground and perspective on domains of referential interpretation. *Journal of Memory and Language*, *49*, 43–61. http://dx.doi.org/10.1016/S0749-596X(03)00022-6

Harris, P. (1996). Desires, beliefs, and language. In P. Carruthers & P. K. Smith (Eds.), *Theories of theories of mind* (pp. 200–220). http://dx.doi.org/10.1017/CBO9780511597985.014

Horton, W. S., & Gerrig, R. J. (2005a). Conversational common ground and memory processes in language production. *Discourse Processes*, *40*, 1–35. http://dx.doi.org/10.1207/s15326950dp4001_1

Horton, W. S., & Gerrig, R. J. (2005b). The impact of memory demands on audience design during language production. *Cognition*, *96*, 127–142. http://dx.doi.org/10.1016/j.cognition.2004.07.001

Insel, T. R. (2013). *Director's blog: Transforming diagnosis*. Bethesda, MD: National Institute of Mental Health. Retrieved from http://www.nimh.nih.gov/about/director/2013/transforming-diagnosis.shtml

Irvine, C. A., Eigsti, I. M., & Fein, D. A. (2016). Uh, um, and autism: Filler disfluencies as pragmatic markers in adolescents with optimal outcomes from autism spectrum disorder. *Journal of Autism and Developmental Disorders*, *46*, 1061–1070.

Kamio, Y., Robins, D., Kelley, E., Swainson, B., & Fein, D. (2007). Atypical lexical/semantic processing in high-functioning autism spectrum disorders without early language delay. *Journal of Autism and Developmental Disorders*, *37*, 1116–1122. http://dx.doi.org/10.1007/s10803-006-0254-3

Kanner, L. (1971). Follow-up study of eleven autistic children originally reported in 1943. *Journal of Autism & Childhood Schizophrenia*, *1*, 119–145. http://dx.doi.org/10.1007/BF01537953

Keysar, B., Barr, D. J., Balin, J. A., & Brauner, J. S. (2000). Taking perspective in conversation: The role of mutual knowledge in comprehension. *Psychological Science*, *11*, 32–38. http://dx.doi.org/10.1111/1467-9280.00211

Kjelgaard, M. M., & Tager-Flusberg, H. (2001). An investigation of language impairment in autism: Implications for genetic subgroups. *Language and Cognitive Processes*, *16*, 287–308. http://dx.doi.org/10.1080/01690960042000058

Korkman, M., Kirk, R., & Kemp, S. (1997). *NEPSY*. San Antonio, TX: Harcourt Assessment.

Korkman, M., Kirk, U., & Kemp, S. (2007). *NEPSY–II* (2nd ed.). San Antonio, TX: Psychological Corporation.

Krauss, R. M., & Fussell, S. R. (1991). Perspective-taking in communication: Representations of others' knowledge in reference. *Social Cognition*, *9*, 2–24. http://dx.doi.org/10.1521/soco.1991.9.1.2

Lake, J. K., Humphreys, K. R., & Cardy, S. (2011). Listener vs. speaker-oriented aspects of speech: Studying the disfluencies of individuals with autism spectrum disorders. *Psychonomic Bulletin & Review*, *18*, 135–140. http://dx.doi.org/10.3758/s13423-010-0037-x

Landa, R. J., & Goldberg, M. C. (2005). Language, social, and executive functions in high functioning autism: A continuum of performance. *Journal of Autism and Developmental Disorders*, *35*, 557–573. http://dx.doi.org/10.1007/s10803-005-0001-1

Lazenby, D. C., Sideridis, G. D., Huntington, N., Prante, M., Dale, P. S., Curtin, S., . . . Tager-Flusberg, H. (2016). Language differences at 12 months in infants who develop autism spectrum disorder. *Journal of Autism and Developmental Disorders*, *46*, 899–909. http://dx.doi.org/10.1007/s10803-015-2632-1

Loveland, K. A., Landry, S. H., Hughes, S. O., Hall, S. K., & McEvoy, R. E. (1988). Speech acts and the pragmatic deficits of autism. *Journal of Speech & Hearing Research*, *31*, 593–604. http://dx.doi.org/10.1044/jshr.3104.593

Maclay, H., & Osgood, C. E. (1959). Hesitation phenomena in spontaneous English speech. *Word-Journal of the International Linguistic Association*, *15*, 19–44.

Mesibov, G. (1992). Treatment issues with high-functioning adolescents and adults with autism. In E. Schopler & G. Mesibov (Eds.), *High-functioning individuals with autism* (pp. 143–156). http://dx.doi.org/10.1007/978-1-4899-2456-8_8

Mirman, D., Dixon, J. A., & Magnuson, J. S. (2008). Statistical and computational models of the visual world paradigm: Growth curves and individual differences. *Journal of Memory and Language*, *59*, 475–494. http://dx.doi.org/10.1016/j.jml.2007.11.006

Mirman, D., Yee, E., Blumstein, S. E., & Magnuson, J. S. (2011). Theories of spoken word recognition deficits in aphasia: Evidence from eye-tracking and computational modeling. *Brain and Language*, *117*, 53–68. http://dx.doi.org/10.1016/j.bandl.2011.01.004

Mitchell, S., Brian, J., Zwaigenbaum, L., Roberts, W., Szatmari, P., Smith, I., & Bryson, S. (2006). Early language and communication development of infants later diagnosed with autism spectrum disorder. *Journal of Developmental and Behavioral Pediatrics*, *27*(Suppl. 2), S69–S78. http://dx.doi.org/10.1097/00004703-200604002-00004

Mundy, P., Sigman, M., Ungerer, J., & Sherman, T. (1987). Nonverbal communication and play correlates of language development in autistic children. *Journal of Autism and Developmental Disorders*, *17*, 349–364. http://dx.doi.org/10.1007/BF01487065

Nadig, A. S., & Sedivy, J. C. (2002). Evidence of perspective-taking constraints in children's on-line reference resolution. *Psychological Science*, *13*, 329–336. http://dx.doi.org/10.1111/j.0956-7976.2002.00460.x

Naigles, L. R., & Chin, I. (2015). Language development in children with autism. In E. L. Bavin & L. R. Naigles (Eds.), *The Cambridge handbook of child language* (2nd ed., pp. 637–658). http://dx.doi.org/10.1055/s-0033-1353446

Nilsen, E. S., & Graham, S. A. (2009). The relations between children's communicative perspective-taking and executive functioning. *Cognitive Psychology*, *58*, 220–249. http://dx.doi.org/10.1016/j.cogpsych.2008.07.002

Norbury, C. F. (2014). Sources of variation in developmental language disorders: Evidence from eye-tracking studies of sentence production. *Philosophical Transactions of the Royal Society: B. Biological Sciences*, *369*, 20120393. http://dx.doi.org/10.1098/rstb.2012.0393

Norbury, C. F., & Bishop, D. V. (2003). Narrative skills of children with communication impairments. *International Journal of Language & Communication Disorders*, *38*, 287–313. http://dx.doi.org/10.1080/136820310000108133

Norbury, C. F., Gemmell, T., & Paul, R. (2014). Pragmatics abilities in narrative production: A cross-disorder comparison. *Journal of Child Language*, *41*, 485–510. http://dx.doi.org/10.1017/S030500091300007X

Paul, R. (2007). Communication and its development in autism spectrum disorders. In F. Volkmar (Ed.), *Autism and pervasive developmental disorders* (2nd ed., pp. 129–155). http://dx.doi.org/10.1017/CBO9780511544446.005

Paul, R., Augustyn, A., Klin, A., & Volkmar, F. R. (2005). Perception and production of prosody by speakers with autism spectrum disorders. *Journal of Autism and Developmental Disorders*, *35*, 205–220. http://dx.doi.org/10.1007/s10803-004-1999-1

Paul, R., & Cohen, D. J. (1985). Comprehension of indirect requests in adults with autistic disorders and mental retardation. *Journal of Speech & Hearing Research*, *28*, 475–479. http://dx.doi.org/10.1044/jshr.2804.475

Paul, R., Shriberg, L. D., McSweeny, J., Cicchetti, D., Klin, A., & Volkmar, F. (2005). Brief report: Relations between prosodic performance and communication and socialization ratings in high functioning speakers with autism spectrum disorders. *Journal of Autism and Developmental Disorders*, *35*, 861–869. http://dx.doi.org/10.1007/s10803-005-0031-8

Pickering, M. J., & Garrod, S. (2013). An integrated theory of language production and comprehension. *Behavioral and Brain Sciences*, *36*, 329–347. http://dx.doi.org/10.1017/S0140525X12001495

Rajendran, G., Mitchell, P., & Rickards, H. (2005). How do individuals with Asperger syndrome respond to nonliteral language and inappropriate requests in computer-mediated communication? *Journal of Autism and Developmental Disorders*, *35*, 429–443. http://dx.doi.org/10.1007/s10803-005-5033-z

Rapin, I. (1996). *Preschool children with inadequate communication: Developmental language disorders, autism, low IQ* (pp. 58–97). London, England: MacKeith Press.

Rapin, I., & Dunn, M. (2003). Update on the language disorders of individuals on the autistic spectrum. *Brain & Development*, *25*, 166–172. http://dx.doi.org/10.1016/S0387-7604(02)00191-2

Roid, G. (2003). *Stanford–Binet Intelligence Scales* (5th ed.). Itasca, IL: Riverside.

Rubin, R., Brown-Schmidt, S., Duff, M., Tranel, D., & Cohen, N. (2009, October). *Common ground representations in hippocampal amnesia.* Paper presented at the Society for Neuroscience, Chicago, IL.

Rutter, M., & Lockyer, L. (1967). A five to fifteen year follow-up study of infantile psychosis. I. Description of sample. *The British Journal of Psychiatry*, *113*, 1169–1182. http://dx.doi.org/10.1192/bjp.113.504.1169

Schuh, J. M., & Eigsti, I. M. (2012). Working memory, language skills, and autism symptomatology. *Behavioral Science*, *2*, 207–218. http://dx.doi.org/10.3390/bs2040207

Schuh, J. M., Eigsti, I. M., & Mirman, D. (in press). Referential communication in autism spectrum disorder: The roles of working memory and theory of mind. *Autism Research.*

Schuh, J. M., Eigsti, I. M., Mirman, D., & Gustafson, T. (2009, April). *Do you see what I see? The influence of working memory on shared knowledge in children and adults.* Presented at the Society for Research in Child Development Biennial Meeting, Denver, CO.

Schuh, J. M., Mirman, D., & Eigsti, I. M. (2016). *Finding common ground: The impact of individual differences in working memory on referential communication for children and adults.* Unpublished manuscript.

Semel, E., Wiig, E. H., & Secord, W. A. (1995). *Clinical evaluation of language fundamentals* (3rd ed.). San Antonio, TX: Psychological Corporation.

Semel, E., Wiig, E. H., & Secord, W. A. (2003). *Clinical evaluation of language fundamentals* (4th ed.). San Antonio, TX: Harcourt Assessment.

Shriberg, L. D., Paul, R., McSweeny, J. L., Klin, A. M., Cohen, D. J., & Volkmar, F. R. (2001). Speech and prosody characteristics of adolescents and adults with high-functioning autism and Asperger syndrome. *Journal of Speech, Language, and Hearing Research*, *44*, 1097–1115. http://dx.doi.org/10.1044/1092-4388(2001/087)

Simmons, J. Q., & Baltaxe, C. (1975). Language patterns of adolescent autistics. *Journal of Autism & Childhood Schizophrenia*, *5*, 333–351. http://dx.doi.org/10.1007/BF01540680

Stone, W. L., & Caro-Martinez, L. M. (1990). Naturalistic observations of spontaneous communication in autistic children. *Journal of Autism and Developmental Disorders*, *20*, 437–453. http://dx.doi.org/10.1007/BF02216051

Tager-Flusberg, H., Paul, R., & Lord, C. (2005). Language and communication in autism. In F. R. Volkmar, R. Paul, A. Klin, & D. Cohen (Eds.), *Handbook of autism and pervasive developmental disorders* (3rd ed., pp. 335–364). New York, NY: Wiley.

Tek, S., Jaffery, G., Fein, D., & Naigles, L. R. (2008). Do children with autism spectrum disorders show a shape bias in word learning? *Autism Research*, *1*, 208–222. http://dx.doi.org/10.1002/aur.38

Uchiyama, H., Seki, A., Kageyama, H., Saito, D. N., Koeda, T., Ohno, K., & Sadato, N. (2006). Neural substrates of sarcasm: A functional magnetic-resonance imaging study. *Brain Research*, *1124*, 100–110. http://dx.doi.org/10.1016/j.brainres.2006.09.088

Van Bourgondien, M. E., & Woods, A. (1992). Vocational possibilities for high functioning adults with autism. In E. Schopler & G. Mesibov (Eds.), *High functioning individuals with autism* (pp. 227–242). http://dx.doi.org/10.1007/978-1-4899-2456-8_12

Volden, J., & Lord, C. (1991). Neologisms and idiosyncratic language in autistic speakers. *Journal of Autism and Developmental Disorders*, *21*, 109–130. http://dx.doi.org/10.1007/BF02284755

Volkmar, F. R., & McPartland, J. C. (2014). From Kanner to *DSM–5*: Autism as an evolving diagnostic concept. *Annual Review of Clinical Psychology*, *10*, 193–212. http://dx.doi.org/10.1146/annurev-clinpsy-032813-153710

Walenski, M., Mostofsky, S. H., & Ullman, M. T. (2014). Inflectional morphology in high-functioning autism: Evidence for speeded grammatical processing. *Research in Autism Spectrum Disorders*, *8*, 1607–1621. http://dx.doi.org/10.1016/j.rasd.2014.08.009

Wetherby, A. M. (1986). Ontogeny of communicative functions in autism. *Journal of Autism and Developmental Disorders*, *16*, 295–316. http://dx.doi.org/10.1007/BF01531661

Williams, D., Botting, N., & Boucher, J. (2008). Language in autism and specific language impairment: Where are the links? *Psychological Bulletin*, *134*, 944–963. http://dx.doi.org/10.1037/a0013743

Williams, K. T. (1997). *Expressive Vocabulary Test.* Circle Pines, MN: American Guidance Service.

Lesley Stirling, Graham Barrington,
Susan Douglas, and Kerrie Delves

10 Recall, Structure, and Complexity in Story Retellings by Children With ASD

The research described in this chapter was motivated by a case study of spontaneous written story retellings by an 8-year-old boy with autism spectrum disorder (ASD).[1] Lincoln had demonstrable difficulties in conversational interaction but had produced a range of retellings of familiar children's stories such as "The Three Little Pigs" and "The Three Billy Goats Gruff," which exhibited interesting structural and perspectival characteristics (Stirling & Barrington, 2007). On the basis of this experience and the literature on ASD and narrative then available, we hypothesized that providing children with ASD with the opportunity to produce narratives within a maximally comfortable environment might lead to outputs more likely to exhibit their strengths. Alternatively, outputs produced in more challenging environments, such as in laboratory settings where the children were asked to orally produce story retells to unfamiliar adults, could provide a profile emphasizing deficits at the expense of children's abilities. Our focus thus reflects Happé's (1999) maxim that "success is more interesting than failure."

The importance of narrative abilities for development and everyday functioning is well established. As a genre within which to explore linguistic and cognitive abilities of children with developmental delays, narrative has a number of advantages. The production of a narrative text potentially results in a self-contained sample of language data for analysis, and narrative production also presents the study participant with a complex cognitive task that may reveal areas of ability and

---

1 We take this story to translate roughly as:
"The three little wolves and the big bad pig
Once upon a time there were three little wolves and the big bad pig. They built a house of flowers. The pig smelled the flowers and they lived happily with(?) him(?). The end."

This research was supported by a grant from the Australian Research Council (ARC DP 0662936). Particular thanks go to the children, families, and teachers who took part in this research and to the Catholic Education Commission, Victoria; Amaze (formerly Autism Victoria); Ivanhoe East Primary School; and Cheryl Dissanayake and the Olga Tennison Autism Research Centre for assisting with participant recruitment. We are grateful to Eric Huang, who developed the StoryLincs software; to Graham Hepworth for assistance with statistical analyses; and to Priscilla Samuel, who assisted with some of the IPSyn coding. Some of the research tools used were developed in conjunction with Tessa Plueckhahn for her unpublished Honours thesis in linguistics (Plueckhahn, 2009), and we are grateful for her contribution to this project.

http://dx.doi.org/10.1037/15964-011
Innovative Investigations of Language in Autism Spectrum Disorder, L. R. Naigles (Editor)

deficit in, for example, the ability to remember and relate a series of events sequentially organized in time and space and linked by causal connections, the ability to construct a story world and maintain representation of differing perspectives on this, and the ability to comprehend and represent a global structure or point. It is therefore unsurprising that an extensive literature on narrative in ASD exists, comprehensively summarized in Stirling, Douglas, Leekam, and Carey (2014), but growing all the time, including recent work on languages other than English (e.g., on Finnish, see Mäkinen et al., 2014).

The research has persistently identified narrative as a site of difference for individuals with ASD; however, results from published studies have been variable and sometimes inconsistent, as Stirling, Douglas, Leekam, and Carey (2014) showed in their review of a core group of studies of oral elicited narrative, most using as the stimulus the wordless picture book *Frog, Where Are You?* (Mayer, 1969). Some but not all studies found narratives from ASD groups to be shorter and grammatically less complex (with better-matched higher functioning groups showing no differences). All studies surveyed that addressed global coherence reported significant differences between the control and ASD groups, noting a focus on minor details (e.g., Waterhouse & Fein, 1982) or problems with global coherence or gist (Diehl, Bennetto, & Young, 2006; Loveland, McEvoy, Tunali, & Kelley, 1990) and linking (Landa, 2000); difficulties in understanding global structure had also been observed for narrative comprehension studies (Norbury & Bishop, 2002). Some studies reported less frequent or sophisticated use of causal language to establish global coherence, for example, Diehl et al. (2006), who used a detailed causal connectedness analysis based on the work of Trabasso and colleagues (e.g., Trabasso & Sperry, 1985). These observations are consistent with claims of broader cognitive preferences for local over global processing among individuals with ASD (cf. Koldewyn, Jiang, Weigelt, & Kanwisher, 2013). Additionally, some studies reported differences in perspectivization: the ability to view the narrated events from the point of view of multiple characters, or narrator versus characters (García-Pérez, Hobson, & Lee, 2008; Stirling & Barrington, 2007). The research reported here aims to further explore these observed differences using a range of novel analyses but focuses on written story retelling using a culturally more familiar stimulus than *Frog, Where Are You?*

The StoryLincs project was an exploratory and descriptive study of the abilities of high-functioning children with ASD attending mainstream primary schools to produce written narratives and of the similarities and differences in their productions compared with typically developing (TD) children. Taking the lead from our case study of Lincoln's culturally familiar narratives, the aim was to design an appealing story retelling task closely aligned to familiar story reading and writing activities children already engage in at school and at home and that would take advantage of the tightly structured nature of culturally honed texts. Our goal was to identify features that showed developmental changes in the acquisition of narrative ability and that better differentiated between ASD and TD groups in narrative skills and deficits. Here we focus on exploration of features of global coherence, connectedness, and perspectivization identified by earlier work as potentially differing between these two populations.

Methodology

Study Structure and Participants

The research reported here is based on data collected in two studies. Study 1 surveyed a large number of TD children across the 7 years of primary school in one state school in Melbourne, Australia. For Study 2, we recruited as many children with ASD as we could who were attending mainstream primary schools in Melbourne or the surrounding area. For the quantitative and qualitative analyses reported here, we profile the results from the ASD group in Study 2 against the normative background of the larger number of TD children in Study 1.

Table 10.1 displays participant details for both studies. One hundred forty-eight TD children took part in Study 1. For the ASD study, 35 participants were recruited, primarily through the Catholic Education Commission, Victoria, with some children recruited through the Olga Tennison Autism Research Centre, La Trobe University, and through advertising via Amaze. All participants were competent speakers of Australian English, had been diagnosed with ASD, and attended mainstream primary schools. Based on records provided by families, none of the children had a formal diagnosis of intellectual disability. Two participants were excluded from analyses due to technical/methodological issues. Table 10.1 shows the details for the final 33 children.

The research team was not in a position to confirm diagnoses for the children but sought diagnostic and test information from parents. For children entering the study via the Catholic Education Commission, the school system had independently determined that they were suitable for additional assistance at school due to social communicative

Tab. 10.1: Participant Details for Study 1 (TD) and Study 2 (ASD)

	Male		**Female**		***n***	
Grade	**TD**	**ASD**	**TD**	**ASD**	**TD**	**ASD**
0 (Prep)	11	1	8	0	19	1
1	16	3	15	1	31	4
2	13	5	12	2	25	7
3	8	5	4	0	12	5
4	6	7	10	1	16	8
5	23	2	14	2	37	4
6	4	3	4	1	8	4
Total	81	26	67	7	148	33

Note: ASD = autism spectrum disorder; TD = typically developing.

difficulties with a recognized diagnosis of ASD (including Asperger syndrome). Because of the range of availability of information and the variety of test instruments provided, it was not possible to compare the children on variables such as IQ or severity of ASD symptoms. For 22 of the children, the diagnostic label reported was *ASD* or *ASD (HFA)* or *HFA*, where *HFA* indicates high-functioning autism. Eight of the children had been diagnosed with AS, and three had been diagnosed with pervasive developmental disorder—not otherwise specified. Age at diagnosis ranged from 2 to 10 years old. Five participants were noted to have comorbid attention-deficit/hyperactivity disorder, and an additional two were noted to have a comorbid anxiety or mood disorder.

Elicitation Task

The StoryLincs Internet-based story-elicitation environment was developed specifically for this project as a context within which the children could create stories and save them to an online library. It differs from commercially available products in that it does not provide automated pagination or spelling or grammar checking. All children in both studies undertook the same task, administered under the same conditions, with one difference as indicated subsequently.

The task was administered by pairs of researchers according to an agreed protocol. Children did the task over 2 consecutive days. On the first day, they were introduced to the StoryLincs computer program and asked to write a practice story using it, assisted as needed by the researcher. They were then read the stimulus story, "The Three Little Wolves and the Big Bad Pig" (Trivizas, 2003), either by their regular classroom teacher or by one of the researchers. On the next day, the children were read the story again and were then given 40 minutes to produce a retell of the story using the StoryLincs program. During this task, they were unassisted except for help with occasional technical difficulties.

The only difference between Study 1 and Study 2 was that in Study 1, the TD children were read the story as a class group within their normal classroom environment and then produced their retell using classroom computers in groups of three to seven children. For Study 2, the children with ASD undertook the task individually, in pairs or in small groups with a researcher, either in a quiet room within their school or in their own home, as preferred.

The story production task we set the children turned out to have several interesting characteristics. The stimulus story is long but highly structured and is seeded with somewhat sophisticated lexis and descriptive detail. It is similar to the culturally familiar "The Three Little Pigs and the Big Bad Wolf" (which itself exists in various versions) in that it involves three main protagonists, in this case, three little wolves, who attempt to build progressively stronger houses for themselves, while a villain, in this case a big bad pig rather than a big bad wolf, progressively destroys the houses. In the original version, the wolf is vanquished and either dies or flees. In the Trivizas version, there are four different houses built, and the final house of flowers smells so beautiful that it brings about a change of heart in the Big Bad Pig, who then becomes friends with the Little Wolves and lives with them happily ever after. The stimulus story is thus on a highly familiar model but also models the possibility of creative variation of the storyline. We did not want the children to treat the task as primarily a memory task and were interested in trying to gauge their ability to construct stories more generally, so we explicitly allowed them to vary their retells. The script used by the researchers in introducing the retell task included the following components:

> Now we would like you to retell the story of 'The Three Little Wolves and the Big Bad Pig' in your own words, using the computer program. We are interested in your own special story, however you want to retell it. [and if they asked any further questions about the actual story writing]: We're interested in your own special story that you can write, so we can't help with that, but I'm sure you can work out what to do and it will be absolutely fine. [and if children specifically asked whether or to what extent they could depart from the original story]: We want you to tell the story of 'The Three Little Wolves and the Big Bad Pig.' As long as you do this, I'm sure whatever you do will be fine. [at the 35-minute mark]: You have 5 more minutes to finish your story. Maybe you would like to start thinking about how to finish it.

Because the task was time-delimited for practical reasons, it challenged most children to make decisions about prioritizing provision of detail as against producing a finished retell. We return to these features in the section Qualitative Analyses of Children's Approach to the Story Retelling Task later in the chapter.

Analyses

We report here two sets of analyses. Further details for individual analyses are given in the presentation of the findings later in the chapter. Analyses were conducted over minCHAT versions of the stories where applicable (MacWhinney, 2000).

Quantitative Analyses of Length and Linguistic Complexity

The following microlevel analyses of length and linguistic complexity were performed: total number of words (TNW); number of different words (NDW); type-token ratio (TTR); and Index of Productive Syntax score (IPSyn). We used Scarborough's (1990) Index of Productive Syntax analysis as an approximate indicator of grammatical complexity of the stories. This measure was designed for oral language and to be applicable primarily to language samples from children aged 2 to 4 years old; it is also sensitive to sample size. However, even in its original form, IPSyn analysis can be used for written language samples to provide a useful comparator that distinguishes between children at broadly constituted distinct developmental levels. Samuel (2009) evaluated IPSyn using 145 of the corpus of 148 TD story retells from Study 1 and showed that the interaction between IPSyn score and grade level was highly significant for this cohort, $F(1,144) = 59.24$, $p < .001$, and that a linear regression analysis showed a straight line fit with a correlation coefficient of .79, indicating that overall this analysis measures developmental progression. In Samuel's study, IPSyn also highly correlated with other measures of length and complexity including TNW, NDW, and TTR, and with a subjective rating analysis of the grammatical complexity of the stories by a group of primary school teachers. Thus, the IPSyn score can be taken to provide a representation of the grammatical complexity of the piece of writing under analysis.

Qualitative Analyses of Approach to the Task and Overall Structure of the Stories

In addition to the relatively standard analyses just described, which provide a broad but superficial overview of the character of the data, we developed a series of qualitative analyses designed to investigate the topics of perspectivisation, global coherence, and causal connectedness identified as of particular interest in the narratives of children with ASD. We were also interested to explore the way in which the children approached the task as a whole. The requirement to produce a written story retell of a complex stimulus within a defined time period, along with license to depart from the original story, effectively constituted the task as one of how to manage to produce a globally coherent retell on a broad, supplied model. Hence, we considered the following analyses, more fully explained in the next section:

- What was the complexity of the retell in terms of inclusion of represented character speech and thought as a measure of perspectivisation?
- Approach to the Task 1: To what extent was the story presented as a direct retelling of the stimulus or as the child's own alternative version of the stimulus story?
- Approach to the Task 2: Was the story presented as finished or complete or as unfinished and truncated (generally due to the child running out of time)?
- Similarity to the stimulus story: Which of the elements of the stimulus story were given parallel representation in the child's retell?
- Sensitivity to the causal connections between events in the story in the retells.

Findings

Engagement With the Task

Virtually all children who took part indicated that they enjoyed the task. In Study 1, we surveyed all the children after completion of the retell, and the results indicated a high level of engagement with and enjoyment of the task.

All but two of the 33 participants with ASD produced a text that clearly counted as an attempt at a retell of the stimulus story (the two children who did not wrote on other topics). Thus, although for these two participants the task was evidently not engaging or manageable, the remaining children in this group did engage with the task.

Because the task was time limited and consistent across all ages and grades, there was variation in output as to both the degree to which the entire story was covered in the retell and the length of the retell. Ability to produce a longer retell due to higher literacy or computer skills did not necessarily correlate with production of a retell that attempted to give a complete version of the story: Some younger children produced "complete" but short versions of the story, whereas some older children produced long but incomplete versions of the story. Example 1 is a story from a Grade 1 girl with ASD who has captured core elements of the stimulus story in a short, heavily truncated text, which nevertheless is clearly intended as complete and finished:

1. the 3 little wlle and the big bad, pig. [Title]
   ons upn a time trer. werr 3littlewlls and, thebigbadpig. they bld a hoseof flos. the, pig sml the flse.and theylv hppyl hti hit, the ead.[1]

Profile of the Story Retells Using Quantitative Measures

We first provide a broad overview of the data using the range of measures of length and morphosyntactic complexity listed earlier.

Linguistic Complexity at the Microlevel

As an indicator of linguistic complexity, story length in TNW is a measure that shows a stepwise incremental progression as neurotypical children proceed through the years of primary school education (cf. Stirling, Barrington, Douglas, & Delves, 2009b). Comparison of the retells from the ASD group with those from the baseline TD group as to overall length in TNW revealed that the ASD retells were significantly shorter than the TD retells taking grade level into account: ASD: $M = 179.24$; TD: $M = 212.34$; $F(1,180) = 21.26$, $p < .001$. To overcome heterogeneity of variance, log transformations of the TNW and NDW scores were used in statistical inferences.

Analyses of NDW and TTR were performed to give a different perspective on lexical complexity of the texts. There was again a significant difference in NDW by diagnostic group, controlling for a highly significant effect by grade level: ASD: $M = 74.7$; TD: $M = 93.34$; $F(1,180) = 25.53$, $p < .001$. There was also a significant difference between the groups in TTR: ASD $M = .622 \pm .03$; TD $M = .536 \pm .01$; $F(1,180) = 8.97$, $p = .003$, although, interestingly, the groups converge at higher grades.

To profile grammatical complexity of the retells, an IPSyn analysis was performed as described in the Methodology section of this chapter. The overall mean score for the ASD students was 56.12, and for the TD students, it was 62.57. There was a significant effect for grade level, and taking account of this, a significant effect for diagnostic group, $F(1,180) = 25.65$, $p < .001$), indicating that the children with ASD were in general lagging behind the TD group in use of more complex syntactic constructions in their writing.

Interim Discussion

While acknowledging the relatively small numbers of participants, especially at some grade levels, in the ASD group, it can be seen that the overall profile of the story retells produced by this group in comparison with the larger TD baseline study is consistent with some of the findings from other work on oral narratives by children with ASD. Overall, the stories are somewhat shorter in word length and the children use smaller numbers of different lexical items. On average, the grammatical complexity of the stories is behind that of TD children at comparable grade levels.

Is it simply the case that the children with ASD are developmentally behind the TD children in their story writing abilities, or are there more interesting differences in the way they approach the task? To explore this question, we turned to a series of qualitative analyses targeting the children's approach to the retelling task and the overall nature and structure of their stories.

Qualitative Analyses of Children's Approach to the Story Retelling Task

Perspective Space Analysis

An alternative measure of complexity and sophistication of storytelling focuses on the ability and propensity to represent the perspectives of multiple characters, something that García-Pérez et al. (2008) reported as differing for children with ASD. To test this in our written story retells, we developed an analysis in which stories are divided into *perspective spaces* (PS) marking contiguous stretches of the narrative presented from a consistent perspective (that of the narrator, a character's represented speech or thought, or represented stretches of dialogue between characters). Example 2 is an excerpt from a Grade 3 retell by a TD child showing the coding into PS, with a shift from the narrator perspective, to represented dialogue between the three little wolves and a zebra (an example of a *complex* or *dialogic perspective space* [CPS], and later a shift to represented (joint) speech by the wolves (a *single perspective space* [SPS] in that there is no reply represented).

2. <PS1 = Narrator>Once there was three little wolves that decided to build a house but there mother warned them about the big bad pig. They were looking for some materials when they saw a zebra carrying bricks.
   <PS2 = CPS>"can we borrow some of your bricks?" asked the three little wolves "sure" said the Zebra.
   <PS3 = Narrator>So the little wolves built there house of bricks. The three little were playing crochet when they saw the big bad pig coming there way.
   <PS4 = SPS>"run inside!" cried the little wolves.
   <PS5 = Narrator>Then the big bad pig knoked on the door . . .

These analyses allow for an alternative measure of complexity of the story in terms of the number of shifts between PS so defined. They also provide a means of analyzing the amount of represented speech in the retells and the extent to which dialogue is represented. Stirling, Barrington, Douglas, and Delves (2009a) gave a preliminary analysis of a subset of data from this study, and Stirling, Barrington, Douglas, and Delves (2013) presented results for the entire set of study participants and further discussed the application of this measure; we summarize the findings here.

Stirling et al. (2009a, 2009b) had shown a strongly linear relationship between grade level and total number of PS for the baseline TD group of 148 children, whereby the mean total PS increased by 2 PS per grade level. Even after correcting for story length in TNW, there was an increase of 0.5 PS per grade level, suggesting that the TD children were developing more sophisticated skills in narrative production through time, over and above their ability to write longer stories.

Results for the ASD group also showed a highly significant effect of grade level on Total PS ($p < .001$). In this case, however, the effect is completely correlated with length of story in TNW: In other words, for the children with ASD, the amount they wrote was as good an indicator of the sophistication of their PS management as their grade in school. To overcome heterogeneity of variance, a log transformation was done for all statistical inferences. Difference in mean Total PS was significant, $F(1,180) = 5.853$, $p = .017$, despite the small difference in means (see Table 10.2 and Figure 10.1). There was more variability

Tab. 10.2: Mean Total Perspective Spaces by Group and Grade

Grade	ASD	TD	Total *n*
0 (Prep)	1.00	1.26	20
1	2.50	4.10	35
2	5.86	6.08	32
3	7.00	7.33	17
4	9.50	9.69	24
5	11.00	11.95	41
6	11.50	12.50	12
Total	7.67	7.35	181

Note: ASD = autism spectrum disorder; TD = typically developing.

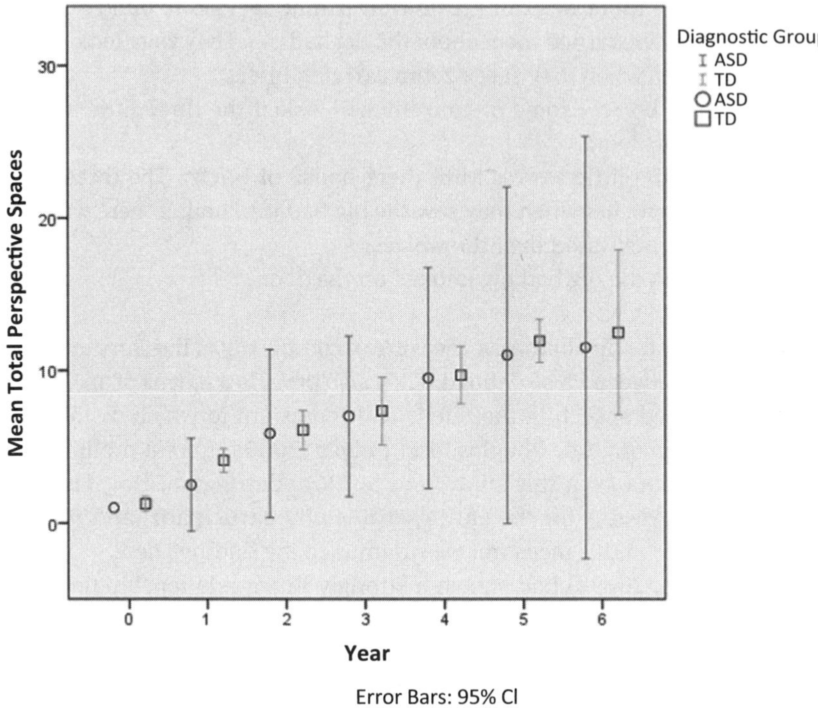

Fig. 10.1: Mean total perspective spaces across grade levels for autism spectrum disorder (ASD) and typically developing (TD) groups showing error bars.

for the ASD group. The ASD group performed proportionately more poorly at younger grades, then seemed to catch up, but fell behind again in the oldest primary school years.

We also compared differences in children's representation of single instances of represented speech or thought (SPS) and differences in their representation of character exchanges of dialogue (Complex PS). There was no significant difference in mean SPS for diagnostic group, although the ASD group showed on average a higher number of such spaces ($M = 2.00$, $SD = 2.291$), compared with the TD group ($M = 1.33$, $SD = 1.500$). However, the difference for mean Complex PS was significant (ASD group $M = 1.55$, $SD = 1.641$; TD group $M = 2.01$, $SD = 1.868$; $F(1,180) = 6.118$, $p = .014$). Correcting for length in TNW removed this significant difference; however, the results suggest a different pattern overall in the preferred management of represented interaction and perspectivisation by the children in the two groups.

We noted earlier that the particular constraints of the task used in this research meant that it effectively functioned as a challenge to produce a globally coherent story within time constraints and with license to depart from the stimulus to do so. Our preliminary observations of the way the children approached the task and the strategies they used to complete it indicated that children took different approaches and made choices as to whether to attempt an accurate representation of the stimulus story or to take up the offer to creatively and playfully depart from it and also whether to prioritize production of a finished story, and if so, what strategies to use to achieve this.

We now discuss a group of analyses in which we explore these differences between the children, focusing on stories from children in Grades 4 through 6 inclusive. Berman (2009) noted that age 9 to 10 is a key age after which children demonstrate greater sophistication in story construction, and in our own analyses of the TD cohort, we have some evidence that this is the case (Stirling et al., 2009b). For the ASD group, many children in years Prep to Grade 3 were minimally productive in their output, whereas most children in Grades 4 through 6 produced a competently written attempt at a retell. In Grades 4 through 6, there were 61 TD children in Study 1 and 16 children with ASD in Study 2, giving a subset of 77 stories to be considered here.

Completeness and Creativity

To explore whether children took the approach of attempting a close, accurate recount of the stimulus story, we divided the retells into two types: *Direct Retells* and *Alternative Retells*.[2] Direct Retells were those that presented as a clear attempt to retell the stimulus story as accurately as possible in all essential details, preserving the overall structure and point, with only minor changes. Counted as allowable minor changes were the following: omission of events or episodes or combination of episodes; minor changes in the type of animals met (e.g., wombat vs. beaver), materials used for house construction or instruments used in their destruction; changes in identity of major characters if everything else remained the same (e.g., "the three little mice and the big bad cat"); and "quick fix" different endings when the child found they were running out of time (usually involving the sudden death or escape of one side or other in the conflict). Alternative Retells were stories in which the children clearly departed from the model and introduced their own variations. In addition to any minor changes, these involved major changes in structure or point or pervasive minor changes resulting in a story with a different overall flavor. There were usually major changes to the suite of characters (e.g., one hero and three villains) or to the way in which the characters interact; there might be pervasive differences in theme or worldview (e.g., recasting the story as a Mafioso drama), and there were usually differences in structure, although the story might retain its own repetitive structure of episodic cycles along the lines of the stimulus.

An additional distinction was made between stories that presented as finished and complete and those that simply stopped when the children ran out of time (in some cases, midsentence or even midword). Finished stories were taken to be those that reached a resolution to the main conflict, and the ending was often

2 This distinction was developed in conjunction with Tessa Plueckhahn, who performed a preliminary study of a subset of the data (Plueckhahn, 2009).

accompanied by formulaic phrases (e.g., "lived happily ever after," "the end"). Unfinished stories lacked such a resolution. The most borderline cases were stories that stopped abruptly at the end of an episode.

Both TD and ASD groups included some children who attempted a Direct Retell of the stimulus story and some who produced an Alternative Retell. Table 10.3 shows the pattern for the 16 children with ASD from Grades 4 through 6 and for the 61 children with TD in the same grade levels.

Note first that the only children in the study who did not attempt some version of the target story were two from the ASD group, one of whom was in Grade 4 (a further Grade 4 child with ASD produced a very minimal story). All the TD children made an attempt. Second, the children with ASD were more likely than the TD children to produce an Alternative Retell of the story rather than a Direct Retell (60% Alternative overall), in contrast to the TD group who were more likely to produce a Direct Retell (only 27.9% Alternative overall). This difference is statistically significant: $\chi^2(1, n = 76) = 5.523$, $p = .019$. None of the 16 Grade 4 TD children attempted an Alternative Retell.

However, when the TD children in this age range did produce an Alternative Retell, without exception, they finished the story; in fact, they were more likely to finish than if they attempted a Direct Retell (54.5% finished). Conceivably, varying the original story made it easier for children to bring the story to a satisfactory conclusion of some kind within the time limit available. The TD children produced finished stories in 67.2% of cases overall, and none of the Grade 6 TD children produced unfinished stories.

Tab. 10.3: Profiles of Story Retells by Grades 4, 5, and 6 TD Children and Children With ASD: Completion of Stories and Direct or Alternative Retell

	Grade	ASD direct retells	ASD alternative retells	ASD all retells	TD direct retells	TD alternative retells	TD all Retells
Finished	4	3	0	3	9	0	9
	5	0	3	3	12	12	24
	6	0	2	2	3	5	8
	Total	3	5	8	24	17	41
Unfinished	4	1	3	4	7	0	7
	5	1	0	1	13	0	13
	6	1	1	2	0	0	0
	Total	3	4	7	20	0	20
Total	4	4	3	7	16	0	16
	5	1	3	4	25	12	37
	6	1	3	4	3	5	8
	Total	6	9	15	44	17	61
Not an attempt		1					

Note: ASD = autism spectrum disorder; TD = typically developing.

The children with ASD were about equally likely to produce finished or unfinished stories (53% and 47%, respectively, of the 15 stories that count as attempts at a retell). Whereas choosing to write an Alternative Retell was associated with 100% completion rate for the TD group, for the ASD group, only 55.6% of their Alternative Retells were finished, similar to the proportion of their finished Direct Retells (50%). However, the differences between the mean number of stories finished and unfinished were not significant across the two groups: $\chi^2(1, n = 76) = 1.013, p = .314$.

It is worth noting that the children with ASD, like the TD children, are clearly aware of and able to reproduce a story structure with an iterative pattern of episodes, and their stories tended to be symmetrical in their episode structure even if they differed from the stimulus or were truncated. Of the 14 stories that counted as an attempted retell and that were more than minimally long, five of the six Direct Retells and five of the eight Alternative Retells included a repeated episodic structure in which characters progressively attempted to solve the problem of providing themselves with a home; younger children with ASD also made use of this structure.

Similarity to the Stimulus Story

As a further exploration of children's approach to the task, all stories were evaluated as to which of the events or elements in the stimulus were represented in children's retells, whether these were Direct Retells or Alternative Retells. The stimulus story was divided into 135 component events or elements (cf. Plueckhahn, 2009, after Trabasso & van den Broek, 1985). Each child's contribution was then coded as to whether for each of these 135 elements in the stimulus, there was a corresponding element in the child's retell.

Correspondence was based on propositional content and equivalence of function in the story rather than identical expression, and order of events was not taken to be important (although there was minimal reordering). For the Direct Retell stories, this comparison was a relatively straightforward process. For the Alternative Retell stories, more flexibility was required, and an event was counted as equivalent if it served the same structural function in the story as a similar event in the stimulus. For example, in the stimulus story, the three little wolves meet with four minor characters, all animals, who provide them with materials to build the four houses. Then for the first three houses, there are three instruments of destruction used by the big bad pig after simple huffing and puffing fails to destroy the house. One common way in which children took advantage of the license to introduce their own creativity was in choosing to make use of different animals, different types of house-building materials, and different instruments of destruction at what is structurally the same point in the story. Example (3) shows a portion of one story illustrating the way in which events in alternative retells were counted as corresponding with numbered events of the stimulus story.

Tab. 10.4: Profiles of Story Retells by Grades 4, 5, and 6 TD Children and Children With ASD: Similarity to Stimulus Story in Number of Stimulus Elements Retold

	Grade	ASD retells, mean	ASD retells, range	TD retells, mean	TD retells, range
Number of retold elements	4	21.25	0–61	29.81	15–60
	5	29.25	6–68	33.05	6–57
	6	14.50	5–32	18.88	0–36
	Total	21.56		30.34	

Note: ASD = autism spectrum disorder; TD = typically developing.

3. a. Stimulus story—Episode 3 (House 2: house of concrete)
   (28) He went and fetched his sledgehammer (29) and he knocked the house down. (30) The little wolves only just managed to escape, (31) before the bricks crumbled.
   b. Retell—Episode 3 (House 2: house of newspaper)
   (28′) He fetched his watering can (29′) and poured water onto the house. (30′) [no correspondence] (31′) Slowly, the cardboard started melting away.

This analysis, along with those reported in Completeness and Creativity later in the chapter, was conducted by the first author and an intercoder reliability check was performed where the second author blind-coded 12 (15%) of the 77 stories, selected randomly with equal representation of diagnostic and grade-level categories. There was an average of 96.3% agreement between the two coders, and any discrepancies were resolved through discussion. Differences primarily resulted from error or from different decisions on a small number of truly borderline cases.[3]

Results from this analysis indicate that both TD and ASD groups were more likely to include events from the beginning of the stimulus story. Table 10.4 shows the mean number of retold events per story for each subgroup of participants; a one-way analysis of variance indicated that there was no significant difference between the TD children and the children with ASD on this measure, $F(1,76) = 1.492$, $p = .226$, and there was greater variation within the ASD group (ASD: $M = 21.56$, $SD = 21.08$; TD: $M = 30.34$, $SD = 13.53$).

However, beyond these relative similarities between the TD and ASD groups, there are interesting differences between the groups in the pattern of retold elements. In evaluating whether there were any patterns as to which events from the stimulus were more likely to occur in the retells, we investigated whether more causally connected events from the stimulus were more likely to be retold in the children's stories.

3 Intercoder reliability checks performed for the same subset of 12 stories also showed few differences in the decisions as to story type (Direct Retell vs. Alternative Retell) and completeness (Finished vs. Not finished) for these 12 stories, with one disagreement for the former classification and two for the latter. Both were resolved through discussion.

Previous research has shown that story comprehension by neurotypical individuals involves structured mental representations for which the differential salience of story events is critical and that this also affects which events get recalled and retold, with the salience of events modeled in terms of their number of causal connections to other events (e.g., Trabasso & van den Broek, 1985). For this analysis, we used a causal network analysis of the stimulus story produced by Plueckhahn (2009) based on protocols from Trabasso and Sperry (1985). This categorized each of the 135 stimulus story events or elements in terms of its causal importance for the story by the numbers of causal connections between it and other events/elements: Each of the 135 elements was assigned a *connectedness value* of between 0 and 6. (Diehl et al., 2006, conducted a similar analysis of their oral retellings of *Frog, Where Are You?*)[4]

Table 10.5 lists the set of 23 events that were retold in some form in 50% or more of the 61 Direct and Alternative Retells from TD children, and also highlights the small number of events that were also retold in a majority of the ASD stories (the events in bold). Table 10.5 shows that events commonly occurring in TD retells all come from the first part of the stimulus—up to the building of the second house (of concrete). Of those included, six have three or more causal connections, and only two (the first and the event of playing croquet in the garden) have no causal connections. For the ASD group, only six of the 135 events from the stimulus story are consistently included in 50% or more of the retells. Most of these six have two or more causal connections. However, clearly a majority of the children with ASD do not include a majority of those events that are most causally connected in their retells.

In contrast, 20 events are omitted from 100% of the TD retells. These all come from the second half of the stimulus story (from Event 58 on, none of the earlier events are excluded from all retells), and also all have at most one causal connection (all but four have zero), reflecting the relationship of causality to recall observed by Trabasso and van den Broek (1985) and Trabasso and Sperry (1985). These events all involve provision of minor detail or elaboration, and many are in subordinate clauses. All but two are also omitted from all ASD retells.

Almost twice as many events are excluded from all ASD retells as are excluded from all TD retells: In addition to the 18 noted earlier that are also excluded from the TD retells, there are a further 22 elements from the stimulus which occur in none of the ASD retells. This group of excluded events includes events with zero to at most two causal connections, and for all but five of them, they are also represented in small numbers of TD

4 Plueckhahn (2009) also analyzed the causal structure of a set of the story retells themselves using the protocol developed by Trabasso and colleagues (e.g., Trabasso & Sperry, 1985). The set of retells examined consisted of the first 10 available stories from the ASD group of children in Grades 4 through 6 (also included in the analyses in this chapter), compared with nine stories collected from TD children in the same grade as these children at the same schools. Unlike Diehl et al. (2006), this analysis showed no significant differences between the two groups on mean number of causal connections per story and on percentage of events per story with causal connections. However, group sizes were small, and there was a large amount of variation in both groups.

Tab. 10.5: Stimulus Story Events Recounted in 50% or More of TD Retells

Event no.	Event content	No. of causal connections	% ASD stories containing event
1	**Once upon a time there were three cuddly little wolves with soft fur and fluffy tails**	**0**	**86.7**
5	And [the mother] said "My children, it is time for you to go out into the world."	3	46.7
6	**"Go and build a house for yourselves."**	**5**	**60.0**
7	"But beware of the big bad pig."	6	40.0
9	and they set off.	1	46.7
10	Soon they met a kangaroo who was pushing a wheel-barrow full of red and yellow bricks	1	40.0
11	"Please, will you give us some of your bricks?" asked the three little wolves.	3	26.7
12	"Certainly," said the kangaroo,	2	20.0
14	**So the three little wolves built themselves a house of bricks.**	**1**	**53.3**
15	The very next day the big bad pig came prowling down the road	1	40.0
17	The three little wolves were playing croquet in the garden.	0	26.7
19	they ran inside the house	2	20.0
22	**And [the pig] grunted "Little wolves, little wolves, let me come in!"**	**2**	**53.3**
23	"No, no, no," said the three little wolves. "By the hair on our chinny-chin-chins, we will not let you in, not for all the tea leaves in our china teapot!"	3	46.7
24	**"Then I'll huff and I'll puff and I'll blow your house down!" said the pig**	**2**	**60.0**
25	So he huffed and he puffed and he puffed and he huffed	2	40.0
26	but the house didn't fall down.	1	20.0
28	He went and fetched his sledgehammer	1	26.7
29	**and he knocked the house down.**	**4**	**66.7**
30	The three little wolves only just managed to escape	1	46.7
34	Just then, they saw a beaver who was mixing concrete in a concrete mixer.	2	26.7
35	"Please, will you give us some of your concrete?" asked the three little wolves.	2	26.7
38	So the three wolves built themselves a house of concrete.	1	33.3

Note: Events that were retold in a majority of the stories by the children with autism spectrum disorder (ASD) are in bold.

stories—only between one and three retells. Three of these five events that are excluded from ASD retells but included in a number of TD retells have two causal connections, and one of the three is included in 44% of TD stories: It reports the agreement of the first animal approached to supply the wolves with house-building materials, early in the story. The other two of these three causally connected events report key changes in the pig's mental state (his heart becomes tender, and he realizes how horrible he has been). It is notable that the group of 22 events excluded from all stories in the ASD group but not excluded from all TD stories does include eight of the 12 events in the story that report mental or emotional states or evaluations. However, the numbers of TD stories including these events is also small (at most four), and most of the events belong to the poorly recalled second half of the story, so this observation must be treated with caution.

In addition, there is a subset of events with more causal links that occur commonly in the TD stories but rarely in the ASD stories. Of the 135 elements in the stimulus story, 41 have two or more causal connections and so can be thought of as relatively highly causally connected. Of these 41 highly causally connected events, only four (9.8%) are represented in more than 50% of the ASD stories, whereas 13 (31.7%) are represented in more than 50% of the TD stories.

An additional observation is that a large number of these highly causally connected events (22 of the 41 with more than two causal connections) incorporate representation of character direct speech. For the first part of the story, TD retells are much more likely to include these instances of represented speech than ASD retells. Nineteen of the 22 highly causally connected elements including direct speech appear in fewer than 50% of ASD retells. This requires further exploration (cf. the earlier discussion in Perspective Space Analysis).

As noted, there is a greater likelihood of the children with ASD producing Alternative Retells than the TD children. However, a number of the ASD group attempt Direct Retells of notable detail and accuracy: In fact, the child who retells the greatest number of stimulus story elements belongs to this group. This Grade 5 girl had recounted 68 of the 135 elements from the stimulus story—virtually every element up to Event 87 (78% of the story to this point)—when she clearly ran out of time. In contrast, a number of retells by TD children clearly began as Direct Retells but were transformed into Alternative Retells or gained a brief, alternative conclusion at the point at which the children evidently realized they needed to do something to bring the story to completion, thereby privileging the production of a coherent and complete story over the accurate rendition of the sequence of events in the stimulus.

Causal Connectedness of Stimulus Story Events and Proportion of Events Retold

A Pearson product–moment correlation coefficient was computed to assess the relationship between the connectedness value of an event from the stimulus story (from 0 to 6 connections) and the number of children's retells in which that event was represented. For each of the ASD group and the TD group considered independently, there was a positive correlation (ASD: $r = 0.476$, $n = 135$, $p < .001$; TD: $r = 0.470$, $n = 135$, $p < .001$). This suggests that both groups of children are sensitive to a differential status of events to be retold, as reflected in the number of causal connections these events have with other events in the story. However, the two groups nevertheless differ in their sensitivity to connectedness.

We calculated three indicators of the amount of material each child represented from the stimulus story. First, we calculated the *number of events* from the 135 in the stimulus that the child represented in his or her retell; this result was reported in the previous section. Second, we calculated the child's *retell event span*: how far through the stimulus story he or she progressed in constructing a retell, as indicated by the final stimulus event reproduced by the child out of the series of 135. Finally, we measured the amount of stimulus story material represented, weighted by the connectedness value of each of the 135 events. As indicated earlier, each of the 135 events was assigned a connectedness value from 0 to 6 representing the number of connections between it and other events in the story. The connectedness values for events in the stimulus story were not evenly distributed but were, as expected, higher for events in the first part of the story. For each child's retell, we calculated a *causally weighted event score* (CWES), which was the result of multiplying each event the child retold by its connectedness value and summing over all retold events. We then calculated a baseline measure, $CWES_{max}$, consisting of the maximum CWES possible if the child had represented all stimulus events in his or her *retell event span*, by multiplying each event in the span by its connectedness value and summing the results. Finally, we took the child's CWES as a proportion of the $CWES_{max}$ for the span, and we treat this as a measure of how much of the span the child chose to represent in his or her story, weighted as to the causal connectedness value of the events selected for retelling—the *retell connectedness measure* (RCM).[5]

For example, the child who produced Retell 639 included events from the stimulus story belonging to a range spanning Events 1 through 106 (this child's retell event span). Within this span, they represented 32 of the 106 events, which together had a CWES of 47 (the sum of each of the 32 events multiplied by its connectedness value from 0 to 6). The total span of 106 events had a $CWES_{max}$ of 144 (the sum of each of the 106 events multiplied by its connectedness value). The child's CWES of 47 as a proportion of the $CWES_{max}$ of 144 is 0.326, and this is the retell's RCM, a measure of the amount of material the child represents from the span he or she is working with,

5 For this analysis, we excluded Event 135, which was the formulaic "and they all lived happily together ever after" and also excluded two TD and two ASD stories with two or fewer represented events from the stimulus.

weighted by the connectedness values of the events chosen to retell. In other words, the RCM is an indication for each child's retell of both the amount of material represented from the span of the story he or she gets through in the 40 minutes allowed for the task and the child's choices from stimulus story events in terms of how important those events are causally for the story. Figure 10.2 illustrates the difference between the two groups on this measure.

There is a significant difference between the mean score for the ASD group ($M = .40 \pm .24$) and that for the TD group ($M = .56 \pm .19$), $t(71) = -2.803$, $p = .007$. There were no significant differences by grade, so we treat the Grade 4 to 6 children as a single group here.

As indicated earlier, there was no significant difference between ASD and TD groups in the mean number of events retold, nor was there a difference in the mean size of the retell event span (as measured by the furthest event represented in the retell). So the children are not differing in how much of the stimulus story they retell, but there is a difference in RCM, which reflects the sum causal connectedness of the events they choose to represent.

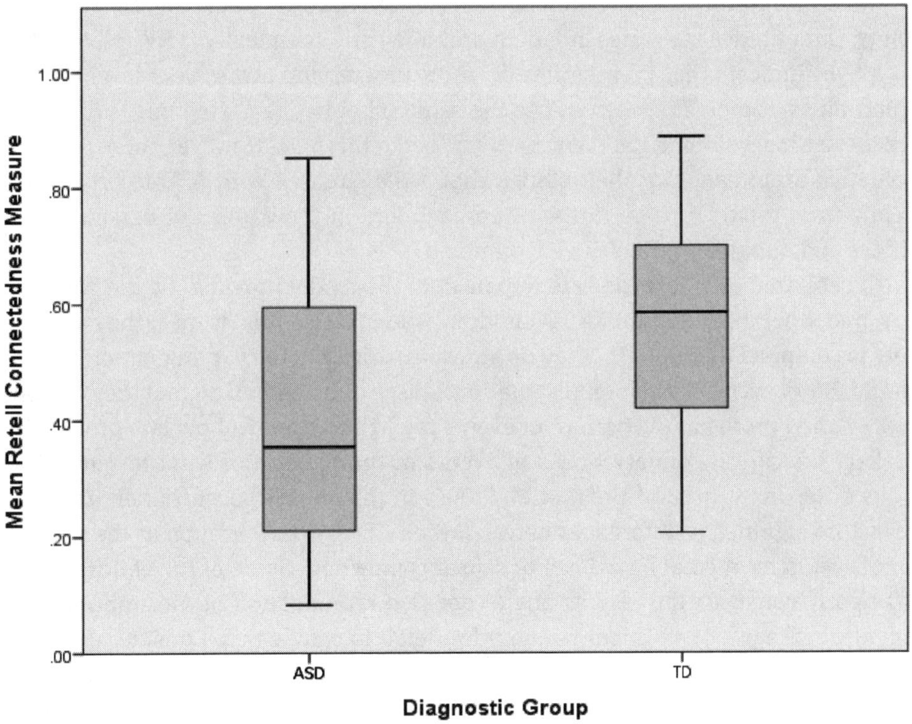

Fig. 10.2: Mean Retell Connectedness Measure for autism spectrum disorder (ASD) and typically developing (TD) retells.

Discussion and Conclusion

With the exception of Carey (2007), this study is unique in considering written narratives by children with ASD. Although some research has looked at the written stories of adults with ASD (e.g., Brown & Klein 2011), we know of no other study that has focused on younger ages and the development of literacy in this genre. The task we set for the children is also unique in research on narrative in ASD in that it allows for an exploration of a difficult-to-measure aspect of narrative production—the management of global coherence—other than through subjective rating analyses of children's finished stories. It created an environment that tapped into the ability of children to maintain global coherence in a way that could not have been examined through observation of naturally occurring stories or oral narratives.

We have shown that the high-functioning children with ASD attending mainstream schools who participated in our study are generally able to tackle the task of retelling a story of a culturally familiar, structured type, especially at older grades. They understand what it is to write a story, can manipulate a repeated episodic structure, and are statistically no more likely to leave their stories unfinished than TD children of the same age range.

There are, nevertheless, differences in performance between the TD and ASD groups. Quantitative measures of length and linguistic complexity (TNW, NDW, TTR, and IpSyn) indicate that their stories do show progression across year level but lag behind those of their TD peers within the same school system. One might therefore hypothesize a developmental delay with respect to this task. However, more detailed qualitative examination of their stories shows the children with ASD to profile differently from their TD peers in their approach and in the pattern of demonstrated abilities and apparent difficulties encountered.

The children are more likely to depart from the model provided by the stimulus story, and when they do, unlike TD children who exercise this license, they are less likely to complete their retells. They do show sensitivity to the varying importance of stimulus story events in their representations, just as TD children do, but they present a more varied profile in the pattern of events retold and overall show less propensity to reflect the causal connectedness of events in their choice of what to retell. Our results differ from those of Diehl et al. (2006) in this regard because their analyses showed no significant differences between their TD and ASD groups in the proportion of events recalled at each level of causal connection. Some of the children with ASD clearly construct the task as one of detailed reproduction of the stimulus and evidently make use of excellent memory for detail to enable this. Consider the child we described who accurately retold 78% of the events in the stimulus story until she ran out of time is in this category: Her case, although not characteristic of the ASD group, is perhaps illustrative of one of a number of strategies being used to give the impression of competence where there may be underlying difficulty.

The observed difference between the ASD and TD groups in propensity to tackle an Alternative Retell rather than a Direct Retell raises questions that are not easy to answer on the basis of the data available here. One interesting question is the degree to which genuine creativity is demonstrated in the productions of the children with ASD, compared with the TD group. A number of possible factors may be relevant here, from degree of willingness to call on native creativity in this institutional, task-oriented context, to an inclination to gravitate to fixed domains of interest. Linked is the question of why, when they do depart from the model, these children are significantly less likely to complete the story than TD children who tackle an Alternative Retell. It is possible that the children with ASD are less able to manage the executive function demands of the complex task of completing a narrative under time pressure while departing from the model. It may be that preferences for local over global processing mean that they have difficulty planning for a globally complete and coherent alternative retell in a way that, in contrast, appears to come readily to the older TD children. Additional detailed analysis of the nature of the creativity exhibited in the Alternative Retells of the TD children and children with ASD may help answer these questions.

The participant numbers in this study are small given the variation in age and school grade, so the findings should be interpreted as preliminary and a starting point for further investigation. The study design does not discriminate between possible differences in comprehension and memory of a stimulus story and differences in reconstructing a story for telling to an audience.

Nevertheless, the findings reported and discussed here show the value of detailed qualitative examination of children's narratives, in addition to broader-brush quantitative analyses. They progress research on narrative in ASD by describing new measures which have been used to identify additional differences in stories from this group, in particular indicating some significant differences between the retells by the children with ASD and the TD children in aspects of perspectivization (the representation of dialogic interaction by characters), in approach to the task (readiness to produce alternative retells but inability to complete these) and in subtle aspects of sensitivity to the importance of story events in selecting them for retelling (a more mixed pattern of events consistently retold by children within the group, with less sensitivity to the causal connectedness of events in selection for retell). The task design has provided a new way of investigating children's management of competing factors of accuracy and detail in retelling and achievement of a globally coherent story, and the findings provide additional evidence of differences in the ability of children with ASD to maintain global coherence in their production of discourse.

These findings have potential implications for interventions and educational strategies intended for high-functioning children with ASD. The positive message from the findings is that, irrespective of the degree to which they succeed, the children with ASD do demonstrate an understanding of the story retelling task. Many of them integrate new material into the Alternative Retells, showing an ability to work within the prescribed story schema. To this degree, they show evidence of creativity. The most readily identifiable difficulties appear to relate to global coherence and planning, causal connectedness, perspectivisation, and the representation of character interaction. There appears to be a difference in the profile of their learning needs rather than simply a developmental delay. The children may go about the task in a different way, but it is a way that nevertheless lends itself to assistance through appropriate educational interventions. Future research should be directed to how this is best achieved.

References

Berman, R. (2009). Language development in narrative contexts. In E. L. Bavin (Ed.), *The Cambridge handbook of child language* (pp. 354–375). http://dx.doi.org/10.1017/CBO9780511576164.020

Brown, H. M., & Klein, P. D. (2011). Writing, Asperger syndrome and theory of mind. *Journal of Autism and Developmental Disorders*, *41*, 1464–1474. http://dx.doi.org/10.1007/s10803-010-1168-7

Carey, L. (2007). *Structural narrative analysis: Assessing language abilities in autism* (Unpublished doctoral dissertation). University of Durham, Durham, England.

Diehl, J. J., Bennetto, L., & Young, E. C. (2006). Story recall and narrative coherence of high-functioning children with autism spectrum disorders. *Journal of Abnormal Child Psychology*, *34*, 87–102. http://dx.doi.org/10.1007/s10802-005-9003-x

García-Pérez, R. M., Hobson, R. P., & Lee, A. (2008). Narrative role-taking in autism. *Journal of Autism and Developmental Disorders*, *38*, 156–168. http://dx.doi.org/10.1007/s10803-007-0379-z

Happé, F. (1999). Why success is more interesting than failure: Understanding assets and deficits in autism. *The Psychologist*, *12*, 540–546.

Koldewyn, K., Jiang, Y. V., Weigelt, S., & Kanwisher, N. (2013). Global/local processing in autism: Not a disability, but a disinclination. *Journal of Autism and Developmental Disorders*, *43*, 2329–2340. http://dx.doi.org/10.1007/s10803-013-1777-z

Landa, R. (2000). Social language use in Asperger syndrome and high-functioning autism. In A. Klin, F. Volkmar, & S. Sparrow (Eds.), *Asperger syndrome* (pp. 125–158). New York, NY: Guilford Press.

Loveland, K., McEvoy, R., Tunali, B., & Kelley, M. L. (1990). Narrative story telling in autism and Down's syndrome. *British Journal of Developmental Psychology*, *8*, 9–23. http://dx.doi.org/10.1111/j.2044-835X.1990.tb00818.x

MacWhinney, B. (2000). *The CHILDES project* (3rd ed.). Mahwah, NJ: Erlbaum.

Mäkinen, L., Loukusa, S., Leinonen, E., Moilanen, I., Ebeling, H., & Kunnari, S. (2014). Characteristics of narrative language in autism spectrum disorder: Evidence from the Finnish. *Research in Autism Spectrum Disorders*, *8*, 987–996.

Mayer, M. (1969). *Frog, where are you?* New York, NY: Puffin.

Norbury, C. F., & Bishop, D. V. M. (2002). Inferential processing and story recall in children with communication problems: A comparison of specific language impairment, pragmatic language impairment and high-functioning autism. *International Journal of Language & Communication Disorders*, *37*, 227–251. http://dx.doi.org/10.1080/13682820210136269

Plueckhahn, T. (2009). *"Ill blow your house down by your cinie cin chin": Narrative recall, causality and coherence in children with autism spectrum disorder* (Unpublished honours thesis). School of Languages & Linguistics, the University of Melbourne, Melbourne, Australia.

Samuel, P. (2009). *Redeveloping the IpSyn metric to code the grammatical complexity of children's written language* (Unpublished honours thesis). School of Languages & Linguistics, the University of Melbourne, Melbourne, Australia.

Scarborough, H. (1990). Index of productive syntax. *Applied Psycholinguistics*, *11*, 1–22. http://dx.doi.org/10.1017/S0142716400008262

Stirling, L., & Barrington, G. (2007). "Then I'll huff & I'll puff or I'll go on the roff!" thinks the wolf: Spontaneous written narratives by a child with autism. In A. Schalley & D. Khlentzos (Eds.), *Mental states: Language and cognitive structure* (pp. 133–172). http://dx.doi.org/10.1075/slcs.93.09sti

Stirling, L., Barrington, G., Douglas, S., & Delves, K. (2009a). Analysis of perspective management and reported interaction in story retellings by children with ASD and typically developing children. *E-Journal of Applied Psychology*, *5*, 31–38.

Stirling, L., Barrington, G., Douglas, S., & Delves, K. (2009b). The developmental profile of editing and repair strategies in narrative structure: A cross-sectional study of primary school children. *Proceedings of the 31st Annual Boston University Conference on Language Development* (pp. 504–515). Somerville, MA: Cascadilla Press.

Stirling, L., Barrington, G., Douglas, S., & Delves, K. (2013, May). *The developmental profile of perspective-taking in written story production by children with ASD.* Poster presented at the International Meeting for Autism Research 2013, Donostia, Spain.

Stirling, L., Douglas, S., Leekam, S., & Carey, L. (2014). The use of narrative in studying communication in autism spectrum disorders: A review of methodologies and findings. In J. Arciuli & J. Brock (Eds.), *Communication in autism* (pp. 169–215). http://dx.doi.org/10.1075/tilar.11.09sti

Trabasso, T., & Sperry, L. (1985). Causal relatedness and importance of story events. *Journal of Memory and Language*, *24*, 595–611. http://dx.doi.org/10.1016/0749-596X(85)90048-8

Trabasso, T., & van den Broek, P. (1985). Causal thinking and representation of narrative events. *Journal of Memory and Language*, *24*, 612–630. http://dx.doi.org/10.1016/0749-596X(85)90049-X

Trivizas, E. (2003). *The three little wolves and the big bad pig.* London, England: Egmont.

Waterhouse, L., & Fein, D. (1982). Language skills in developmentally disabled children. *Brain and Language*, *15*, 307–333. http://dx.doi.org/10.1016/0093-934X(82)90062-1

Joyce Suh, Inge-Marie Eigsti, Allison Canfield, Christina Irvine, Elizabeth Kelley, Letitia R. Naigles, and Deborah Fein

11 Language Representation and Language Use in Children With Optimal Outcomes From ASD

Autism spectrum disorder (ASD) has typically been considered a lifelong condition; however, studies have identified a subset of children (estimates suggest 3%–25%) who improve to such an extent that they no longer meet diagnostic criteria for ASD (Anderson, Liang, & Lord, 2014; Fein et al., 2013; Helt et al., 2008; Sallows & Graupner, 2005; Sutera et al., 2007; Szatmari, Bryson, Boyle, Streiner, & Duku, 2003). These children have been characterized as having "optimal outcomes" (OO). Globally, results indicate no significant difference on the Autism Diagnostic Scale (ADOS) or the Vineland Adaptive Behavior Scales for youth with OO and their typically developing (TD) peers (Fein et al., 2013).

Given the significance of communication and language deficits in the ASD presentation, it is critical to evaluate more specific and fine-grained aspects of communication and language to probe for subtle residual deficits in children who achieve an OO, and to look for early prognostic indicators of an OO. Although the factors involved in determining which individuals will experience OO are not fully explained, they include earlier, more intense intervention (specifically, applied behavior analysis), stronger early cognitive and language skills (e.g., higher IQ, better receptive language), and better imitation abilities (Helt et al., 2008; Orinstein et al., 2014). Language learning and use is intricately tied to social functioning, as language ability could facilitate social experiences, and improvements in social functioning may encourage more frequent use and further development of language skills.

This chapter describes the results of a series of studies of fine-grained aspects of language in the context of globally intact functioning in communication and socialization in ASD. We describe the extent to which improvement in ASD symptomatology relates to improvement in language functioning. A second goal is to explore the mechanisms that may underlie optimal outcomes in ASD, by examining which aspects of language show plasticity and recovery and which continue to show subtle impairments. We also discuss the individual characteristics and adaptive pathways that may have facilitated this improvement in functioning.

http://dx.doi.org/10.1037/15964-012
Innovative Investigations of Language in Autism Spectrum Disorder, L. R. Naigles (Editor)

Initial Studies of Language Functioning in Children With an Optimal Outcome

Kelley, Paul, Fein, and Naigles (2006) studied the language functioning of 14 children (aged 5–9 years) with OO and compared their scores on a series of standardized language tasks with those of 14 children with a history of typical development. The children with OO performed in the average range on all measures: the Peabody Picture Vocabulary Test (PPVT), a measure of receptive vocabulary; the Expressive One-Word Picture Vocabulary Test, a test of expressive vocabulary; the Test of Auditory Comprehension of Language, a measure evaluating vocabulary, grammatical morphemes, and elaborated phrases and sentences; and the Stanford–Binet Memory for Sentences subtest, a test of verbal memory.

The OO and TD groups were largely indistinguishable in lexical and grammatical aspects of language. However, the OO group lagged behind on measures of semantic language, including knowledge of mental state verbs and verbal theory of mind (ToM). *Theory of mind* refers to the ability to understand others' emotions, beliefs, and intentions, and ToM deficits are thought to contribute to the communication deficits in ASD (Baron-Cohen, Leslie, & Frith, 1985). The OO group also struggled with some aspects of pragmatic language (the use of verbal and nonverbal cues for social communication). Pragmatic language requires the complex integration of language and social knowledge and is a particular weakness in ASD (for review, see Eigsti, de Marchena, Schuh, & Kelley, 2011). The participants with OO also showed impairments on a task measuring categorical induction, or the ability to extend properties of a category of items; this capacity is associated with language learning and linked to lexical and pragmatic abilities (Naigles, Kelley, Troyb, & Fein, 2013). Finally, narrative production was also an area of relative weakness, a finding that is further explored later in the chapter.

A follow-up study examined many of the same children, now 8 to 13 years old (Kelley, Naigles, & Fein, 2010), and added a comparison group of children with high-functioning ASD (HFA; defined as having IQ > 70). As in the 2006 study, the OO group did not differ from the TD group in receptive vocabulary (PPVT). Semantic and syntactic language scores, measured by the Clinical Evaluation of Language Fundamentals (CELF) were also in the normal range; the OO group did not differ from either the TD or HFA group on this measure, with mean scores falling between the two group means. On three measures of pragmatic language (Test of Pragmatic Language, and the Making Inferences and Figurative Language subtests of the Test of Language Competence), the OO and TD groups did not differ. Therefore, when evaluated by standardized measures, pragmatic language appeared to normalize fully as children with OO matured (it should be noted that categorical induction and narrative tasks, areas of relative weakness in the 2006 study, were not included in this report).

Language Functioning in Children From the Optimal Outcomes Study

A large project was designed to describe the OO phenomenon in detail (Fein et al., 2013); the findings described in the rest of this chapter draw from this study. Participants with OO were stringently defined. In addition to a diagnosis of autism before age 5 from a clinician specializing in the disorder, documented by written reports that were verified by expert raters naive to diagnostic status, these children did not show symptoms on the ADOS, the primary diagnostic tool for ASD, at the time of the study; they had scores in the normal range on the Communication and Socialization scores on the Vineland Adaptive Behavior Scales; and they were not receiving any special education services related to autism (e.g., participation in a social skills group). Details of subject recruitment and characterization are provided in Fein et al. (2013). In these studies, analyses probed for any indication of functional differences in participants with an OO, compared with TD peers; a lack of such difference suggests full normalization. Analyses also probed for results in which the HFA and OO groups did not differ, suggesting residual, ASD-like characteristics. Participants included 34 children with OO, 44 children with HFA, and 34 children with TD, ranging in age from 8 to 21 years (12 years on average). The studies described here draw on this sample or a subset.

Standardized Assessments

To evaluate language abilities, the comparison of performance scores on age-appropriate standardized language tests provides a logical starting point. In one study (Tyson et al., 2014), the OO group scored in the average range or above on all language measures, including receptive vocabulary (the PPVT) and subtests of the CELF (Semel, Wiig, & Secord, 2003), which assess the ability to listen to and follow complex, orally presented instructions (Concepts and Following Directions); create sentences using unmarked verb, subject, and object prompts (Formulated Sentences); repeat orally presented sentences (Recalling Sentences); explain semantic relationships between pairs of words (Word Classes); and define words (Word Definitions). All HFA and OO group scores were in the average range. The primary measure on which the OO and TD groups differed was the Formulated Sentences subtest, on which the OO group had lower scores than the TD group (whose scaled scores, notably, were at a mean of 13, in the high average range), and the HFA group performed worse than both the OO and TD groups.

Reading and Written Language: Academic Skills

Also using standardized measures, Troyb, Orinstein, et al. (2014) evaluated academic abilities, focusing in particular on reading and written language. The following measures were administered: (a) the Woodcock–Johnson—III Tests of Achievement, Word Attack and Passage Comprehension subtests; and (b) the Test of Written Language—3. As the authors predicted, there were no group differences in phonological decoding (Word Attack), which involves the ability to read aloud an unfamiliar or nonsense word. Passage comprehension is a more complex process in that it involves abstract reasoning, the ability to distinguish essential from nonessential details, and the ability to make inferences ("read between the lines"), aspects that are all weaknesses that have been observed in ASD (Griswold, Barnhill, Myles, Hagiwara, & Simpson, 2002; Mayes & Calhoun, 2003). In our study, the HFA group performed significantly worse than the TD group; as for the OO group, scores did not differ from either group (although the OO–HFA difference approached significance, $p = .07$). On the Test of Written Language, the children were instructed to write a story about an outer space scene. The HFA group's stories were significantly shorter (contained fewer sentences) than those of the OO and TD groups. However, controlling for length, there were no group differences in total number of words, mean sentence length, or mean word length (indices of structural complexity), and no differences in spelling or punctuation (i.e., *Contextual Conventions*), vocabulary or syntax (i.e., *Contextual Language*), or the use of prose and action (i.e., *Story Construction*). These results suggest that the skills involved in passage comprehension (e.g., inference, abstract reasoning), normalize in OO but continue to be a relative weakness in HFA; general aspects of writing were intact in both OO and HFA.

Subtle Assessments of Language Ability in OO

Because of the structured nature of standardized language measures, they are limited in their ability to capture what may be more subtle language deficits (Diehl, Bennetto, & Young, 2006; Eigsti et al., 2011; Kjelgaard & Tager-Flusberg, 2001; Naigles & Chin, 2015). Communication does not take place in a vacuum; it involves language knowledge, as well as ToM, working memory, and other executive processes. Narrative elicitation and other ecologically valid tasks may better approximate communication in everyday life, that is, in vivo language ability. Furthermore, although deficits may not be detected using untimed, structured, experimenter-led standardized assessments (for further discussion of this point, see Eigsti & Schuh, Chapter 9, this volume), they may become apparent in the context of more sensitive measures. Assessing narrative production or language in the context of more complex tasks could extend our understanding of the degree of normalization of subtle semantic and pragmatic language abilities among OO individuals.

As noted earlier, Kelley et al. (2006) found narrative weaknesses in OO children at ages 5 to 8 years. When telling a story from a picture book, the OO group was less likely to identify the goals and motivations of the characters, more likely to misinterpret story events, and less likely to give causal explanations (consistent with Diehl et al., 2006). The OO group was also more likely to repeat story elements and to make ambiguous references to characters and events. These narrative qualities are critical; to tell a good story, the speaker must specify which characters and events she is describing and explain causal relationships between events. The mild deficits seen in the young OO sample suggested a more limited understanding of and interest in the internal mental states of characters (possibly associated with ToM) and a more limited understanding of social dynamics.

Suh and colleagues (2014) extended this research in the current OO project by evaluating narrative skills in an older subset of OO, TD, and HFA participants (aged 9–15, $n = 15$ per group). Children told a story while paging through a (largely) wordless picture book, *Tuesday* (an activity on the Autism Diagnostic Observation Schedule, or ADOS; Lord, Rutter, DiLavore, & Risi, 2002). The resulting narratives did not differ in length or lexical diversity (e.g., number of different words and word types produced), factors associated with morphological and syntactic language skills. These skills have been found to be within the average range for many children with HFA (Kjelgaard & Tager-Flusberg, 2001). Additionally, the OO group did not differ from their TD peers in several important narrative features: the presence of "gist" descriptions (Jolliffe & Baron-Cohen, 1999), the production of ambiguous pronouns (Arnold, Bennetto, & Diehl, 2009), and the presence of repetition disfluencies (e.g., *They all—they all were flying*). However, the OO group had residual ASD-like characteristics in some regards: more self-correction disfluencies (*They were all/those crows were all sitting on the wires*) and the use of idiosyncratic language (e.g., *congregating around a human suburb*). Idiosyncratic language involves a less conventional way of speaking, overly formal use of language, and a reliance on clichéd or formulaic phrases (*Stay tuned for the sequel*). Therefore, a subset of OO children appeared to continue to display subtle weaknesses in pragmatic language. However, it should also be noted that a small majority of participants with OO (eight of 15) produced narratives without any idiosyncratic characteristics.

Disfluencies during speech have particular significance vis-à-vis pragmatic language. Lake, Humphreys, and Cardy (2011) reported that high-functioning adults with ASD produced more self-repetitions during spontaneous speech but fewer speech revisions (*My fat . . . favorite . . . best animal is a dog . . . my favorite animal is a cat*) than age-matched control subjects. The authors postulated that revisions may be listener-oriented pragmatic speech devices that clarify information for the listener and communicate the speaker's intentions. Consistent with this hypothesis, Suh et al. (2014) reported more repetitions by the HFA group compared with the TD group; the OO group did not differ from either one. Repetitions in spontaneous speech may also reflect executive demands in planning and inhibitory control, as more effortful processing (including greater syntactic complexity) is found to elicit more repetition (Arnold, Kam, & Tanenhaus, 2007).

Filled pauses or fillers (i.e., *uh* and *um*) are also thought to also serve pragmatic functions, announcing momentary delays in speech or signaling intent to hold the conversational floor (Clark & Fox Tree, 2002; Maclay & Osgood, 1959). There were no differences in the overall production of *uh* and *um* (considered together) in Suh et al.'s (2014) study. Using a nonnarrative spontaneous speech sample involving picture description under conditions of cognitive load (to elicit greater filler production; Schachter, Christenfeld, Ravina, & Bilous, 1991), Irvine, Eigsti, and Fein (2016) examined *uh* versus *um* disfluency. *Uh* and *um* are thought to serve different functions, and they present in (somewhat) complementary distribution: *uh* typically precedes shorter delays in speech, and *um* precedes longer ones; *uh* is produced more within utterances, whereas *um* is produced at utterance boundaries (Clark & Fox Tree, 2002; Smith & Clark, 1993). Given the "hold-the-floor" placement of *um*, it is thought to communicate mental-state information to the listener and thus to serve a more listener-oriented function. Analyses revealed no differences in rates of *uh* disfluencies, but fewer *um* disfluencies from the HFA group compared with both TD and OO groups (with no OO–TD differences). Less frequent *um* production was also associated with greater ASD symptom severity. Irvine et al. concluded that the normalized rate of *um* production in OO suggests a fundamental improvement of pragmatic language abilities.

Story Structure

There is a strong relationship between completeness and organization in narratives, defined as *story goodness*, and pragmatic deficits (Lê, Coelho, Mozeiko, & Grafman, 2011). Whereas the previous studies examined detailed aspects of narrative production, Canfield, Eigsti, de Marchena, and Fein (in press) used *story structure* to characterize the narratives from the OO project. Participants looked through six pictures (the monkey cartoon from the ADOS) and then told the story from those pictures. Measures included *story completeness* (e.g., number of core story events expressed) and *story organization* (a type of story grammar that captures how prototypical story structures are expressed; Liles, Duffy, Merritt, & Purcell, 1995). A story composite score was calculated to capture global narrative quality. The HFA narratives received lower story composite scores than the TD group, and the OO group did not differ from either group. Results did not indicate significant deficits for the OO group but suggested greater variability in story goodness for both the OO and HFA groups.

Story Ratings From Naive Observers

In addition to researcher-based analysis of the transcribed narratives, both Suh et al. (2014) and Canfield et al. (in press) gathered naive impressions of narrative quality from college students. Suh and colleagues found that the OO group's narrations were rated as indistinguishable from their TD peers in all domains, but that narratives from the HFA group were rated as lacking in overall quality, harder to comprehend, and containing more odd content and language. Canfield and colleagues also found that the HFA narratives were rated as less easy to follow, less reflective of the actual story, "less good" as stories, and as more odd or unusual, confirming that deficits in ASD narratives were detectable by naive raters. However, unlike in Suh et al., raters found narrations from the OO group to be less easy to follow and "less good" as stories (similar to the HFA group). Canfield et al.'s narrations required more planning; rather than paging through a book, and telling a story as they did so, participants were asked to review the picture stimuli and then to tell the story. This difference may have contributed to narrations being less well organized and less easy to understand. The results suggest that slight impairments in pragmatic language, detectable by naive raters, may persist in OO, despite their otherwise normalized language performance.

Category Knowledge

Semantic organization can reveal subtle language deficits without using speech as an outcome measure. Naigles and colleagues (2013) conducted a categorical induction task. Consistent with results from Kelley et al. (2006), participants with OO and HFA showed residual weaknesses in the ability to extend category knowledge to novel exemplars (e.g., if all snakes in a diverse group have gray eyes, does a new, differently colored snake also have gray eyes?). Although most children were able to extend category properties, a substantial subgroup of OO (22%) and HFA (33%) participants did not extend on any trial; no TD participants displayed this profile. Task performance, controlling for IQ and vocabulary scores, was associated with scores on the Test of Pragmatic Language, suggesting that categorical induction captures an ability that is important in pragmatic language. Residual deficits in semantic generalization skills thus may in turn influence pragmatic language functioning.

Potential Mechanisms and Predictors of Symptom Remission in OO

Further research into language in OO has investigated some of the mechanisms through which OO children may achieve an OO. Results could reflect *preexisting characteristics*, which drive improvement in ASD; characteristics that *changed with remission of ASD symptoms*; or *compensatory mechanisms* through which children with OO compensated for initial developmental difficulties. Results could also reflect a combination of these factors. It is exciting that, in addition to informing our understanding of symptom improvement, study of these mechanisms may illuminate models of typical language acquisition.

Weak Central Coherence

The OO project identified a classic feature of the ASD diagnosis that appears to modulate along with symptom remission: *weak central coherence*. As early as 1943, researchers in the field remarked that affected individuals display an interest in parts of objects rather than the whole—seeing the “trees” rather than the “forest” (Kanner, 1943). This cognitive pattern, called weak central coherence, involves enhanced attention to local features and difficulty integrating elements of a complex stimulus set (Frith & Happé, 1994) for both visuospatial (Happé, 1996) and verbal (Happé, 1997; López & Leekam, 2003) domains. Because children with ASD tend to focus on local rather than global details, they have more difficulty generalizing and learning language and social rules.

Given that this pattern is characteristic of ASD, we examined whether detail focus was present in OO (Fitch, Fein, & Eigsti, 2015). While engaged in a finger-tapping dual task, participants described a series of oil paintings. Descriptions were coded for global focus (descriptions of the main character in the painting, summary or gist descriptions of the painting as a whole, and statements evaluating the painting’s quality) versus detail focus (descriptions of background elements, and statements describing something related to, but not present in, an element of the painting), based on previous reports (Barnes & Baron-Cohen, 2012; Glosser & Deser, 1991). Findings indicated that although all participants produced more global than local details, the HFA group produced significantly more local details than OO and TD groups, which did not differ. Linear regression analyses indicated that full-scale IQ, history of communication difficulties (Autism Diagnostic Interview [ADI]—Lifetime score), and executive functioning predicted global–local focus in the OO (but not the HFA) group. Individuals with a history of more severe communication and social symptoms displayed a greater focus on details relative to gist; however, current symptom severity was not a predictor of global/local focus in HFA. This suggests that the relative severity of childhood ASD symptoms, but not current symptoms, is a predictor of global–local focus.

The results of the weak central coherence study are consistent with two possibilities. First, the OO group may never have shown the global–local focus that characterized the HFA group’s performance. Their typical processing style may have been present throughout development, including the period when they had active symptoms of ASD, such that this processing style may have been instrumental in their improvement. Alternatively, participants with OO could have had HFA-like global–local focus early in development and lost it over time (i.e., OO group “overcame” local focus, much as they “overcame” ASD symptoms). The study is not longitudinal and thus prevents us from making interpretations about causality; however, results suggest that global–local focus may be a useful index of symptom remission.

Tone Discrimination

The OO project evaluated another nonlinguistic factor potentially associated with language acquisition: heightened acuity for auditory pitch discrimination. Multiple studies have demonstrated exceptional pitch perception and discrimination in both children and adults with ASD (reviewed in Mottron, Dawson, Soulières, Hubert, & Burack, 2006), and our group hypothesized that hyperacuity for pitch could contribute to overly detailed representations of phonological information, thereby delaying the development of phonological categories and subsequent word learning in ASD (Eigsti & Fein, 2013). The ability to build abstract categories rather than focusing on immediate perceptual qualities may be critical in early language development (e.g., Son, Smith, & Goldstone, 2008). In this way, superior pitch processing in ASD might reflect the overdevelopment of low-level perceptual processes in general (Bonnel et al., 2003), consistent with local neural overconnectivity (Belmonte et al., 2004).

Participants completed a tone discrimination task in which they had to make a same–different judgment about pairs of tones (Eigsti & Fein, 2013). Results showed that the HFA group had the best pitch discrimination, followed by the OO group, followed by the TD group. Furthermore, symptom severity accounted for unique variance in pitch discrimination, even controlling for age and IQ, in linear regression analyses, such that better discrimination was associated with greater symptom severity. In addition, parents reported the timing of first word production (for HFA and OO groups only, as part of the revised ADI). The OO group was similarly delayed in this important language milestone, with first words at an average age of 27 months (21 months in the HFA group). Comparing on-time versus delayed (no words at 24 months) groups, results showed an interaction of delay status and pitch condition, with the delay group displaying generally better performance. Findings were consistent with the possibility that heightened pitch discrimination is associated with early language delays and suggest that early language delays can be overcome. Heightened sensitivity to acoustic signals may impede the extraction of communicative meaning from these signals, possibly by impairing the formation of phonological categories. Our findings also suggest that heightened acuity is an index of symptom remission in OO.

Compensatory Mechanisms

This chapter has two primary goals: to describe language abilities in youth with optimal outcomes from ASD and to tackle the question of how symptom remission happens, in part by describing the individual characteristics and adaptive pathways that may have facilitated improvements in language-related functions. What are the mechanisms responsible for this impressive normalization? We hypothesized that, across many domains and abilities, we might observe three distinct patterns of language functioning. First, we anticipated *full normalization* in some domains, such that functioning in the OO group would resemble that in the TD group, where both differed from the HFA group. Second, we anticipated *residual ASD* functioning in some domains, such that the OO group would resemble the HFA group (and thus reflecting the ASD history of OO individuals), and both would differ from the TD group. Finally, we expected evidence of compensatory functioning, defined as characteristics in the OO group that differ from both the groups with HFA (indicating that they do not simply reflect residual ASD symptomatology) and with TD (such that they may reflect exaggerations or extensions of normative function). To restate, the three expected patterns: *normalization*: HFA ≠ OO, TD; *residual* ASD: HFA, OO ≠ TD; and *compensation*: HFA, TD ≠ OO. Although many of the behavioral studies reviewed here suggest full normalization of function in OO, other findings suggest compensatory processes, providing hints about the mechanisms underlying OO.

Personality

One potential early characteristic that could serve as a positive prognostic indicator is personality style, linked in some studies to early language development (Reznick, Corley, Robinson, & Matheny, 1997). In one study, positive affect (i.e., the tendency to show positive emotions, seek novelty and environmental stimulation) and extraversion were associated with better expressive language at age 14 months, potentially because subjects had more frequent social interactions in which to practice language skills (Laake & Bridgett, 2014). Our group evaluated the Big Five personality characteristics of *Extraversion*, *Agreeableness*, *Conscientiousness*, *Openness to experience*, and *Neuroticism* (Suh et al., in press). The OO group was higher in Extraversion, even compared with the TD group, and both TD and OO groups were higher in Agreeableness, Conscientiousness, and Openness, and lower in neuroticism, than their HFA peers. Children who achieved an OO may have been initially more sociable and motivated to communicate, and these traits may have provided them with more language experience.

Verbal Memory

Another candidate process for compensation leading to language improvements is verbal memory. Strengths in memory domains could compensate for language and social impairments. For example, declarative memory (i.e., memory for facts and experiences) could be used to explicitly learn language formulations or social rules and schemas (Ullman & Pullman, 2015). Correlations between aspects of verbal memory and language abilities (e.g., sentence comprehension) have been reported in both typical and atypical development. Verbal memory deficits in HFA individuals have been tied to deficits in both language and nonlanguage domains, including social skills (Schuh & Eigsti, 2012). This suggests that verbal memory may be one compensatory strategy that facilitates language processing and social development in OO and HFA children.

In a study of children with a past history of language impairments, nonword repetition deficits were as large as those in a group with current language impairment, suggesting that short-term phonological memory is a marker of impairment even after surface language abilities have normalized (Baird, Dworzynski, Slonims, & Simonoff, 2010). Verbal memory impairments are clinically salient in ASD. Fein et al. (1996) found that children with HFA, compared with a group with specific language impairment, had the least difficulty remembering digits, more difficulty with sentences, and the most difficulty with stories, suggesting that verbal memory impairments increase in parallel with the complexity of the material.

In the Tyson et al. (2014) study described earlier, participants completed the CELF and PPVT language assessments; in addition, they completed assessments of verbal memory, including a nonword repetition task and a list-learning measure. The TD group performed significantly better on nonword repetition than the HFA group, and the OO group scores did not differ from either TD or HFA groups. On the list-learning task, mean group scores were all in the average range; the TD group performed significantly better than the HFA group, and the OO group did not differ from either. Furthermore, and relevant for the discussion of mechanisms, linear regressions indicated that verbal memory and short-term phonological memory predicted language abilities in the OO and HFA groups, but not for the TD group; these relationships were particularly strong for the OO group.

These results raise the possibility that verbal memory is a compensatory ability that facilitates language processing. Verbal memory has been shown to play a critical role in language acquisition (de Abreu, Gathercole, & Martin, 2011; Gathercole & Alloway, 2006; Gathercole, Alloway, Willis, & Adams, 2006). Children who can hold sentences in short-term memory longer can better analyze those sentences into their components. Children with better short-term memory might also have more stable lexical representations, such that incoming words are more efficiently recognized, categorized, and parsed. During the course of language acquisition, children in the OO and HFA groups may have relied more than their TD peers on their verbal memory abilities in developing language skills. This possibility is also consistent with the finding that executive functioning scores in OO are within the average range, even for functions that are impaired in HFA (Troyb, Rosenthal, et al., 2013), because verbal memory is tightly linked to executive control. If children with an OO had initially stronger verbal memory skills, this may have provided an early compensatory advantage for language acquisition.

Neural Circuitry of Language Processing

The results reviewed so far suggest normalization of essentially all basic language functions (Tyson et al., 2014), including many but not all subtle pragmatic processes. This raises an interesting question: To what degree does normative language performance reflect normative brain function? Studies of language processing in ASD have shown atypical activations during language processing, including impaired functional connectivity (Catarino et al., 2011; Kleinhans, Müller, Cohen, & Courchesne, 2008; Verly et al., 2014), abnormal lateralization (Boddaert et al., 2003; Eigsti, Schuh, Mencl, Schultz, & Paul, 2012; Grèzes, Wicker, Berthoz, & de Gelder, 2009; Groen et al., 2010; Hesling et al., 2010), and some recruitment of brain regions not typically involved in language (e.g., Catarino et al., 2011; Knaus et al., 2010; Mizuno et al., 2011; Redcay & Courchesne, 2008). Additionally, studies of ASD have found greater activation in the medial temporal lobe (an area associated with declarative memory) during language and social processing tasks compared with TD peers, suggesting that this area is activated as a compensatory pathway (Ullman & Pullman, 2015).

Our group collected functional brain imaging data during language comprehension (Eigsti, Stevens, et al., 2016), anticipating three possible patterns of activation. As described earlier, we expected evidence of some neural normalization in which neural systems should function similarly in OO and TD, as has been reported in successfully treated dyslexia (Aylward et al., 2003; Simos et al., 2002) and resolved aphasia (Saur & Hartwigsen, 2012). A normalization pattern was reported in an electroencephalograph study of toddlers with ASD who completed intensive early intervention (Dawson et al., 2012). A second pattern, residual ASD, would describe activations in the OO group that resemble those seen in individuals with ASD. Finally, we anticipated some evidence of neural compensation, as is observed in studies of healthy aging (Ansado, Marsolais, Methqal, Alary, & Joanette, 2013), in which processing inefficiencies cause the aging brain to recruit additional neural resources in the same or different regions to achieve computational output equivalent to that of a younger brain; and in successfully remediated dyslexia in adults, who show normalization of activity in the left hemisphere as well as compensatory right hemisphere (language homologue) activation (Eden et al., 2004).

Participants made true–false judgments for written sentences (a task modeled on Kana, Keller, Cherkassky, Minshew, & Just, 2006). The groups did not differ in behavioral indices of task performance (e.g., accuracy and reaction time). Imaging results indicated that the task engaged a broad bihemispheric network across all groups. Somewhat surprisingly, there was no evidence for neural normalization (i.e., OO = TD ≠ HFA). Several regions showed residual ASD activation (i.e., OO = HFA ≠ TD); these included regions of left dorsolateral prefrontal cortex, left inferior parietal lobule (supramarginal gyrus), bilateral posterior cingulate gyrus, and right superior and middle temporal gyrus (the right-hemisphere homologue of Wernicke's area).

The vast majority of group differences followed a neural compensation pattern in which the OO group showed heightened activation relative to both HFA and TD groups (i.e., OO > HFA = TD). These regions included motor and supplementary motor regions of the right hemisphere, right middle and superior frontal gyrus, right supramarginal gyrus, right superior temporal and parahippocampal gyrus, left precentral and inferior temporal gyrus, left precuneus, left superior temporal gyrus, left occipital gyrus, and several regions of both anterior and posterior cerebellum.

The OO group showed ASD-like and heightened activation of brain regions often implicated in language comprehension and prosody, cognitive control, and using motivation in decision making and also in the right-lateralized regions of brain, which, on the left, are often associated with language. Additionally, there was heightened or ASD-like activation in regions that have been associated with cognitive control and motivation in decision making. This is consistent with a body of previous work showing less left-lateralized, more bilateral, and more right-lateralized activation during language tasks in ASD (Knaus et al., 2010; Knaus, Silver, Lindgren, Hadjikhani, & Tager-Flusberg, 2008), and suggests that the OO group retains this somewhat atypical "signature" of language processing. Reorganization during aging may serve as an analogue to the developmental plasticity observed in OO in that the recruitment of right-homologue tissue facilitates behaviorally normal language. These findings highlight the impressive plasticity of neural circuits underlying language and suggest that symptom remission relies more on compensatory mechanisms than on the complete normalization of language functions and pathways in the brain.

The Next Steps

The many findings described in this chapter paint a detailed picture of the degree to which language abilities normalize in individuals who achieve optimal outcomes from ASD. In each of the reported studies, the OO group's standardized scores were always in the normal range, indicating intact functioning; for a small number of standardized assessments, scores were lower in the OO than in the TD comparison group but that TD group had scores in the above-average range (i.e., TD participants were "supranormal"). At a young age (5–8 years), children with OO produced narratives that were less causally connected and produced fewer ToM character features; these difficulties seemed to be fully resolved by age 8 to 21 years. In the large OO study, narratives from OO participants differed only from the TD group in showing more disfluency and idiosyncratic phrases, and narratives were rated by naive observers as more difficult to follow. The OO group also had residual deficits in semantic generalization skills (categorical induction). This represents the total of language measures on which the OO group showed deficits compared with a TD group. In contrast, for a large set of measures, the OO group had fully normal scores, with no differences from the very high-functioning TD group. Their academic language abilities were intact, they had typical rates of speaker-oriented disfluencies in narratives, and they used good story structure; narratives produced with less planning (e.g., while participants paged through a book) were rated similarly to TD narratives by naive listeners. The OO participants were typical in the degree to which they described the gist of a painting; they also had typical tone discrimination skills.

The OO studies consistently yield results indicating the presence of genuine impairment early in development, followed by a trajectory of rapid growth. An important step for the future is to explore the mechanisms driving these impressive behavioral improvements in language and communication skills. The chapter has provided some hints about possible mechanisms; for example, the greater extraversion characterizing the OO participants, if it were present early in development, may have led to increased experience with social interaction and language. Similarly, the OO participants have good verbal working memory skills and executive functioning, which may have allowed them to make more rapid gains in language skills. The imaging data also suggest the possibility that the OO group has adaptively compensated for atypical early language organization via significant compensation using a variety of brain systems. One fundamental question for the future is whether areas of cognitive strength and compensatory brain activation are consistent across OO participants, or whether each child finds his or her own path to obtaining an OO. Longitudinal studies will provide an important means of establishing whether children who achieve an OO did so because of strong extraversion and verbal memory, for example, such that these factors led to remediation of ASD and language development or whether these processes showed gains concurrently with symptom remission. Longitudinal studies will also provide a crucial means of identifying predictors that may be present early in development (but not measurable later in life).

Studies of OO provide an exciting window into the factors underlying the language deficits of ASD and shine a powerful light onto the processes critical for typical language development.

References

Anderson, D. K., Liang, J. W., & Lord, C. (2014). Predicting young adult outcome among more and less cognitively able individuals with autism spectrum disorders. *Journal of Child Psychology and Psychiatry*, *55*, 485–494. http://dx.doi.org/10.1111/jcpp.12178

Ansado, J., Marsolais, Y., Methqal, I., Alary, F., & Joanette, Y. (2013). The adaptive aging brain: Evidence from the preservation of communication abilities with age. *European Journal of Neuroscience*, *37*, 1887–1895. http://dx.doi.org/10.1111/ejn.12252

Arnold, J. E., Bennetto, L., & Diehl, J. J. (2009). Reference production in young speakers with and without autism: Effects of discourse status and processing constraints. *Cognition*, *110*, 131–146. http://dx.doi.org/10.1016/j.cognition.2008.10.016

Arnold, J. E., Kam, C. L., & Tanenhaus, M. K. (2007). If you say thee uh you are describing something hard: The on-line attribution of disfluency during reference comprehension. *Journal of Experimental Psychology: Learning, Memory, and Cognition*, *33*, 914–930. http://dx.doi.org/10.1037/0278-7393.33.5.914

Aylward, E. H., Richards, T. L., Berninger, V. W., Nagy, W. E., Field, K. M., Grimme, A. C., . . . Cramer, S. C. (2003). Instructional treatment associated with changes in brain activation in children with dyslexia. *Neurology*, *61*, 212–219. http://dx.doi.org/10.1212/01.WNL.0000068363.05974.64

Baird, G., Dworzynski, K., Slonims, V., & Simonoff, E. (2010). Memory impairment in children with language impairment. *Developmental Medicine & Child Neurology*, *52*, 535–540. http://dx.doi.org/10.1111/j.1469-8749.2009.03494.x

Barnes, J. L., & Baron-Cohen, S. (2012). The big picture: Storytelling ability in adults with autism spectrum conditions. *Journal of Autism and Developmental Disorders*, *42*, 1557–1565. http://dx.doi.org/10.1007/s10803-011-1388-5

Baron-Cohen, S., Leslie, A. M., & Frith, U. (1985). Does the autistic child have a "theory of mind"? *Cognition*, *21*, 37–46. http://dx.doi.org/10.1016/0010-0277(85)90022-8

Belmonte, M. K., Allen, G., Beckel-Mitchener, A., Boulanger, L. M., Carper, R. A., & Webb, S. J. (2004). Autism and abnormal development of brain connectivity. *The Journal of Neuroscience*, *24*, 9228–9231. http://dx.doi.org/10.1523/JNEUROSCI.3340-04.2004

Boddaert, N., Belin, P., Chabane, N., Poline, J. B., Barthélémy, C., Mouren-Simeoni, M. C., . . . Zilbovicius, M. (2003). Perception of complex sounds: Abnormal pattern of cortical activation in autism. *The American Journal of Psychiatry*, *160*, 2057–2060. http://dx.doi.org/10.1176/appi.ajp.160.11.2057

Bonnel, A., Mottron, L., Peretz, I., Trudel, M., Gallun, E., & Bonnel, A. M. (2003). Enhanced pitch sensitivity in individuals with autism: A signal detection analysis. *Journal of Cognitive Neuroscience*, *15*, 226–235. http://dx.doi.org/10.1162/089892903321208169

Canfield, A. R., Eigsti, I.-M., de Marchena, A., & Fein, D. (in press). Story goodness in adolescents with autism spectrum disorders and in optimal outcomes from ASD. *Journal of Speech, Language, and Hearing Research.*

Catarino, A., Luke, L., Waldman, S., Andrade, A., Fletcher, P. C., & Ring, H. (2011). An fMRI investigation of detection of semantic incongruities in autistic spectrum conditions. *European Journal of Neuroscience*, *33*, 558–567. http://dx.doi.org/10.1111/j.1460-9568.2010.07503.x

Clark, H. H., & Fox Tree, J. E. (2002). Using uh and um in spontaneous speaking. *Cognition*, *84*, 73–111. http://dx.doi.org/10.1016/S0010-0277(02)00017-3

Dawson, G., Jones, E. J., Merkle, K., Venema, K., Lowy, R., Faja, S., . . . Webb, S. J. (2012). Early behavioral intervention is associated with normalized brain activity in young children with autism. *Journal of the American Academy of Child & Adolescent Psychiatry*, *51*, 1150–1159.

de Abreu, P. M. J. E., Gathercole, S. E., & Martin, R. (2011). Disentangling the relationship between working memory and language: The roles of short-term storage and cognitive control. *Learning and Individual Differences*, *21*, 569–574. http://dx.doi.org/10.1016/j.lindif.2011.06.002

Diehl, J. J., Bennetto, L., & Young, E. C. (2006). Story recall and narrative coherence of high-functioning children with autism spectrum disorders. *Journal of Abnormal Child Psychology*, *34*, 87–102. http://dx.doi.org/10.1007/s10802-005-9003-x

Eden, G. F., Jones, K. M., Cappell, K., Gareau, L., Wood, F. B., Zeffiro, T. A., . . . Flowers, D. L. (2004). Neural changes following remediation in adult developmental dyslexia. *Neuron*, *44*, 411–422. http://dx.doi.org/10.1016/j.neuron.2004.10.019

Eigsti, I.-M., de Marchena, A. B., Schuh, J. M., & Kelley, E. (2011). Language acquisition in autism spectrum disorders: A developmental review. *Research in Autism Spectrum Disorders*, *5*, 681–691. http://dx.doi.org/10.1016/j.rasd.2010.09.001

Eigsti, I.-M., & Fein, D. A. (2013). More is less: Pitch discrimination and language delays in children with optimal outcomes from autism. *Autism Research*, *6*, 605–613. http://dx.doi.org/10.1002/aur.1324

Eigsti, I.-M., Schuh, J., Mencl, E., Schultz, R. T., & Paul, R. (2012). The neural underpinnings of prosody in autism. *Child Neuropsychology*, *18*, 600–617. http://dx.doi.org/10.1080/09297049.2011.639757

Eigsti, I.-M., Stevens, M. C., Schultz, R. T., Barton, M., Kelley, E., Naigles, L., . . . Fein, D. A. (2016). Language comprehension and brain function in individuals with an optimal outcome from autism. *NeuroImage: Clinical*, *10*, 182–191. http://dx.doi.org/10.1016/j.nicl.2015.11.014

Fein, D., Barton, M., Eigsti, I.-M., Kelley, E., Naigles, L., Schultz, R. T., . . . Tyson, K. (2013). Optimal outcome in individuals with a history of autism. *Journal of Child Psychology and Psychiatry*, *54*, 195–205. http://dx.doi.org/10.1111/jcpp.12037

Fein, D., Dunn, M. A., Allen, D. M., Aram, R., Hall, N., Morris, R., & Wilson, B. C. (1996). Neuropsychological and language findings. In I. Rapin (Ed.), *Preschool children with inadequate communication: Developmental language disorder, autism, low IQ* (pp. 123–154). London, England: MacKeith Press.

Fitch, A., Fein, D. A., & Eigsti, I.-M. (2015). Detail and gestalt focus in individuals with optimal outcomes from autism spectrum disorders. *Journal of Autism and Developmental Disorders*, *45*, 1887–1896. http://dx.doi.org/10.1007/s10803-014-2347-8

Frith, U., & Happé, F. (1994). Language and communication in autistic disorders. *Philosophical Transactions of the Royal Society B: Biological Sciences*, *346*, 97–104. http://dx.doi.org/10.1098/rstb.1994.0133

Gathercole, S. E., & Alloway, T. P. (2006). Practitioner review: Short-term and working memory impairments in neurodevelopmental disorders: Diagnosis and remedial support. *Journal of Child Psychology and Psychiatry*, *47*, 4–15. http://dx.doi.org/10.1111/j.1469-7610.2005.01446.x

Gathercole, S. E., Alloway, T. P., Willis, C., & Adams, A. M. (2006). Working memory in children with reading disabilities. *Journal of Experimental Child Psychology*, *93*, 265–281. http://dx.doi.org/10.1016/j.jecp.2005.08.003

Glosser, G., & Deser, T. (1991). Patterns of discourse production among neurological patients with fluent language disorders. *Brain and Language*, *40*, 67–88. http://dx.doi.org/10.1016/0093-934X(91)90117-J

Grèzes, J., Wicker, B., Berthoz, S., & de Gelder, B. (2009). A failure to grasp the affective meaning of actions in autism spectrum disorder subjects. *Neuropsychologia*, *47*, 1816–1825. http://dx.doi.org/10.1016/j.neuropsychologia.2009.02.021

Griswold, D. E., Barnhill, G. P., Myles, B. S., Hagiwara, T., & Simpson, R. L. (2002). Asperger syndrome and academic achievement. *Focus on Autism and Other Developmental Disabilities*, *17*, 94–102. http://dx.doi.org/10.1177/10883576020170020401

Groen, W. B., Tesink, C., Petersson, K. M., van Berkum, J., van der Gaag, R. J., Hagoort, P., & Buitelaar, J. K. (2010). Semantic, factual, and social language comprehension in adolescents with autism: An FMRI study. *Cerebral Cortex*, *20*, 1937–1945. http://dx.doi.org/10.1093/cercor/bhp264

Happé, F. G. (1996). Studying weak central coherence at low levels: Children with autism do not succumb to visual illusions. A research note. *Journal of Child Psychology and Psychiatry*, *37*, 873–877. http://dx.doi.org/10.1111/j.1469-7610.1996.tb01483.x

Happé, F. G. (1997). Central coherence and theory of mind in autism: Reading homographs in context. *British Journal of Developmental Psychology*, *15*, 1–12. http://dx.doi.org/10.1111/j.2044-835X.1997.tb00721.x

Helt, M., Kelley, E., Kinsbourne, M., Pandey, J., Boorstein, H., Herbert, M., & Fein, D. (2008). Can children with autism recover? If so, how? *Neuropsychology Review*, *18*, 339–366. http://dx.doi.org/10.1007/s11065-008-9075-9

Hesling, I., Dilharreguy, B., Peppé, S., Amirault, M., Bouvard, M., & Allard, M. (2010). The integration of prosodic speech in high functioning autism: A preliminary FMRI study. *PLoS ONE*, *5*, e11571. http://dx.doi.org/10.1371/journal.pone.0011571

Irvine, C. A., Eigsti, I.-M., & Fein, D. A. (2016). Uh, um, and autism: Filler disfluencies as pragmatic markers in adolescents with optimal outcomes from autism spectrum disorder. *Journal of Autism and Developmental Disorders*, *46*, 1061–1070.

Jolliffe, T., & Baron-Cohen, S. (1999). The Strange Stories Test: A replication with high-functioning adults with autism or Asperger syndrome. *Journal of Autism and Developmental Disorders*, *29*, 395–406. http://dx.doi.org/10.1023/A:1023082928366

Kana, R. K., Keller, T. A., Cherkassky, V. L., Minshew, N. J., & Just, M. A. (2006). Sentence comprehension in autism: Thinking in pictures with decreased functional connectivity. *Brain: A Journal of Neurology*, *129*, 2484–2493. http://dx.doi.org/10.1093/brain/awl164

Kanner, L. (1943). Autistic disturbances of affective contact. *Nervous Child*, *2*, 217–250.

Kelley, E., Naigles, L. R., & Fein, D. A. (2010). An in-depth examination of optimal outcome children with a history of autism spectrum disorders. *Research in Autism Spectrum Disorders*, *4*, 526–538. http://dx.doi.org/10.1016/j.rasd.2009.12.001

Kelley, E., Paul, J. J., Fein, D., & Naigles, L. R. (2006). Residual language deficits in optimal outcome children with a history of autism. *Journal of Autism and Developmental Disorders*, *36*, 807–828. http://dx.doi.org/10.1007/s10803-006-0111-4

Kjelgaard, M. M., & Tager-Flusberg, H. (2001). An investigation of language impairment in autism: Implications for genetic subgroups. *Language and Cognitive Processes*, *16*, 287–308. http://dx.doi.org/10.1080/01690960042000058

Kleinhans, N. M., Müller, R. A., Cohen, D. N., & Courchesne, E. (2008). Atypical functional lateralization of language in autism spectrum disorders. *Brain Research*, *1221*, 115–125. http://dx.doi.org/10.1016/j.brainres.2008.04.080

Knaus, T. A., Silver, A. M., Kennedy, M., Lindgren, K. A., Dominick, K. C., Siegel, J., & Tager-Flusberg, H. (2010). Language laterality in autism spectrum disorder and typical controls: A functional, volumetric, and diffusion tensor MRI study. *Brain and Language*, *112*, 113–120.

Knaus, T. A., Silver, A. M., Lindgren, K. A., Hadjikhani, N., & Tager-Flusberg, H. (2008). fMRI activation during a language task in adolescents with ASD. *Journal of the International Neuropsychological Society*, *14*, 967–979. http://dx.doi.org/10.1017/S1355617708081216

Laake, L. M., & Bridgett, D. J. (2014). Happy babies, chatty toddlers: Infant positive affect facilitates early expressive, but not receptive language. *Infant Behavior & Development*, *37*, 29–32. http://dx.doi.org/10.1016/j.infbeh.2013.12.006

Lake, J. K., Humphreys, K. R., & Cardy, S. (2011). Listener vs. speaker-oriented aspects of speech: Studying the disfluencies of individuals with autism spectrum disorders. *Psychonomic Bulletin & Review*, *18*, 135–140. http://dx.doi.org/10.3758/s13423-010-0037-x

Lê, K., Coelho, C., Mozeiko, J., & Grafman, J. (2011). Measuring goodness of story narratives. *Journal of Speech, Language, and Hearing Research*, *54*, 118–126. http://dx.doi.org/10.1044/1092-4388(2010/09-0022)

Liles, B. Z., Duffy, R. J., Merritt, D. D., & Purcell, S. L. (1995). Measurement of narrative discourse ability in children with language disorders. *Journal of Speech, Language, and Hearing Research*, *38*, 415–425. http://dx.doi.org/10.1044/jshr.3802.415

López, B., & Leekam, S. R. (2003). Do children with autism fail to process information in context? *Journal of Child Psychology and Psychiatry*, *44*, 285–300. http://dx.doi.org/10.1111/1469-7610.00121

Lord, C., Rutter, M., DiLavore, P. C., & Risi, S. (2002). *Autism Diagnostic Observation Schedule (ADOS)*. Los Angeles, CA: Western Psychological Services.

Maclay, H., & Osgood, C. E. (1959). Hesitation phenomena in spontaneous English speech. *Word*, *15*, 19–44. http://dx.doi.org/10.1080/00437956.1959.11659682

Mayes, S. D., & Calhoun, S. L. (2003). Ability profiles in children with autism: Influence of age and IQ. *Autism*, *7*, 65–80. http://dx.doi.org/10.1177/1362361303007001006

Mizuno, A., Liu, Y., Williams, D. L., Keller, T. A., Minshew, N. J., & Just, M. A. (2011). The neural basis of deictic shifting in linguistic perspective-taking in high-functioning autism. *Brain: A Journal of Neurology*, *134*, 2422–2435. http://dx.doi.org/10.1093/brain/awr151

Mottron, L., Dawson, M., Soulières, I., Hubert, B., & Burack, J. (2006). Enhanced perceptual functioning in autism: An update, and eight principles of autistic perception. *Journal of Autism and Developmental Disorders*, *36*, 27–43. http://dx.doi.org/10.1007/s10803-005-0040-7

Naigles, L. R., & Chin, I. (2015). Language development in children with autism. In E. L. Bavin & L. R. Naigles (Eds.), *The Cambridge handbook of child language* (2nd ed., pp. 637–658). http://dx.doi.org/10.1017/CBO9781316095829.029

Naigles, L. R., Kelley, E., Troyb, E., & Fein, D. (2013). Residual difficulties with categorical induction in children with a history of autism. *Journal of Autism and Developmental Disorders*, *43*, 2048–2061. http://dx.doi.org/10.1007/s10803-012-1754-y

Orinstein, A., Helt, M., Troyb, E., Tyson, K., Barton, M. L., Eigsti, I.-M., . . . Fein, D. A. (2014). Intervention for optimal outcome in children and adolescents with a history of autism. *Journal of Developmental and Behavioral Pediatrics*, *35*, 247–256. http://dx.doi.org/10.1097/DBP.0000000000000037

Redcay, E., & Courchesne, E. (2008). Deviant functional magnetic resonance imaging patterns of brain activity to speech in 2–3-year-old children with autism spectrum disorder. *Biological Psychiatry*, *64*, 589–598. http://dx.doi.org/10.1016/j.biopsych.2008.05.020

Reznick, J. S., Corley, R., Robinson, J., & Matheny, A. P. (1997). A longitudinal twin study of intelligence in the second year. *Monographs of the Society for Research in Child Development*, *62*, i–vi. http://dx.doi.org/10.2307/1166193

Sallows, G. O., & Graupner, T. D. (2005). Intensive behavioral treatment for children with autism: Four-year outcome and predictors. *American Journal on Mental Retardation*, *110*, 417–438. http://dx.doi.org/10.1352/0895-8017(2005)110[417:IBTFCW]2.0.CO;2

Saur, D., & Hartwigsen, G. (2012). Neurobiology of language recovery after stroke: Lessons from neuroimaging studies. *Archives of Physical Medicine and Rehabilitation*, *93*(Suppl. 1), S15–S25. http://dx.doi.org/10.1016/j.apmr.2011.03.036

Schachter, S., Christenfeld, N., Ravina, B., & Bilous, F. (1991). Speech disfluency and the structure of knowledge. *Journal of Personality and Social Psychology*, *60*, 362–367. http://dx.doi.org/10.1037/0022-3514.60.3.362

Schuh, J. M., & Eigsti, I.-M. (2012). Working memory, language skills, and autism symptomatology. *Behavioral Science*, *2*, 207–218. http://dx.doi.org/10.3390/bs2040207

Semel, E., Wiig, E. H., & Secord, W. A. (2003). *Clinical Evaluation of Language Fundamentals* (4th ed.). San Antonio, TX: Harcourt Assessment.

Simos, P. G., Fletcher, J. M., Bergman, E., Breier, J. I., Foorman, B. R., Castillo, E. M., . . . Papanicolaou, A. C. (2002). Dyslexia-specific brain activation profile becomes normal following successful remedial training. *Neurology, 58*, 1203–1213. http://dx.doi.org/10.1212/WNL.58.8.1203

Smith, V., & Clark, H. (1993). On the course of answering questions. *Journal of Memory and Language, 32*, 25–38. http://dx.doi.org/10.1006/jmla.1993.1002

Son, J. Y., Smith, L. B., & Goldstone, R. L. (2008). Simplicity and generalization: Short-cutting abstraction in children's object categorizations. *Cognition, 108*, 626–638. http://dx.doi.org/10.1016/j.cognition.2008.05.002

Suh, J., Eigsti, I.-M., Naigles, L., Barton, M., Kelley, E., & Fein, D. (2014). Narrative performance of optimal outcome children and adolescents with a history of an autism spectrum disorder (ASD). *Journal of Autism and Developmental Disorders, 44*, 1681–1694. http://dx.doi.org/10.1007/s10803-014-2042-9

Suh, J., Orinstein, A., Barton, M., Chen, C.-M., Eigsti, I.-M., Ramirez-Esparza, N., & Fein, D. (in press). Zero acquaintance ratings of broader autism phenotype and personality traits in optimal outcome individuals with a history of autism spectrum disorder. *Journal of Autism and Developmental Disorders.*

Sutera, S., Pandey, J., Esser, E. L., Rosenthal, M. A., Wilson, L. B., Barton, M., . . . Fein, D. (2007). Predictors of optimal outcome in toddlers diagnosed with autism spectrum disorders. *Journal of Autism and Developmental Disorders, 37*, 98–107. http://dx.doi.org/10.1007/s10803-006-0340-6

Szatmari, P., Bryson, S. E., Boyle, M. H., Streiner, D. L., & Duku, E. (2003). Predictors of outcome among high functioning children with autism and Asperger syndrome. *Journal of Child Psychology and Psychiatry, 44*, 520–528. http://dx.doi.org/10.1111/1469-7610.00141

Troyb, E., Orinstein, A., Tyson, K., Helt, M., Eigsti, I.-M., Stevens, M., & Fein, D. (2014). Academic abilities in children and adolescents with a history of autism spectrum disorders who have achieved optimal outcomes. *Autism, 18*, 233–243. http://dx.doi.org/10.1177/1362361312473519

Troyb, E., Rosenthal, M., Eigsti, I.-M., Kelley, E., Tyson, K., Orinstein, A., . . . Fein, D. (2013). Executive functioning in individuals with a history of ASDs who have achieved optimal outcomes. *Child Neuropsychology, 3*(3).

Tyson, K., Kelley, E., Fein, D., Orinstein, A., Troyb, E., Barton, M., . . . Rosenthal, M. (2014). Language and verbal memory in individuals with a history of autism spectrum disorder who have achieved optimal outcomes. *Journal of Autism and Developmental Disorders, 44*, 648–663. http://dx.doi.org/10.1007/s10803-013-1921-9

Ullman, M. T., & Pullman, M. Y. (2015). A compensatory role for declarative memory in neurodevelopmental disorders. *Neuroscience and Biobehavioral Reviews, 51*, 205–222. http://dx.doi.org/10.1016/j.neubiorev.2015.01.008

Verly, M., Verhoeven, J., Zink, I., Mantini, D., Peeters, R., Deprez, S., . . . Sunaert, S. (2014). Altered functional connectivity of the language network in ASD: Role of classical language areas and cerebellum. *NeuroImage: Clinical, 4*, 374–382. http://dx.doi.org/10.1016/j.nicl.2014.01.008

Index

About the Editor

Letitia R. Naigles, PhD, is a professor of psychological sciences at the University of Connecticut. After earning her PhD in psychology from the University of Pennsylvania, she taught at Yale University for 10 years. She has held visiting professor positions at Koç University in Istanbul, Turkey, and at the MIND Institute at the University of California, Davis. Dr. Naigles became a Fellow of the Association for Psychological Science in 2009. At UConn, she is currently head of the Developmental Division in Psychological Sciences, founding head of the university-wide Kids In Developmental Science research and recruitment consortium, and a member of the Executive Committee of the Cognitive Science Program. She has conducted research on language acquisition with children learning a variety of languages, including English, French, Spanish, Mandarin Chinese, Turkish, Japanese, German, Hindi, and Korean, and has been engaged for the past 15 years in an intensive longitudinal investigation of the language development of children with autism spectrum disorder. Her research has been funded by grants from NIH (FIRST, DCD, and CHD), NIMH, NSF, and NAAR. Dr. Naigles is the coauthor of an SRCD Monograph (2009: *Flexibility in Early Verb Use*), and coeditor of the *Cambridge Handbook of Child Language* (2nd ed., 2015).